Harriet and Neil Pike (above, in Bolivia) updated this third edition. They met trekking in Chile in 2002 and together began exploring the world's mountains on foot. A chance Caspian Sea ferry encounter with a cyclist in 2007 led to a switch to cycle touring, and a trip across Europe was followed by a few years in the Andes and Himalaya, during which time they fell in love with riding on traffic-free dirt roads. Neil spends hours poring over maps and scouring satellite images for routes; Harriet is the gear geek and team bike mechanic. Peruvian climbs, ice cream, the Puna de Atacama and Argentinian *facturas*: any of these make them happy bikers.

Stephen Lord (above, in Spiti, India) wrote the first two editions of this book. He graduated from Trinity College, Oxford, then worked in banking for 12 years, living in Japan and the USA. He has toured in Asia, North America and Europe on mountain- and touring-bikes. He also enjoys kayak-touring, long-distance walking, skiing and all other forms of exercise and is currently training to be a corrective exercise coach.

Authors

Adventure Cycle-Touring Handbook
First edition: 2006; this third edition: 2015

Publisher
Trailblazer Publications
The Old Manse, Tower Rd, Hindhead, Surrey, GU26 6SU, UK
info@trailblazer-guides.com   www.trailblazer-guides.com

British Library Cataloguing in Publication Data
A catalogue record for this book is available from the British Library

ISBN 978-1-905864-68-3

Editor: Nicky Slade
Series Editor: Bryn Thomas
Typesetting: Nicky Slade **Layout**: Nicky Slade **Proofreading**: Henry Stedman
Cartography: Nick Hill **Index**: Jane Thomas

Photos: Front cover: Riding to volcanoes on the Puna de Atacama, Chile.
This page: Saharan face-off with a camel. © Logan Watts **Overleaf**: Heading onto the
Salar de Uyuni, Bolivia. © Anna Kortschak **Back cover**: Chang La, India.

For more detail about this book see **adventurecycle-touringhandbook.com**
Printed in China; print production by D'Print (☎ +65-6581 3832), Singapore

Adventure
Cycle-Touring
HANDBOOK

NEIL & HARRIET PIKE

with

STEPHEN LORD

and contributions by
SARAH BEDFORD, JOHN BURNHAM, JAMES BUTCHER, EMILY CHAPPELL,
GAYLE DICKSON, PETER GOSTELOW, NATHAN HALEY, ANNA KORTSCHAK,
ALIA PARKER AND AMAYA WILLIAMS

and

Tara Alan, Tom Allen, Jean Bell, Lars Bengtsson, Joe Cruz, Mark Elliot,
Stephen Fabes, Edward Genochio, Friedel Grant, James & Jane Hall,
Steve Halton, Loretta Henderson, Lars Henning, Alastair Humphreys,
Jonathan Kennett, Maria Leijerstam, Helen Lloyd, Matt McDonald,
Anna McNuff, Scott Morris, Tim & Laura Moss, Laura Mottram,
Andy Peat, Matt Pierle, Scott Richardson, Lorenzo Rojo, Mike Roy,
Kurt Sandiforth, Chris Scott, Sonya Spry, Laura Stone, Shirine Taylor,
Rob Thomson, Elmar & Ellen van Drunen, Charlie Walker, Logan Watts,
Bill Weir, Paul Woloshansky and Mirjam Wouters

TRAILBLAZER PUBLICATIONS

INTRODUCTION

PART 1: PRACTICALITIES

Planning and preparation A plan 13 – What kind of ride? 14
Which continent? 15 – Seasons and climate 16 – Budget and time 18
Travelling companions 20 – Research: Getting information 23

Documentation Passports 25 – Visas 26 – Insurance 26 – Money 27

Health preparation Inoculations 30 – Malaria 31

PART 2: BIKES, CLOTHING & CAMPING GEAR

Bikes Narrowing down your choices 34 – Expedition touring bikes
34 – Traditional touring bikes 34 – Mountain bikes 35 – Fat bikes 36 –
Recumbents 36 – Tandems 36 – Narrowing it down further 37 –
Frame material 37 – Wheel size 38 – Derailleur gears vs hub gear
39 – Rim brakes vs disc brakes 39 – Drop bars vs straight bars 40

Choosing a new bike Surly 40 – Thorn 41 – Koga-Miyata 42 –
Santos 43 – Recumbents 43 – More dream bikes 44 – Cheaper touring bikes 45 – Mid-range MTBs 46 – Build your own bike 46

Gears, brakes and wheels Gears 47 – Choosing brakes 51
Wheels 54 – Bottom brackets 58 – Headsets 58

Comfort zone Finding the sweet spot 59 – Love in the saddle 60
Handlebars 62 – Suspension forks 63

Carrying luggage Racks 65 – Panniers 68 – Bikepacking setup 71

Pimping your ride 73

Tools and spares Essentials 73 – Other things to consider 75

How much stuff? Light vs heavy 76

Clothing Layering 82 – Footwear 85

Camping Tents 87 – Bike touring tents 89
Sleeping bags 91 – Sleeping pads & air mattresses 93
Stoves 93 – Treating drinking water 96 – Kitchen essentials 96
Toilet bag 97 – Electronic devices 98 – Other useful kit 98

PART 3: ON THE ROAD

Transporting your bike By air 99 – Boxing your bike 100
On buses & trains 102 – On horses & mules 103

Navigating the adventure cycle-touring world Paper maps 104
Asking as you go 104 – GPS units 105 – Smartphones 106

Staying in touch on the road To blog or not to blog 107

Health on the road Mosquito-borne diseases 108 – Altitude sickness 109 – Hygiene 110 – Women's health 111 – Pacing yourself 112

Food and water A healthy diet 112 – Food hygiene 113
Purifying water 113

Staying safe Avoiding accidents 114 – Theft & robbery 115
Dealing with dogs 115

Dirt-road (off-road) riding 117

PART 4: ROUTE OUTLINES
EUROPE TO ASIA & AUSTRALASIA

Europe 121 – Ready-made routes 121– To the continent 121
The call of the Orient 124 – To West Africa via Spain 126

Asia 127 – Main routes 130 – **The southern route** 132 – **Turkey**
132 – **Iran** 135 – **Pakistan** 140 – The Karakoram Highway 142
India 144 – The North-East, and to Myanmar 148 – Ladakh, Spiti &
Kinnaur 148 – Manali to Leh 149 – North of Leh 149 – To Srinagar
or Zanskar 150 – Rajasthan 151 – **Nepal** 153 – The Caucasus 155
Georgia 155 – **Azerbaijan** 157 – **Armenia** 158

Central Asia 160 – **Turkmenistan** 164 – **Uzbekistan** 165
Tajikistan 166 – The Pamir Highway 167 – **Kyrgyzstan** 169
Kazakhstan 170

The northern route 172 – **Russia** 172 – **Mongolia** 177

East Asia 181 – **China** 181 – Sichuan 185 – Yunnan 188
Chongqing 190 – Guizhou 190 – Guanxi 191 – **Tibet** 191
The Friendship Highway 192 – Kashgar to Lhasa 192
Lhasa to Markham 193 – **Taiwan** 193 – **South Korea** 195 – **Japan** 197

South-East Asia 201 – **Thailand** 206 – **Cambodia** 208
Vietnam 209 – **Laos** 210 – **Malaysia** 212 – **Indonesia** 213
Sumatra 214 – Java, Bali, Lombok 215 – Sumbawa, Flores, Timor
216 – Sulawesi, Borneo 217 – **Philippines** 217 – **Myanmar** 218

Australasia 221 – **Australia** 221 – Red centre, West coast, Nullarbor
Plain 224 – Tasmania 225 – East coast 226 – **New Zealand** 227

PART 5: ROUTE OUTLINES – AFRICA

Main routes 229

The Nile route 236 – Egypt 237 – Sudan 237 – Ethiopia 241

East and Southern Africa 241 – Kenya, Uganda 242 – Rwanda,
Burundi, Tanzania 243 – Malawi, Mozambique, Zimbabwe, Zambia
245 – Namibia 246 – Botswana, South Africa, Lesotho, Swaziland 247

West and Central Africa 248 – Morocco, Mauritania, Mali 249 –
Senegal & The Gambia, Guinea Bissau, Guinea, Sierra Leone 251 –
Liberia, Ivory Coast 252 – Ghana, Nigeria, Cameroon 253 – DRC,
Angola 254

PART 6: ROUTE OUTLINES – THE AMERICAS

Introduction 255

North America 256 – **USA & Canada** 256 – PanAm route ideas 258
Riding Alaska to the Lower 48 258 – Pacific Coast Route 263
Riding the Great Divide 265

Mexico and Central America 269 – **Mexico** 273 – Yucatán
Peninsula/**Belize 275** – **Guatemala** 275 – **Honduras** 276
Nicaragua, Costa Rica 277 – **Panama** 278 – **Cuba** 278

South America 279 – **Colombia** 283 – **Ecuador** 287 – **Peru** 289
Cordilleras Blanca & Huayhuash 294 – The Huascarán Circuit 294
Cusco and the Sacred Valley 295 – **Bolivia** 296 – The Salars 300
Chile 303 – **Argentina** 303 – Patagonia 305
The Carretera Austral 307 – **Venezuela** 308

PART 7: TALES FROM THE SADDLE

The Wild Corner of Myanmar – Stephen Fabes   311
Kidnapped by Comedians – Emily Chappell   316
Crossings and Encounters – Anna Kortschak   320
Go with the Flow – John Burnham   325
Now or Never – Charlie Walker   330
Alaskan Epiphanies: Finding My Roads – Nathan Haley   335
Just Don't Stop! – Helen Lloyd   339

APPENDIX   Bicycle maintenance 345

GLOSSARY   355

ACKNOWLEDGEMENTS & CONTRIBUTORS   356

INDEX   359

A request

Every effort has been made by the authors and the publisher to ensure that the information contained in this book is as up to date and accurate as possible. Nevertheless things change; even before the ink is dry. If you notice any changes or omissions that you think should be included in the next edition of this book, please write to the authors at pikes@trailblazer-guides.com or c/o Trailblazer (contact details on p2).

Contents

INTRODUCTION

Pedalling through far-flung lands, immersed in the landscape, listening to the birds, absorbing the local culture from chats with new-found friends. Being in the moment: it's you, your bike, the road and a never-ending string of fascinating encounters and experiences. These are just some of the many joys of Adventure Cycle-Touring.

While backpackers spend their hours cooped up in old buses, racing from one 'sight' to the next, with a bike the whole world is your oyster. Take advantage of the great freedom to explore those places in between that public transport doesn't reach, to head out on quiet roads through villages where you'll feel like you've gone back in time, and to enjoy the beauty and simplicity of a biking-camping lifestyle. Fifteen kilometres an hour is the perfect speed for making satisfying progress across countries and continents, and you'll always have time to pause for chai when beckoned over by a welcoming villager's smile.

And the crowning glory is that almost anyone can embark on a cycle tour; the forty-plus contributors to this book are not elite athletes. The only prerequisites are a thirst for adventure, the ability to ride a bike, and the strength of mind to convert your desire for a big trip into actually setting off. As many tourers will tell you, that first act of setting off is the hardest part.

This isn't to say your tour is **all** going to be easy or fun; it wouldn't be an adventure if it was. There'll be plenty of challenging days, particularly to begin with as you find your rhythm, and later when you can no longer resist the urge to head out onto rougher, more remote roads. But stick with it after making those first few pedal strokes and you'll find a world of exciting riding awaits.

ABOUT THIS BOOK

This book is primarily concerned with the practicalities of going on lengthy and adventurous cycling trips, of exploring by bike countries your friends back home might not even have heard of, and certainly can't pinpoint on a map. Preparation is key to your tour running smoothly and the *Adventure Cycle-Touring Handbook* aims to give you the necessary knowledge, inspiration and confidence to set forth and discover the world on two wheels your own way. Read on to find out what today's bike tourers are choosing to ride and what gear they are using, which countries are being explored and what kind of riding to expect in each.

Initially, taking the decision to head off on a big trip can seem daunting with a lot to take in and learn. But rest assured that it's nothing too difficult, and by preparing and planning the most important aspects of your trip, you'll soon work out the details that suit you best on the road. By the time you return home you'll be surprised at the myriad of transferable life skills you've developed.

Part One: Practicalities will help you understand the major issues which are thrown up as a consequence of deciding to embark on a tour and we'll navigate you through the bureaucratic and practical factors to consider when planning a ride in the world's adventurous zones.

You may want to jump ahead to the **Route Outlines (Parts Four, Five and Six)** after this to get more ideas and detailed information about riding in exotic countries all over the globe; it's well worth reading about the terrain and

Below: Tso Kar, Ladakh, India.

environments you can expect to find on any route you're considering taking before you begin thinking about sorting out a bike and kit.

Part Two will help you prepare the bicycle and equipment that are best suited to your ride, and we'll lead you through the most important decisions that need to be taken without complicated or confusing jargon, drawing on advice from a whole gamut of experienced tourers with hundreds of thousands of kilometres under their tyres.

There's some handy On the Road advice in **Part Three**, and after the Route Outlines we wrap up with the **Tales from the Saddle** – some rip-snorting but not atypical accounts of encounters that have taken place out there on two wheels. Dip into those as and when; but for now, a plan.

Overleaf: The Adventure Cycle-Touring World.

Alaska – The Dalton Highway
Ride through the Alaskan wilderness –
a wonderful way to begin a Pan-Am tour.
Pages 259-61.

The USA – The Great Divide Route
The longest mapped unpaved route in
the world: a 4500km-long workout for
you and your bike, with wild camping
for most of the way. Pages 264-9.

Africa
The ideal way to see Africa is on a bike,
the most popular form of transport on
the continent. Go local and ride the
backroads. Pages 229-54.

Bolivia
High altitude salt flats, multi-coloured
deserts, volcanoes and flamingos.
With few paved roads this is no place
for skinny tyres! Pages 296-301.

The Peruvian Cordillera
Take on the 2000-4000m challenge
in one of the most vertical
countries on Earth. Pages 289-96.

Chile – Carretera Austral
One of the best cycle routes in South America
and the most glorious in Chile. This largely
unpaved 1240km road also offers a back-door
route into Argentina open only to hikers and
bikers. Pages 305-7.

ARCTIC

Greenland

Iceland

Alaska

Canada

Norway

Denmark

Ireland

UK

France

Germany

NORTH ATLANTIC OCEAN

Portugal

Spain

Morocco

USA

Mexico

Cuba

Haiti

Dom. Rep.

Belize

Jamaica

Guatemala

Honduras

El Salvador

Nicaragua

Costa Rica

Panama

Venezuela

Guyana

Suriname

French Guiana

Colombia

Galapagos
Islands

Ecuador

Peru

Brazil

Bolivia

Paraguay

Argentina

Chile

Uruguay

Algeria

Tu

Mali

Nig

Senegal

Gambia

Guinea
Bissau

Guinea

Burkina
Faso

Sierra
Leone

Ivory
Coast

Ghana

Togo

Benin

Niger

Liberia

Equatorial
Guinea

G

C

SOUTH

ATLANTIC OCEAN

SOUTH

PACIFIC OCEAN

Falkland
Islands

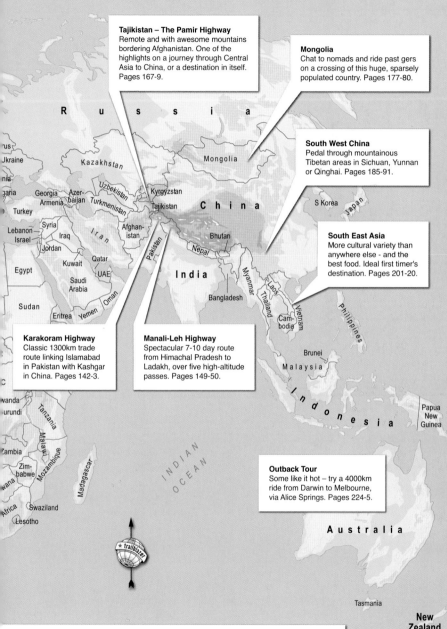

Tajikistan – The Pamir Highway
Remote and with awesome mountains bordering Afghanistan. One of the highlights on a journey through Central Asia to China, or a destination in itself. Pages 167-9.

Mongolia
Chat to nomads and ride past gers on a crossing of this huge, sparsely populated country. Pages 177-80.

South West China
Pedal through mountainous Tibetan areas in Sichuan, Yunnan or Qinghai. Pages 185-91.

South East Asia
More cultural variety than anywhere else - and the best food. Ideal first timer's destination. Pages 201-20.

Karakoram Highway
Classic 1300km trade route linking Islamabad in Pakistan with Kashgar in China. Pages 142-3.

Manali-Leh Highway
Spectacular 7-10 day route from Himachal Pradesh to Ladakh, over five high-altitude passes. Pages 149-50.

Outback Tour
Some like it hot – try a 4000km ride from Darwin to Melbourne, via Alice Springs. Pages 224-5.

The Adventure Cycle-Touring World
Selected Highlights

PRACTICALITIES

Planning and preparation

A PLAN
Before beginning to think about details and specifics, it is important to consider the wider aspect of your trip. Ask yourself what **type of tour** you want to take, **where you want to go** and what you hope to **get out of it** and from the ideas that flow from you and the information provided in this section, a plan will begin to take shape.

A major attraction of cycle-touring is the immense freedom and flexibility it affords you, so think about what inspired you to travel by bicycle and indulge in a bit of blue-sky thinking about dreams, destinations and goals. You may doubt you have it in you, but **aim high** – your abilities will surprise you and what was, or seemed, impossible before the trip will gradually become reality as you become a stronger, more confident tourer.

One of the aims of this book is to prepare you to ride in places most people would not even consider visiting – a sure way of providing a wealth of indelible memories – but those big ideas need to be tempered by realism. Independent biking in Tibet isn't legally possible and the Morocco-Algeria border has been closed for years; that road across the Darien Gap still ain't done, and do you really want your first experience of cycle-touring to be taking on the infamous wall of Patagonian wind? Good preparation will foresee and outmanoeuvre these problems, meaning you can spend more of your trip doing what you're there for, whether it be riding, soaking up culture or socialising.

Having a plan doesn't take the spontaneity out of things – you'll still stop when you want, take on board travel advice gleaned from roadside conversations and change your route at regular intervals when that enticing track that catches your eye at a crossroads proves just too tempting to resist. But investing time in preparing a plan saves the inconvenience of cycling into dead ends from which it will take time and money to extricate yourself: stumbling upon a shut border post for example; or reaching a country where you needed to apply for a visa months in advance; or hitting passes in winter when they're closed by snow.

(Opposite) A nice spot for a rest, Uzbekistan. © Scott Richardson

TRIAL TOUR, ON A BUDGET

Our first tour was a no frills affair: £200 hybrid bikes bought in Istanbul, a dry bag stuffed with camping gear and clothes,

A simple and cheap setup for a trans-Europe ride.

lashed on the back with bungees and wrapped in a high-vis vest. Cycling for pretty much the first time in 15 years, we started slowly and learnt the art of wild camping the hard way, from a first-day low where at 11am we were to be found pitching the tent by a rubbish dump, too tired to continue. Spokes began pinging before arrival home in the UK, but with bike shops never far away we were able to get to mechanics for anything that repulsed the usual super glue or gaffer tape fix. This setup and approach worked fine for that initial tour, a journey which was enough to convince us we loved the simple lifestyle and that it was worth investing in stronger expedition bikes for more ambitious future rides.

WHAT KIND OF RIDE?

There are different ways of touring on a bicycle. You could stick to tarmac, or hunt down unpaved roads; you could pile your panniers full of gear for every eventuality and comfort, or get by on the bare minimum; you could go on shorter, focussed trips or decide to set aside a few years of your life to cycle the globe.

If you haven't toured before, by far the best way to start working out which suits you best is to **go on a short practice tour** or two – it's a personal experience and only by being out on the road can you discover what you truly enjoy. Keep it simple, and to avoid shelling out on a new bike and gear right away try to use a bike you already own (or borrow from a friend) and go off for a few days or weeks. Head out on different surfaces and with different amounts of equipment to see which you prefer. For Brits, a route such as Land's End to John O'Groats is a perfect introduction and a good way to ascertain whether you even like the touring lifestyle. Not everybody does and it's better to find out in the vicinity of Chester rather than Chengdu.

Tarmac or unpaved?

Nowadays it's almost possible to cycle the length of every continent without leaving tarmac; conversely if you search hard and plan well you can avoid the blacktop and wend your way across landmasses on dirt and gravel roads. All adventure cycle-tourists mix and match the two, albeit to varying degrees, so you'll want to tailor your bike and how much gear you carry to the surface on which you will be spending most of your time. Almost everything is possible on a bike (see box p294), so you can tackle unpaved roads on road-orientated touring bikes and tarmac on knobbly tyres; it just happens to be faster and a lot more enjoyable, rideable and comfortable if you have the right steed for the terrain you expect to concentrate on.

Level of comfort

You need to decide on the level of comfort that is right for you and this in turn will help determine how much kit you carry. Do you want to travel with a spacious tent, multiple pans to prepare gastronomic delights when you're camping in the middle of Mali, and carry changes of clothing to stroll around town in on your day off? Or will you be happy in a 1kg tarp-tent, cooking and eating out of the same one pan with just a change of t-shirt for rest days? There are more details on p75, and some riders' thoughts and explanations for what's packed in their bags.

Length of trip

A ride of a month is a very different undertaking from a year-long tour across a continent, so having an idea of how long you wish to be (or can be) away will help you decide not only where to head and what's achievable but also how much equipment to take and how hard wearing it needs to be.

There are no right or wrong answers to any of these issues. Pick what appeals to you most as you'll have an adventure whatever you do, but they're all factors to consider before starting to look for new kit.

WHICH CONTINENT?

You may always have dreamed of visiting a certain place – to hear that crunch of tyre on Bolivian salt-flat or experience the thrill of pedalling past Zanskari *gompas* and glaciers. Perhaps your aim is to cross continents from Cairo to Cape Town or Alaska to Ushuaia? If this is the case your first decision will already have been made and you can home in on the particular section of the Route Outlines to delve deeper into those destinations. But for those who've made up their mind to embark on a bike trip but haven't settled on a destination, here are some classic trans-continental rides to whet your appetite.

From the UK and Europe, it's possible to wheel out of your front door, point east, and cycle to China or South-East Asia. The most popular route slices through Turkey, Iran, and Central Asia, with detours via Siberia and Mongolia possible. Routes through Asia (see p127) offer a wealth of fascinating cultures and history, and astounding scenery; visa issues and avoiding the paralyzing winter cold and lassitude-inducing summer temperatures will be your biggest logistical challenges.

Cycling the length of **Africa** (p229) is the least common of the trans-continental rides. Despite the attractions of wide open spaces, wild animals, and friendly locals, it can be a draining continent to traverse; but from challenges, the strongest and fondest memories are often forged. Cairo to Cape Town is by far the most popular north-south route, though taking an exciting ride down West Africa is another option. The heat of a Saharan summer is the main season to side-step.

Descending from the Sani Pass, one of the most exciting in Africa. © Logan Watts

RIDING EVERY INCH OF THE WAY

Many cycle tourers set off with a vow to cycle all the way, except when absolutely unavoidable – usually ferries to cross seas or rivers, or rides across motorway bridges or through tunnels. Indeed first timers often assume it ought to be done this way, that they've somehow cheated themselves and betrayed the greater cause should they take the train or a bus when a perfectly rideable road exists. From this viewpoint the ride is an act of purification or a political statement; it's just you, your bike and the world. Recognise this as a not uncommon over-adventurous reflex to the humdrum and predictable life you may be leaving behind; you're up for it and want to get your teeth into a challenge!

In the car-dominated West the environmentally affirmative activity of cycling as full-time transportation (as opposed to widely practised recreation) encourages a certain zeal which might eschew any form of engine-powered assistance. It's something that most experienced riders get over once they realise **it's not necessarily about riding, it's about the experience of travelling**. This doesn't mean you have to hail down a local farmer in a pickup every time a stiff climb or an annoying headwind presents itself; it merely recognises that a bicycle's many advantages include its natural portability – and that one of the better lessons learned on the road is flexibility (see Bikes on Transport p99).

Riding it all is challenging stuff indeed and the downside of this kind of commitment is clear: a fair amount of discomfort and even danger at times, heading out of towns on busy motorways or through run-down shanty-towns, riding in extremes of heat and cold, unable to catch up with the favourable seasons for travel.

With your bike lashed to a bus roof, in a train or on a ferry or plane, you can cut out a busy or boring stretch and have a chance to meet some more locals and so enrich your experience. Refusing to consider these options is to make a rod for your own back. So you slogged your way resolutely across the endless Kazakh steppe. Was it a month well spent? Or would you rather have shot ahead to ride the alpine meadows and heavenly mountains of Kyrgyzstan before the first winter snows?

If your time is unlimited, you might want to ride every inch of the way. Otherwise, you'll have a lot more fun and get further if you press 'fast-forward' once in a while. This is the key: it's your ride, not someone else's. Any rules you decide on are your own.

The **Americas** (p255) draw an increasing number of adventure cycle-tourers, lured by the lack of bureaucracy, the convenience of needing to add only Spanish to their repertoire in order to be able to communicate with everyone en route, and the magical scenery that rarely abates as you migrate with the seasons along the longest continental landmass on earth.

SEASONS AND CLIMATE

A bike tour involves being outside most of the day, most days; this is one of its great joys. It also means that weather will play a far more significant role on your existence and morale than it does in a sheltered, indoor lifestyle back home. Most people agree hauling your bike up Sikkim's steep gradients in

CHECK THE FORECAST BEFORE YOU GO...

Settling on an idea of where and when you want to tour, then forcing it through despite all climatic evidence pointing to the fact it's not a good time, rarely works. If you can only ever get January and February off work, but you really want a back-roads tour in British Columbia, you'll have to either quit your job, or invest in some very warm gear and a fat bike (see p36)... Once you decide where you'd like to go, find out when it's good to go there, before setting your heart on it.

monsoon season is silly – your clothes will grow mould and Kangchenjunga will remain swathed in cloud for the entirety. And who likes cycling in the rain anyway?

Despite increasing weather insta-bility across the globe, **ensure your plan takes into account the climate** at the time you'll be visiting as this can be key to enjoyment. British riders in particular should be aware that the weather in many parts is nowhere near as benign as back home. Just as

Now, where did those brakes go?

important in relation to climate is the fact that **many of the world's most beau-tiful roads are seasonal**: snow, mud, impassable landslides or water keep them off-limits to cyclists at the wrong times of year, so even being hardy enough to stick out the elements doesn't guarantee you'll be able to cycle that longed-for route.

Factoring favourable seasons into a ride is essential, so devour the Route outlines section for information, whilst noting that for a longer ride it's simply not feasible to always be in the right place at the right time. Reading up will enlighten you about some of those climates that regularly catch cyclists out. For example don't make the mistake of thinking Turkey is all beach resort – *Speedos* and towel won't keep you warm in a winter blizzard in Kurdistan when it's -20°C and the next tea house is still 50km away.

Which direction?

For trans-continental rides, the question of which is the best direction to travel is usually most pertinent in the context of getting your seasons right. For short-er, more-focussed tours however, never ever underestimate prevailing winds. The simple decision of choosing which way to go can make or break a ride, as cycling into a head wind day after day can be soul destroying. To glance at a Patagonian tree, hear a monologue of half-crazed nonsense vomited by a lone-wolf two weeks into a northward ride from Ushuaia, or survey the sand-blast-ing damage on a kilometre marker in the Puna de Atacama (see below) will

Left: The eastern-facing side of a roadsign on the Puna.
Right: The western-facing side.

PLANNING SCHEDULE

With a well set-up bike, experience, and having ascertained the bureaucracy and climate situations, riders who regularly take adventurous tours can leave planning till the last minute. If it's your first big trip with a new bike and new gear, begin planning well ahead, or the mistakes you make in those last weeks when you should be out having farewell drinks with friends will cost you time and money on the road.

One year before departure
● Research your destination to work out a rough plan, taking into account the seasons.
● Try some short practice tours to get an idea of the kind of riding you enjoy.
● Think of the key gear choices that take time to get right, not least your bike.
● Take test rides, ask around, visit bike shops or manufacturers and trawl the internet.
● Consider beginning to learn languages that'll be of use on the road.

Six months before departure
● The rest of your gear – camping equipment, electronics and camera – have to be pinned down, bought and tested, and don't forget racks and panniers to carry it all.
● Decide which inoculations you need (see p30); immunisations such as hepatitis B need a course over a period of six months.
● Begin looking into flights – early booking can be rewarded with cheaper fares.

● If needed, get a new passport.

Three months before departure
● Start applying for any visas that are easier to obtain in your home country.
● Work out who's going to feed your cat, pay your mortgage and store your stuff.
● Get your affairs in order: online banking, bank cards and a PayPal account (see p27).
● Start researching travel insurance.
● Identify gear you haven't got but think you'll need.
● Consider starting light fitness training if you don't exercise regularly.
● Begin loaded test rides and short camping trips to test your system and setup.

One month to go
● Begin stocking your first aid kit.
● Pick up spare parts for your bike and supplies such as batteries or memory cards.
● Have your bike shop look over your bike and service it, or better still, do it yourself.

Two weeks to go
● Get a bike box or packing material from your local bike shop, if flying out.
● Leave spares and kit you don't want to take initially, but may need later, with a friend who's able to send them out as needed.
● Start packing and leave your panniers packed.

---

make it blindingly obvious which way you'll want to be tackling a route. And the Andes by no means have a monopoly on the world's winds – Mongolia, Western Sahara, Iceland, they're all breezy too, so if you're concentrating on one region, factor that into your planning.

It is sometimes easier logistically with visas or border crossings to head in a particular direction so take note when these are mentioned in the Route Outlines.

BUDGET AND TIME

The cost of kitting out a tour and daily expenses on the road, as well as the length of time taken to pedal across continents, varies significantly between riders as we all have different styles.

Touring can certainly be done on a shoestring but if you have the resources then investing in strong, durable, tried and tested gear is a sensible policy. With confidence in the reliability of your bike you can forget worrying about it breaking down and you'll save time and money on the road if the need for repairs is kept to a minimum.

Most tourers from the UK spend at least £700 on a bike, racks and panniers for a long trip; £1500 gets you a new expedition bike with strong racks and panniers that have been purpose-built for a tough transcontinental tour. If you don't already own it, good quality camping kit and hard-wearing outdoor clothing that'll survive a year or more of touring will cost upwards of about £800.

Camping in the shadow of Cotopaxi, Ecuador. © James Butcher

The sky's the limit in terms of what it's possible to spend on biking and outdoor equipment. If you're on a tight budget, don't lose sight of the fact your last £500 is much better invested in a few months on the road than on titanium handlebars or a jacket that was designed with the West Face of K2 in mind.

On the road

On the road, bicycle touring is arguably the cheapest form of long range travel. Having amassed all necessary gear and made it to the start of your ride, you can live frugally, if desired, as many of the major costs of backpacking and other ways of travelling simply do not apply.

Except when you choose to throw your bike on a vehicle, take a flight, or need to fix a worn-out or broken bike-part, you'll be spending no money day to day on **transport**. Though you'll stay in hotels and guesthouses, many nights are spent wild camping and if you're lucky there'll be times where you are hosted as someone's guest, saving on **accommodation**, which would normally be the biggest expense of the day.

Food will be a major expense; enormous amounts of fuel disappear down cyclists' gullets at each and every pit-stop, but as you'll find yourself off the beaten track, stocking up on local food at small shops and eating at cheap restaurants in non-touristy places, you'll discover that food prices in most of the world are lower than at home.

Insurance and any **visas** complete the last of the major categories of expenditure on a bicycle tour. The latter is dependent on where you choose to head; there are no visa fees for EU nationals in the Americas, whereas in Asia and Africa getting hold of those little stickers and blurred stamps in your passport adds significantly to total costs.

Bear in mind that while it's possible to do a trip incredibly cheaply, and you'll come across the odd rider boasting of having survived for years on US$2 a day, do you really want to penny-pinch this much? It's nice to splash out on a decent meal and a bed every now and then after a tiring period out on the road.

ONLINE HOSPITALITY

Online hospitality websites are a good way to meet local people and to overnight cheaply in towns. Check out:
- **warmshowers.org**, which is specifically for cyclists
- **couchsurfing.org**
- **hospitalityclub.org**

In Latin America, Casas de Ciclistas are a fantastic resource similar to Warm Showers – information can be found on blogs, or by word of mouth, as there is no central website.

Daily costs and timings by continent

Costs vary between countries on the same continent and with different riders' styles of touring, so take these numbers from a survey of book contributors as **ball-park low-end figures** only.

Daily costs on trips across **Asia** are the cheapest, with US$10-15 a day being an achievable budget. A **year** to **18 months** is a common length of time taken to cycle from western Europe to SE Asia.

Africa tends to be a little more expensive, so expect to spend a minimum of US$15-20 per day, and for it to take **at least 6 months** to pedal down the east side, and **a year or more down the west**.

A ride the length of the **Americas** generally takes people at least **18 months**: 6-9 months in North and Central America, and 9-12 months in South America. US$10-20 per person per day in Latin America and US$15-25 in the USA and Canada are doable.

TRAVELLING COMPANIONS

For most people, the decision is already made; it's merely a matter of recognising your situation for what it is. Either you have a partner or friend with a like-minded commitment, or you don't.

Alone?

If you do go alone, people will quiz you about whether it's safe and if you'll have a good time on your lonesome. This is understandable; we are a gregarious species and solo travel does not come naturally to everyone. There's no two ways about it, touring solo is tougher than being with a companion, but it also has many advantages. You'll have the complete freedom of the open road with no compromise necessary when it comes to route choice, daily distances, where and how long to lay up resting. You'll have more interactions with local people, as without a touring partner you'll seek out encounters and you'll appear more approachable too. The experience will undoubtedly be more raw, with no-one to share the highs or later reminisce about those times you kipped in storm drains under Uzbek desert roads to escape the searing summer sun. The testing moments will be all the harder for having no-one to share the mental strain or allay fears about wild camping in bear or lion country. Your moods will likely swing wildly, but once you survive it you'll be all the stronger and more confident for having done so.

Travelling solo means you can stop where you want for as long as you wish.
© Daisuke Nakanishi

If you don't have a riding partner and still want company, you can post on various bike-touring forums, outlining your plans and asking if anyone might be going your way. The good thing about these arrangements is that they aren't set in stone, so you can go your separate ways if riding styles or personalities clash.

Many riders who set off alone spend time touring with company anyway. Life on the road can involve meeting many fellow riders who easily become friends, and camping companions either for the evening or longer if you're both heading the same direction. Adventure cycle touring encourages a certain comradeship and it's unheard of for long-distance riders to pass each other and not stop for a chat. There are those who prefer to ride alone for the most part but enjoy a week or two with others now and again, particularly on a remote or challenging stretch of road. This can be seen as a chance to learn new things and experience different styles of travel, and the real challenge can be in readjusting to being with other people and the compromises required.

With a partner or friend

If you're in a committed relationship with someone, count yourself lucky indeed if you have the same aspirations and both want to take on the same big trip. Companionship means you can share the trip's load – the hours of planning, the tent and stove, the spare parts, the bad times, the learning of mechanic skills and languages. And then there are the simple, though important, things like always having someone to look after your bike while you head into the market to hunt down pastries. Overall it tends to be more fun, and people are braver in a pair than they would be alone, but there's the need for compromise that solo riders just don't have. You also must work hard to get along when you're in each other's company 24/7; trust us, that isn't easy to do. Having a partner to chat to or moan at generally leads to fewer (though still a lot of) interactions with local people, as you can insulate yourselves, when wanted, from the world through which you're travelling.

SOLO WOMEN

If you're travelling on your own, you'll get very used to people telling you how brave (or intrepid, or plucky, or feisty) you are. The secret, you'll quickly discover, is that very little bravery is actually required. Solo women often have a much easier time of it – their very presence tickles people's protective instincts, and they'll often find themselves being invited in for a hot meal and a bed for the night, while their less fortunate male counterparts camp in the snow. And while you may soon tire of the knights in shining armour who insist on 'fixing' your bike when in fact you're a qualified mechanic and built it yourself, if you are genuinely in need of help (or just feeling lazy) – well, they can sometimes have their uses.

The main challenge solo female cyclists face, which their male counterparts don't, is sexual harassment. There are parts of the world where you'll experience a certain amount of harassment, though women travelling through remote areas by bike are statistically much safer than if they were partying in beach resorts. It's very unlikely you'll experience a serious attack, but even a few days of catcalling and flashing can take its toll on your happiness. Everyone evolves their own coping strategies – I've found that appealing to the protective instincts of an older/kinder-looking man can help, if there's one around. Otherwise, ignoring or shouting tends to see off the vast majority of the sex pests. Taking one or two self-defence classes before you set off can be helpful if only in that it improves your confidence, but you are unlikely ever to need to defend yourself physically.

Travelling solo isn't for everyone, but a lot of women who initially thought they could never possibly manage without someone else for safety, company and confidence end up cycling thousands of miles alone and loving it. You're no safer with someone else, even the finest company may grate after a few days, and there's no confidence boost like rolling into a town you never thought you'd reach, thousands of miles away from home, after cycling all day and fixing several punctures, and realising that you did it all by yourself.

Emily Chappell

The couples that ride together most happily tend to be fairly equal in their physical abilities, but a basic thing to consider is the importance of acknowledging differences, such as body mass. When loading your bikes, aim to distribute the weight (bike plus gear) roughly in proportion to each rider's weight. A quick maths teaser for you: if an 80kg man and a 60kg woman travel as a couple on 15kg bikes and with a total of 40kg gear, how should they aim to divvy up the gear? Roughly 25kg : 15kg should work well, in order that the weight of each bike plus gear is the same percentage of each rider's body mass. Often couples just split the gear equally, which causes problems for the lighter rider, generally the woman, carrying proportionately more weight, and consequently having a much harder time of it. If they stick it out, they invariably end up becoming much stronger, and over the course of many months most couples find their endurance abilities, though not their speeds, converge.

Out on the road, couples who find themselves travelling at very different speeds should consider redistributing weight to address this. It's no fun for anyone being left behind, and it soon gets tedious and chilly on a mountain pass waiting for your partner to grind their way to the top. Couples whose physical abilities are very dissimilar might want to think about riding a tandem – see p36 for some pros and cons of this way of travel.

Friendships with origins back home don't always survive the transition to the road where old rules or loyalties are no longer relevant. Travel gives you the freedom to find your own style as a process of self-discovery, and that is often easiest done in the company of strangers where you can re-invent yourself as the kilometres unroll. If you're riding with a friend from home, you need to talk about all these possibilities and agree that expectations may

With a partner there'll always be someone to take your photo.

TRAVELLING WITH KIDS

When our son Luke was born, many people suggested we do something 'more sensible' than bike touring and camping. We decided not to listen and instead looked for ways of reconciling our love of cycling with family life. We embarked on this journey with a large degree of uncertainty and trepidation.

Would Luke enjoy being on a bicycle for hours at a time? How well would he sleep in a tent? What would we do when it rained? And most importantly: how would we make room in our bike bags for the diapers, toys and other things that go along with a child?

There's nothing like experience as a teacher. After a few short trips close to home under our wheels we'd already learned the basics of touring with a kid. First and foremost, go slowly. Our days of 100km have been traded in for lazy days of 30-40km. We are never bored. There are far too many playgrounds to explore, flowers to pick and ice creams to be eaten.

A bit of wiggle room in your budget also helps, to allow for luxuries like meals out and hotels when the weather is really nasty. Prepare to change your packing style (we swapped panniers for a trailer, to make room for a child seat on the bike) and upgrade to ultra-light, compact gear, to make the burden of carrying family-size luggage a little easier.

Luke is now an energetic toddler, with a few thousand kilometres of touring to his name. It hasn't always been easy and we've had stressful moments when rain starts pouring down or when we find ourselves on an unexpectedly busy road, but overall we've had far more positive experiences than negative ones. In addition to being a wonderful way to disconnect from the busyness of everyday life and spend more time together as a family, bike touring has always been a great way of connecting with local people. This is even more the case when you have a child to break the ice.　　**Friedel Grant**

Smiles all round. © Andrew Grant

change on a long ride, and have to be accommodated, which in many cases means splitting up and heading your separate ways.

It may seem obvious to some, but needs mentioning, that those setting out in a pair will benefit from choosing to travel on the same model of bike – there'll be less weight to carry in spares and tools, and fewer online mechanic videos to have to watch and learn from.

Larger groups

Riding for an extended period in a group larger than two is rare, though that's not to say it's impossible or doesn't ever happen. Finding such a group of like-minded individuals with the same ambitions and goals is hard enough to do, but keeping those goals aligned out on the road is even more difficult and often results in the group fragmenting.

RESEARCH – GETTING INFORMATION

Online

The internet is awash with cycle-touring information and one of the joys of beginning to plan a tour is immersing yourself vicariously in other peoples' journeys. You instantly feel you've joined that band of tourers, and people you first came across online are sometimes surprisingly encountered on the road, or else become virtual friends.

Forums

What you'll read on cycling and travel forums is not checked for accuracy but has qualities that books such as this lack, being both interactive and up to date. If you're desperate to find out if the rainy-season mud has engulfed the high passes in the Peruvian Cordillera this year, how far the Chinese have got laying paving on the road to Lubumbashi, or whether the Tajik consul in Tashkent has thrown a tantrum and won't be handing out visas until the next new moon, get online for the latest – someone will have found out and spread the word.

Internet forums such as those at ⌨ crazyguyonabike.com, ⌨ lonelyplanet.com/thorntree/forums/on-your-bike, ⌨ horizonsunlimited.com/hubb and the Touring forum at ⌨ bikeforums.net are great places to search for specific information or ask questions if your query hasn't previously been covered. Facebook and Google groups are also good for picking up real gems of useful information.

Websites and blogs

Established personal websites are excellent sources for gleaning reliable and relevant information. Good places to start are ⌨ travellingtwo.com and ⌨ tomsbiketrip.com, which both house a wealth of knowledge about cycle touring. Friedel and Andrew Grant of Travelling Two produce the *Bike Touring Survival Guide* which answers almost any bike-touring question you might dream of thinking of, while Tom Allen's *Essential Gear for Adventure Cycle Touring* ebook provides a cornucopia of gear advice. Try ⌨ sheldonbrown.com for the answer to your bicycle mechanics-related queries. Other good sites for practical information include ⌨ cyclingabout.com and ⌨ bicycletouringpro.com. Tim and Laura Moss' ⌨ longdistance.bike is packed with stats about tours, and ⌨ crazyguyonabike.com has thousands of bike-trip journals and articles.

A quick internet search about biking in the region that interests you will soon throw up some blogs; most of these will have links to other touring blogs, and in this way it's possible to travel virtually through the best sites, finding information and tales about your chosen route. We've mentioned particularly useful websites within the Route Outlines, but for initial inspiration try checking out: Cass Gilbert's ⌨ whileoutriding.com, Amaya Williams and Eric Schambion's ⌨ worldbiking.info, Logan Watts' ⌨ pedalingnowhere.com, ⌨ gobicycletouring.info, as well as the list of contributors on pp356-8, and expand your touring universe outwards from there.

Cycling e-publications which are well worth perusing include *Bunyan Velo* and *Bicycle Traveler*.

In print

Destination-specific guidebooks such as Lonely Planet and Rough Guides are extremely useful for sightseeing ideas in the country you're headed to, and the tips therein will save you the price you've shelled out on the guide many times over. With an ebook reader, loading up with books won't slow you down on those climbs either, so some people find it makes sense to buy relevant country guides for their ride. Many cyclists, particularly grizzled and more worldly pedallers, travel with maps but no guidebooks as there is so much information in the blogosphere about good routes and sights worth seeing.

It's not a bad idea to read a book on cycle maintenance (see p353) before you go and possibly even before you buy a bike. Haynes' *The Bike Book* is a great place to start though there's no need to delve too deep; the internet has 'how-to' guides for everything, and there'll be a demonstration video on YouTube too. It's not worth the weight taking paper reference books (including this one) on a trip, so digest them before you go or hunt down the digital version.

Other riders

On the road you'll be surprised how frequent meetings with other riders are, particularly if you take popular touring routes and stay in cyclist havens in towns. If they're heading the opposite direction and don't ride with their head in the clouds, they should be the most reliable source of knowledge for what awaits up ahead. You can at least guarantee they'll be the most up-to-date; likewise be prepared for them to ply you for information too.

Documentation

PASSPORTS

If you need a new passport, try and get a '**diplomatic passport**' (if your country issues them) with more pages than the standard issue. Passports aren't cheap and it's amazing how fast they fill up in certain parts of the world.

If you're planning on using an existing passport, make sure it has **at least six months validity** well after the last possible entry date to your last intended country, and apply for a new one if it doesn't. Plenty of places insist on this validity when you enter, and as your plans evolve you'll need all the flexibility you can get.

Hang on to your passport, in spite of dodgy officials who want to take it out of your sight, or guest-houses who want to keep it overnight. Police and other officials may have no legal authority to hold your passport and even honest guest houses experience loss or theft. Carrying photocopies of the photo page and current visa will save time whenever a copy is needed and may suffice in hotels or with police requests to see your passport details. As a backup it's highly recommended to carry scans of every page of your passport on a USB stick or other electronic device. Back up those, and all other important documents, on a cloud or email account before leaving home, so you can access it anywhere you can log on in the world.

Passport pages soon start filling up with stamps and visas.

VISAS

Outside of the Americas, Australia and Europe, bikers will find they become more familiar than they'd ever imagined with the waiting rooms (or outside steps) of consulates and embassies. Visas have become a nice little earner for many African or Central Asian countries that don't rank high as dream travelling destinations and in these places visas will account for a high proportion of overall expenses. Look in the Route Outlines sections for information on visas which are particularly troublesome and may need to be planned for well in advance, or even before departure from your home country, as is the case with Pakistan.

Many of these countries are desperate for foreign currency and demand payment in US$, so check online what you'll need for your next couple of countries and scan further ahead for places that might have become off limits in case you're forced to start planning an alternative route. Some countries want new banknotes, others won't like the curtain in the background of your photos and some Muslim countries insist on women covering their hair in visa application photos.

To help you navigate some countries' tumultuous bureaucratic waters, visa agents can be helpful. They come at a cost, but sometimes are the only way for you to get hold of that closely-guarded stamp. Iran and certain of the 'Stans are examples of places where these agents are invaluable.

Many of the tricky countries have varying entry requirements for different nationalities and policies often differ between embassies of the same country. China is well known for changing rules regularly, and for allowing a month's visa from some embassies but three months from others. For visa issues such as these researching ahead really pays off, and can be the difference between being able to cycle your whole route as planned, and being forced onto a bus or train to get to an office where an extension can be obtained (or even having to get out of the country before your visa expires). Internet forums are more likely to be up to date than possibly-stale official advisory websites.

BIKE DOCUMENTATION

If you've ever met a motorcyclist or overlander being hounded for papers at a border, you'll realise just how easy us cyclists have it when it comes to bureaucracy and documentation. To cross borders you need no paperwork for your bicycle and if a border guard does ask for some, just stay patient – it may well just be them trying to conjure up an excuse to ask for a bribe.

INSURANCE

Insurance is a sensible thing to buy before embarking on an adventurous cycle tour; after all you'll be exposing yourself to hazards such as traffic, exotic diseases and bike theft. Start probing deeper and you'll soon find that the cycle-touring niche isn't actually that well catered for. For a start, you won't be able to cover your bike for tours of more than a couple of months, meaning the best 'bike insurance' you can take is to look after it with sensible precautions like carrying it into your hotel room at night, and avoiding leaving it out in the street unattended in a large city while you go shopping.

Most tourers elect to get travel insurance for peace of mind in the event of disaster – serious injury, big medical bills, personal liability or repatriation. Some standard travel policies will cover this and the loss of smaller articles of kit, which are seen as less of a theft risk than a bike. Another option a minority of bikers choose is to only take out specific medical cover.

It's imperative you **check any policy's small print** and usually it pays to phone up to clarify, or negotiate, terms and premiums. Most 'annual' policies have limits on the length of individual trips and some companies don't make it clear that cycle touring is covered only when incidental to the trip, not the main purpose for it. Intercontinental touring is often specifically excluded, so don't fall into the trap of invalidating your policy when you cross the Bosphorus and continue on to tackle a new continent.

For trips up to a year in length it isn't difficult finding someone to cover you, albeit with a less comprehensive policy than you might like. Renewing or taking out a policy when you've been on the road a year is more tricky and expensive (try ⌨ **worldnomads.com**), and a significant minority of contributors to this book stated they didn't renew cover. This isn't as rash a tactic as it may first appear – in many countries in the developing world medical fees for non-catastrophic incidents will be lower than insurance premiums; it all depends on your appetite for this kind of risk. It's a tedious and time consuming task to research insurance, so don't leave it until the last minute.

MONEY

In terms of money, travelling today is easier than it's ever been as foreign bank cards and cash are ever more widely accepted. There are a number of options for how you handle money on the road, but most see it as essential to set up **internet banking**, which makes it simple to manage your finances whilst abroad. Enabling **telephone banking** as well is useful as a backup, and with a little planning ahead you'll always have some way of getting cash locally no matter what situation you find yourself in.

Before you leave home

Fees for **withdrawing cash from ATMs** abroad can soon rack up, so well before your departure date look into which bank or building society offers the cheapest (or free) withdrawals. Look at ⌨ moneysavingexpert.com for up-to-date articles on the subject. The bother of jumping through the many hoops required to open a new account will become worthwhile when you're able to save hundreds of pounds in fees on the road, as well as have the freedom to take only small amounts out of ATMs at a time.

For existing accounts, consider getting new debit and credit cards if they are a year or two old as once the magnetic stripes wear out the cards will be almost unusable. Even if you don't already use a credit card, it's useful getting one for your big trip for the advantages of protection against loss or disputes with retailers and for emergencies like buying plane tickets, for which sometimes debit cards aren't accepted. If you only take one card, VISA has the edge, particularly with ATMs, and none of the other cards come close to VISA and MasterCard global reach.

Inform your card issuer where you're going, ensure that your own contact details are up to date on their systems, and make yourself a note of the numbers to call from abroad in emergencies. It is all but certain that your bank cards will be suspended for security reasons at some point in your travels, so double-check you know your internet and telephone passwords and security questions and answers as well as the bank contact numbers. Set up your credit card so it's automatically paid off in full each month – when you're gallivanting around with Mongolian nomads it's easy to forget to make the payments and incur hefty interest penalties.

The convenience of internet banking is undeniable but on the road it can never be 100% safe, so don't use it any more than necessary. Carrying your own laptop or tablet is considerably safer for handling banking or any internet purchases you need to make. Using USB drives and portable hard drives is more troublesome as they easily pick up viruses or trojans at internet cafés. Don't forget to bring your **card reader** for logging onto, and making fund transfers from, your online account.

Lastly, a **PayPal** or similar account can come in handy for receiving money or making payments, as it can avoid extortionate bank charges for overseas transfers and exchanges currencies at reasonable rates. You can easily transfer money you have received from others in your PayPal account to your bank account at home and thus access it via an ATM.

Debit and credit cards

As they can be used in almost every country to obtain local currency from ATMs, nearly all travellers take debit and credit cards nowadays, and carry backup amounts of US$ and euros to change only when they cannot use their cards. Debit and credit cards can also be replaced if lost or stolen, though check your card issuer's policy on replacement cards as some will send only to your home address or may send out an emergency card that is valid for only a few months.

To reduce the chances of being a victim of card fraud it's best to withdraw cash from ATMs and pay for things in cash, even when it is possible to pay by debit or credit card. By doing this you reduce the likelihood of someone cloning your card details and using them to make fraudulent purchases. Even though suspicious transactions are usually refunded, it's still a big nuisance having your details cloned as the card will be blocked and you'll have to contact your bank to remedy the situation. Always read your monthly statements online when on the road to check all transactions are legitimate.

Travellers' cheques are becoming increasingly obsolete – their big advantage that they can be replaced if lost or stolen no longer being that important as in most countries it's not necessary to carry enormous cash sums.

Stock up on cash before heading into the ATM-free Nepali hills.

How much cash to carry

With cash machines becoming increasingly widespread, there's less need to carry vast amounts of cash, and in some countries it's possible to with-

SPONSORSHIP

Getting financial sponsorship is hard at the best of times and – wonderful though they are to those of us in the know – cycle tours are sadly just not sexy enough for the media or big business. I could count on one finger the number I've heard of with corporate backing. So, unless you have a really unique and saleable idea – and some good contacts – then save yourself the time and heartache. On a more positive note, however, sponsorship in kind (eg. kit) is much more common. Whatever you're looking for, the following advice still applies.

There are no concrete rules for how you approach a sponsor. The person reading your pitch will have their own preferences: some will find a phone call annoying, others will hate opening post. Just go with whatever you think best (I email).

1 Do your research: find the company's sponsorship policy then see how cheaply you can get the product on eBay or Amazon to check it's actually worth the effort.

2 Consider your audience and what you can actually offer. Local coverage is good for a local store but not a national company. Product feedback may help small companies with new products but not bigger, established brands. Offering advertising on your blog is no good if you just started it yesterday but if you have an established audience then shout about it.

3 Be succinct. Don't give them a chance to dismiss you without having read your best bits. My sponsorship emails are normally four sentences, three bullet points and an attachment. I use a highlighter on the really good bits too, just to be sure.

Finally, don't forget that with great gear comes great responsibilities. Some companies will be happy just knowing you're wearing their kit but others may want the rights to your photos, regular progress updates, routine positive exposure and more. Whether that's a hassle you don't need or a price worth paying is entirely up to you. Either way, good luck.

Tim Moss

PART 1 – PRACTICALITIES

draw US$ or euros as well as local currency from ATMs. Cash machines can be used in almost every country in the world except for the most undeveloped (and therefore inexpensive), and a few quirky ones you need to be aware of. In Iran, your debit card's most useful purpose is to toe in brake pads and the same goes for Sudan and Turkmenistan. In some countries, like Venezuela and Argentina, you won't want to use ATMs due to the low official exchange rate – bring in US$s and take advantage of unofficial street rates.

There are other reasons for carrying convertible cash too. Payment for visas sometimes has to be in US$ or euros, while at other times banks simply run out of cash or the phone networks are down and the ATMs won't work. An emergency cash reserve will get you through these tricky times. It's best not to carry too many large denominations – US$100 and €100 notes may save space, but they're rarely seen abroad so will be viewed with suspicion. Small denomination notes are better, and make sure they're in good condition for the fussier embassies.

Which foreign currency to carry depends on where you are going; the US$ still rules in the Americas, Asia, and Southern and East Africa, while the euro is better accepted in North and West Africa.

In countries with usable ATMs we've never felt the need to carry more than a few hundred US$ each at any one time, however you need to prepare for countries without usable ATMs well in advance – either by bringing hard currency from home, or withdrawing from ATMs (preferably ones which dispense US$ to avoid an extra conversion) on your route beforehand. In these cases you can end up having to carry an uncomfortably large amount, sometimes over US$1000 per person.

Keeping your money safe

It's best not to carry all your money, cards and passport in one place. Get a purse for day money, which could be your 'fake wallet', the one with the expired credit cards that is reluctantly handed to a mugger. It's all you need show the world and the value is so low you can afford to keep it in an outside pocket or a bar bag. As bar bags look like obvious targets for thieves, keeping cash in there works best if you're strict about taking the bag off the bike every time you're away from it.

Next, have a money belt with your main stash of cash, real cards and passport – avoid flashing this unnecessarily. The safest place to carry this is about your person, either as a chest pouch (waterproof-lined to cope with sweat) or a waist pouch, but as these generally aren't comfortable while riding, most cyclists hide it in a pannier when on the bike.

Store further, emergency, cash in a couple of locations – deep in panniers (never near the top where casual thieves will soon find it) or maybe hidden in the seat tube of your bike.

Health preparation

INOCULATIONS

Seek medical guidance from your doctor or health clinic staff; this section provides suggestions only. If you have not travelled to developing countries before, a visit to a travel health clinic can be an expensive proposition involving several repeat visits for follow-up doses of vaccines. It's a good idea to make your first visit six months prior to departure, to ensure enough time for all courses to be administered. Although many of these immunisations are good for several years and you may well be up to date with a number, the first appointment at the travel clinic is the time to sort out which you have or haven't had and to get them all listed on an official, multi-lingual **vaccination certificate**. This certificate may be required at some borders in Latin America and Central Africa, to prove you've had a Yellow Fever shot.

The World Health Organisation (💻 who.int), the US Centers for Disease Control and Prevention (💻 cdc.gov), and the Fit For Travel website (💻 www.fitfortravel.scot.nhs.uk) are good places to start your research. Much will depend on where you travel, but there are a number of immunisations that are good for all travel, no matter where you go.

The most common immunisations are:
- **Hepatitis A** A single dose gives protection for a year; a booster after 6-12 months extends this protection to 20 years.
- **Hepatitis B** Three doses at 0, 1 and 6 months. The disease is transmitted through contaminated blood so the inoculation is advisable for long trips.
- **Tetanus** The single dose adult booster jab is one of those you can get and forget about for a very long time. The disease itself is omnipresent in spore form and the risk of catching it from dirty wounds can be high.

● **Rabies** Three doses at 0, 7 and 28 days. Though rare, rabies is 100% fatal; it is found mostly in Asia and Africa. Cyclists are, of course, an 'at risk' group from infected dog bites or scratches. Having the pre-departure course buys you time to get to a clinic for essential post-bite jabs and also means fewer post-bite jabs over a shorter period of time, provided the right vaccine is available locally. There's more at: 🖥 who.int/rabies/en, and also see p117.

● **Yellow fever** A single dose provides protection for 10 years. The certificate to say you have been inoculated is required to enter some African and Latin American countries.

● **Typhoid** A single dose. Typhoid is uncommon but found throughout the Developing World; it is prone to appearing as an epidemic and, like any other water-borne disease, is most common during the wet/monsoon season, so make sure your plans take this into account.

● **Polio and diphtheria** These are vaccinations you probably already had in childhood – check when you visit a health professional.

● **Japanese B encephalitis** Three doses at 0, 7 and 28 days. A regional disease found in south and east Asia which, though rare, can be fatal.

● **Meningitis** A single dose. The disease is most commonly found in the 'meningitis belt' of sub-Saharan Africa, which runs from Senegal to Ethiopia.

MALARIA

In affected areas, malaria is the biggest headache for cyclists; it's not that uncommon to hear of cycle-tourers contracting it. Carrying bulky boxes of prophylactics is a pain but if you buy locally you risk buying counterfeits, especially in the subcontinent and Thailand, so you're better off paying full price at home. The prescription is always specific to an area and despite the expense it's not a good idea to use leftover tablets from a previous trip.

Take malaria seriously, it's one of the world's biggest killers, especially in Africa where the more dangerous cerebral malaria is present. Reducing your exposure to malarial mosquitoes (see p108) is very important as malaria prophylactics are not 100% effective, they may merely slow down the onset of symptoms.

TAKING HEALTH INFORMATION WITH YOU

It's useful to save information about diseases, inoculations, and medicines from one of the above mentioned websites onto your laptop or smartphone prior to travel. This will enable you to have something reassuring and reliable to refer to if you fall ill out on the road, far from a doctor, the internet or mobile phone reception.

2 BIKES, CLOTHING & CAMPING GEAR

Bikes

You can enjoy the freedom of pedal-powered adventure travel on almost any type of bike. People have ridden across continents on recumbents, tandems and $50 Chinese cheapies. A single speed has been cycled the length of the Manali-Leh Highway and South America has been explored on a 1940s road bike. All it takes is two pedals, as many wheels, a chain and the desire to do it.

There's no guarantee you'll complete your mission even if you spend thousands on a made-to-order, expedition-ready beauty because, like all bicycles, it won't pedal itself, but starting out with a well-chosen and equipped machine stacks things massively in your favour.

These are the most important things to consider when looking for an adventure touring bicycle:

• **Comfort** is non-negotiable. Always test-ride a bike you are considering taking on a big trip and, if it is comfortable, keep it on your list of potentials. Never be tempted by a cheap price into buying the wrong size bike or something that doesn't suit you.

• **Strength** should be considered with every part of the bicycle, from the frame to the screws that attach your rack. Select components that are hardwearing and long lasting.

• **Simple designs** and standard, generic components are best as you will find replacement parts and tools to fix your bike far more easily. If you choose exotic parts you'll need to carry the spares and specialised tools with you.

• **Ride a bike you love**. Some bikes will take a bit more effort to convert to a world tourer but touring is a very personal, customisable thing and you should consider your own tastes and instincts. If you love your low-down recumbent or feel more comfortable on your 700c-wheeled hybrid, work through all the issues in this chapter and adapt the bike to suit your own style and needs.

• **Weight** should not be the priority when choosing a touring bicycle as the factors above are more important. However, consider the extra weight before you are lured into fitting that double-pronged kickstand or over-engineered rack: keep the kilos down and your whole ride will be easier and more enjoyable.

Touring Bike Anatomy

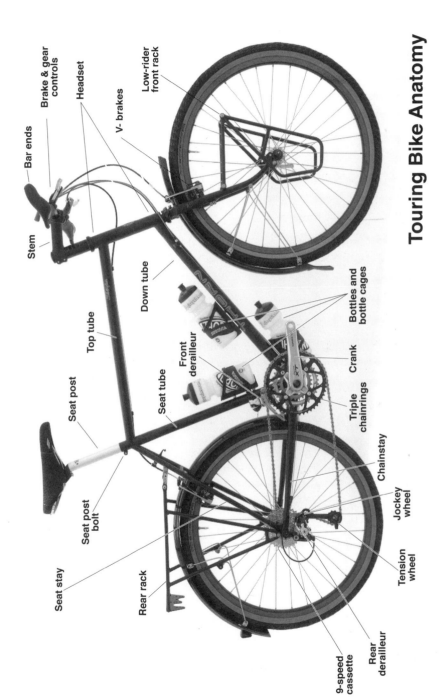

Bar ends

Brake & gear controls

Headset

V- brakes

Low-rider front rack

Stem

Down tube

Top tube

Bottles and bottle cages

Front derailleur

Crank

Seat post

Seat tube

Triple chainrings

Chainstay

Seat post bolt

Jockey wheel

Seat stay

Rear rack

Tension wheel

9-speed cassette

Rear derailleur

NARROWING DOWN YOUR CHOICES

Expedition touring bikes

Features: 26" or 700c wheels, any handlebar, comfortable frame geometry, rim or disc brakes, low bottom bracket, forks will accept up to ~2" tyres

These bicycles are made to circumnavigate the globe and are normally a cross between a traditional touring bike (see below) and a mountain bike. The geometry is designed with all day, every day comfort in mind and is intended to be easy to manoeuvre when loaded up with heavy panniers. A long

chainstay prevents your heels from hitting your rear panniers and provides stability, as does the low bottom bracket. Some expedition tourers are designed with paved roads in mind, others are dirt road oriented.

A new expedition touring bike will roll for thousands of kilometres with little more than the occasional puncture to repair – reliability which is achieved through a combination of simple, durable and functional components which are hard to break and easy to fix.

Thorn Raven Tour. © James Butcher

You can buy an expedition touring bike from about £1000, or go for a highly customised and handmade bike that will fit your dimensions perfectly, and set you back considerably more.

Traditional touring bikes

Features: 700c wheels, drop handlebars, long chainstays, comfortable frame geometry, rim brakes, low bottom bracket, tyres up to 1.5"

If you go into your local bike shop (LBS) and ask for a touring bike, this is likely to be the sort of bicycle you'll be shown. These kinds of bikes were perfect in the days when touring meant pedalling on paved roads from youth hostel to youth hostel in the British hills; nearly all traditional touring bikes have 700c wheels, and are designed to run tyres up to 1.5" wide.

DEMYSTIFYING TYRE SIZING

There exist many different wheel sizes – from those used on kids' bikes up to 29" – and different ways of measuring and describing these sizes. The width of the tyre is traditionally measured in inches for mountain biking and millimetres for road biking.

The International Organisation for Standardisation (ISO) has standardised sizes, defining tyre size (in millimetres) as the bead seat to bead seat diameter. Mountain bike tyres described as 26" are ISO 559. The 700c tyres which are used on road bikes are ISO 622. Many modern mountain bikes come with 29" tyres, which are also ISO 622, but are wider than 700c tyres. The 27.5", or 650b, tyre is a compromise between 29" and 26" and is gaining popularity with mountain bikers; it is ISO 584. The standardised way of displaying tyre size is width-diameter (in mm) e.g. 50-559.

Adventure touring nowadays is likely to mean carrying camping gear and travelling on rougher roads, and traditional touring bikes run into difficulties here. They don't handle heavy loads well or have the fatter tyres necessary for dirt road riding. As such they are more suited to paved roads in Europe or North America rather than a more rugged tour to far flung corners.

Mountain bikes

Features: 26" or 29" wheels, flat handlebars, aggressive frame geometry, usually disc brakes, high bottom bracket, tyre width normally >1.75"

If you plan on spending a significant amount of time on dirt or gravel roads then a mountain bike can make an excellent steed. It is also a good option for a first tour if you already have a mountain bike and would rather spend more money on the tour itself than on buying a new bike, or if you are purchasing your bike in a country where touring-specific bicycles aren't easily found.

Felt Nine 30 aluminium 29er mountain bike. © Jukka Salminen

Hardtail mountain bikes need a little work to make them tour-ready, but they are strong, and their low gearing is perfect for hauling a load up insane Ecuadorian inclines. Their wide handlebars and upright riding position are ideal for confidently controlling a heavy rig on unpredictable mountain roads or rough surfaces. Many mountain bikes now have 29" wheels rather than traditional 26" wheels – see p38 for a discussion on the pros and cons of these.

If you're going round the shops testing mountain bikes, or already own one, here are some touring-specific features to consider:
● Small adjustments notwithstanding, can you foresee day-long comfort? Is the handlebar height roughly level with the saddle, or is the riding position too stretched out (see p59)?
● Are there threaded eyelets ('braze-ons') on the frame and front fork for fitting racks? (See p67 for racks that might work if there are no braze-ons on your bike.)
● Is the rear wheel so close to the seat tube that you may have problems with heel clearance once panniers are fitted?
● Is the bottom bracket so high you feel unstable when riding the bike fully loaded?
● Are the wheels, forks or frame made of carbon fibre, or a complex construction which would be difficult to repair in the field?
● Some parts, such as the suspension fork and disc brakes may not be of sufficient quality for touring. How much will it cost to switch these out for better alternatives?

If your finances are tight, the old skool frames of the '90s make perfect touring bikes and can be built up with new parts for a budget ride. Look for something like a '90s Specialized Stumpjumper or Trek 830, and see p44 for details of how to magic junkyard salvage into a fully functioning tourer.

PART 2 – BIKES, CLOTHING & CAMPING

Fat bikes

Features: 26" or 29" wheels, flat handlebars, disc brakes, high bottom bracket, 3-5"-wide tyres

A recent and very much niche addition to the adventure cycle-touring bike list, but one guaranteed to put the adventure into your tour and earn you adulation from every teenage boy you pedal past. Where a normal bike will start to skid in snow, sand and mud, the fat bike will simply keep on rolling. This type of bike is often used by the new breed of lightweight bikepacker, who seeks out rough roads and singletrack. It is best for shorter tours in a narrower range of environments, however a few hardy souls have successfully crossed continents on fat bikes – see p78 and p118. Fat bikes will hinder your speed on paved roads, and other disadvantages which merit consideration include that you will never find spare parts for your wheels outside of Europe or North America. This is a choice for the few whose desire to ride challenging terrain outweighs these drawbacks.

Pedalling a recumbent through Thailand.
© Ben Dugauquier

Recumbents

The comfortable seat of a recumbent bike is a great place from which to see the world; the riding position is relaxed and natural with a reduced frontal area that slices through headwinds effortlessly. The low eye-level makes you less conspicuous to other road users, but saddle sores, wrist and back trouble are rare and the more upright position of your head and neck is perfect for enjoying the scenery. They are a great choice for those who suffer from back or knee problems. Carrying their loads low, recumbents are ideally suited to fast road rides, but cope much less well off-road and on steep hills where their greater weight and the rider's inability to stand on the pedals slows them down. They're also a pig to carry up steep and narrow guest house stairs to your room, and boxing them for a flight is a challenge.

For comfort, they can't be beaten and if you love yours, these criticisms won't deter you from riding a recumbent around the planet. But you have to be an extrovert to enjoy the attention a recumbent attracts or you'll soon tire of it.

Tandems

The rewards of tandem riding are a fast bike and close company. Tandems are excellent for couples of different abilities who might otherwise be left cycling miles apart. These days tandems are built for the heavier rider to sit up front (most are sold to mixed couples) and so have a relatively smaller cockpit at the back. There's much less space for each person's gear compared to riding two single bikes, so many loaded tandems tow a trailer as well as carrying panniers. This makes the whole rig as long as a car, nearly as heavy and slow on unpaved roads so if possible try to limit yourself to four panniers and a rack pack.

It's clearly an eye-catching and spectacular way to go, and like a recumbent attracts attention, but don't expect to save any money buying a tandem instead of two single bikes: for adventure touring on a tandem you need the best quality you can afford. Tandems need to be very strong in every aspect to support the weight and pedalling force of two riders, and fare best on flat roads. They're fast in a straight line but slower on hills as it's harder to co-ordinate pedal stroke, and they're not as nippy in traffic as a solo bike.

If you're thinking of buying a new tandem, consider having one made for you. That way the fit for each rider is closer to ideal and you could specify S&S couplings (clamps which separate the frame midway, allowing you to break the bike down to a more manageable size), which is very helpful given that some planes and even trains won't take the length of a tandem frame.

NARROWING IT DOWN FURTHER

Frame material

A purpose-built expedition touring frame from a good manufacturer will be stiff enough to take a heavy load and strong enough not to break under the stress of rugged, corrugated routes, whether it is made from **chromoly** steel or **aluminium**. All touring bikes used to be made from chromoly steel because aluminium frames often suffered from fatigue failures, but with the advent of oversized aluminium tubing and some clever frame-design, aluminium frames can now be built strong enough for touring. If a touring frame breaks it is likely to be because of an impact collision and whichever material it is made from it will be hard to make a long term repair unless it is only a small crack.

In order to be strong enough, aluminium frames are built stiffer than steel frames. Some riders like the springiness of steel and traditionalists can't imagine bikes made of anything but chromoly tubes, but countless aluminium bikes such as Koga-Miyata have toured the world and the preference for steel is more about personal taste than anything.

Aluminium's low density means that despite the oversized tubing used, an aluminium frame will be as light, or lighter, than a chromoly frame. Another consideration is the cost: chromoly frames cost less than good aluminium frames. If travelling on an aluminium frame, ensure that the

---

WHAT'S IN A NUMBER?

Different grades of steel and aluminium are classified using different number systems: 4130 steel (as specified by the Society of Automotive Engineers) is often used in good quality steel bicycles. Reynolds Steel, a market leader in Britain, describe their different steels using three digits. Reynolds 520 or 525 chromoly is used in low end bikes – the steel is cheaper because it hasn't been strengthened by heat treatment. Reynolds 853 has been heat treated, is stronger and is used in high end bikes. Reynolds 969 is made especially for Thorn (see p41) and is supposed to be the strongest Reynolds steel.

A good aluminium frame will have been manufactured from aircraft-grade aluminium. This will be designated two codes: a four digit number that denotes the composition, and a letter and number which denote the type of heat treatment. While there are quality differences between the various aluminium types, the method of construction and welding is highly important in determining overall frame strength and it's too simplistic to decide from the material alone whether one frame is stronger than another.

derailleur hanger is replaceable, and carry a spare as it is easy to break, which would render your gears unusable.

Quality touring frames can also be made out of **titanium**, but as these are far more costly than chromoly or aluminium frames, they are a much less common choice.

Wheel size

It's possible to build a wheel suitable for heavy touring in either 26", 700c or 29" sizes (see box p34), but outside of the developed world you will usually only find 26" wheels, tyres and inner tubes for sale. The quality may not be very good but you'll find something that fits and keeps you riding; not so with 700c or 29" wheels. The advantages of touring on a bike with these larger wheel sizes include that they are better for tall riders, have slightly lower rolling resistance and roll better over bumps, but if you go for this you need to think about how you'd fix a wheel in the event one suffered serious damage.

TOURING WITH PLUS-SIZE TYRES

When an upcoming tour promises a hefty percentage of unpaved terrain, the perfect bicycle becomes the focus during the planning stage. There are many factors that play a part in putting it together. Will you be travelling over rocky, technical bits? How about soft sand? How much water does it need to carry? Will the size of tyres you need be available in the country you're touring in, and does it matter?

These are all legitimate questions in the decision making process, although that last one is increasingly ignored by intrepid dirt-tourers. Folks are using 29ers, fat bikes, 650b, and even mid-fat 29+ to reach far corners of the globe. The typical safe choice is a 26" bike; standard 26"x 1.75-2" tyres are available in most countries. But there are benefits that 29ers and fat bikes have to offer. For starters, large tyre volume can increase the ability of a bicycle to perform well off road, without suspension. When off-the-tarmac is

where the adventure beckons, a rigid bike can serve up a beating; bigger tyres eat up the vibrations that this terrain dishes out, for kilometres on end.

So what about the *risk*? Say you are in Timbuktu, and your 3" 29er tyre blows a hole in the sidewall the size of a Malian Franc coin. What can be done? They probably don't stock 29er tyres in the local corner store in Timbuktu. Several online retailers, such as SJS Cycles and 🖳 JensonUSA.com, claim shipping availability to most countries, worldwide; maybe not Mali though. More than likely, if you are a fairly resourceful person (which is assumed since you got yourself to Timbuktu) you will find a way to get replacement tyres shipped to you... it might just take a while, and some money. Otherwise planning in advance and carrying a spare is an option. If your trip is through a more developed country, even a country such as South Africa, 29er tyres are readily available.

True fat tyres are another story. Although it is a rapidly growing trend, fat bikes don't have high statistics outside of the USA and parts of Western Europe. However, some 26" fat bike rims of a reasonable size (around or under 65mm) can also fit a standard 26x2.25" tyre in the event of a catastrophe.

The rulebook has definitely been burned, and with a big world shrunken by the internet, anything is possible. Just make sure you think about the options and possibilities based on location.

Logan Watts

In Morocco with a 29+ Surly ECR.
© Logan Watts

Where would your nearest in-country shop be? Would you have to get a new wheel shipped from home? If wheel spares are unobtainable en route, you'll need to carry extra inner tubes and a spare tyre. With the popularity of 29" wheels increasing, replacements are slowly becoming more easily available in some of the world's capital cities and adventure hubs, but for those who want minimum bike fuss whilst touring, it's recommended to stay safe and opt for 26". See opposite for an alternative view on the merits of using plus-size tyres.

Derailleur gears vs hub gear

We'll get into details of gears on p47, but quite early on you need to decide whether you want derailleur gears or a hub gear – both have their merits. Although you may be able to adapt a frame to both Rohloff (by far the most used hub gear for touring) or derailleur, they are usually designed for one or the other.

Derailleur gears are what you see on most bicycles; one to three chainrings at the front and a cassette of sprockets on the back with a derailleur hanging down. They are widely used throughout the world, so should something go wrong or wear out, you will be able to source replacements. Downsides include that the working parts are exposed to the dirt and dust which means you need to maintain and clean your gears regularly; the rear derailleur is also vulnerable, so more care needs to be taken than with a hub gear.

The German Rohloff Speedhub is an ingenious 14-speed internally-geared system; all the gear changing goes on inside the hub, protected from dust, grime and knocks. The Speedhub is an expensive option, but it is tough, has proved to be reliable, and compared to a derailleur it needs very little maintenance. However, if your Rohloff breaks, it can put the brakes on your tour for weeks. A local mechanic will not be able to fix it, so you will be at the mercy of the international courier system to ship replacement parts from home.

Rim brakes vs disc brakes

Loaded touring bikes need powerful brakes, not least when descending from mountain passes. **Rim brakes** (of which V-brakes and cantilever are the most commonly used for touring) use a pair of brake pads that are squeezed against the rim to stop progress; **disc brakes** (which can be mechanical or hydraulic) have a disc or rotor that is mounted at the centre of the wheel and brake pads are squeezed against this to bring your bike to a halt.

The advantage of a rim brake is its worldwide availability and mechanical simplicity though they provide less powerful braking than disc brakes and rim brake pads will eventually wear through your rims. Most bikes come with mounts for either disc or rim brakes (not both) so you need to decide whether to play it safe with rim brakes, or go for improved performance with discs, before buying your bike. More detail about different types of brakes is on p51.

Tektro Oryx cantilever rim brakes.

PART 2 – BIKES, CLOTHING & CAMPING

Drop bars vs straight bars

Drop bars best suit those who plan on pacing along on paving: they have a number of comfortable hand positions and you can tuck up when heading into headwinds. But for adventure touring they simply aren't as good as **straight bars**. Straight bars really come into their own on dirt roads, where the bar's additional width gives you better control over steering on a bad surface, and you'll also appreciate the more powerful braking. Switching a setup between drops and straights can be done, but be cautious here. Nearly all bikes are designed for one kind or the other and you may run into issues, not least in relation to finding a comfortable riding position.

Choosing a new bike

Expedition touring bikes are the ideal choice as they are specifically designed for the kind of tour this book is all about. But don't assume you must have a bike like this for your big trip. Plenty of cyclists, especially those on tight budgets, set off with an adapted mountain bike or a budget touring bike and most will do just fine. Out on the road they may realise there are better choices, but the main thing is they got on a bike and did it.

As with many products, big bicycle manufacturers need to be seen to update models every year, even though it might just add up to a paint job. You can save a great deal by buying last year's near-identical model, but be cautious if tempted by a great bike that's one size too big or small as it may be difficult to achieve that all-important comfortable fit.

It's always helpful to head to your nearest bike shop that stocks expedition touring bicycles to look at and try out some bikes, have a chat and seek advice. If you know a lot about bikes it is possible to buy a frame, select components, and build up your perfect touring bike from scratch (see p46).

Here is a selection of bikes that make a superb choice for an adventure cycle tour:

EXPEDITION TOURING BIKES

Surly

The Surly **Long Haul Trucker** (LHT) is a great blend of road and mountain bike and is equally at home with straight bars and 2.1" tyres as it is with 700c wheels and drops. You can buy a complete bike which comes with drop bars, but if you'll be riding some dirt it makes more sense to buy just the frame and fork and build up the bike with straight bars from there. The frame is 4130 chromoly with all the braze-ons a touring cyclist could dream of: racks, mudguards, spare spokes, three bottle cage mounts, brake hangers and even mounts for gear shifters on the down tube. Everything on the LHT is a standard easy-to-find size, it's got relaxed, stable steering and long chainstays (a generous 18"). It comes with 26" wheels and also in 700c for larger frame sizes. I've found it fun and easy to ride on both pristine paving and rotten *ripio*.

The complete bike is fantastic value (it retails at £1150), light (under 13kg), with dependable, long lasting and easily sourced parts. The guys at Surly have invested in good components where it matters and left you to customise it with saddle, pedals, tyres and mud guards.

An overloaded Surly Long Haul Trucker.

The **Disc Trucker** (£1300) is the disc brake equipped version of the Long Haul Trucker and comes with dependable Avid BB7 cable disc brakes.

The **Troll** (£1300) is a more off-road bike than the LHT, and is perhaps the most versatile expedition touring bike there is. With 26" wheels, and braze-ons for everything (rim or disc brakes, derailleur or Rohloff) this is an anything-goes bike described by the makers as a "go to utility tractor". Designed with gnarly dirt road tourers in mind, if you are inclined to bikepack some singletrack on your trip then the Troll can even be fitted with a 100mm travel suspension fork. The ingenious Surly Tuggnut will keep your chain taut when you fit a Rohloff Speedhub.

Surly Troll. © Cass Gilbert

Surly design some of the most innovative bikes around. Having produced the **Pugsley**, the first commercially available fat bike, in 2005, the **ECR** is their touring mid-fat (29+) bike, equipped with all the braze-ons you need for winter or desert riding. The **Ogre** is the 29er version of the Troll and is another that is great if you want to include some bikepacking routes as part of a longer tour.

Thorn

Thorn pioneered the making of expedition touring bikes. With a workshop in Somerset, you can book an appointment to go and see Thorn's touring experts, who'll help you choose the model that suits you best, and then customise it for your tour. The **Sherpa** (£1300) is the entry-level derailleur bike in Thorn's adventure touring range, though in all respects it is a premium quality bike, available in short and long frames in varying sizes. The frame is made with oversized 4130 chromoly in Taiwan, where most high-quality steel frames are made.

Loaded touring on a Thorn Sherpa.
© Paul Schmidt

PART 2 – BIKES, CLOTHING & CAMPING

You can upgrade everything on a Sherpa and still have a bike designed for hard touring at a lower price than the Rohloff models (see below). It's a perfect touring set up with all the fixings for bottle cages, racks, and mudguards with very solid geometry for easy control of a heavily-loaded bike.

In 2004 Thorn produced their first model designed specifically for the Rohloff 14-speed hub gear system, the **Raven Tour**. The Raven Tour (£2170) is extremely versatile; it's not the lightest bike in the world but it is one of the strongest, built from oversized chromoly made exclusively for Thorn. If you want a stronger frame, your only choice is another Thorn, the **Nomad** (£2300), which has thicker seat tube and stays and can take a shock fork as an option. It's also available with S&S couplings, making it much easier and quicker to pack the bike down for transport in a package small enough to avoid airline surcharges.

Thorn Nomad. © Nathan Haley

The advantages of designing Thorn's expedition tourers from the ground up for Rohloff are that the torque arm needed to hold the hub in place on many conversions is not needed, nor is the chain tensioning wheel. Instead, Thorn use an eccentric bottom bracket held in place by two easy-to-adjust bolts. Cable routing is designed for friction-free shifting without tight bends in the cable, for more effortless gear-changing. Most buyers choose Thorn's own wide and swept riser bar, as the Rohloff shifter will not fit on drops.

Thorn offers a unique 100-day return policy on Rohloff-equipped bikes, enough time to take your new bike on a short tour and return it if you're not happy.

Koga-Miyata

Dutch-made Koga-Miyatas are designed from the ground up for an adventurous tour and they're fully equipped for it too. Koga shocked the hardcore touring world when it switched to aluminium for its trekking bike frames (the forks are still chromoly). The off-the-peg version of their top-end model, the **World Traveller**, costs €2250 and comes with everything you need already fitted, including Tubus racks, Ergon grips and a Brooks B17 saddle. The Koga Signature tool (🖳 koga-signature.com) is really neat for custom-building your bike online. Start with the frame and select 26" or 29" wheels, derailleur gears or a Rohloff and customise it with different racks, saddles, rims and handlebars.

Koga Miyata World Traveller.
© Amaya Williams

For steely types, the chromoly-framed 700c **Randonneur** is only slightly heavier than the World Traveller.

Santos

Another from the Dutch School of expedition touring bikes and similar in many ways to the Koga Miyata; Santos have also made the shift from steel to aluminium-framed touring bikes. The **Travel Master 2.6** is the pick of the adventure tourers in the troop, fitted with 26" wheels, XT derailleur gears and XT rim brakes. It is also available with hydraulic rim brakes and in a 700c and 29" wheel size. Santos bikes are designed around a Rohloff hub and can also be fitted with a Gates belt drive (see p50) instead of a chain, which makes

for even less maintenance. Take your pick from 7 different sizes and 24 different colours. The **Travel Lite** is an alternative for lightly loaded touring cyclists.

The bikes come with so many choices that it is worth going for a fitting in order to get a customised bike. In the UK you could head to MSG Bikes in West Sussex who will help you fit the bike and customise it with racks, bottle cages, handlebars and anything else you can think of.

Santos Travelmaster. © Cass Gilbert

Recumbents

If you're going to tour on a recumbent, the aluminium-framed **Street Machine GTE** is probably the pick of the bunch. It is compact for a recumbent, weighs the same as a conventional tourer, and has a good load-carrying capacity – it handles four panniers well. Rear panniers sit behind the rider and there's space for a cargo bag too, all low down for added stability. The Street Machine is a great ride on a good road: stable, fast and fairly responsive with its 20" front wheel; it has rear suspension right under the seat. A recumbent will make your life a bit more complicated, but if you're rarely off paved roads and

want to cover big mileage every day, the Street Machine will do it in style and comfort.

The **Azub Max** is another aluminium recumbent which is able to carry big loads. Its front and rear wheels are the same size – choose the 26" option for touring. Having a larger front wheel than the Street Machine makes it a better choice if you're tempted to ride some dirt roads, and it'll make you a bit more visible too. Neither of these bikes are cheap options – they both retail at over €2000.

Customs inspection of an HP Velotechnik Street Machine GTE in Central Asia.
© Rob Thomson

More dream bikes worth considering

There are many small chromoly frame builders in the UK who can build your perfect custom-made bike. If you take this (expensive) route, spend time going to see a few to work out who you get on with and who best understands your needs. **Oak Cycles** are one such frame builder; **Oxford Bike Works'** Expedition Bike is too new to have been pedalled round the world, but looks like a worthy competitor to the expedition bikes already discussed.

If you're prepared to look further afield, there are numerous alternatives. The **Tout Terrain** Silk Road is a Rohloff- or Pinion-based (see p51) bike with an integral stainless steel rack. **VSF Fahrrad Manufaktur** make a few different expedition bikes from the derailleur-equipped TX-400 to the Pinion P1.18-equipped TX-1200. **Van Nicolas** make beautiful titanium frames and the

ADAPTING AN OLD MOUNTAIN BIKE

You may be on a tight budget or perhaps you're turned off modern mountain bike designs with the near inevitability of ending up with an aluminium frame fitted with potentially fiddly suspension forks, or 29" wheels. In which case looking for an old MTB is a flash of inspiration; not only will you save money but you'll also get a bike that may be better suited to the kind of riding you have in mind: simple, reliable and easy to maintain on the back roads of the world. Out there you can still find inexpensive parts easily enough as locals still ride bikes with technology or equipment from yesteryear; it's the latest gear that can be hard to find.

Here's what to look for when checking out older (1990s or earlier) bikes:

• Avoid suspension or be wary of early generation suspension systems. Don't even consider rear suspension bikes.
• Stick with chromoly frames; aluminium welding is much better nowadays; in older bikes fatigue is more likely. If you prefer aluminium, go with a bike not much more than about five years old that has had 'one careful owner' and not been thrashed around MTB parks.
• Older mountain bikes were generally cross-country designs, so you'll find them to be good all-rounders in terms of handling. Chainstays shorter than 17" (43cm) may be too short for big feet to clear the rear panniers.
• An 8-speed cassette can be upgraded to give as wide a gear range (ie: between highest and lowest gear) as today's 9-speed. For 7-speeds it is a stretch, so look for an 8-speed bike if you're heading for the hills.

• Bar-top shifters are worth looking out for; a simple design, easy enough to use and fix. They are hard to find now, though sometimes turn up in odd places like Romania or India. Bar-top shifters, however, can be built up using the bar-end gear levers sold for touring bikes which fit in the ends of drop bars.
• Non-compact frames. Older bikes usually had full-length seat tubes and near-horizontal top tubes, giving more room inside the triangle to fit frame bags (see p71), bottle cages and other essentials such as your growing flag sticker collection.
• Threaded headsets (as opposed to modern threadless systems – see p58) made it very easy to adjust your handlebar height as well as turn or remove the handlebars altogether without altering the headset adjustment.
• Cantilever brakes are as old as the hills and when well-adjusted, nearly all will stop you fast enough. Plus it's easy and inexpensive to upgrade these to more powerful V-brakes.

Remember it's primarily the frame you're looking out for. Assuming it's in good shape don't be put off if everything else is junk as long as the price is right; it can all be changed.

Where to find them and what to look for

A walk to my local train station finds a classic 1986 Stumpjumper, a '90s Diamond Back and an old Marin hybrid chained up every day. It's the sad fate of so many once-great MTBs to be relegated to commuter hackbikes when they could be wheeling with the condors across the Cordillera Blanca. There's

Pioneer is a bike for a serious tour with a Gates belt drive-driven Rohloff Speedhub. **CoMotion** cycles make tandems and singles – the 26″ Pangea is built like a tank from Reynolds 725 tubing.

CHEAPER TOURING BIKES

With cycle touring being in vogue, a number of entry-level touring bikes are appearing. If you need a bike for a rough, long trip then go for a more robustly equipped expedition bike or mountain bike, but for less demanding terrain these cheaper tourers will serve you well. The Country Explorer by Edinburgh-based **Revolution Bikes** is built on a solid Reynolds 525 steel frame, has Avid BB5 mechanical disc brakes and is good value at £600. The STI shifters, less-strong 700c wheels and lower-spec gear set may not be ideal, but

little incentive for their owners to sell them because they're virtually worthless to most people and they're becoming harder to find. Good examples often show up on eBay, Gumtree or Craigslist but are hyped in a 'they don't make them like this any more' way as if the seller knows what treasures they are. Rather than trawl eBay with separate searches for models you're interested in, check out the AuctionWatch feature, which searches eBay sites worldwide, at 🖳 retro-bike.co.uk/auction. Bike forums are also great places to look, especially for serious old touring bikes. In the UK, the CTC has a good small ads forum for buying and selling secondhand bikes, as does the Adventure Cycling Association in the US.

Above all you need to make a close inspection of the frame, and not just aluminium frames. The most common type of damage is from a front-end crash which shows up as a bump underneath the down tube, right at the top where it joins the head tube. Look also for cracks around the welds; the bottom bracket is a likely place, especially on an old aluminium frame. Forks that appear to be bent backwards, even if a tiny amount, is not a good sign. A weakened frame may not crack up until you're hammering with a full load down the KKH, but eyeing up a bike from the front, top and side will identify anything out of alignment, as should a test ride. Try riding the bike no-handed to see if it's balanced or if it wobbles. Look for any roughness in the steering: the headset might need some work. Old bikes can grind and click down in the bottom bracket, but these are cheap and easy to replace.

There are many good bikes out there but the big names like Trek, Specialized, Giant and Marin will be easiest to find. Look for chromoly Treks such as the 830 or 950 models or a MultiTrack. Specialized Rockhoppers and Stumpjumpers were classics until they went to aluminium and the frame design changed radically. Late model steel HardRocks are fine too. Marin's bikes in the 1990s were all steel and were versatile designs, as were Giants. GT bikes like the old Avalanche are a bit trickier to fit racks to but the oldies are good strong designs, if pitched as a little racier.

Don't go back beyond 7-speed cassettes; the axle spacing was narrower for 6-speeds. Seven-speed cassettes were the first Hyperglide models with indents and ramps cut into the sprockets to ease shifting. Later 7-speed hubs were wider, 135mm, the same as today's 8 and 9-speeds – and are the ones to go for.

Stephen Lord

1992 Rockhopper still going strong.

to get you out on your first tour this bike will work fine. Similarly the **Dawes** Galaxy AL is a 700c aluminium touring bike with rear rack which would be fine on a light, paved tour; it also costs £600. It comes fitted with cantilever brakes and Schwalbe Marathon tyres.

In a 700c wheel and with TRP-Spyre disc brakes, the **Genesis** Tour de Fer is worth a look – it retails at £900. **Ridgeback**'s World Expedition is a 26" tourer with a Reynolds 520 chromoly frame, bar-end shifters, and a reasonable chainset but weaker wheels than you normally want from an expedition bike. It is another priced at £900, but if you can spare the extra £250 I think it's worth going for a Surly LHT. In the US, the Novara Safari by **REI** is a double butted steel touring bike with 700c wheels, Deore components and Microshift thumbies for US$1100

MID-RANGE MTBS

Buying and converting a mid-range mountain bike used to be a common way of creating your own adventure tourer. After all, adventure touring bikes are all about using mountain bike technologies and components on a heavy-duty tour-ready frame. Off-the-peg mountain bikes are becoming less and less suitable for touring and therefore more expensive to adapt while at the same time, Surly, Thorn, Salsa, Genesis, On-One and many other brands are producing frames and bikes well-suited to round the world trips and with all the braze-ons for racks and bottle cages that mountain bikes lack.

If you are drawn to mountain bikes or perhaps favour shorter, off-road trips, look to the low- to mid-range bikes from top makers to avoid fussy frills you will want to swap out, such as long-travel shocks. You will probably also want to change the tyres and fit racks (see p65) but if a mountain bike is the ride you like, then go for it.

BYOB: BUILD YOUR OWN BIKE

A number of bike manufacturers offer frame-only or frame and fork deals, including Surly and Thorn (their Sherpa model). Mostly these are smaller outfits offering chromoly frames built in Taiwan rather than expensive made-to-order or full custom-builds. The Inbred MTB chromoly frame from **On-One** is a cheaper option for building up a 26" or 29" tourer from scratch; it can be matched with a rigid chromoly fork compatible with disc or rim brakes. The **Genesis** Longitude frame is a 29er that has every braze-on imaginable and looks wonderfully customisable; it even takes a 3" tyre if you substitute your triple chainring for a double.

On-One Inbred chromoly mountain bike, customised with Tubus racks, Shimano Deore groupset, Brooks saddle and Marathon Mondial tyres. © Lars Henning

Buying a frame and fork like this is a great way to go if you have a mountain bike with good components but a frame that is too compact, won't take racks or is too specialised (or valuable) to work as a tourer. Just transfer the groupset and you're ready to roll. Unless you have a donor bike you'll spend much more on transmission, brakes, wheels and so on, but you'll have the satisfaction of your own custom-specified bike for less than the high-end names mentioned earlier. Your local bike shop can assemble it all for you, or you can learn those skills yourself on a course (see p353).

A word of caution for all self-builders: try to avoid building a Frankenbike, a mish-mash of components that may not work well together, such as mixing road and mountain bike groups and different brands of transmission kit. Sometimes this works, sometimes not, so research well and be prepared to take advice, including this advice, which says be moderate in your tinkerings, the most difficult of which is to switch between dropped and flat handlebars.

Gears, brakes and wheels

Now you've got your bike, new or used, you need to assess what works and what needs upgrading. If you've gone for a new bike you'll ideally have bought something with decent componentry (see p48) and may need only tyres (see p56), a rack or two for the panniers (see p65) and a dialled-in seating position (see p59).

GEARS

Derailleur gears

Your chainrings, chain and sprockets are the hardest working areas on your bike. Expedition touring bikes use mountain bike derailleur gear groups, which offer durability and a far wider, as well as lower, range of gears than road bikes. Their relative cheapness and worldwide availability make them great for cycle touring, even though they need a fair bit of maintenance and tweaking to keep them running well.

Derailleur gears have 1, 2 or 3 chainrings on the front and 7 to 11 sprockets on the rear cassette; a maximum of 33 different gears. Until recently the standard gearing on a mountain bike was a triple chainring of around 22, 32 and 42 teeth, which was matched with a 7-, 8- or 9-speed cassette with a range of 11-34T (a high gear of 11 teeth and a low of 34). With the advent of 10 and 11 sprocket cassettes with a range of up to 11-40T, double and even single chainrings have become more popular on high end mountain bikes. These keep the weight down, but it's best to stick with a

Paul Woloshansky's well-pimped Tech Pulse, with home-made racks, licence-plate fenders and army-surplus canvas bag panniers.

triple-ring setup for touring as fewer chainrings means you spread the wear less, which will shorten the chainrings' lives.

Most expedition touring bikes now pair a triple chainring with an 8-, 9- or 10-speed cassette. If you have an 8-speeder, don't see a 9- or 10-speed cassette as an essential upgrade. An 8 speed might not shift quite as slickly, but the thicker sprockets last a bit longer and the cassette is narrower so there is less dish to the wheel (see p52) making it all a little more durable – the overall priority for adventure touring. The chain is also wider on 8-speed set ups and if regularly cleaned and maintained lasts longer too. Riders building a tourer from scratch will often choose an 8 speed system (and a 9- over a 10-speed) because of this durability. Get a high quality chain like those by SRAM or KMC as these have greater longevity and also increase the lifetime of your chainrings and cassette.

In the mountains, you'll appreciate low gearing on steep gradients. A 24-tooth granny gear (the small chainring) and 11-34T cassette has always worked for me on my 26er, though in the lowest gear I travel no faster and weave no less than the local drunk on his stumble home. If you're heavily loaded or ride a bike with 700c/29" wheels you may require even lower gears, but you'll also need good balance to avoid falling off. When switching chainrings or cassettes you always need to be wary of compatibility issues with derailleurs/shifters and ensure that there isn't too big a leap between chainrings; it's a good idea to consult your local bike shop before making any changes.

Componentry
The largest manufacturer of derailleur gears by far is Shimano and you will find their spares, and mechanics familiar with the designs, in bike shops worldwide. They have a hierarchy of different qualities of MTB components, starting with Acera and Alivio – both good entry level kit but not as refined or

---

COUNTING GEARS

It's not just young boys who try and count your gears.

The reason for having so many gears is that it's easier to shift between similar sized cogs and so maintain an optimal cadence or pedalling rhythm. It's worth knowing that with a 3 x 9 (the most popular touring choice) you don't really have 27 different speeds as there is a lot of overlap; middle chainring 4th cog may be the same as big chainring 2nd cog, but the latter selection will give a cross-over chain alignment which will rattle and accelerate chain wear. In reality you only use the bottom couple of cogs when in the smallest chainring and the top few cogs when in the largest chainring so this adds up to around 15 usable speeds in all (and is why Rohloff's sequential 14-speed Speedhub is not so far off the mark; see p50).

lightweight as Deore, Deore LX, SLX, Deore XT or XTR which is the very top high-end groupset. For a tour of a year or more Deore components should be the minimum quality you look for; don't bother upgrading to XTR components as they are expensive, less durable and you won't get the benefits of their lower weight.

Shimano's better derailleurs (Deore, SLX, XT and XTR) use the Shadow design. This is great for touring because the derailleur sits behind the cassette and inside of the axle skewer, so the derailleur is well protected if the bike falls over or your panniers hang low.

SRAM has a smaller range of gear groups and as with Shimano don't go for the pricey top of the range X0 components. X5 is the minimum quality I would recommend and is roughly equivalent to Deore, whilst X9 components will offer you a good durability to weight ratio.

Gear shifters

You have three options for gear shifters and it's worth trying them out to see which you prefer. On the road, it's not all about super-slick shifting which you might appreciate while racing to work; it's about simple, robust and even repairable designs that won't get easily damaged in a crash or while lashed to the roof of a bus. Old fashioned **bar-end shifters** (such as Shimano's Dura-Ace) are simple, durable and low maintenance as they are friction shifters and don't need indexing. They can be used on a drop bar, or using mounts from Paul Component Engineering you can convert them to a straight bar thumbie shifter. Microshift SL-T09 shifters are a similar, simple, straight bar shifter.

With no vulnerable or exposed levers, **twist-grip shifters** are the simplest and so are well suited to touring (Rohloff hub gears use a twist-grip control – see below). The best known is SRAM's GripShift, which brought twist-grip shifters back from the dustbin of history and became the first competitive alternative to Shimano.

Thumb and forefinger **trigger shifters** are the most common type on flat bar bikes. The XT Shimano RapidFire shifters are great for touring, however they do lack the simplicity of the Microshift or Dura Ace bar-end friction shifters, and require regular mainte-nance to keep them aligned.

Dual-control levers (a brake lever that also clicks up and down to change gears) are not a great choice for adven-ture cycle touring. These integrated brake/gear shifters work well on drop bars but are less useful on straight bars, and are over-complex for tour-ing. You can't change your brakes without changing the gear levers and you can't fine tune the position of either as they're a single fixed unit.

Shimano Dura-Ace shifters have a habit of changing gear when your back's turned…

Rohloff Speedhub: a black box.
© Stephen Lord

Rohloff – the hub gear option

The Rohloff Speedhub 500/14 goes against the usual touring simplicity mantra; it is a complex bit of engineering, so much so that you are unlikely to be able to fix one if it seriously malfunctions on a tour. However its durability and reliability is such that many tourers consider it ideal for long range travels. Speedhubs cost the best part of £1000, which is three or four months on the road to most world travellers, and also a large lump of cash to have parked outside your tent at night.

Maintenance-wise there is very little to do as all the workings are contained within the central hub. Cable replacement and oil changes are a bit more complex than servicing a derailleur, but an oil change might only be necessary every 5000 kilometres or so, the suggested service interval. You must be diligent in performing this oil change or you are likely to encounter problems down the road. Replacing cables every 20-30,000km is also a good idea, rather than waiting till they break.

A Speedhub's 14 speeds are evenly spaced and are a touch lower than the lowest possible derailleur gears while being just one gear shy of the highest gear a 9-speeder can manage (the gear a loaded touring rider hardly ever uses). The chain always runs in the same plane between the chainring and sprocket and so ought to last much longer, especially if you use Rohloff's own extra-strong chain. The single sprocket can be reversed as it wears, which gives more kilometres before replacement is needed. The hub also gives a symmetrical spoke profile (no dishing is required as there is equal spoke size and tension) adding up to a much stronger wheel with less risk of broken spokes on the drive side (which can be a common problem with derailleurs). And, if you do break a drive-side spoke, it's easier to replace, as there is no cassette to remove. You can fit a Rohloff-equipped bike with a Gates belt drive instead of a chain and this will mean even less maintenance as the belt will not get rusty, no oil is needed and cleaning is simpler.

ROHLOFF SPARES

Recommended spares to carry if touring with a Rohloff hub outside of Europe/North America/Australasia:
- Full oil change kit – part #8410 – an oil change is recommended every 5000km.
- Hub cable easy set – part #8573 – cables usually need replacing between 20,000 and 30,000km.
- Bayonet connectors, female type – part #8273 – given how difficult these are to source, and how small and light (6 grams) they are, I recommend carrying two spares

for a long tour of over a year, just in case you need to replace them.
- Spare spokes for the Rohloff wheel; these are shorter than standard spokes, and near-impossible to find outside of the western world, so I recommend carrying 5-10 spares.
- If you are running a Gates belt drive, carry a replacement (with exactly the same number of teeth as the belt on your bike). A belt drive usually lasts over 10,000km.

Matt McDonald

There are slightly different Speedhubs to fit different dropouts, axles and brakes. The Speedhub finder on 🖥 rohloff.de will help you select the right one for your bike. Fitting a Rohloff hub to a bike not designed for it can be a major conversion and is best done by a Rohloff specialist rather than your local bike shop.

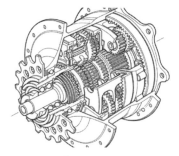

Inside a Rohloff 14-speed Speedhub – planetary gears.

The problem for the touring cyclist of using an internal hub is that if something should go wrong, you're on your own. Go to 🖥 rohloff.de and download the technical manual to troubleshoot and determine if you can diagnose the problem; chances are it's cabling or time to change the oil. In the unlikely event that it's something internal, you'll have to send it back to Rohloff.

You'll read on the web about Rohloff disaster stories, such as the flange cracking where the spokes mount. These are such a show stopper that it is worth considering where you are going and what the effect of a complete breakdown would be. Even if the necessary replacement is quickly sent out, the process for getting parcels through customs in many countries of the world is tortuously slow, which can lead to weeks of thumb twiddling whilst you wait for a spare to arrive.

See box opposite for a list of recommended spares to carry, in order to give yourself a chance to fix an external problem with the hub. If you break a spoke and don't have a spare you can always try and get a good bike shop to cut a longer spoke down and thread the end.

Finally, there are aesthetic considerations too when choosing your gears and this is not unimportant for something you will notice every time you turn the pedals. Some find the simplicity of using the Rohloff system and the ability to change gears while the bike is stationary to be winning arguments; others find the grinding noise and slight drag in seventh gear can get irritating; it's a regrettable characteristic of the design, not something broken.

Pinion gearbox

Designed by two Porsche engineers, the new Pinion p1.18 gearbox hasn't yet been ridden round the world nearly as many times, but looks like a promising rival to Rohloff and derailleur systems, if a little pricey. The 18-speed gearbox sits adjacent to the bottom bracket so your gears won't be exposed like on a derailleur system and you won't have the added revolving weight of a hub gear. Bike frames have to be specially designed for the Pinion, which means that if anything went wrong you would *really* be in a tight spot.

CHOOSING BRAKES

As discussed on p39, your main choice is between rim brakes (V-brakes or cantilever) and disc brakes (mechanical/cable or hydraulic). To play it safe maintenance-wise, go with the simplest setup: either rim brakes or mechanical disc brakes.

Avid Single Digit 7 V brakes. © Nathan Haley

Rim brakes

Most mountain bike rim brakes are the V-brake design, which is a kind of cantilever with extended direct-pull arms (meaning the brake cable pulls the arms together, rather than upwards as in older cantilever models). V-brakes and cantilevers fit on the same brake bosses and swapping your cantis for V-brakes is about the easiest and most effective upgrade you can do – it will improve the power of your braking. All V-brakes are powerful but the better quality V-brakes offer more refinement.

For both canti and V-brakes choose one that uses brake pad cartridges. Worn brake pads are replaced by sliding them out of the cartridge, and as cartridge pads are light and slim it's easy to carry plenty of spares from home.

Rim brakes are simple and easy to maintain on the road but quite fiddly in that fairly frequent tweaks are needed to keep them at optimal performance. Properly adjusted rim brakes give a lot more braking force than those that haven't been looked after. The downside of rim brakes is that they depend on a clean dry wheel rim and don't work well in rain. They also shorten the life of your wheels considerably by wearing down the side of the rim, but you can mitigate this to a certain extent by cleaning the rim and the brake pads to remove grit which will otherwise act like sandpaper on your rims.

Disc brakes

Disc brakes are a big improvement over rim brakes in terms of performance – you won't want to go back to rim brakes once you've used discs. Their large braking force for little effort means you only need one finger on the brake lever, leaving three fingers to control the handlebars – something you'll appreciate as you dodge the potholes bouncing down from Ladakh's high passes. Unlike rim brakes, braking in the wet is as good as in dry weather and your rims won't

---

DISHING

One of the drawbacks of derailleur gears is that they weaken the rear wheel because the spokes on the cassette (right-hand) side are at a very shallow angle. This is called 'dishing', and the more the wheel is dished due to a wider cassette, the weaker it becomes. Spoke tension on the drive side spokes has to be greater to compensate for the dished shape and you will find you break more spokes on the drive side of the rear wheel (see p74 for the tool you need to carry to replace drive-side spokes). Drive side spokes are shorter than left-hand side spokes and

you should carry a couple more of them, but with good quality hand-built wheels and moderate loads, breaking spokes should be a rare event. Light riders will find they break far fewer spokes than heavier counterparts. If you only weigh 60kg and carry minimal kit, your spokes are under far less force – it wouldn't be unusual for such a rider to go tens of thousands of kilometres without ever breaking a single spoke. Beyond a certain age spokes will start to break more often; that's a sign to replace them all and probably the rim too.

overheat on long downhills (though the disc and pads certainly will). Discs also avoid wear on the wheel rim, greatly extending the rim's longevity, and if your wheel is knocked out of true, braking is not affected so you can re-true the wheel at the end of the day rather than at the roadside.

Disc brakes cannot be fitted to a fork or frame that isn't designed for them because the braking forces are much more tightly concentrated than on a wheel rim. Though it is possible

Avid BB7 cable-operated disc brakes – powerful and easy to adjust. © Stephen Lord

to buy a rigid fork (see p63) that will take a disc brake, calipers can make fitting a rack awkward (options for disc-friendly racks are on p67). Rather than go through all the complications and expense of fitting something your bike was not designed for, get a bike which is disc-ready.

Mechanical disc brakes use a cable to pull brake pads onto the disc to stop the wheel; with hydraulic brakes, fluid is pushed along tubes to close the brake pads against the disc. Mechanical disc brakes require no particular skills or tools for maintenance. They are far simpler than hydraulics and you can easily source spare cables and housing; they are thus a better choice for adventure touring. Popular models such as the standard-setting Avid BB7s are simple to install (though the tool-free pad adjustment is fiddly) and feature confidence-inspiring modulation, or 'feel', as good as any hydraulic brake. A recent arrival on the market is the TRP Spyke, which has received great reviews for its dual-sided braking (the pads on the Avid BB7 only push on one side of the rotor), easier set-up and pads which are compatible with Shimano's M525/M515, making them easier to find on the road.

If you choose to go with the sexier **hydraulic** discs you will get more powerful and even braking. The major downside of hydraulic setups is they can get damaged and leak (albeit more commonly in transit) and the thin brake hoses and couplings are not something you'll find in a Punjabi back street where brake cables hang thick like spaghetti. To keep things as simple as possible with hydraulics, opt for brakes that use the standardised DOT brake fluid rather than a proprietary mineral oil favoured by Shimano and Magura so that you can resupply along the way.

Maintenance of hydraulics may seem daunting, but is an easy skill to learn. Bleeding mushy brakes by purging tiny air bubbles from the fluid (much as you would a domestic radiator at home) is a very infrequent and not-too-difficult task with quality units – check out the online video tutorials by whichever company produces your brakes. Include 100ml of appropriate brake fluid and a bleed kit (which normally includes two small syringes – one for the caliper end and the other for the lever end) in your spares. Servicing the brake pistons may be necessary too, typically involving opening, cleaning and replacing the seals in the caliper. Whenever you remove the wheel and transport the bike, it is very important that you remember to wedge the pads open (with a coin, for example) or they may lock together.

Whether you have mechanical or hydraulic disc brakes, brake pads and rotors are generally different for each brake model and therefore cannot easily be found on the road. They are light and don't take up much room, so it's wise to carry spares from home. Go for ceramic brake pads in preference to metallic or sintered, as ceramic pads last longer, are quieter and cope better with the heat a loaded bike will generate on long descents. A 6-bolt rotor will be easier to find in a spares shop in Ouagadougou than the CentreLock style which requires a matching hub.

WHEELS

Bicycle wheels are designed to balance the competing needs of strength and speed. Because weight has a much more noticeable effect on rotating parts like wheels, bike manufacturers are tempted to fit fairly light wheels that give a bike a much livelier feel than the heavier wheels that adventure tourers need. Nonetheless, the wheels on any decent mountain or touring bike are designed to take some abuse and are likely to be good enough for a year or more of hard touring before you need to think about replacing them.

High end expedition bikes will come with hand-built wheels, as these are much better than machine-built wheels. If you are starting out on a bike with machine-built wheels, you should stress-relieve the spokes (instructions at 🖳 sheldonbrown.com/wheelbuild.html#seating) to reduce the stress on each and help them become properly seated.

Choosing a new wheel

Wheels do wear out in the normal course of things and if you're headed for the back of beyond you might want to upgrade what you've got so your bike is ready for the toughest roads you can find, even when it's loaded down with a few weeks' supply of Snickers and dried noodles. Only very cheap wheels come ready made, and as you can choose hubs, rims and spokes individually, bike shops usually only build wheels when someone orders them. Strong wheels are the most important element of your bike to invest money in, so that's your chance to upgrade and have some great hand-built touring wheels made that will see you through thick and thin.

Hubs

Wheel hubs are one of those components we like to fit and forget, so the better the hub you get, the longer you can afford to leave it before opening it up, cleaning it out and replacing the bearings. Keep life easy by getting something standard like Shimano Deore LX or Deore XT as going for major brands always simplifies things in terms of repair, replacement, availability of parts and compatibility. If your hubs continue to run freely with no play, you might need to service them only once a year. These days you can find out what bearing sizes or parts you need for a hub service from the web (for Shimano, go to 🖳 si.shimano.com). Ball bearings come in standard imperial sizes everywhere in the world so you don't need to bring them from home, but knowing the size helps if you've worn them down when it comes to service time. If you've got cash to splash, then Phil Wood or Hope hubs will go the extra (few thousand) miles. For a dynamo hub to generate power for your gadgets see p98.

Rims

Bicycle wheel rims are made of aluminium alloy for lightness and rigidity; 'eyelets' (small washers) around the spoke holes help spread the load and are a sign of good quality. Double-walled rims are stronger and are what you want for touring. It's also better if they come with eyelets on each wall (double eyelets) to help prevent the spoke nipple from pulling through.

End of the road for this rim. Though you are risking a crash on a cracked rim, it may carry you a few hundred kilometres from when you first notice the crack developing.
© Stephen Lord

New MTBs are usually sold with a mid-weight rim but these aren't designed specifically with touring in mind. Consider fitting something a little heavier but be cautious because rotating weight has a greater effect on performance than static weight. Ryde (formerly Rigida) make the cheap and bombproof Sputnik (670g) for derailleur equipped bikes and the Andra 30 for Rohloff equipped bikes. Both of these have the option of 26" or 700c and you can get a CSS (Carbide Supersonic System) coating which will make the rims last an age. If you go for the CSS coating make sure that you use blue brake pads.

Unless you're very heavily loaded or the worrying type, you don't need a rim this heavy but could get by with Sun's 550g-Rhyno Lite XL. It's a wider rim suited to fatter tyres and sometimes recommended for downhill but works fine for adventure touring. Light riders should find Sun's CR18 (440g) strong enough for touring. The French brand Mavic is the biggest manufacturer of bike wheel rims but there are complaints from some tourers that Mavics are prone to cracks around the spokes.

Even if your bike has disc brakes, bear in mind that disc-specific rims are built without the thick braking surfaces on the sides. You might want the option of fitting rim brakes some day, so stick with a more traditional and solid construction which has the braking surfaces.

Make sure your rims are compatible with the fatter Schrader valves which you are much more likely to find on inner tubes throughout the world. If your rims are designed specifically for the narrower Presta valves, you may need to widen the hole with a file or a drill in order for a Schrader valve to fit through. Beware also of rims that are too deep for Schrader valves (which are shorter than Prestas); this can result in you being unable to inflate a tube as you can't attach your pump to the valve.

Spokes

The ideal spoke count for a strong touring wheel is 36 holes. Good quality mountain bikes usually have 32 spoke wheels, which are good enough and are more commonly found around the world, though there are exceptions (in Iran rims and hubs are available in 36H only). I have seen tourers riding bikes with four empty holes where spokes should be, either at the hubs or at the rims, because they could not find a new rim or hub with the right number of holes.

Any less than 32 holes (the next possible figure is 28 spokes) is too weak for touring. Go for the heavier-gauge DT Swiss, Wheelsmith or Sapim spokes, the most common high-quality brands.

Tyres

Fitting good tyres is probably the biggest single improvement you can make to any bike to turn it into a world tourer. Tyres are the most basic form of suspension and are the only kind you need for road riding and most unpaved roads. Fitting 2-inch wide tyres will protect against a multitude of sins such as an overloaded bike, weak racks and wheels or a frame unsuited to bad roads in the first place. Take care not to overinflate tyres this wide as you risk cracking your rims. If you go for narrower tyres – and even a 1.75" tyre will give a noticeably harsher ride – you'll pedal with less effort for sure but unless you lighten up, you're risking broken spokes and rack bolts and buckled wheels. I've watched numerous riders on 1.75", or narrower, tyres descending beautiful mountain passes at a crawl because they were overloaded or their wheels weren't strong enough to risk going faster. Downhills are one of the greatest and hardest-earned pleasures of cycling and it's a shame to miss out on the fun because your bike isn't tough enough for it.

If you have a mountain bike with knobbly off-road tyres, change them for something that is designed for the job; touring calls for tougher and heavier tyres than mountain biking. Whatever machine they're on, most users judge a tyre by its tread, but it is the quality of the carcass that defines a tyre's load-carrying and shock-absorbing capacities. The tread pattern is a secondary matter but you'll soon learn that a smooth tread rolls more efficiently, is more predictable on bends and in the wet, and lasts much longer than an off-road tyre. Riding unpaved roads, having a tread pattern rather than a smooth or slick tyre becomes more important, especially on loose surfaces.

Folding tyres are more expensive than rigid bead tyres but are lighter and much more convenient to carry as a spare as they take up less space and can fit in a pannier.

Unlike wheels, where almost everything in 26" size is designed for mountain bikes, there are some excellent tyres designed specifically for adventure touring. Make sure you check the maximum width of tyre your fork will accept before ordering. These are the best options for long trips:

Schwalbe Marathon Mondial

Marathon Mondial tyre. © Nathan Haley

The Mondial is the ultimate adventure touring tyre and was designed for everything from sandy roads on a Saharan crossing to the loose gravel on a Chilean back road. The Mondial is the successor to Schwalbe's fabled (and sadly now discontinued) Marathon XR, with which cycle tourists faithfully shod their bikes for years. Marathon Mondials roll well on paving for their weight and size and have good grip on gravel roads. Their tough sidewalls provide protection against cuts from rocks. The durability of these tyres means you can fit and forget – it's not unusual for them to last well over 10,000km. For 26" wheels they come in 2.0" and 2.15"; for 700c wheels the 47mm (1.85") and 50mm (2.0") widths are most useful for touring. The 26x2.0 tyre weighs in at a heavy 740g, so only consider the Mondial if you plan on long tours or rough, remote routes as they will slow you down on shorter paved jaunts.

If you want something even more durable than the Mondial, look at the Marathon Plus Tour; they're very heavy (the 26x2.0 is 1.1kg) but will outlast everything else.

Schwalbe Marathon Supreme

The Marathon Supreme has a slick-tread design with low rolling-resistance, which is what you'll want if you stick to paved roads most of the time. This tyre doesn't have the longevity of a Mondial, but at 565g for a 26x2.0 tyre the rolling speed is much better. As long as you're not riding lots of loose dirt or gravel, the Supreme will be a very efficient tyre. It's well-suited to rides round India or South-East Asia while still versatile enough for the odd diversion onto mountain tracks.

Schwalbe Marathon Supreme.
© Stephen Lord

The Supreme was released at the same time as the knobbier Marathon Extreme. This was an awesome tyre for dirt road tourers – light, grippy and puncture proof – but is another that Schwalbe has discontinued. Look out for any left-overs online.

Continental Travel Contact

Less expensive than Schwalbe's Marathon range, the Travel Contact comes in rigid and folding versions. It offers a great combination with a hard and smooth centre ridge for low rolling resistance on roads, and small shoulder knobs for a bit of bite in loose bends. The result is a fairly efficient tyre – the 26x1.9 is 50g lighter than a Marathon Mondial and may have better off-road cornering. The 26" size comes in two widths – 1.75" and 1.9" –

Continental Travel Contact. © Stephen Lord

while the 700c size is most usefully available in 42mm (1.65") and 50mm (1.9").

Schwalbe Smart Sam Plus

Riders who seek out dirt roads need a nubbier, wider tyre with better grip – it makes for a much more fun and comfortable ride. The Smart Sam Plus is the answer – it is hard wearing, has solid sidewalls and has the added benefit of rolling well on asphalt. It is available in 26x2.1 and 26x2.25, as well as 29x2.1. If you want a 29x2.25 you'll have to go for the less puncture-resistant Smart Sam.

BOTTOM BRACKETS

Unseen and overlooked, the bottom bracket (or 'BB') is the large bearing inside the BB shell between the cranks. It's likely to be a sealed unit and there's no servicing to be done, but if you know yours is old and you're setting off to circle the globe, replacing it is a good and inexpensive precaution. It takes shop tools to install a BB and any bike shop that sells MTB-style bikes should have something that will fit, though first check if tightening your old BB will solve any clicking or loose play in the cranks. Mechanics the world over will be familiar with one of the standard Shimano BB designs and have the tools for it, whereas if you've got a high-end BB made by anyone else you could struggle to get help.

HEADSETS

Almost every bike sold today uses a threadless headset – the bearings (one set at the bottom of the head tube, one at the top) which allow the fork to rotate within the head tube. They're simpler and easier to adjust than the old thread-

ed kind and you don't have to carry a large 32mm wrench to tighten it. It's also very easy to get at the headset bearings to service them and they are always cartridge bearings so they don't spill out when you open up the headset. Although threadless headsets are nearly all 1^1/$_8$", if you are replacing a cartridge bearing you must look for one of exactly the same shape as well as size. If you've got a non-standard width headset such as one by Cannondale, be sure to carry spare

A threadless headset and stem.

bearings for a long trip. Other ultra-wide headsets such as Koga-Miyata's are non-standard in other ways and though a very strong design, will not be easy to service except at a dealer. The best headsets are made by Chris King – if you are replacing yours, and have the cash, consider installing one of these. Cheaper headset options are the Ritchey Comp Logic V2 or the Cane Creek 40, which are still reliable for a year or more of touring.

Comfort zone

You will leave your comfort zone many times whilst on your cycling adventure but don't let that have anything to do with the setup of your bike. Once you've got your mechanicals sorted you will want to fine tune your setup so you are comfortable and ready to spend six (or four, or eight) hours per day in the saddle. A saddle and handlebars that conform to your body and preferred posture are absolutely non-negotiable. Suspension, on the other hand, is certainly not essential – few tourers use it on a long tour.

You should not have to reach so far forward that your back arches, which will give you backache on tour.

Having set the saddle height, adjust your **handlebars** so they are level with the saddle. If you have drops, the top of the bar is where to measure.

Your kneecap should be above the pedal spindle. Move your **saddle** back and forth to find that position, then road-test it as you may find your riding position on the saddle is a little different to how you sit on it while stationary.

Don't hunch your shoulders; keep them relaxed and keep your spine straight as it goes up into your head.

Start with your **saddle** horizontal. If you have to tip it up or down, it may not be the right saddle for you.

It's easy to change the **stem** for one with more height or extension. Too long and you will strain to reach the bars; too close and you will be too upright and not have enough power over the steering.

Set the **saddle height** so your legs are almost fully extended when the pedals are furthest away from you. Your ankle should be relaxed, at a right angle to the leg and not pushed up or stretching down.

PART 2 – BIKES, CLOTHING & CAMPING

FINDING THE SWEET SPOT

A lot of research has been done into finding the ideal cycling position, but it's all in the name of increasing racing-oriented efficiency, not trans-continental comfort. It's another area where the touring cyclist has to spend time and put thought into adjusting their bike until it's as comfortable as possible. You'll be spending as much time perched on your saddle as you ever did on a chair in the office and it's vital to get the right saddle and in the right position for long-term happiness. More than just a sore butt, if you get your riding position wrong you could end up with back, neck or wrist trouble that jeopardises your trip, but get it right and there will be nothing stopping you.

Plan well ahead and experiment with all comfort-related issues – remember it's a top priority in choosing a bike. You need to put in some long rides on your bike as well as a short shake-down tour to check it out for comfort. If you make amendments to the riding position, you need to be sure they work for you: last-minute changes to a stem or saddle may be quickly regretted on tour.

One shortcut to finding your ideal riding position is to go for a bike fitting at a bike shop. Whether you elect a more traditional fitting where you sit on a frame and get measured up, or a computerised fitting, make it clear that you want a touring setup and that you're looking to maximise comfort, not power output.

Here are some starting points for finding a good riding position. It's easiest if you can get a friend to help you by looking at your position while you are sitting on the bike.

1. Get the saddle height sorted first. The right spot will probably feel higher than you think is natural. At the correct height you should be able to only just touch the ground with one foot when sitting on the saddle. With one foot on the pedal in its highest position, the other foot should be able to reach the lower pedal with a slight bend in the knee (and the foot horizontal).

2. Now fine-tune the saddle angle. Start with a level (horizontal) saddle. This spreads your weight best and allows you to move around more easily while riding.

3. Move the saddle fore and aft to find the spot where your kneecap is over the axle of the pedal when that pedal is horizontal and pointing forward.

4. Finally check your handlebar stem is the ideal length and height. Your handlebars should be roughly level with the saddle because this balances your weight between hands and seat and avoids placing excessive stress on either. You may be able to adjust the height of your handlebars using spacers on the steerer tube (if not, see below). A general guide for the stem length is that when sat on the bike and looking down at the front axle, the centre of the handlebar should be in line with the axle, not in front nor behind it.

Remember that these are just guidelines – it is much more important to go with what feels right and then take a long ride to confirm it. Getting the right stem is the biggest hassle because you're simultaneously looking for two measures, the angle of the stem and its length. Bike shops may have a box of used stems to loan out or swap so you can find the right one for you. Otherwise buy an adjustable cheapie to pin down your optimum position. When you've found the right spot, get a bombproof rigid stem that won't snap on you when you least want it.

Generally speaking, tall riders converting compact-framed MTBs for touring are looking to substantially increase handlebar heights. Sometimes so-called 'riser handlebars' and the typical range of threadless 1 1/8" stems are inadequate, partly because threadless stems merely clamp to the available steerer tube (part of the fork) which may itself be insufficiently long. A fork with an adequate length of steerer tube to spare is best, but an inexpensive way of getting the same result is to fit a stem raiser clamp which can add up to 80mm of height to a steerer tube.

LOVE IN THE SADDLE

The most difficult aspect in the fraught quest for comfort is finding the right saddle. Almost every touring biker will tell you a firmer saddle works best in the long run as it will support your nether regions on the hips' sit bones, rather than letting them sink in to soft foam or gel. But with saddles more than any-

thing, advice from others is only their humble opinion, it can never be a hard (or indeed 'soft') rule. You have to go entirely by your own impressions and the only way to do that is to experiment by spending plenty of time on your saddle before committing to a long ride.

You may never find a saddle you'd want to take down the aisle but you ought to be able to find one where the discomfort doesn't carry over from

Brooks B17 saddle. © Jenny Bell

one day to the next or build up over time. There are a couple of characteristics that make a good touring saddle. Firstly, a reasonably large area to sit on rather than a racing blade will spread your weight and so reduce pressure points. A larger saddle will also give you some room to move around to relieve aches or boredom, or to sit forward a little when climbing. It needs to be broad enough at the tail to support your sit bones, and women are likely to need a broader saddle than men as their sit bones are typically wider.

Secondly, saddles with a groove down the middle work well by relieving pressure on the pudendal nerves and arteries which pass on the saddle side of your sit bones. These types of saddle are now very common. It doesn't have to be a massive groove, even a faint depression and softer material along the centre will do the job.

Among tourers the classic Brooks range of leather saddles is the most popular brand. You'll see many a touring bike fitted with the B17 touring model – something Brooks claim was the world's first anatomic saddle, back in 1930. It may not feel like a classic after the first long ride, but like a good shoe, a leather saddle will wear in with age and outlast other kinds of saddle – which helps justify the £80 price tag. Although incredibly durable, Brooks saddles are vulnerable to getting wet. They need waxing, either with Brooks' own Proofide or something like Nikwax. I often just put some suncream on mine as I don't carry the wax. You need to keep the saddle as dry as you can even when it's thoroughly proofed, which includes protecting it from spray from underneath. The thinner models like the B17 break in quicker but are more prone to losing their shape than the thicker hide examples such as the Team Pro or Swift.

The worst situation is to have to ride on a wet Brooks saddle, as that is when it will stretch the most. Carry and use the tensioning spanner to keep the saddle taut, but take care not to over-tension a wet saddle; there's a risk of it shrinking and ripping off the rails as it dries. Lastly, like your best school shoes, a shiny leather saddle will scratch easily, but it's only cosmetic damage and can probably be polished out by the first shoe shine-wallah you come across. A smooth slippery surface has benefits in making sliding around the saddle easier, something the more common gel examples don't do so well. Not everyone bonds with a Brooks, but those that do swear by them. A recent addition to the Brooks stable, the Cambium is said to be comfortable without needing much 'riding in'. Made of rubber and canvas it could be the answer to wet climate leather woes.

Selle Anatomica are the most beautiful and, some say, comfortable saddles on the market. Made in the US, they are leather with a slit down the middle that allows your sit bones to move, meaning there is no perineal pressure. Unlike the Brooks they can easily be tensioned with an Allen key. At US$159 they are quite an investment but if nothing else is working, this may be the answer.

Specialized make a lot of channelled saddles; their much-imitated BG (Body Geometry) range is worth a look, particularly the less expensive all-round models rather than racing or triathlon-specific items. In saddles more than any other component, comfort has little to do with cost – that factor more commonly relates to lightness and racing needs where potential customers have money to spare. Another brand worth investigating is WTB, known for the Rocket V saddles. The characteristic dip isn't always a good sign in a saddle (it can mean too much contact and less ease moving around) but oddly it works for some riders. The Rocket Vs also have a slightly dropped nose to make it easy to climb on the front of the saddle and avoid getting jabbed in the rear if you hit a bump.

HANDLEBARS

Different handlebars will greatly affect your comfort and the handling of your bike. Drop bars are generally used only by those who stick mostly to paving; on the dirt switchbacks of Ayacucho you will want flat bars so you can benefit from the improved handling on the climbs and stronger braking on the descents.

Hold your hands out in front of you in a fist and mime holding a straight bar; now mime holding two parallel vertical bars. You should find that neither of these positions is totally comfortable, but that somewhere in between is: this is the position you are looking for with a handlebar. You can achieve it with the 'hoods' of a drop bar or the sweep of a slightly bent flat bar. Whether you choose drops or straights, get a simple design to start with – you can always change to a fancier bar if you decide (after many happy hours spinning along mentally fine tuning your setup, if you're anything like me) it will enhance your ride.

With a flat bar you don't want a completely straight bar, and most bars nowadays have a bit of a backward sweep to reduce wrist strain. The extreme sweeping On One Mary Bar and the Jones H-Bar are both comfortable and relaxed. The Thorn MK2 Comfort bar is good if you want a less extreme sweep.

No flat handlebar should head off over the horizon without a pair of Ergon grips. These are the most comfortable grips going, offering a flat platform for your palms that spreads the pressure and allows you to keep your wrists straighter than wrapping your hands round a circular grip. The rubber version can get sweaty if you don't wear gloves but is more durable than the cork alternative.

A good dropped touring bar is the same width or slightly wider than your shoulders. The On One Midge bar is a nice relaxed dropped bar; both On One

A well-used Ergon grip. © Jenny Bell

and Nitto make a number of interesting looking bars. There is nothing like Ergons available for drop bars, but double-wrapping drops with tape or adding some foam padding and then a further layer of tape will make them more comfortable for long days on the bike as well as insulating your hands in cold weather.

Some tourers get on with butterfly bars, even though it means extra weight. These may look tempting as they have a lot of hand positions, but what you really need is one good position, not three or four imperfect ones. Another problem is the brakes are too far back and not where you need them: on the ends of the bars where your hands naturally rest when controlling going downhill.

SUSPENSION FORKS

Suspension forks are not necessary or recommended for a long-distance tour. For a short off-road tour they are a lot of fun and improve your bike's handling, but for pedalling across continents they simply do not have the reliability, loading capacity and easy serviceability of a rigid fork and also make it challenging to fit a front rack. Air forks require far more frequent servicing than is feasible on a long tour, and coil forks of sufficient quality for touring are increasingly hard to find. If you'll spend a large proportion of your time hammering along on rugged routes, get larger tyres which you can run at lower pressure to eat up vibrations, rather than suspension.

If you do go with a suspension fork

Some people who buy a MTB choose to keep the suspension fork, thinking it will come in handy somewhere along the way or because it's an extra expense to replace it with a rigid fork (see box below if you are considering this option). In typical touring conditions of high mileage mostly on roads and with a minimum of maintenance, a suspension fork will slowly seize up as the ingress of grit and moisture causes internal corrosion. To prolong the life of your fork you need to keep dirt and grit from the upper legs, or stanchions, so it cannot damage the seals. Give them a good wipe with a dry cloth every day and wash the forks fairly often.

More problematic would be an air fork collapsing through a broken seal. All good quality forks can be locked out, meaning turned into a rigid fork at the turn of a knob, bringing your problems to an end, but if that's not possible, the fork is finished and you will have to try other means of eliminating all

---

REMOVING SUSPENSION FORKS

The longer your trip, the less sense a suspension fork makes as it will need a proper service or repair at some point. Most of them weigh over 2kg so you will save around half that weight and have an easier time fitting racks by removing it and installing a rigid fork. What you need is a so-called suspension-corrected rigid fork that will mimic a suspension fork's geometry.

Thorn offer the Mt. Tura suspension-corrected fork with the extra length necessary to replace a suspension fork running around 80-100mm of travel without altering your bike's geometry and handling. You get all the braze-ons for racks, rim brakes (not disc) and a dynamo in a classic raked and tapered design.

If you still want to run disc brakes, you need a straight fork but you will lose the suppleness and shock absorption of a good quality touring fork. On One do a 26" disc and rim brake compatible straight fork. In the US, Vicious Cycles (🖥 viciouscycles.com) and Surly (🖥 surlybikes.com) make a range of 'straight blade' forks with optional braze-ons for lowrider racks and fenders (mudguards to Brits), and mounts for disc brakes if desired.

Thorn's
Mt. Tura fork.

movement in the forks, such as filling the lower legs with sand to fill the void. Servicing requirements are unique to each fork, so look online for specific details from the manufacturer. Fitting racks to suspension forks calls for a little ingenuity, or buying a rack designed for suspension forks (see p67).

Suspension seatposts

If you crave some sort of rear suspension, a suspension seatpost is by far the easiest way to achieve it; the many ingenious downhill-racing rear suspension

designs are not suited to carrying baggage or irregular maintenance. With a simple elastomer design requiring no maintenance, the Cane Creek Thudbuster offers a noticeably plusher ride with up to double the play and none of the initial 'stiction' (static friction) of telescopic seatposts. The short-travel model (shown here) is all you need for touring. If you are touring on a tandem, these are endorsed by all stokers, and may well help save the relationship between stoker and pilot!

Cane Creek Thudbuster. © Stephen Lord

Carrying luggage

Once you've got a bike and fitted it with the components that will last a long tour across a continent, you need to work out how to carry your stuff. Your setup will be determined by how much kit you choose to lug around, so have a look at p75 for four different cyclists' thoughts. Always tailor your setup to the trip in question – cycling around the Indian plains you could get by with just a few tools and a change of clothes, by staying in cheap accommodation and eating at the numerous *dhabas*. Crossing Siberia in winter requires a whole different wardrobe and camping kit.

Four panniers – two large ones on the back, two smaller ones on the front – and a handlebar bag has in recent decades been *the* way to set up your bike for a long cycle-touring expedition. For most tourers this is still the preferred amount of capacity, providing sufficient room for all necessities as well as some comforts and luxuries too. If you wish to carry more equipment, it's easy to strap a dry bag on the back, and some front racks can accept a lashed-on bag as well. In case you haven't guessed, touring with a backpack is a short route to posterior misery and a sweaty back. For ideas of how fully loaded tourers like to pack, peruse the gallery of bike pictures posted on ⌨ loadedtouringbikes.com – currently numbering nearly 500 and many of them adventure tourers.

There is a certain amount of machismo about having a bike so heavy that you can't lift it off the ground, but increasingly people are experimenting with lighter setups on long tours. This will involve ditching the front panniers (and in extreme cases the rear ones too), and introducing other bags such as a frame bag or seat post bag. If you want to go fast, extra-light and off road then a pannier-free bikepacking setup works well, though it is better suited to short tours where everyday comfort isn't a priority. See p71 and take a look at 🖥 bikepacking.net/category/individual_setups for some inspiration.

RACKS
Racks are a relatively recent invention for bike touring. Blackburn made the first modern racks for bike touring some 30 years ago from aircraft grade aluminium tubing and though strong for their weight and great for light camping trips, heavily-loaded adventure tourers nowadays pick something stronger. Luckily several manufacturers are waiting to supply your needs.

Tubus
German-made Tubus are the best chromoly racks available. Their long-running Cargo model has a dog-leg rear strut to stabilise the load against swaying and a triangular middle strut to provide exceptional rigidity. If you want to set your panniers a little lower or need a little more heel clearance, Tubus' Logo rack should work for you. The Cargo and Logo are rated for 40kg loads, but aim for less than half of that and your rack will never break on tour. I've seen a rack that was run over by a car and still worked fine. If you are going fast and light the Vega is a minimalist rear rack rated to 25kg.

Tubus also make four great front racks including the Tara which is elegant and light, and has become a touring classic. They're available for both 26" and 700c/29" wheels.

Old Man Mountain (OMM)
Whereas Tubus come from a road touring tradition, OMM are all about fitting racks to mountain bikes. Their first rack was created in order to fit a rack to a suspension fork. OMM make innovative designs and theirs are the strongest aluminium racks available. To avoid any risk of flex and therefore metal fatigue to which aluminium is prone, OMM racks are exceptionally rigid. The base is made of solid CNC-milled aluminium with double bolts connecting the struts of the rack. Long welds curving round the top platforms make a solid structure; weld failures are unknown. OMM racks are designed with mountain bikes in mind and work well with suspension forks or disc brakes, even if your fork has no rim-brake bosses or rack eyelets. Most OMM models are designed to carry the weight on the axle by using extra-long skewers to hold the rack mounts

A Tubus Cargo rack on a Long Haul Trucker.

Old Man Mountain's Cold Springs rack.
© Stephen Lord

Left: Surly front rack. **Right**: Thorn Expedition Steel rear rack. (Both © Stephen Lord)

against the wheel dropouts. There are a couple of conventional eyelet-mounted models too. The high-mount front racks have a useful platform for carrying gear on top of the front wheel. The racks are available for both 26" and 29" wheels.

Surly

US bike-builder Surly make chromoly racks and their front rack is the business if you want a large capacity rack that carries panniers either high or low. It carries the load over the axle and though it weighs a hefty 1.4kg, that's nothing compared with its 32kg capacity. If you're going heavy, this is the rack for you.

Thorn

Thorn's racks are available only from the maker but will fit any bike with braze-ons. These are uncomplicated triangular 531 steel designs (easily repaired if need be by brazing) with thick welds and an extended top for carrying tents. The Expedition rear rack is said to be good for up to 60kg on surfaced roads (but stick to a more normal load of 15-20kg). They also make an excellent tandem rack.

Fitting, repairs and DIY racks

Make sure your rack comes with the best bolts you can buy; choose stainless steel with a little extra length so you have something to work on if the bolt shears off inside the braze-on. Backing up with vibration-resistant Nyloc nuts is also a good idea, as is dabbing on some blue Loctite to prevent bolts working loose. A few hose clamps in your repair kit can cover some possible rack

Left: A stronger replacement for a cheap rack that snapped on day 2 of a Himalaya tour. **Right**: A home made framebag. © Anna Kortschak

disasters; your ingenuity will have to cover for the rest – duct tape and tent pegs will probably be involved.

If you're tempted to have a rack made for you, clamps and bolts will give the strongest join. Bending and welding tubes weakens them; this is where most home-made racks break.

Weight distribution considerations

Front racks and panniers are intended to carry less than rears; if you are touring with four panniers, you only want about a third of the weight in the front. Some riders carry large 'rear' panniers on the front as well as the back, but larger panniers are prone to sway more and will interfere with the steering. It's not recommended, but if you need to carry more up front, look for larger racks such as those by Nitto.

If you choose to go with just rear panniers there's a need to balance your weight and to try not to overload your back wheel and rack. Putting just a few kilos in your front bag or framebag, or carrying water attached to the frame or forks can make all the difference on steep inclines between being able to ride, and having to focus all your attention on not pulling wheelies.

Fitting a front rack for panniers allows you to carry more weight and makes it easier to better balance your load – the price is much heavier steering but you'll get the benefit of a more stable ride.

Fitting racks to a suspension fork

Suspension forks weren't designed with touring in mind and make no provision for racks, but a couple of well thought-out racks will do the trick, or you can make your own. Old Man Mountain's racks will work on any fork but are easiest to fit on forks that have bosses for rim brakes. Suspension forks increasingly do not have brake bosses, so OMM make band clamps (hose clamps in the UK) to fit round the forks to stabilise the rack while the weight is borne by the axle. Tubus makes the Smarti, a good simple option if you want a chromoly rack but need some brake bosses to attach to. Because it is so hard to find a front rack that works well with front suspension, bikepackers developed handlebar slings to carry gear on bikes with suspension forks.

RACK COMPATIBILITY WITH DISC BRAKES

If your bike has disc brakes you need to be careful when selecting racks to make sure they will fit. A hub-skewer mounted Old Man Mountain rack (see p65) may be the answer, or the Topeak Super Tourist DX, which is a budget aluminium option designed to fit around disc brakes. Tubus also have a light design called the Disco. Like most OMM racks it mounts on an extra-long skewer, but you should check that it clears the disc brake before buying. You can also use a Tubus rack extension on the Logo or Vega racks to make them compatible with disc brakes. Surly's Disc Trucker is designed so that there is room for disc brakes and an ordinary rack.

Tubus Disco rack:
a close fit round a disc brake.
© Stephen Lord

THE TRAILER ALTERNATIVE

If you cannot, or do not want to, fit racks on your bike, and aren't an ultralight tourer, a trailer is the way to go. They are rarely seen on RTW rides, but are common on off-road routes like the Great Divide Mountain Bike Route (see p264). Popular with riders who want the feel of a light and more responsive bike on singletrack and washboard, they also hold appeal for those who want to increase carrying capacity – always an issue for tandem riders who have limited pannier space.

A trailer can be removed quickly, unlike racks, returning your bike to its original light and racy condition for short side trips around town or into the mountains. They are also good for spreading the load appropriately between two people with different physical abilities, without overloading the stronger rider's panniers.

There are many different models out there but look only at single-wheel models which are more efficient for touring. The well-established BoB (Beast of Burden) Yak is the oldest and most popular trailer; the best of the other options is the Extrawheel Voyager, which is lighter than a BoB and carries loads in panniers either side of its single wheel.

Trailers of course make for a much longer and more cumbersome rig – ground handling is trickier and you can't just move your bike sideways to lean it up against a wall. You have extra weight when you take a plane and it's another awkward carry up rickety guesthouse stairs. Manoeuvring through crowded traffic is more difficult too and you have to worry about the hub, the connection and pivot, the extra rim and tyre; ensure your trailer's tyre is as puncture-proof as your bike tyres.

With a BoB in Argentina. © Jane Hall

PANNIERS

Good panniers last for years, over which time you'll appreciate their dependability and strength. When selecting a set, there are a couple of things to look for. Firstly, they need to have a good system of fitting to your rack without rattling around or wearing out. If you compromise here, you may well end up with clumsy and weak rack attachments which will break at your first meeting with Cameroonian corrugations. Secondly, your panniers need to seal tightly in order to keep your belongings dry and dust free. Cheapies tend to be stitched nylon where the waterproofing wears off quickly, followed soon after by the stitching.

At times like this, you'll be glad your bags are 100% waterproof. © Janne Corax

German-made **Ortlieb** panniers are by far the most popular panniers among long-distance cyclists. Ortlieb revolutionised pannier design by developing a 3D welding technique for a totally waterproof, stitch-free pannier. This welding is covered by a 5 year warranty and the company are true to their word. Their bags come with the most simple and long-lasting closure of all: a fool-proof roll-up/clip-down fastening as used in canoeists' dry bags. Ortlieb was also the first to use locking clips to hold the pannier onto the rack and their system is still the easiest to use. Initially the bottom, stabilising hook may fly off now and again but keep tweaking the position of the hook and this should stop happening. Despite many attempts at imitation, Ortlieb remain the market leaders. A pair of Back Roller Classics will set you back about £100.

Other options include **Vaude** Aqua Pros; some swear they're better in certain details than Ortliebs. If you like lots of pockets, and have deep pockets of your own, consider **Arkel** panniers. What Arkel considers a light-touring pannier, the T42, has 42L capacity per pair (about the same as rear Ortliebs). The size of the GT-54 (which will set you back £285) is excessive for most needs;

On the road in South America, with some home-made front panniers. © Anna Kortschak

remember, you have to carry whatever you stuff in them! A virtue of Arkels is the strong aluminium frame on the back of the pannier, which won't twist or flap about on your bike.

The traditional-looking Carradice Super-C panniers are made out of tightly woven waterproof and dustproof canvas, and win the pannier beauty contest. They may not be a match for an Indian monsoon season or a roll-up Ortlieb bag that can actually float, but on the plus side the canvas is very hardwearing and can be easily patched and repaired. At 54 litres a (rear) pair the volume matches the Arkels, and there are extra large pockets big enough for a

PART 2 – BIKES, CLOTHING & CAMPING

MAKING YOUR OWN GEAR

High quality touring gear can be expensive. In order to keep costs down and maximise the length of their trip, some bike tourers decide to make their own gear on a sewing machine. You can buy a variety of outdoor fabrics and supplies for making superlight clothing, bike bags, tarp tents, etc. All you need to get started is a basic home sewing machine, some tough needles and thread and a bit of patience.

One basic yet incredibly useful first DIY project for bicycle touring is the frame bag. Every bike frame has different dimensions, so frame bags tend to work best when they are custom made to fit the frame. You can buy custom-made frame bags from several companies on the web, but they are not cheap. There are a few good tutorials online which demonstrate how you can measure your own frame to create a sewing pattern for the design. Try looking at 🖥 bikepack ing.net. The rest is just a matter of getting

accustomed to your sewing machine with the fabrics of your choice.

The more advanced could consider some more elaborate bag designs, custom waterproof clothing, bivvy sacks and tarp tents. After honing your skills on your first few projects, you will better appreciate the value of well-made custom gear!

Lars Henning

Making a frame bag. © Lars Henning

PANNIER PACKING TIPS

The more you travel, the better you become at packing. What may have taken half an hour to jam into panniers that first day can be pared down to just a few minutes as you become an efficient touring machine. A good way of keeping all your kit in order within panniers is to use small dry bags such as those by Exped and Alpkit, or packing organisers like Eagle Creek's Pack-It Cubes. Try and balance out the weight of each side's panniers, and once you've got your system sorted, stick with it so you always know where things are or if anything is missing.

Most of us get off the bike on the left-hand side and lean it against a wall on its right-hand side, so put the things you need most often during the day in your left-side panniers. This should include clothing, which I put in the left rear as changes are likely several times a day; wrapping up for an early start, stripping off for a long midday climb and then wrapping up again against the wind chill for the descent. In the right rear pannier I put food and spares, electronics, books and a spare tyre at the bottom. The front panniers are the 'kitchen' and 'bedroom': the stove and pots are on the left side with bowls and cups (easy to get at for a quick roadside brew-up) and the right side has the Therm-a-Rest and sleeping bag. The tent is strapped on top, packed in a cheap and cheerful thin nylon daypack to provide extra UV and damage protection, but with a bit of extra space for a padlock and cable and a mat to sit on for lunchtime.

If you don't have a kickstand, and find you lay your bike down on the ground on its left side more often than you lean against a wall, simply swap the contents of your panniers over so the right-hand ones are more accessible.

Stephen Lord

---

bottle of burgundy on each side. Carradice are known for making old-style saddle bags which would be all you needed for a tent-free tour of South-East Asia, for example, and are also great as part of a bikepacking setup. They aren't hi-tech in any respect and the locking clips, though very secure, are a fiddle every time you try to get the bags off the bike.

Handlebar bags

Handlebar bags allow you to keep your valuables, including camera, right in front of you on the bike – almost every rider uses one. They're easily unclipped from the handlebar and carried on the shoulder when off the bike.

A waterproof Ortlieb handlebar bag.

Ortlieb makes the most reliably waterproof handlebar bags, good enough for cameras and other electronics, especially if you get the optional padded camera insert. The medium size is perfect and will (just) take an SLR. Make sure you get the latest version which comes with magnetic fastenings, rather than the brass poppers which used to rattle on corrugations and drive some riders to distraction.

On many bikes, having a front bag means you are unable to see your front wheel. To avoid this, you could wear a compact camera on your hip, where it is even more readily accessible. A mini bag mounted on your top tube, such as the Revelate Designs Gas Tank, is another good way to store valuables close at hand.

BIKEPACKING SETUP

Bikepacking is effectively mountain biking with enough camping equipment to overnight. A bikepacking setup will include a **handlebar roll**, a **framebag** and a **seat pack**. The idea is to enable you to travel fast and light and not be impeded by your luggage. If need be, you can carry your loaded bike and hike it over a pass. This is not an ideal setup for years on the road, unless you are really prepared to rough it (see p118), but is great for up to a couple of months and will mean you can cover a greater distance on gnarlier terrain in that time. Some riders now tour with rear panniers and bikepacking bags, shedding the panniers now and then to ride short, challenging routes with a lighter bikepacking setup, before returning to continue their tour with a full load.

A bikepacking setup is also a great option if you have a bike which doesn't have braze-ons for a rack and you just want to get on the road. It's a setup that can be used on any type of bike, so also works for a road-bike blacktop-burst from London to Istanbul or Seattle to Boston.

PART 2 – BIKES, CLOTHING & CAMPING

BIKEPACKING AND DIRT-ROAD TOURING

As long as people have been touring on bicycles, people have been packing too much stuff. While the traditional ways of packing, and the traditional types of touring bikes, are well and good for most people, for others who like to find their way via dirt tracks and rocky roads, maybe not so much. Both the idea of bicycle touring and the idea of mountain biking have recently been upended, with the advent of new types of gear, new types of bikes and a new type of touring: bikepacking.

Over the last couple of years this has become quite the industry buzz word. It's been attached to a wide range of bikes and tossed about when describing everything from multi-day singletrack expeditions to gravel road odysseys and greenway explorations. The lines are blurring between bikepacking and bike touring. However, when it comes to off-road multi-day bike travel, for the purpose of discussing bikes, and gear, there are two breeds:

Bikepacking

Multi-day rides over terrain typically reserved for mountain bikes, a healthy ration of singletrack and dirt roads that make an ultralight and rackless setup more relevant for technical surfaces. Generally, the bikepacker travels light with minimal equipment for a trip of up to about a week, using soft bags (a frame bag, seat pack, and handlebar roll). Emphasis is placed on riding; gear is sacrificed in order to maintain the feel of mountain biking.

Dirt-road touring

This involves longer trips of a few months or even years, through various countries, over mixed terrain including dirt, gravel, and pavement. More gear is needed for diverse situations and extended travel. Racks are employed to handle heavier loads or to carry extra water. The love of off-road riding is still a motivator but the capacity for shredding lines suffers as the idea of long-distance exploration takes the lead. Gear choices for dirt-road touring often lead to the use of two panniers on a rear rack, with no panniers in the front; bottle cage mounts on the fork may be employed with the combination of a framebag; a large saddlebag is also a possibility.

Logan Watts

The Surly Troll makes a great
steed for a dirt tour of Africa.
© Logan Watts

STRAPS NOT BUNGEES!

A strap will hold things more securely on your bike than a bungee, which allows items to bounce around and wriggle free. I find straps come in handy in all sorts of situations, from attaching kit to your bike to holding your trousers up, carrying your bike like a backpack or rigging a harness for dragging your bike through sand. They weigh nothing, so I carry two or three.

Left: Podsacs straps come in useful when dragging through sand.

Bikepacking grew up around the Great Divide Mountain Bike Route in the USA (see p264) where a handful of cottage industries began making custom framebags. Framebags need to be custom made to fit every frame and size of frame, which means they're pricey, so you could follow Lars' example and make your own (see p69). Revelate Designs bags are the most universally available – they work with Surly and Salsa to produce bags that fit their frames.

A handlebar roll can be used to attach a tent and/or dry bag to your handlebar without it flopping around. A seatpack can swallow up as much as a front pannier would and is a great place to stow a small sleeping bag, compact mat, tarptent and an alcohol burner stove. UK-based Apidura's regular seat pack is a whopping 17 litres; the classic Carradice Longflap is also huge; Alpkit and Wildcat Gear are worth checking out too. Alberta-based Porcelain Rocket can craft you a beautiful custom-made bag from an array of different weight and colour of fabrics.

Pimping your ride

Your bike will come with two or three **bottle cage** mountings on the frame. Carry your **fuel bottle** in one of them – you don't want it inside a pannier where the fumes will contaminate clothes and food. The small 600ml fuel bottles fit in a standard bike bottle cage, but get hold of a larger cage to take a one-litre fuel bottle.

Ordinary cycling **water bottles** soon become grimy and they leak when you lay your bike down, so it is better to have something with a screw top such as a Nalgene bottle; plastic won't rattle in the way metal will. I often use fizzy drink bottles, and make sure I switch them every week or so as sunlight causes the plastic to degrade and begin leaching into your water.

Go for the most robust cage, not the lightest one. Small cages, such as the Profile Design Stryke Kage, will take a 1 litre bottle, however **oversized cages** give more bottle-size flexibility. The Topeak Modula XL design works well and mine have lasted years. SJS Cycles have a similar Alloy XL and the BBB Fueltank

XL is also worth a look. The Salsa Anything cage can, err, carry anything, and is another option – earlier versions had problems with breaking welds but the newer HD design is stronger. Oversize cages can be mounted on forks if you don't have front panniers.

Get some respect with this pump-horn, found in Lahore. © Stephen Lord

A **kickstand** is very much an optional accessory. It's easier to load panniers on a free-standing bike and easier to work on one too, but you can always lean your bike against something, or lay it down, so consider whether the stand-up convenience is worth that extra half-kilo in weight. If you decide yes, hunt down the Esge twin leg model by Pletscher which weighs 550g; it holds the bike upright as you kick the legs down, then you rock the bike back onto the stand just like a motorbike. Always check a kickstand is compatible with your bike before buying (Long Haul Truckers, for instance, can't take the pressure of a kickstand attached to a chainstay).

Is a **bell** really necessary on a touring bicycle? No, but it will be greatly appreciated the world over by children as something to twang and as a friendly warning to pedestrians that you are coming through. A 150db siren goes down especially well on the Indian subcontinent.

A **bike computer** is nice to have if you're a statto, but also if you're following route notes or road signs and need to know when you'll hit your next turning. VDO make good units with barometric altimeters; it's considerably cheaper to buy a computer which measures only distance and speed.

If you are mostly touring on paved or well consolidated roads and visiting wet countries, get some **mudguards** (fenders). If you tend to gravitate towards dirt roads, which get muddy in the wet, mudguards can get clogged and be a hindrance. An effective mudguard can be rigged with a series of plastic drinks bottles, some cable ties and a dose of ingenuity.

Tools and spares

Your toolkit and spares should be chosen with your own bike in mind so that it comprises only the things you need. Split your tools into those you frequently use – like pump, multitool, puncture repair kit, oil – and the rest which you rarely use. Store the latter at the bottom of a pannier and keep the others somewhere accessible like your handlebar bag or frame bag.

ESSENTIALS

A **pump** such as Topeak's Mountain Morph is ideal; a miniature trackstand pump that can deliver much higher pressure than other compact pumps and is robust yet small enough to conceal in a pannier. Don't necessarily trust the gauge: it's possible to crack a rim by over-inflating with this pump! Another option is the Blackburn Mammoth Anyvalve Mini-Pump which is compact, has a robust aluminium body and a comfy handle. Having a good, reliable pump is important, as a pump-failure in the middle of nowhere would leave you in the lurch. Check your pump fits both Schrader (used in car tubes) and Presta (thinner, screw-shut) valves; you never know when you'll need this flexibility. It's also an advantage if you can buy a rebuild kit for your pump so that you can carry this and replace the innards in case of failure, rather than carrying a spare pump.

Tools you must ensure you have include: **Allen keys** in a variety of sizes (to fit every bolt on your bike), a **flat screwdriver**, a **Philips screwdriver**, **pliers**, **spoke key**, **chain splitter**, and a **cassette remover**.

A cycling **multitool** is good for providing many of the tools needed in one place. Topeak's Alien series are well-equipped but there are dozens of different multitools and you should buy whatever feels comfortable in your hand while looking for the highest quality you can find. The multitools that split in two are more useful than having all the tools on one unit.

A **Leatherman**, or similar general purpose multitool with pliers, is versatile and another essential thing to carry. The larger Leathermans are a bit heavy but all the tools are good quality and useful, whereas lightweight tools don't always perform well. You don't need to bring a dedicated wire-cutter – the Leatherman one isn't great – but you can just leave cables uncut until you find a workshop with decent wire-cutters.

Carry a **chain splitter** (often part of a cycling multitool) and a few universal chain links such as SRAM's PowerLink (make sure you get the right size e.g. 9-speed width). A couple of extra links saved from your last chain should be carried for replacing damaged links.

When it comes to a **cassette remover** the tiny NBT2 is all you need. It's essential (for those with derailleur gears) when replacing broken spokes on the drive side of the rear wheel as you can't fit them without removing the cassette. In the UK you can get NBT2s from 🖳 spacycles.co.uk. The Unior Lockring Remover performs the same function; Harris Cyclery in the USA (🖳 harriscyclery.net) sells a similar tool, the Stein Mini Cassette Lockring Tool.

On longer tours, carry a **spare tyre** (foldable is best so it fits in a pannier), unless you are going ultra-light and are happy to take a chance with a sticky **tyre boot** (a small patch of rubber which can be used as a temporary fix on a tyre gash). You can improvise a boot with a piece of inner tube (or toothpaste tube and gaffer tape), and this can be enough to get you to the nearest bike shop for an emergency local tyre (that's why you're running 26ers, right?).

It's sensible to have up to five **spare spokes** for the drive side and three for the left-side of the rear wheel/the front wheel. Rohloff users won't find the correct spoke length for their rear wheel out in the adventure cycle-touring world, so may want to carry more (see box p50), although a good bike shop can shorten spokes. The ingenious FiberFix offers a quick, temporary solution to a broken spoke.

Bring three plastic **tyre levers** (Park Tools make a good, strong set), **spare inner tubes** (at least one if you're touring on 26" wheels and regularly passing through towns with bike shops; more if you're using a tyre size not available locally, or are going remote), **brake pads** (and **rotors** if running disc brakes), a **puncture repair kit** (if you buy locally, make sure the glue and patches are decent quality), a spare **brake cable**, a spare **gear cable**, some **cable ends**, good **duct tape**, **electrical tape**, **superglue**, **Seam Grip glue**, some **cable ties** in various sizes, a small selection of **bolts**, **nuts** and **washers**, a couple of **hose clamps**, an old **toothbrush** for cleaning gears and **WD40** or similar solvent.

It's handy having a decent plastic bottle for your **chain oil** – preferably with a screw lid that won't leak, and with a removable dropper so you can refill it. Small amounts of oil can often be scrounged from motorbike shops you pass.

Other things to consider

A quality 15mm **wrench** that is wider than a cone wrench but still narrow enough to fit between pedal and crank will be handier than you think for taking pedals off when you put your bike on buses, or to prevent your shins from getting bashed when pushing. Make sure that your pedals are tight if you have to refit them without a pedal wrench, and get them greased and tightened properly as soon as you can.

A proper **spoke key** will do a better job of truing a wheel than the little one you will find on almost any cycling multitool. You may have to rebuild your wheel at some point, and spoke keys are easier on your hands and are less likely to round off a spoke nipple (which would then need to be replaced). The Park Tools Triple Spoke Wrench has served me well.

A small pot of synthetic **grease** is useful for big cleaning jobs like headsets and for installing pedals; but again, you can always find some when you need it.

People often carry **spare chains** and switch between them on the road, in order to make their drivechain teeth last longer. However, a chain weighs nearly half a kilo, so I prefer not to lug all that metal around.

If you have any specialist parts on your bike that you know you won't find spares for when on tour, then ensure you carry these spares with you. Those with Rohloff hubs should see the list on p50.

How much stuff?

You'll find the question of how much gear to take on an adventurous bike tour gets bandied about endlessly on the internet and on the road. We all think we're carrying the absolute minimum and that everything we have on our bikes is there for a good reason; but it's a strange coincidence that no matter what their setup, bikers always manage to fill their bags to the very brim.

The important thing about your bike trip is that **it's your bike trip**: take as much or as little as you want to make the whole experience as fun and rewarding as possible. But before embarking on a shopping spree, you might want to take the following into account:

LIGHT VS HEAVY

The main advantage of carrying more gear is the additional comfort you'll be able to enjoy *when not riding*. All riders need to carry the essentials for surviving the elements, but having luxuries means nicer clothes for towns, fancier cooking equipment, more electronic gadgets and campground comforts. Many cycle tourers like to combine cycling with other outdoor activities, and if you carry hiking kit or a fishing rod you'll be able to have plenty of off-bike adventures walking in the Tian Shan, or pulling fish from the Urubamba. It's very unusual, though not unheard of, for cyclists to carry pack rafts, and I once encountered someone with base-jumping kit – in these cases the extra weight was more than compensated for by the added enjoyment provided off the bike.

Carrying more spares and tools means you're less likely to lose time and money if you break down halfway across the Taklamakan. Having that essential item with you can mean avoiding the need to catch transport to a mechanic or a shop selling parts, or getting a bike piece shipped from home.

The downside of loading up your bike with all this stuff is that when riding, every kilo makes a difference. Of course your trip isn't a race and it doesn't matter if you're 100% efficient; but, particularly in the mountains and on unpaved roads, the lighter your bike, the easier and more enjoyable it is to ride. **The most common mistake inexperienced tourers make is to take too much stuff.** Couples have an advantage over lone riders in being able to share communal kit like the tent, stove, tools and spares, which usually adds up to a saving of 3kg or more per rider. Another important consideration is how much food and water you need to carry – mould it to fit the local circumstances.

It also pays to be flexible. You might not always be going in a straight line, heading for some far-off goal – if you're cycling a loop or dead-end valley road, why not leave all the non-essentials behind and pick them up afterwards? If you won't be needing warm weather gear for a while, look into whether you can send it on or home. Consider buying or giving away smaller items of kit, as your need for them arises or disappears.

Only you can decide what your 'perfect weight' is, because it's different for everyone and you may well find that it changes as you go anyway. It's noticeable from blogs how some bikers' gear gets larger as the trip progresses, the bike becomes a home, and after a while they look like a Bactrian camel with two great humps, front and rear. For a minority the opposite happens and they shed weight the longer they stay on the road.

Here different cyclists tell what's in their bags and why.

Lightweight – 10-15kg

Harriet Pike

I've toured with everything from 15-50kg and I tailor my gear and setup to each trip. After a few years of fine tuning, I feel like the 15kg I carried on a month-long trip in vertical Peru was just right for the mountainous, dirt road riding I love.

This setup enabled me to enjoy the long mountain climbs and opened up opportunities to ride roads that on a heavy bike would feature frustratingly long pushes. Carrying what for me was the bare minimum, I had a comfortable enough campsite at the end of the day (I like to have a really warm -17C sleeping bag – it is quite literally my security blanket) and sufficient clothing to keep me happy even in bad weather. I love the increased simplicity of a light load – having fewer things to worry about looking after and it being quicker to pack up camp – as well as being able to shoulder my loaded bike up to hotel rooms.

You'll want to go light in the Peruvian hills.

Sharing all the communal kit with Neil meant my 15kg of kit fitted nicely into rear panniers and a bar bag (Neil also had a tent strapped across his back rack). This weight included everything needed for a wild camping trip in the high Andes. For chilly descents: full waterproofs, full thermals, big gloves, a fleece and a couple of buffs. For exposed campsites: a mountaineering tent, 4-season bag, lightweight Therm-a-Rest, two pans and a WhisperLite International stove. Luxuries came in the form of a camera, a GPS, a diary, a tablet, some chargers and a spare t-shirt for days off the bike. Going light on spares meant only taking one inner tube for four wheels, some tyre boots but no spare tyre, one brake and one gear cable, a couple of PowerLinks, glue, patches and a few spokes. For tools: a pump, NBT2, multitool, Leatherman, spoke key, chain breaker and tyre levers. I carried gaffer tape and cable ties in case some bodging was called for – anything that couldn't be fixed with all of this would've meant hitching a ride to a town, which fortunately didn't happen, but wouldn't have been the end of the world.

Medium weight – 15-25kg

Tim Moss

When my wife and I cycled around the world, we stripped down our kit until it fitted easily within four panniers. This meant our luggage never felt overly burdensome (ie. we could carry it all into a train/hotel in one go) but after 16 months on the road, we weren't wanting for anything extra.

I've never needed more than three sets of clothes: one for cycling, one for evenings and shorts and t-shirt for laundry days, swimming and sleepovers. I carried a cheap fleece and Primaloft jacket for warmth. For the rain, I had Gore-Tex Active jacket and trousers (light but tough) and SealSkinz socks. I took a paper-thin microfibre towel (big enough to wrap around my waist but small enough to hold in my fist) and I always carry a flannel – highly recommended for that end-of-day wipe down.

For sleeping we had a lightweight, free-standing tent (2kg) and super-light bivvys (200g) to sleep under the stars.

A medium weight four-pannier setup.
© Tim & Laura Moss

We took a slight hit on weight with synthetic sleeping bags but it meant we didn't have to worry about them getting damp or dirty and could chuck them in washing machines. Similarly, I used a polycotton liner as it's cheaper and tougher than silk with only a small weight penalty. I slept on a three-quarter-length inflatable mattress. Inflating every night took a bit of effort and they filled a lot of space in the tent but they were embarrassingly comfortable on even the rockiest ground. I also used a super-thin foam mat underneath for protection and something to sit on during the day.

We carried a Primus multi-fuel stove but, through 25 countries, we never needed to use petrol as gas canisters were always available. We used Primus Eta pots which have heat exchangers – they were a little bigger and heavier but used less fuel and cooked faster (tested in my kitchen before departure!).

We had a 7-inch tablet for navigating, video editing, email and Skype, and a Kindle each for reading – all stored in a clip-lock tupperware pot. I got obsessed with podcasts and audiobooks so bought a thumb-sized MP3 player which, along with our cheap Chinese mobile and headtorch batteries, could all

ULTRALIGHT BIKEPACKING – UNDER 10KG

For six months in South America—Ecuador to southern Argentina—I sought unpaved routes on remote terrain between villages. I chose my most capable wheel, a fat bike, as I envisaged this trip as one where I would be on broken stair step single track descents at 3500m, where I would face day-long climbs out of Andean canyons, and where I would sometimes have to hike-a-bike into the unknown. I wanted to remain light, fast, and agile though, in spite of the heavier machine. Consequently, I pared down my kit to the ultralight essentials. I now aim for under 9kgs, no matter what bike I'm on.

Base outfit

Thinly padded baggy shorts (ideally pad cleaned daily); small change in pocket
Football jersey
Merino socks
Low cut hiking shoes
Baseball cap
Sunglasses (take them off when making friendly eye contact!)

Dry bag strapped to fork leg carrier

eg. Salsa Anything cage
1 spare short sleeved top; I prefer a merino polo for lounging and for looking respectable off-bike, riding when the other top is wet.
1 pair arm warmers
1 pair thinly padded merino undershorts, wear under trousers or tights as necessary
1 spare pair merino socks
1 pair ultralight trousers for off-the-bike

Mesh bag of toiletries: toothbrush, paste, salt odor crystal fragment, spare contact lenses, micro saline solution bottle, fragment of soap, earplugs, nail clippers
Mesh bag of meds: ibuprofen, zithromycin, malarone, zolamide, benadryl allergy, immodium, dayquil sinus, steri strips, transparent dressing, antiseptic wipes, bandaids

Saddle bag

Down quilt rated to -5C
Puff pullover, synthetic fill
Waterproof / windproof tights
Merino liner gloves
Merino buff
Gore-Tex booties
Titanium cup strapped outside
(Food overflow is accommodated by extending roll closure on saddle bag)

Handlebar sling

Single wall one person free standing tent
Flip flops
Three-quarter-length foam pad

Front bag, strapped to handlebar sling

Map
Gore-Tex hooded jacket
Micro 4/3 camera with versatile lens, packed in ziplock bag
Smartphone + earbuds
Toilet paper stash
Passport + travel paperwork, eg. air ticket, insurance forms, immunisations
Credit cards / cash

be charged by USB. As such, we just needed one travel adaptor with a USB slot to charge everything.

Finally, we each had a saddle bag filled with repair stuff. Combined, this amounted to:

• For tools: pen knife, bike tool, Allen keys, chain breaker and cassette remover.
• For bike repairs: 2-4 tubes, 12 spokes, kevlar emergency spoke and two repair kits with extra glue and patches.
• For the rest: tape, cable ties, cord, mat/tent patches and glue.

Heavyweight – over 25kg

Lorenzo Rojo

Last time I weighed my bike – one year ago in Missoula, Montana – the scales said 72kg. Heavy, are you thinking? *Not a bike but a cart?* someone said. OK... but first of all come in please, come and see from inside what has been my home for the past 17 years.

PART 2 – BIKES, CLOTHING & CAMPING

2-3 pages from small notepad
Space pen
Gore-Tex Shell mittens clipped to front bag, used to carry snacks

Gas tank bag
Snacks
Lip balm, doubles as sunscreen

Frame bag
Breakfast and dinner food
Light small stove
Titanium pot
Pot scrubby
Titanium spork
Lighter
SteriPEN
Headlamp
Rear light
Chargers
Spare memory cards
Spare batteries for camera and SteriPEN
Spectacles
Repair kit in small nylon sack: lube bottle, small piece of rag, patch kit, 2 spokes, 4 brake pads, quick link, 6 zip ties, 1 tube

Small bag at junction of top tube and seatpost
4cm knife
Tiny cable lock
Tools in small nylon sack: #4 and #5 Allen keys, torx wrench, tyre levers, chain tool, spoke wrench, Stein hypercracker cassette tool, Park MT-1 backup tool

On frame
Pump wrapped with gorilla tape
Stove fuel bottle, downtube bosses
2L water bottle attached to fork leg carrier, eg. Salsa Anything cage
x2 1L water bottles rear triangle
(add two more on forks when necessary)

The above kit list assumes a trip in unpredictable weather of a few weeks to indefinitely long world travel. For a shorter trip, or for places known to have warm weather, I'd substitute a tarp and Tyvek ground sheet for the tent, and leg warmers for the heavier tights. The list also assumes that there will be times spent in civilisation; if it is a completely backcountry trip, there may be no need for off-bike trousers or a bike lock.

Joe Cruz

An ultralight setup. © Joe Cruz

Let's start with the kitchen: two stoves, a multi-fuel MSR and an alcohol-Trangia. The latter very useful for cooking indoors, as it is completely silent and leaves no odours or fumes. Also a ceramic water filter.

Tools room: everything you need to assemble and disassemble the bike completely, plus a good selection of nuts and bolts. Never in 190,000km was I stranded on the road because of a breakdown (I am proud, yes, you may have noticed). I also try to go to bicycle shops as little as possible, I prefer to repair and replace parts myself. Parts: Always a new tyre (ideally Schwalbe Marathon), a chain, cables, two inner tubes, some spokes.

Now we come to one of the most important places of the home, the bedroom – come in, don't stand at the door. A two-person tent (2.5kg); down sleeping bag (-7C); two mats, one Thermarest (recent acquisition) and the previous foam one which is completely puncture-proof and for all-terrain-use (good for a roadside picnic or nap). Now let's open the wardrobe: Gore-Tex jacket and trousers and shoe covers, winter clothing (non-technical and slightly heavier as a result), cotton T-shirts, cycling shorts to pedal in, walking and

A heavy bike means some home comforts.
© Lorenzo Rojo

cycling shoes; also normal street clothes, including jeans, which in this world of globalised cities makes me an anonymous being (or near...) almost anywhere.

Next door, multi-use room: books, maps, a small laptop, camera, shortwave radio, first aid kit and a wide selection of small items and spare parts (bag-hooks, stove parts...).

Is that all? No, we are missing one of the most important and assorted corners of the home: the pantry. Out of those 72kg, 20 correspond to the bike and about 10-12 to food and water. I always have food for 2-3 days, sometimes for 8. Why? Well, sometimes it's necessary, and it's almost always cheaper. When I was riding the Great Divide Mountain Bike Route the food in the villages was too expensive, so I would buy at supermarkets in towns and transport it. I also believe that honey is to a cyclist what magic potion is to Asterix (it makes us invincible) so it's always in my bags and if the quality is good I don't mind carrying up to a kilo.

Summarising: 50 kilo-luggage implies home comforts, self-sufficiency and autonomy; and – very important – economy, as the smaller your budget, the heavier your bike. And coming to the questions at the beginning: can you ride comfortably pulling such a burden? The answer is yes, and for me that's also a condition. I like unpaved roads and mountains and am always on the lookout for high passes and wild places. I enjoy them the most. Only if someday the weight of the bike prevents me from getting as far or as high as I want – hasn't happened yet – will I consider throwing away a few things. Except the honey, of course.

Clothing

Every trip will call for its own choice of clothing depending on the climate, seasons and type of ride you're doing. A short summer jaunt around France needs something very different from an overland trip to Australia. Whereas on short rides back home you may deck yourself out in Lycra for sheer efficiency, you will find that when you wear the same clothes day in day out on tour, comfort, durability, fitting in with your surroundings and wearing fabrics that don't retain odour are all more important considerations.

If you're going round the world, don't expect to be able to carry clothing for every eventuality of climate you'll meet. Bring the most important items of clothing from home and then just buy anything else on the road as the need arises. Sending home, sending on, or giving away what you aren't using is a good way of keeping your wardrobe streamlined.

Cycling shorts

Wearing padded cycling shorts is a matter of personal preference – most, but not all, cyclists prefer them. Give padded shorts a go but if you find them uncomfortable, try going without – I've met people whose comfort problems were thus instantly cured.

The reason cycling shorts work is not just the padding, but because they become a slippery second skin. This slides over, rather than snagging on, the saddle, and reduces friction and consequent soreness. No one ever tells you to wear padded bike shorts without underwear, but 'going commando' like this is the most comfortable way for both men and women, as chafing from seams on your undies is avoided. Perhaps the best approach is to wear cycling shorts just some of the time (bring a couple of pairs for hygiene reasons) and give your loins some air on other days. If you go with padded shorts, note that traditional chamois-lined shorts are more comfortable than synthetic ones, but they are more expensive and take longer to dry.

If you choose to use regular underwear, try a few different pairs to find which ones give greatest comfort. Look for flat-seamed underpants made from natural fibres; merino boxer shorts are great for both men and women as they are comfortable and remain stink-free for much longer.

Lycra-clad women may attract unwanted attention and not all men like to walk around with their family jewels exposed in such an acutely sculpted profile; additionally, in most Muslim and Buddhist countries (and others) close fitting clothing is bad form, so riders often wear baggy shorts on top. Three-quarter-length padded baggy shorts are very popular; an exposed shin and calf seems to be non-controversial and off the bike they hang lower, while on the bike they ride up and ventilate better.

LAYERING

Layering is generally accepted as the best way to regulate body temperature. Layers keep you warmer by trapping air, and can be added or taken off as you ride, depending on how warm or cold you feel. This layering system extends from your thermal underwear to the waterproof mitts over your gloves.

Performance clothing is generally broken down into three levels: base, insulating (or mid-layer) and shell (or outer-layer).

Base layer

Merino wool base layers are favoured by many riders as they are very comfortable in mild climes, look smart, and remain odourless far longer than synthetics. However, they are more expensive than synthetics or cotton, dry more slowly and need a little looking after – you won't want to give your prized merino top to a dhobi-wallah to bash clean on the banks of the Ganges. Thinner merino tops only last a few months of constant use and may begin to become ragged not long after your beard/underarm hair starts to look unseemly. More and more cycle-specific merino tops are hitting the market – check out Icebreaker and Ground Effect NZ.

One of the aims of a base layer is to transfer sweat away from the body, keeping you comfortable and dry. In outdoor shops and techy sites this is known as wicking. For exercising at intense levels, **synthetic materials** wick sweat away most effectively, meaning a **synthetic top** is the best option for keeping you dry and warm in cold weather. Synthetic materials last longer than merino, and also dry more quickly, however they begin to pong after a short while, and this puts many people off using them as a base layer on a long ride. I have found T-shirts made from a **synthetic/merino mix** are the best compromise between durability and stinkyness; my personal base layer favourites are Rab MeCo and Helly Hansen Lifa Warm.

When cycling at touring speeds in moderate temperatures, you don't need the most efficient performance fabric and you may well feel more comfortable wearing **normal clothes** rather than looking like you just came from the set of Star Trek. A **football shirt** from the local market is often a good way to go – they are cheap and always help generate conversation with new found friends.

A **cotton T-shirt** is the most versatile clothing item for any traveller. Cotton clothing works well for 3-season cycling, is very cheap and you can use it to floss your sprockets when the odour becomes too much.

Essential wardrobe for an Andes ride.

A loose-weave, baggy, 100% **cotton shirt** (not of the travel clothing variety as these are less breathable) is the best option in areas of extreme heat where you don't want your shirt wicking away your precious body fluids. Pop the collar up to keep the sun off your neck and roll the sleeves down to protect your arms. Cheap men's shirts are available everywhere and are good for both men and women. It is worth investing in a new one if you have a few visas to obtain, because by tidying yourself up a little you may be treated better at the embassy, thus speeding up the stamp-collecting process.

Mid layer

Your mid layer should keep you warm. If you are cycling in temperate countries, a **fleece** works best as a mid layer, being lighter than merino and much easier to wash and dry. Good quality fleece also lasts a very long time, but once again merino wins points for style. A cheap fleece can often be picked up at a local market and is a good addition for when you hit the mountains – you can donate it to a local herder when you descend again to the lowlands.

A good shell jacket in bright colours keeps freezing winds at bay on long descents, is very visible and looks great in (colour!) photos.
© Stephen Lord

Nothing beats the warmth-to-weight ratio of down, however a **down jacket** is really only useful when the climate is cold and dry. If you are heading to the Bolivian altiplano in dry season, opt for a down jacket to pull on at the end of the day when the temperature plummets. Down is useless when wet, however, which makes more versatile synthetic insulation a better choice for a long-distance tour. **PrimaLoft** is the gold standard, but Patagonia and Arcteryx versions are also worth a look. A 300g jacket packs small and can be squeezed into the corner of a pannier to be brought out when the mercury drops. You'll really appreciate having one under your waterproof when it's chucking down with rain and you're huddled over the camp stove on a cool night.

Take one or two mid-layers depending on where you are touring and the weather you expect to experience along the way. If you are on a budget, layering up a few micro fleeces is a good option.

Outer layer

If you are going to spend money on one quality item of clothing, make it your waterproof jacket. A jacket provides the wind-proofing that good fleece lacks and adds instant warmth when you throw it on at the top of a pass for protection on the freezing descent. There are two outstanding waterproof and breathable fabric brands to look out for: Gore-Tex and eVent.

Gore-Tex Active is the most breathable fabric in the family, though this added breathability is to the detriment of durability. It makes a great choice if you are going fast and light on a short tour or don't expect to need a rain jacket very frequently.

DRESS TO IMPRESS!

When choosing their wardrobes (and also their panniers), budding photographers should take note that brightly coloured clothing makes for far better shots. Your photos will be improved significantly by having a cyclist heading into the distance wearing a red jacket, rather than one decked out all in black.

PART 2 – BIKES, CLOTHING & CAMPING

CARING FOR YOUR WATERPROOFS ON THE ROAD

When at home, you (are supposed to) care for breathable waterproof membranes by washing them regularly with a specific cleanser such as NikWax Tech Wash or Granger's Performance Cleaner, and then topping up the durable water repellent coat (DWR) by spraying or washing with something like Nikwax XT Direct or Granger's Performance Proofer. It is not often possible to find these products on the road and the last thing you want to do is use a detergent, which may coat the clothing in a layer of gunk that prevents the membrane from breathing. Many cyclists simply neglect their waterproofs but it is important to wash them or the pores will become blocked with dirt and your jacket will cease to be breathable. The solution is to hand-wash your jacket in lukewarm water (without scrubbing it too hard) with a bit of glycerine or natural soap. Make sure you rinse it well afterwards, and pop it in a tumble dryer, if you can find one, to reactivate the DWR.

Gore-Tex Pro garments are the top-of-the-range: rugged and breathable waterproofs with maximum durability. One of the cheaper Gore-Tex Pro jackets makes a good investment for a long distance tour – there's no need to buy a high-end model with a hefty price tag.

Gore-Tex Performance is your bog standard Gore-Tex and is a good option if you are counting your pennies. It is heavier than other types but tends to have more everyday designs, meaning you don't look as flashy.

Less durable than Gore-Tex Pro, eVent lies somewhere between Gore-Tex Pro and Gore-Tex Active in terms of breathability and waterproofness.

When you choose a waterproof jacket, reach forward, like you would on a bike, and ensure the sleeves are long enough that your wrists are covered. Also, check that the jacket is long enough at the back so that your backside will be shielded from spray. The scooped back on a cycle-specific jacket is great for covering your behind, but these will be made of Gore-Tex Active and therefore don't have the ruggedness you usually need for an extended tour.

Despite the hype, breathable waterproof fabrics cannot achieve the impossible. If you're pedalling hard in the rain, you won't stay as dry inside as you would if you were standing still. Riding creates heat and moisture, and waterproof, breathable jackets can only vent moisture slowly, particularly when soaked in rainwater. The simple answer is to ride at a more gentle pace in the rain so that your body generates less heat.

Soft-shell jackets are great for short trips in dry mountain areas. They are more comfortable and breathe better than a hard shell jacket; however, they are not waterproof, so on a tour which passes through rainy areas a soft shell alone will not cut the mustard.

Hands, feet and head

While cycling easily generates heat to warm the body core, feet and hands don't move much and will feel the chill. Layering principles apply to the hands too: a pair of **fleece gloves** is ideal for cold mornings and evenings, and throw a good pair of waterproof **mountaineering gloves** over the top and you won't be reduced to tears by the screaming barfies on mountainous descents. Lycra **leg warmers** and **sleeves** are another good way to keep warm while riding and take up next to no space in panniers. Deploying SealSkinz **waterproof socks** in cold and wet conditions will help keep your toes toasty.

Your head will also feel the cold, so if you're touring in colder climates bring along a warm **hat**. A **Buff** neck-warmer is light and versatile and is almost an essential piece of kit. It can be cinched up as a hat or used as a scarf and also works well as a dust mask (or full-on hijab at a pinch!).

You'll be wearing **sunglasses** most of the day for much of the trip and since we're talking about your eyes, it's worth getting a good pair. Cycling specific frames (which don't

You'll be glad of these when descending in the mountains.

block your peripheral vision) make it easier to spot a speeding moto-taxi when you glance behind before pulling out to overtake a herd of alpacas. Glasses can be pricey, so bring along a crush-proof **case** to protect them.

Footwear

Among long-distance riders it's as common to find standard trainers, sandals or hiking boots being worn as it is cycle-specific shoes with cleats that clip into SPD pedals. You won't hear these people fretting that their pedal stroke might not be efficient enough; footwear is a personal choice, and comfort (both on and off the bike) wins over efficiency on long rides. You can always get the benefit of a stiff-soled cycle-specific shoe without attaching the cleats; many cyclists wear something like a Specialized Tahoe shoe, but use a flat pedal – possibly one with metal pins to help provide extra grip.

There is a huge range of cycle-specific footwear on the market, ranging from sandals to light hiking boots (for example Shimano's MT91 boot), most with a

PART 2 – BIKES, CLOTHING & CAMPING

HELMETS

For a hairy mountain descent, or the no-less-perilous ride into Tehran, using a helmet is just common sense. Many cycle tourists only wear their helmet part of the time and leave it hanging off the back of a pannier the rest. My view is that there's little point stowing it behind you, when you can store it on your head. Once, cycling through a gorge on a quiet road with little traffic in the Himalaya, a fist-sized rock fell with a whistle and smashed into the tarmac one metre in front of my handlebars. A direct head-shot would've meant the end, and this was enough to convince me to always wear my helmet when riding.

Finding a good helmet while you're on the road in a developing country is almost impossible; you've left it too late. As you'll wear it every day, it is worth trying a few out until you find one that fits and suits your

style – make sure you can expand it to put a hood or warm hat underneath. Also bear in mind there are a few countries out there, Australia and Spain among them, where cycling helmets are compulsory.

At least one convert to the helmet brigade. Kinnaur, India.

ALTERNATIVES TO SPDS OR TOE CLIPS

Power Grips. © Stephen Lord

Toe clips consist of a cage and a strap that can be tightened around your foot. I crumpled at traffic lights a couple of times before I got used to removing my feet from them, but they are a cheap and low-tech way of improving the efficiency of your pedalling.

Power Grips, a simple alternative from the 1980s, are also fantastic. These are strips of very tough, robust canvas which bolt diagonally to ordinary flat pedals. You put your foot in at an angle and when you straighten it, the straps hold your foot securely. When you get off the bike, your feet come out easily – they're well worth checking out if you don't like SPDs or toe clips.

recessed Shimano SPD cleat built into the sole of the shoe. Combination pedals such as Shimano's M324 are popular with tourers – they take toe clips if you change your mind about SPDs. The MTB-style M424 is another pedal that works with or without SPD shoes. Though riding with cleats is more efficient, they aren't for everyone and a long trip is the wrong place to find out; some cleated-shoe cyclists develop knee problems because their feet are fixed in one position.

If you plan to do some trekking, then consider taking a trekking boot or a trail shoe to wear for both hiking and cycling. Some approach shoes (a hiking/rock climbing hybrid) make really good cycle touring shoes because the rubber is designed for climbing and hence is more grippy and rigid than your standard trainer; have a look at the offerings from La Sportiva and 5:10.

Sandals (whether cycle-specific, or stiff trekking models such as those made by Keen) are popular – they allow your feet to breathe and keep you comfortable in hot climates. If they get wet they tend to dry out faster than trainers.

Put thought into whether it's worth getting a waterproof shoe. Avoid them if you are headed for a hot climate, but in cool, wet countries waterproof footwear is wonderful for keeping your feet warmer, if not completely dry. A good compromise is a non-waterproof SPD shoe or trail shoe, plus a pair of Neoprene booties or Gore-Tex overshoes to slip over the top on wet days.

Camping

As days turn to months, your tent becomes a home, and many of the sweetest touring memories come when you veer off the road to set up camp in the wild. As with your bike, durability, comfort and reliability are key when choosing camping gear for an adventurous cycle tour. For shorter trips of a few months lightweight kit can work well, but for a longer tour of a year or more you want to go for something that will last the distance.

TENTS

There is always going to be a trade-off between weight, space and price. The vast majority of long distance riders prefer a home away from home even if it weighs a kilo or two more; a simple tarp-tent is sufficient for a hardy few. Take time selecting your tent and visit good outdoor shops where staff will put up several tents for you to try for size. If you buy online, pitch the tent indoors when it arrives, and return it if it fails to meet all your needs.

A sturdy semi-geodesic tent comes in handy in bad weather.

Features to look for in a good bike-touring tent

● **Medium weight** The best and most suitable tents for a bike touring couple are generally in the 2.5-3.5kg range (5½ to 7½ pounds). You can find lighter, but this lower weight is achieved by using thinner materials and smaller flysheets which means they don't stay waterproof for as long. Avoid super-strong mountaineering tents as these will be overly heavy and (usually) you don't need their snow-shedding ability. Look for tents described as three-season.

● **Fabric material** Flysheet fabric is waterproofed either by a polyurethane (PU) coating, which is cheaper, or by impregnating with silicone. PU is used to coat the floors of most tents; it can be coated onto either polyester or nylon. Silicone is always impregnated into nylon (rather than coated on one side) which makes the nylon stronger for its weight, and more waterproof, than its PU-coated equivalent. If you can afford it, go for a 'silnylon' tent. A blast of UV damages any tent (so always take down, shade or cover yours during the day), however PU-coated fabric degrades faster in sunlight than silnylon. The higher the denier of the fabric the more durable, waterproof and heavy it is. Single-wall tents are made from a breathable membrane (similar to Gore-Tex) but I wouldn't recommend this on a tour unless you will be staying in a cold environment for the entirety.

● **Waterproof** The measure used for a fabric's waterproofness is the 'hydrostatic head' (HH); look at the HH of both the flysheet and groundsheet. The higher the number, the more waterproof the fabric but not necessarily the more waterproof the tent, because the design can be as important. Many tents are sold with unsealed seams; seal them with either silicone or PU, (depending on what's used on the flysheet fabric).

● **Strong poles** The strongest tent poles are made of so-called aircraft-grade aluminium, the same used for some bike frames. DAC poles are the best brand. Look for fairly short pole sections as they will be much easier to pack without overhanging the end of your rear rack, and may even fit in a pannier. Most tent poles are around 8.5mm in diameter, anything thicker is a bonus. Poles do occasionally break, usually in high winds, so you need a short section of tube which 'splints' a broken pole. Otherwise use duct tape to strap a tent peg along the broken section.

PART 2 – BIKES, CLOTHING & CAMPING

• **Comfortable size** Most people appreciate a bit more tent space on a long trip, so think in terms of a two-person tent for solo use and a three-person tent for a couple. With a bit more room, your tent will all the sooner become a home rather than an emergency shelter. Don't just look at the floor area of the tent but also consider the height; you want to be able to sit up comfortably which means a height of at least 105cm at the highest point.

• **Storage space** Large porches (vestibules) over each door are useful for storing panniers close by (you won't want them inside the tent if they're wet or dirty), as well as for sheltered cooking. A couple of tents on the market have porches big enough to cover your bike, but it's not needed, although at times you might feel more secure pulling your back wheel under the porch and tying it to something.

• **Good ventilation** Whatever style of tent you choose, ventilation is essential for comfortable camping. Flysheets that reach all the way to the ground will keep the inner drier from rain but make venting less effective. These tents tend to have scoop air-vents on top to encourage air-flow between the inner and outer and so purge the condensation that you produce. Pitching your tent where you can catch a breeze will reduce condensation significantly, as will using a groundsheet to prevent dampness due to evapotranspiration.

• **Free standing** Look for a freestanding design (ie. one that doesn't need pegging out in order to stand up). This will not only mean you can pitch on rocky or stony ground, but also in schools, abandoned buildings or mosquito-infested hotel rooms. The more pole-crossovers there are, the stronger the structure. Look for designs with three or more crossovers or 'hubs'. The time you will be really glad you chose a tough tent is in the mountains, where something solid, at the expense of a pound or two more (in money and weight), will be worth it.

• **Easy to pitch** Some tents have continuous pole sleeves on the inner tent that greatly reduce the airflow between inner and outer; other, cheaper, designs have the pole sleeves in several short sections, which makes the tent maddeningly slow to set up. The clip-type of pole attachment, where the flysheet is clipped on to the inner, is far and away the best way of attaching poles. A variation is the Hilleberg system of having the tent poles threaded into sleeves on the outside of the flysheet, with the inner tent attached with toggles to the fly.

• **Tent pegs** If you can easily bend the tent pegs that come with your tent it is worth upgrading – it won't cost much. The strongest tent pegs with a 3-edge design or V-shaped pegs are best. Pegs with nylon loops (which you can add yourself) are much easier to pull out of the ground. Take a few spares and count them back into the bag when you strike camp to avoid losses.

The problem with tunnel tents: hammering pegs into concrete... © Stephen Lord

• **Footprint** Nearly all tents are now offered with an optional 'footprint', a model-specific groundsheet which protects the floor of your tent. They can seem expensive for what they are, so if you're good with a sewing machine make your own from a piece of cheap tarp for a fraction of the price.

● **Camouflaged** Lastly, but importantly, drab-coloured tents are best suited to stealth camping. Having a bright yellow tent will lead to a far higher number of curious (and sometimes unwelcome) evening visitors.

BIKE TOURING TENTS

Here is a selection of the best bike touring tents around. If one of the listed models doesn't quite suit you, most of these recommended manufacturers offer alternative, similar, designs which use the same materials and have equally good attention to detail.

MSR Hubba Hubba and Mutha Hubba

The MSR Experience Series of tents are currently the most popular tents on the cycle touring circuit. They are cheaper than high-end European offerings and will stand up to most conditions. The **Hubba Hubba** is lightweight, roomy and durable; great for a solo traveller. It comes in two different weights – the heavier green HP (1.9kg), and the grey NX (1.7kg). The NX contains more mesh, so is better ventilated, but can be chilly, and dust will be blown in when it's windy. I would recommend going for the heavier-weight option for durability. The hydrostatic head of the flysheet is low at 1000mm (HP) or 1200mm (NX), but the taut upper of the tent sheds water easily, meaning they perform surprisingly well in the wet. If you are planning to be somewhere with extreme weather then make sure you shelter this tent well, or buy something sturdier.

The 3-man **Mutha Hubba** is perfect for a cycle-touring couple. Inside it is palatial, with 1.17m sitting-up space in the HP version and 1.12m in the NX. The NX weighs 2.2kg, has fewer poles, a less sturdy design, lower roof, and lots more mesh. The HP gets my vote for touring – it only weighs 3.1kg and has a more solid structure, less mesh and a durable groundsheet.

A Mutha Hubba pitched on the Salar de Uyuni. © James Butcher

Vaude Odyssey, Hogan and Space

Vaude make great tents at affordable prices. It's possible to buy many of their designs in different weights but the 'light' or 'ultra-light' models are best for touring. For solo travellers the 1.8kg **Hogan** UL 2P is a nice little tent – sufficiently solid and with enough headspace to sit at the porch-end. The

Vaude Odyssey. © Peter van Glabbeek

Odyssey L 2P, at 2.7kg, is a sturdier semi-geodesic design with three crossovers – much better in the mountains or windy spots. With more head-room and a larger porch it's also well suited to taller riders. Couples should look at the **Space** L 3P (3.6kg). As spacious as its name suggests, it has two doors and porches, meaning plenty of room to pile panniers. The reinforced dome makes it strong too.

Hilleberg Allak and Nallo 2GT

Hilleberg have a reputation for making bombproof tents that will last for years and are popular with many cyclists. Their Red Label range is ideal for touring. However, they are the Rolls Royce of tents in more than one regard; the excellent workmanship comes with a hefty price tag.

The sturdy 2-man **Allak** will survive all weather, making it a great option for adventurous cycle tourists who expect to encounter more extreme conditions and need a really stable haven; it weighs in at 3.3kg. With enough head-room to sit up comfortably, it has two wonderfully large porches which allow good ventilation and room for storing gear.

The **Nallo** 2GT (or 3GT) is one of the tents most commonly used by cycle tourists. The tunnel design means there is masses of space for little weight – it tips the scales at an impressively light 2.8kg – and for many, the comfort provided by this high space-to-weight ratio is the decisive factor. It is not perfect in all situations however: it is not free-standing, can be noisy in high winds, and, as it doesn't ventilate as well as two door designs, condensation can be a problem. Costing double the amount of other quality tents, unless you have plenty of cash I'd suggest spending the extra £400 on your bicycle – or the journey itself.

Hilleberg Nallo – perhaps not as roomy as a yurt but a little more portable.
© Stephen Lord

North Face Tadpole 2

North Face's **Tadpole 2** (EU) is a classic semi-geodesic tent with a stream-lined design that is strong if pitched with its tail into the wind. Brew up in the spacious porch, safe in the knowledge that your shelter is weatherproof – it has been tried and tested by touring cyclists in all conditions and performs well for years. The combination of part pole-sleeves and clips makes it easy and quick to pitch inner first, and on the bike it packs up to a neat little 2kg bundle on your back rack. Note that the green EU version is superior to the lighter, and not-as-sturdy, orange US model.

North Face Tadpole. © Lorenzo Rojo

Marmot Limelight

This is a beautifully simple design: a dome tent with an additional pole which extends the porch enough to ensure rain won't enter when the door's open. It is available as a 2-man (2.3kg, single door) or 3-man (3kg, two door). Marmot have used a thicker and robust fabric and 9mm poles, making it a tough and durable choice. It is another roomy tent with heaps of headroom (1.17m), so you won't get neckache sitting around playing cards, waiting for that storm to pass.

Camping in a Marmot Limelight, Northern Thailand. © Amaya Williams

Budget tents

It's perfectly possible to tour with a less expensive tent which may not be as good as those above, but will still do the job, particularly on a shorter trip. **Vango**'s tents are exceptional value – go for the range with a green flysheet and orange inner (those with blue flysheets aren't of sufficient quality for an adventure-tour, while the orange range are mountain tents which are too heavy). The Mirage, Banshee and Helix models are all good budget choices; they're available in 2- or 3-man versions and with each you'll get change from £150. In the USA, REI's Half Dome 2 and Quarter Dome 2 are options worth investigating.

SLEEPING BAGS

Most bikers go for down sleeping bags, not just for the warmth but for the low bulk. The better the down, the more compact your sleeping bag will be, but also the more fragile. Down is delicate, clogs up and loses all its loft when wet,

PART 2 – BIKES, CLOTHING & CAMPING

FIXING ZIPS

If there's one thing that's guaranteed on a long trip, it's that at some point your zips will begin to fail. Only then will you appreciate just how many zips there are in all the equipment that you rely on. They're particularly prone to breaking in dry environments like the Pamirs of eastern Tajikistan, where the fine sand and dirt finds its way into the zip's teeth and prevents the slider functioning correctly. After one long spell in high and dry regions of the Atacama, fewer than 10 of my 30+ zips still functioned correctly.

To extend the life of your zips, clean them now and then with a toothbrush to remove dirt, and lubricate the teeth with silicon spray or beeswax (running a candle along the teeth works well). If the slider fails and is no longer closing the zip, it's often possible to fix the problem (albeit temporarily) with a pair of pliers. Move the slider to the start, and use the pliers to gently squeeze together the rear corners of the slider, each in turn. Try the zip to see if this has worked – if not, repeat the squeezing process until you get some success.

Sometimes a zip will completely fail to respond to this fix. If you happen to be somewhere like Kathmandu or La Paz, finding a tailor to install a new zip onto clothing should be easy and cheap. Finding a zip long enough for a tent will prove problematic – you'll either have to get multiple zips to replace your old one, or else get one sent out from home. With all tents, the zips are the part most likely to fail so consider getting some spare sliders before you set off.

Neil Pike

and takes ages to dry, so make sure you look after it. If your panniers aren't waterproof (and even if they are) it's wise to invest in a good dry bag to store your precious down bag in – the telescopic ones by Exped are good. It's not the end of the world if your sleeping bag does get a little wet, as long as you get some sunshine and a breeze to dry it out. A tumble-drier with tennis balls or soft shoes in will help bring it back to life all the quicker, but good luck finding one in outback Irian Jaya.

The most important thing to look for is the fill power of the down. This is the amount of volume a gram of down will occupy; the higher the number the better the quality of the down (and fewer feathers in the mix), the more air that is trapped and the toastier the sleeping bag will be. Fill power is measured in cm^3/g in the EU and $inch^3/oz$ in the USA, which can lead to some confusion. A good down bag will have about 650-850 EU fill-power or 550-750 US fill power. If the bag label says something like 85/15, this means the fill is 85% down and 15% feathers, the maximum you'll see is 93/7.

As an indication of warmth, use the lower comfort limit; the lowest temperature at which the average woman will be comfortable (men generally sleep warmer). Everyone feels the cold differently, so if you sleep cold, get a warmer bag. For most people, a three-season bag designed with a lower comfort limit of around -5°C is warm enough until they tackle mountain routes, or hit upon a cold winter. Don't go for a four- season bag if you only need it a few days every year on tour as it's a lot of extra bulk.

If it's really cold, you may want to head to the market and get a fleece liner made up, and also buy a cheap down jacket – at these times you'll be wearing everything you've got inside your bag at night. You could also try and find shelter if the chill is too much, a need readily understood anywhere in the world with the appropriate shivering gestures performed on someone's doorstep.

By minimising the amount of room in the sleeping bag so that you get a snug fit, the bag will perform better. Length is the main difference between men's and women's sleeping bags, so if you are a tall woman get a men's bag, and if you are a short man get a women's. Make sure you buy a bag with a hood (known as a mummy bag) which can be cinched in around your shoulders to prevent drafts. Couples may want to consider getting mirror versions (one with a left zip and one with a right) of the same model sleeping bag, in order to be able to zip the two together.

Rab, Marmot and Mountain Equipment make the best down bags that are available on a UK high street. Alpkit down bags don't pack as small as the big brand bags, but are excellent value. If you are someone who feels claustrophobic in a mummy bag, check out bags by Sierra Designs. Western Mountaineering (⌨ backcountrygear.com) make bags with a more rectangular foot and use the best quality down.

Synthetic sleeping bags are bulkier than down but remain warm when wet and can be machine-washed when that odour becomes overwhelming. The Mountain Hardwear Lamina series are worth considering.

I always use a silk liner inside my sleeping bag – it's light, keeps the bag clean, and is handy in hostels and guest houses to keep bed bugs at bay.

REPAIRING AN AIR MATTRESS

Repairing punctures in air mattresses is much like repairing a bike tyre puncture. If you are carrying a Therm-a-Rest Instant Field Repair Kit, then the job will be done in minutes, as it will be if it's just a pin sized hole you can plug with a speck of superglue.

For those with no repair kit and a larger puncture, urethane glues such as Seam Grip will fix the problem, but need four to six hours to set, so it's bad luck if you discover your puncture in the evening. Set to work immediately, use only a drop of glue and head for the local disco while it dries. On larger holes you'll want to find a piece of mesh to place over the hole to act as a matrix for the glue.

Delamination bubbles mean the beginning of the end for a mattress – they usually spread quickly as air pressure forces the nylon skin off the foam. Therm-a-Rest guarantee all their laminating, so if you get a bubble in a Therm-a-Rest mattress, start looking for the nearest Cascade Designs dealer – the fault is covered by warranty and the mat will be replaced free of charge.

SLEEPING PADS AND AIR MATTRESSES

Don't overlook your sleeping mat when you are sorting camping gear – your weary body will appreciate the comfort of a good mat. I find that sleeping well on tour makes the next day's cycling all the easier. Budget tourers are best opting for a high quality foam mattress such as the Therm-a-Rest RidgeRest SOLite or Z Lite SOL, rather than a low quality inflatable mat which will almost certainly fail early on in a trip. Foam mattresses are bulky, but being 100% puncture proof makes them suited to thorny regions like those found in Africa.

They're handy for sitting on outside the tent, which is where inflatable mats often get punctured. The cheap generic kinds of foam mat are less than a centimetre thick and not that effective.

To save space and for additional comfort, most bikers choose a Therm-a-Rest-style inflatable mat, generally picking the lightest models. Therm-a-Rest mats have been tried, tested and loved by generations of cycle tourers. The ProLite is the lightest self-inflating option but it's worth going for the

Therm-a-Rest backgammon.

added comfort and warmth of the thicker ProLite Plus. At first glance the Therm-a-Rest NeoAir XLite looks too delicate to take on tour; however, it is repeatedly getting good reports confirming its ability to last the distance. It is incredibly comfortable and deals well with the cold; avoid the extremely warm NeoAir XTherm as it's overkill unless you're headed to the Yukon in January.

The Exped SynMat UL looks similar to the NeoAir XLite and is just as comfortable, but some report that it lacks the longevity of its rival.

STOVES

Multi-fuel stoves

A multi-fuel stove is ideal for an extended bike tour because it burns something that is available everywhere: petrol (gasoline). When buying petrol for

A fuel bottle cage attached to front forks.

your stove, choose the lowest octane rating as it contains less ethanol (which blocks camping stove jets). In some countries you will only find high octane fuel – this won't burn at all well, so in these places try to source alternative fuels.

Be aware that fuel poured from a container is more likely to be adulterated than anything coming from a petrol pump; similarly don't expose fuel in plastic drinks bottles on your bike to the sun – once the UV rays have worked their magic you'll find the fuel messes up your stove. While it's nice to have a stove that will burn anything, you'll regret ever filling your bottles with diesel and most types of kerosene too as both are horribly dirty when burnt. In the Americas and Europe you won't have to resort to these as it's possible to find clean burning white gas/Coleman fluid/*bencina blanca*. Carry your fuel bottle in a bottle cage on your frame or forks to avoid stinking out your panniers and contaminating food. It's also a good idea to find an airtight plastic box in which to store your stove in a pannier, for the same reason.

Like so many other pieces of kit, look for a stove which is reliable and durable as well as simple, so that it is easy to fix or clean. **MSR**'s WhisperLite International is the multi-fuel stove that comes closest to ticking all these boxes. It is quiet, as the name suggests, and burns unleaded petrol, kerosene and white gas. The WhisperLite's simplicity makes it a winner – with the manual on your e-reader you can quickly learn how to strip it down, clean blocked fuel lines and rebuild it if needed.

As well as burning liquid fuels, the MSR WhisperLite Universal has an adaptor for gas canisters, and it may prove to be better than the International for long bike tours. It has yet to be pedalled round the globe so it's too soon to tell. MSR's Dragonfly is noisier, more complex and bulkier, but is the chef's choice because of its very useful ability to simmer.

For all stoves, ensure you carry the model-specific spare parts kit for changing O-rings or anything else that can wear out. Keep the pump oiled to ensure it continues operating well.

Swedish brand **Primus** also make very good multi-fuel stoves, which burn gas, white gas, unleaded petrol, diesel and kerosene. Their stoves have a wide base and pot supports – an important consideration, as watching your dinner tip into the sand can really ruin your day. The cheaper Primus MultiFuel has

MAKING A WHISPERLITE SIMMER

One of the downsides of the MSR WhisperLite is your lack of control over the power of the flame. Once you have primed your stove and boiled your pasta, you want it to simmer, and this is difficult to achieve by just turning the flame down to the mini- mum setting. The best way to accomplish it is to remove the pan, blow out the flame, unscrew the pump to depressurise the bottle, screw it back up, pump twice (rather than the 20 times you pumped to boil the water origi- nally), open the valve and relight the stove.

only one control at the fuel bottle. The top-of-the-range OmniFuel has a simmer control as well and has been used by many satisfied bikers on long tours. But as with all multi-fuel stoves, that extra valve adds complexity, which means one more thing that might go wrong. The OmniFuel is a better choice than the OmniLite Ti for a long tour, due to its superior robustness.

MSR WhisperLite International stove.
© Nathan Haley

Primus stoves have to be cleaned the old way, by poking the jet with a very fine wire (a strand of brake cable works as well). The MSR WhisperLite is much easier than the Omnifuel to clean after it's been blocked by a bad batch of fuel, so if you use a Primus make sure you steer clear of all high octane fuels and use gas canisters in countries such as Bolivia and Brazil where the fuel has high ethanol content.

Propane-butane gas stoves

For short trips of a couple of weeks it's easiest to use a gas stove, rather than a multi-fuel one. The majority of camping gas stoves take ISO EN417 screw-on canisters, and this is the type of canister you are most likely to find in outdoor shops the world over. In developing countries you will probably find them only in areas with a mountaineering or trekking scene, or in capital cities. Riders who just use it as a backup, or who don't progress beyond cooking up instant noodle meals, sometimes get by with just a gas canister stove on long tours by making each extra-large canister last weeks on end. This strategy works OK in the Americas and parts of Asia but not in Africa. Other factors to consider include how you'll dispose of your used gas canisters, and the price – at upwards of £5 per canister, they're not cheap. Avoid touring with Camping Gaz stoves unless you are going to France or Spain, as this type of canister isn't widely found elsewhere.

Alcohol stoves

Alcohol stoves are lightweight and reliable and so simple that you can make your own. If methylated spirits, pure ethanol or rubbing alcohol were as widely available as petrol, they would be the choice of many more cycle tourists. Team an alcohol burner made by Trangia, Esbit or Evernew with a Clikstand (🖳 clikstand.com) and you've got a nice light setup. You will find alcohol in the Americas and Europe – for availability in other countries, see 🖳 trangiastove.co.uk. Instructions on how to make five different pop-can stoves can be found at 🖳 pedalingnowhere.com.

An alcohol stove with homemade pot stand.
© Anna Kortschak

TREATING DRINKING WATER

Buying bottled water as you go is impractical and environmentally unfriendly, so it's important to have some way of purifying water.

The compact **SteriPEN** is one of the best solutions – it cleans a litre of water in 90 seconds at the press of a button by using UV light to denature the DNA of the bacteria and protozoa (thus preventing them reproducing). SteriPENs don't work in murky water which the UV can't penetrate, but you probably won't be drinking from puddles every day, and you can always filter the water through a buff or pair of boxers. It means yet another device requiring power, but the AA battery-powered Classic usually lasts a week between chargings. The USB-charged Freedom and Ultra models are the obvious choice for those running a dynamo hub.

The **Sawyer Mini Filter** has a 0.1 micron filter that removes all bacteria and protozoa. Its wonderfully lightweight design weighs just 50g and you can drink straight from the filter or squeeze water through into another container using squeeze bags. The filter is easy to clean and has a 380,000(!) litre guarantee, which should be enough to cover most cycle tours, even Lorenzo's – see p202.

Chemical treatment is good as a back-up but shouldn't be used long term. A little pack of pills takes up no space but purifying this way adds an unpleasant taste to the water, so consider adding a powdered flavouring (such as Tang) to mask this. Chlorine is cheap and found in many pharmacies worldwide, but it doesn't kill Giardia and other protozoa; use **chlorine dioxide tablets** if you can find them.

KITCHEN ESSENTIALS

Any cheap **spoon** will do; a fork isn't essential. Cutlery gets lost easily so don't bother with the expense of titanium. Go for stainless steel; restaurants are usually happy to spare a spoon if you lose yours. People who don't mind living on noodles can get away with any old cooking pot, but slightly thicker pots designed for camping transfer the heat much better and save a bit of fuel. There are many good quality nesting **pot sets** available; look at GSI Outdoors, MSR and Primus. Solo travellers may find taking a single pan is sufficient – it's not unusual to team up with others and communal cooking happens more often than you might expect.

Primus' Eta Power pans are a good choice as they have a built-in heat exchanger to diffuse heat which adds very little weight, but saves fuel. A good non-stick surface is worth getting if you're prepared to look after it and if you plan on preparing more complex meals. A non-stick **frying pan** can work well as a pot lid; carry a plastic spoon or spatula to stir non-stick pans. Many cyclists become quite skilful at whizzing up one-pot gastronomic delights –

THE PERFECT COFFEE?

Having tried most of the coffee-making gadgets out there, I've concluded that the best camp coffee is made by using none of them, though it takes a little longer. You can use any type of coffee, espresso or coarse-ground. Put it in cold water in your pot and bring to the boil, reducing the heat as it warms up and take it off the heat as soon as it begins to boil. Stir once. Bring it to the boil twice more with the heat on low, taking care not to overheat the coffee. The third time it comes to the boil, the coffee grounds will have sunk to the bottom of the pot and you can pour the coffee without a filter.   **Stephen Lord**

CHILI CON CARNE

Prep & cook time: 20 minutes
Makes: 2-3 generous servings
Difficulty: easy

1 onion
3 cloves garlic
½ pound ground beef
1 teaspoon salt
1 14.5oz/411g can diced or whole tomatoes
1 15oz/425g can dark red kidney beans
1 6oz/170g can tomato paste
1 tablespoon chili powder
1 teaspoon cumin
1 teaspoon garlic granules
½ teaspoon chili flakes
½ teaspoon black pepper
¼ teaspoon sugar

First, prepare your ingredients: chop the onion and mince the garlic, then add them to your large cooking pot along with the meat and salt. Open the cans, and get your spice bag and measuring spoons out.

Now, it's time to get cooking: prime and light your cookstove. Sauté the onions and meat over a low flame until the meat is browned and mostly cooked through. Now add the beans (don't drain them), the tomatoes (don't drain them, either), and the tomato paste, stirring to combine. Finally, add the spices and sugar.

Let the chili simmer over low heat for about ten minutes, stirring occasionally. Smash the tomatoes (if whole), and let simmer another few minutes before eating.

Excerpt from *Bike. Camp. Cook.* by **Tara Alan**

Chili con carne: just one of many delicious meals you can prepare on a camp stove.
© Tara Alan

from stews, curries and soups to flat breads, pancakes and even pizza. Tara Alan's *Bike. Camp. Cook.* book is full of useful tips and innovative recipes for spicing up mealtimes on any bike tour – see box above.

Cutting brake housing with your penknife and then using the knife to chop food isn't very hygienic, and penknives don't even make particularly good kitchen knives. I prefer to carry a small **kitchen knife** with a plastic sleeve, and you may also want to carry a single plate or a small chopping board for chopping; alternatively one of the Sea to Summit plates will act as both. Ensure you have at least one 250ml plastic bottle for carrying cooking oil – Nalgene do some great **mini bottles** which are good for condiments such as oil, salt and pepper. Ziploc bags are incredibly useful (be warned: you are likely to wash these up, mend them with duct tape and cherish them) for storing food, and a handful of Ikea's Bevara sealing clips come in handy for fastening food bags. Don't forget a simple **mug**.

TOILET BAG: SOME SUGGESTIONS

• Shampoo by the sachet – avoids carting a whole bottle around
• Dr Bronner's Castile liquid soap
• Skin moisturiser – essential for dry climates
• Suncream – easy to find along the way in cities
• Toothpaste and toothbrush – no problems finding either of these anywhere
• Dental floss – can be used to floss teeth and also for sewing repairs
• Crystal deodorant – buy back home, even the small ones last for years, and it'll greatly increase the longevity of your base layers

● Nail clippers or scissors
● A small mirror – useful for solo travellers

ELECTRONIC DEVICES

There's no need to take along a lot of electronic gadgets on a big trip, however you'll find that most riders pack at least a digital **camera**. Many also carry a laptop for the sheer convenience of accessing the web and storing and editing photos and videos. Laptops with Solid State Drives are less likely to break if dropped or continually jolted, but all your electronics should be stored in robust, padded, dust-proof cases to avoid damage on the road. **Tablets** are light and come in handy for internet, listening to podcasts or Skyping home; **smartphones** have the added bonus of allowing you to make a good old-fashioned phone call (in the vast majority of countries, purchasing a SIM card locally is both cheap and easy to do), can take decent photos and are an alternative to **GPS**s for navigating (see p105). E-readers save a lot of space over proper books, and some tourers also carry **tracking devices** (see p107).

Keeping it all charged

Unless you tour in really remote regions, you are likely to pass a power source at least every few days. I've always kept my electronics charged by using them sparingly out on the road, or by carrying extra rechargeable **batteries** – the latter works well for cameras and items such as GPSs, tracking devices and headtorches which use AA or AAA NiMh batteries. Battery life for laptops, tablets and smartphones is far shorter, so for these consider a **portable power bank** or a **dynamo hub** – the Son 28 is the hub to choose. Team your hub with a dynamo powered USB charger, such as the Sinewave Cycles Revolution or the Tout Terrain Plug III, for charging your USB gadgets as you roll. **Solar chargers** appeal to many cyclists, but for their reliability, superior power output and lighter weight, it's better to go for the extra batteries or dynamo hub option.

OTHER USEFUL KIT

An LED **headtorch** is invaluable to have around camp. They weigh next to nothing and can double up as a front light if you misjudge sunset and find yourself cycling at night. Bring a spare, with a red filter, which can act as a back light. Petzl and Black Diamond both manufacture quality torches – a Petzl Tikka costs around £25 and will do the job on a long tour. Use rechargeable NiMh batteries in the AAA model; or buy one charged by USB.

A **Swiss army knife** such as those by Wenger or Victorinox comes in handy in all sorts of situations, including uncorking that well-earned bottle of Merlot.

For cleaning grease from pots get some E-cloths, the microfibre cleaning cloths. A **metal scourer** will save a lot of time removing burnt porridge from your pans. Don't get bike grease and grime on your cookware cleaning cloths; use rags for cleaning bike gear and tools.

It's worth considering bringing a ten litre Ortlieb or MSR Dromedary **water bag** for occasional use; it gives you freedom to find a camping place away from a water source and is handy when crossing deserts.

Lastly, don't forget a good quality **compass**; anything by Silva, Recta or Suunto will do. A global compass will work better if you're travelling in the southern hemisphere.

Transporting your bike

BY AIR

Regulations for checking bikes onto planes are confusing to say the least. They vary between airlines and airports and sometimes seemingly on what sort of mood check-in staff are in. Forewarned is forearmed, so scour the baggage rules on airline websites and if it's not clear, call the airline before you book in order to know exactly what their rules are for the flight you're looking to take. Make a note of who you spoke to and when, and take a printout of bike rules from the website, so you can show check-in staff in case of disagreements.

The prudent way of preparing your bike for air travel is to box it (see p100) or bag it (see p102) yourself prior to setting out for the airport, and most airlines now insist on this before allowing the bike to be checked in. Though it's still sometimes possible to wheel your bike up to the check-in desk, turn handlebars, remove pedals, deflate tyres and place the bike in a plastic bike bag (such as those sold by the Cyclists' Touring Club (CTC) for £10) we wouldn't recommend this approach, unless you know the airline and airport and are sure it will be allowed, or have been sent prior confirmation in writing by the airline that it will be accepted.

It's also a good idea to use private or public transport to get to and from airports rather than cycling, particularly after a long flight. A boxed or bagged bike makes this an option whereas a fully assembled machine may not be allowed on a bus or fit in a taxi.

When flying into a country whose immigration rules state you need proof of a return flight (or onward travel out of the country) in order to enter visa-free or on the tourist visa in your passport, be aware that airlines are unlikely to accept you pointing at your bike and saying 'I'm riding out on that' as sufficient evidence. If you have no return flight booked, always check well in advance what proof you'll need to muster in order to be allowed to check in.

Bike friendly carriers

There are some generous airlines out there that carry bikes free of charge within the standard baggage allowance – Emirates, Qatar Airways, British Airways, Virgin Atlantic and Thai Airways are some of the bigger names who are currently good to go with, but as rules change so often it's always a good idea to confirm before booking. Some airlines charge a set fee for a bike, while by others you'll be charged a (usually extortionate) rate per kilo of excess baggage. In general, USA-based airlines offer very bad deals for carrying bikes. Always make sure you factor in the amount you will have to pay for your bike carriage before buying your plane ticket.

Be prepared to argue, and arm yourself with knowledge of rules beforehand, if your flight has several legs and an airline tries to charge you for excess baggage on the shorter hop. Get your bike checked through all the way to your final destination, and even if there are months between flights, make sure (or simply bluff and bluster) that you're entitled to the larger allowance for all flight segments. You cannot be expected to shrink your bags for some flights when they were all booked together on a Round The World ticket.

BOXING YOUR BIKE FOR TRAVEL

Seeing your beloved bike disappearing down a check-in luggage belt is one of the most stressful things about bike touring. To avoid additional stress at the airport, box your bike at home or have your local bike shop do it. Bike shops usually do a nice job in padding and boxing your bike for a small fee and are helpful in providing boxes; just give them a few days' notice. If you're flying within the US, a bike shop can box and send your bike via a courier like UPS or FedEx. Though it might cost as much as the airline would charge in bike fees, it does save you the hassle of transporting your boxed bike to and from the airport.

Using a cardboard bike box

On the return journey you will have to box the bike yourself. The best solution is to find a cardboard bike box from a bike shop – this is always how we've packed our bikes for flights, and never had any serious damage to them. Take off the pedals, the front wheel (and possibly the back one and rear derailleur too), the racks and the handlebars, lower or take out the seat post and arrange them all in the box so that fragile parts are protected. Use zip-ties or duct tape to fix loose items so there is nothing that could fall out if the box is damaged mid-flight.

Using any old cardboard box

In the absence of a bike box, any large cardboard box can be broken down and used to pack the bike, before wrapping it in a tarp and tying it up like a parcel, or placing it in a 'tartan' plastic bag. It takes about an hour to wrap or box a bike carefully, much more if you're doing it for the first time. If using any old box, cutting it down to the size of the dismantled bike makes it easier to get in a taxi or bus. To prepare the bike for flight this way, you need to make a dense, tightly packed package so that all components reinforce each other and all vulnerable components are inside this mass.

Airport trolley loaded up with shrink-wrapped and taped bike boxes.

Left: Get packing materials from local market.
Right: Remove racks etc. and arrange round frame. (Both © Stephen Lord)

1. **Remove the pedals**. You'll need a 15mm wrench, though on some pedals you need an Allen (hex) key. Note that the left pedal loosens by turning clockwise; most important! Never just throw pedals (or anything else) in your bike box, they will scratch the paintwork and may fall out. Wrap them in newspaper then tape or zip-tie them to the frame or racks.

2. **Remove the saddle** or lower it all the way down, depending on whether you want to protect the saddle by taping it down somewhere in the middle triangle of the frame, or use it to provide padding for the bike.

3. **Disconnect the brakes and release the wheels**. Your brake arms will spring outwards and are safer if taped tightly together. If you have hydraulic brakes, it is vital to tape something between the brake pads to prevent them popping out if the lever is depressed.

4. **Wheels and tyres**. Remove the quick-release skewers from the wheel axles and tape them to the spokes. Place the wheels either side of the bike and tape them together (as in the photo below left) with some cardboard between wheel and frame to prevent scratches. Aircraft holds are only partially pressurised, so let some air out of the tyres or they could burst in flight. Check-in staff insist on full deflation; it's a waste of time arguing with them but try to keep some air in the tyres to protect the rims and tyres.

5. **Unscrew the derailleur** where it is bolted to the drop-out. This way, you don't have to disconnect the cable; just ensure it is loose enough by pulling it

Left: Find safe places to tuck saddle, racks and handlebars, then add the wheels on either side of the frame with extra cardboard in between wheels and frame and around pedals, gears and chainrings. **Right**: Now wrap it up and rope it up tight and book tuk-tuk to the airport. © Stephen Lord

PART 3 – ON THE ROAD

out of the brazed-on frame guides on the chainstays so it will not get kinked. Wrap the derailleur in newspaper and tape it to the bike frame inside the rear triangle or between the spokes. Wrap up as much of the chain as you can in newspaper or bubble wrap and tape that to the frame.

6. **Remove the handlebars**. You should have enough slack in the cables to do this but disconnect cables entirely if you think they may get kinked in transit. It's best to tape or tie handlebars to the frame; your wheels may be far forward enough to position flat handlebars between them for better protection. You have a lot of important and fragile components on those handlebars, so place them where they are protected and allow for movement. Cardboard and newspaper padding will help.

7. **Mudguards**. The rear mudguard has to come off and is quite well protected if simply wrapped around the rear wheel. The front mudguard may be OK on the bike if it is flexible, as the best SKS brand is. Racks really depend on your bike and the box and how small you want the package to be. They are at greater risk left on the bike but if you plan on riding away from the airport, leave them on.

8. **Some finishing touches**. Screw all rack and mudguard bolts back on the bike. Add some extra padding around the rear stays and especially the derailleur hanger. Taking off the largest chain ring removes a very sharp edge and makes the package easier to stand up. Extra cardboard around the chain rings prevents them slicing their way out. Fitting plastic supports in between the rear stays and the forks protects against the bike being crushed – bike shops will give you these disposable plastic blocks and on shorter tours they're worth keeping with you for the return trip. We put fragile items such as a helmet in the middle of the rear triangle or inside the main triangle and tape them in. A tent can go between the rear stays to add support. Above all, make sure that no small parts are loose in the box, as they will fall through the inevitable holes that will have appeared in the box when it arrives on the baggage carousel.

Bike bags

A reusable nylon zipped bike bag greatly speeds up packing your bike, and good ones such as the Ground Effect Tardis have sleeves to hold the wheels either side of the bike and pockets for sharp items like pedals and quick-release skewers, protecting the frame from scratches. If you're flying in and out of the same city you can leave it with a hotel. In some developing countries, like India or Peru, it's possible to find a local who is a whizz with a sewing machine to knock up a bike bag, if you provide the design sketches.

Ground Effect's excellent Tardis bike bag.
© Roy Hoogenraad

ON BUSES AND TRAINS

You'll almost certainly want, or find it necessary, to hop on land transport with your bike at some point – whether it's to escape a dangerous or dull stretch of road, or because you need to make some rapid progress to avoid winter snows, overstaying a visa or missing a flight. In many developing nations it's straightforward to put your bike on a bus (or coach, minibus or tuk-tuk) for a minimal fee. It always pays to be present when the bike is being loaded so you can temper the driver's eagerness to just chuck it on like a sack of spuds, and to prevent other items being piled on top. In some countries you may be asked to dismantle and package the bike to some extent.

With bikes on the roof of a Nepali bus.

Putting bikes on trains tends to be a bit more complicated and rules vary. Two of the more useful countries to know about are China (p191) and India (p152).

ON HORSES AND MULES
This is another instance where a bike's portability kicks ass (sorry) over any form of motorised transport: you can take it along hiking routes to link up dead-end roads. The most famous and popular bike-hike in the adventure cycle-touring world is between Chile's Carretera Austral, and El Chaltén in

Taking a bike on a trekking route in the Indian Himalaya.

Argentina (see p308), where bikers can employ horsemen to carry panniers, while they push their bikes for a day over the border. It's also possible, in places like the Himalaya, for animals to carry your bike along these kinds of trails (see p151). The horseman will work out what's best for his animal – usually removing the pedals and front wheel – which just leaves you to check as you walk along that the beast is being careful and not smashing your precious bike into rocks!

MINIMUM ENVIRONMENTAL IMPACT CYCLE TOURING

Pack it in, pack it out
Don't leave any rubbish in the outdoors – keep it all in a pannier, or in a plastic bag bungeed onto your back rack, until you reach a town or village with disposal facilities.

Outdoor pooing
If you are cycling in the wilds and need to go, stick to the following rules: make sure you're at least 20m away (the further the better) from any water source or stream; dig a hole to squat over, and cover the hole with plenty of soil once you're done; dispose of your toilet paper properly either by carefully burning it or by burying it deeply in the same hole.

Don't pollute water
Contamination of the world's waterways leads to deterioration in water quality. If you are going to wash yourself, clothes or dishes, carry water well away from streams or lakes and, if necessary, use small amounts of biodegradable soap.

Camping
When wild camping, try to have as little impact as possible on the countryside. Always ask permission if wishing to camp near a farm or small-holding, and when you strike camp make sure you tidy everything up and leave the site as you found it, undisturbed.

Navigating the adventure cycle-touring world

The navigational tools available to cycle tourists keep improving, and with the burgeoning amount of information and electronic mapping online, bike tours in adventurous regions are becoming ever more accessible. Cyclists can add smartphones or GPSs to the paper maps already stuffed in their front bags, and use these, along with information from local people, for navigating and finding routes. Like most riders, we use a combination of navigational aids during tours – here are some of the pros and cons of each.

PAPER MAPS
There's nothing quite like the sense of satisfaction gained from poring over a paper map in camp at the end of a long ride, and tracing a finger along the day's hard-earned progress. Paper maps are fantastic for giving an overview of your trip, are good for high level planning, and will invariably be of interest to local people you meet. They also have the advantage of low value – it's not an item whose replacement cost you'll ever worry about, and using the map in public won't make you feel uncomfortable that you're being flashy and showing off your wealth.

For many countries you are unlikely to be able to find a paper map detailed enough to show smaller roads accurately, meaning that relying solely on this way of navigating can lead to an excessive amount of riding on busy highways. Paper maps are also rarely as up-to-date as electronic mapping, have to be carefully protected from the rain, and need to be held onto with both hands in the Western Sahara winds.

ASKING AS YOU GO
Asking local people for directions can be a goldmine for finding information about roads and sights worth visiting in poorly mapped areas. But you must be wary about the accuracy of information you receive, and learn who to approach for directions. Local drivers are likely to be far more reliable than someone who never strays from the confines of their village, but still, unless you're sure you have been given good information, it's always worth checking with more than one person. You'll often need to stress that you want to take the small, quiet road, rather than the quicker highway route which is the natural way for people to send you.

The question 'how far is it to…?' is inherently difficult to answer if you

Asking directions in Zanskar.

don't own a vehicle with a working odometer and there are no road signs or kilometre markers. There's no point getting worked up if you've been told the next ice cream parlour is 5km away, and your bike computer is now reading 50km and you still haven't happened upon it. Enquiring 'how long will it take to cycle to…?' or 'is it hilly?' are equally unlikely to elicit an accurate response unless the person you ask has actually cycled there. Once, in Peru, we asked a shopkeeper what the route to the next town was like. 'Flat!' was the emphatic response. More than a day, and 2000m, of climbing later, we crested the pass and began the cruise down into the town. 'Flat' had simply meant 'no switchbacks'. Asking how long it takes by bus or on foot, and then applying a conversion factor (that you'll work out for yourself on the road) can be a good way of interpreting distance/time information.

GPS UNITS

GPS (Global Positioning System) units are carried by many tourers but they are by no means a necessity for all. We have found them to be useful when following a particular chosen route, navigating through unfamiliar cities and exploring really remote regions.

Base maps which come pre-loaded on GPSs show very few details and mapping packages which can be bought from GPS manufacturers are expensive. Additionally, many countries described in this book are not even covered by suitable packages. More useful are the free, user-generated Open Street Map (OSM) base maps which can be loaded onto your GPS from sites such as 🖳 garmin.openstreetmap.nl. The detail shown on these base maps is extremely useful for finding alternatives to busy highways and for working out the best route to take as you weave through back streets in larger towns.

Routes and waypoints can be downloaded as .gpx files from sites such as 🖳 mapmyride.com and 🖳 ridewithgps.com, as well as from many personal cycling blogs. These files can be saved onto your GPS, but as with all user-generated information you need to consider the reliability of the source before following a route.

GPSs also come in handy for truly adventurous tours in remote regions which have not yet been mapped electronically. By scouring satellite images on Google Earth, you can mark waypoints and tracks for a route you'd like to take, save these to your GPS and follow the route out in the field. Planning this way is a time-consuming process, but a few hours at the computer can reap huge rewards when you begin riding. Researching like this makes it much easier to get the 'big picture' for a complicated route, and in some areas is the only way to obtain accurate information prior to travel.

Basic precautions to take if you'll be relying on a GPS on tour are to ensure you have sufficient batteries to keep it powered in between charging opportunities, and, if you'll be in cold regions, keep the GPS and spare bat-

Cockpit, complete with GPS. © Cass Gilbert

teries somewhere warm, such as in a jacket pocket. We'd always recommend taking a paper map and compass as back-up to your GPS if you're really heading into the wilds, in the rare event that it does fail.

Look for robustness and good battery life in a GPS for a tour – we are able to get up to 40 hours from a set of NiMh batteries from one of Garmin's basic eTrex series handsets, which retail for as little as £100. This battery life makes it possible to keep a record of your tour, as you can track your ride and way-mark points of interest, such as where you camped each night, for later upload to a laptop. File converters such as 🖳 gpsvisualizer.com can be used to convert between file formats.

Though you could use your GPS to record distances and times in place of a cycle computer, it's not a good idea to rely on these readings, owing to the fact that in areas where reception is poor, readings can go haywire.

SMARTPHONES

Smartphones are an increasingly popular gadget for a cycle tour, and their many functions include the ability to be used as a GPS device. During the day, in the majority of areas covered by this book, there will no wi-fi and only patchy 3G/4G connection at best, so you'll have to download maps for offline use if you wish to navigate using your smartphone. Google Maps (an online app) can be loaded to your cache, for offline use, or alternatively there are many good offline mapping apps (such as Gaia which has worldwide topographic maps), which can be used without an internet connection. Search around to see which app suits you best.

Smartphones tend to be much more intuitive and user-friendly than GPSs, have bigger screens, are great for navigating through cities and are quick to charge. If the route ahead is clear and you don't need the smartphone to navigate, you can make use of its other functions to phone home or take a selfie of that unbeatable Pamir Highway view.

Downsides of smartphones are a lack of robustness, poor screen visibility in daylight, the need to keep them well covered during rain and, most importantly, battery life is far inferior to a GPS's. You'll have to use the smartphone sparingly out on the road, though if your appetite for gadgets hasn't been sated, you could invest in a dynamo hub (see p98).

PART 3 – ON THE ROAD

Staying in touch on the road

It is increasingly simple to keep in touch with friends and family while out on the road, through a combination of email, SMS, Skype, social media, blogs and websites.

Most tourers find it is best to carry an electronic device for communicating; the days of a cybercafé on every corner are gradually fading in many parts of the world such as Latin America and South-East Asia, as more and more locals get hold of their own handheld digital devices. If you choose not to travel with your own laptop/tablet/smartphone, it is probably still safe to say that

TRACKING DEVICES

Tracking devices such as those made by SPOT or DeLorme are useful for letting the folks back home know your whereabouts. At the press of a button you can give worriers some peace of mind by sending a signal which broadcasts your location. Be aware however that not every single location message you send will actually be received, and this can exacerbate any worrying, if signals which are expected don't arrive. The cost of a SPOT handset starts at about £100, and an annual service subscription costs a similar amount again. The DeLorme inReach unit is more costly and heavier than a SPOT, but also allows you to receive messages, and have two-way communication, albeit slow.

in most countries you'll be able to find some sort of computer with internet access in towns if you need it desperately enough. Libraries can be a good bet.

Public access wi-fi is becoming more widely available in many nations – sniff it out in restaurants, cafés, bars, shopping malls and other businesses where it will probably cost you the price of a cup of coffee. In some countries free wi-fi is available in public places, but use your judgement carefully in deciding whether or not it is a good idea to show off your digital jewels in that kind of environment.

Many of the world's hostels and hotels have wi-fi, so if you're striking out elsewhere, checking into accommodation is one way of getting online. Make sure you pick the room closest to the router.

Keep in mind that connections in much of the adventure cycle-touring world are super-slow, so you'll either need the patience of a saint or to reconsider uploading all your photos to a cloud as the most viable way of storing them. Resizing your less-precious photos before uploading is a good way of speeding things up.

If you have an unlocked smartphone, buying a local SIM card will often only cost a few dollars and you can buy data in whatever amounts you need.

A word of warning: in an age where people expect to communicate with you every second of the day, if you go off radar for an extended period you may return online to find impassioned messages from friends and family who are panicking about your whereabouts. Let your mum know beforehand if you're planning on going off to explore a truly wild corner of Siberia or the DRC.

TO BLOG OR NOT TO BLOG

The easiest and quickest way to keep the world informed of your tour's progress is by using social media sites such as Facebook, Twitter and Instagram, or by uploading photos to an image hosting site like Flickr.

Writing a blog requires far more time commitment, but is a nice way of documenting your ride digitally and of keeping interested parties updated, as well as giving you a project for off-the-bike days. Sites such as 🖳 crazyguy onabike.com and 🖳 wordpress.com make it free to create your own blog, and learning the necessary skills to post entries and upload photos won't take very long.

Unless you're already a computer programmer, building your own website requires investing many more hours. A domain name and annual hosting fees will cost you some cash too. If you're not careful, updating your website can begin taking up a large chunk of your touring time, so if the riding is far more important to you, consider carefully before beginning to build. You can always start off with a simple blog and expand it into a full blown website later on if you prefer.

Health on the road

MOSQUITO-BORNE DISEASES

In certain areas, mosquito-borne diseases such as **malaria** and **dengue fever** are real dangers for cyclists. Long-sleeved shirts, bandanas and particularly thick socks or other ankle-level protection are all good precautions to take against being bitten, especially at dusk in affected zones. Long trousers (along with socks) also have numerous other benefits, such as preventing scratches, sunburn and tick bites.

Which repellent you use is a matter of personal choice. Deet has a long shelf life, is very effective in concentrated form and if you have had no reactions to it you are probably safe using a stronger mix than the typically ineffective 10% Deet formulas common in Europe. However, Deet is nasty stuff, and the more you can rely on clothing instead of Deet, the better off you are. The same is true for the insecticide permethrin. You will read suggestions to dip your mozzie net in permethrin and you can buy clothing treated with it, but it is a powerful neurotoxin, the use of which should be minimised. A long-term traveller would do well to avoid it altogether and to minimise the use of Deet by dressing appropriately, using nets and avoiding going outside during peak mosquito-feeding hours.

SUNBURN AND SUNSTROKE

Sunburn is still under-rated as a risk by light-skinned Westerners who are most at risk from it, especially cyclists who are outside all the time. Skin-cancer rates are rising and the risk is much higher in tropical zones and areas in the southern hemisphere where the ozone layer has been denuded. Hats, cycling gloves and long-sleeved clothing are less messy solutions than sun cream, though you need to use all these in some areas. There's a tendency to think that once you have a good suntan, you don't need to cover up or use cream; this is not true. Incremental doses of UV cause incremental cell damage, leading to an increased risk of skin cancer.

Sunstroke (heatstroke) is a related risk, and one which can be fatal.

Thermonuclear protection: a Tilley hat.
© Stephen Lord

Riding in temperatures up to and above normal body temperature (37°C or 98.6°F) is not unusual in many parts of the world. Sunstroke occurs when the body's thermo-regulatory systems can't keep up and is most typically brought on by dehydration. Adequate hydration is vital, helped by not exerting yourself in the hottest time of the day when a hard-working cyclist could be losing several litres an hour.

Glucose drinks and oral rehydration solutions are good for recovering from dysentery and diarrhoea, which bring on dehydration. If the local pharmacy has run out of sachets, the recipe for a homemade oral rehydration solution is: six teaspoons of sugar and half a teaspoon of salt added to one litre of water. Eating plenty of fresh fruit is the best way of absorbing minerals.

ALTITUDE SICKNESS

Most long-distance riders approach their first high mountain range in a state of mild trepidation, though as they conquer their first high pass this becomes euphoria and a fair few go on to become addicted to riding among the world's highest mountains. But to reach this happy state, cyclists must first learn to respect mountains, and that means understanding how to acclimatise properly and avoid Acute Mountain Sickness (AMS). Reading up on the subject at 🖳 altitude.org or the Mountain Medicine section at the International Climbing and Mountaineering Federation website (🖳 theuiaa.org) is a good way to start.

The effects of high altitude can become noticeable at around 2000m (6500ft) and sickness usually becomes a risk at around 3000m (9800ft). Fly in to La Paz or Lhasa at 3600m (11,800ft) and you can expect a headache and other mild symptoms of AMS including nausea, breathlessness and an irritating dry cough – these are uncomfortable, but not dangerous, and will pass in a couple of days. Try not to make the mistake of setting off too soon after flying in to altitude, as you may still not be sufficiently acclimatised for the high passes that undoubtedly await. There is no hard and fast rule as to how long it takes to acclimatise to increases in altitude, as individuals are affected differently and there is no correlation between a person's fitness and their speed of acclimatisation.

Pharmaceutical pain-relievers have little effect on high-altitude headaches, but the South American herbal tea *mate de coca* is recommended for aiding acclimatisation. The most fundamental trick, besides ascending slowly, is to drink considerably more fluid than normal. Altitude sickness is a controllable risk and by acclimatising properly, you'll be able to pedal over the 5000m/16,400ft passes to be found in Ladakh, Peru, and (if it ever reopens to independent biking – see p191) Tibet.

Above 3000m, heed recommended guidance by planning not to sleep more than 300-500m higher than the night before. Most cyclists can knock off a 1500m elevation gain in a day, so try and plan your early days in the mountains so as to get over a pass to a

Drink extra water at high altitudes.

PART 3 – ON THE ROAD

lower camp at a safer altitude on the far side. 'Climb high, sleep low' is the mantra of mountaineers and high altitude bikers should stick to this too; luckily the nature of many routes in Peru (p289) and Ladakh (see p148) is conducive to such a routine.

It pays to research a bit into what's ahead on your route in case your ascent leads to a plateau from which the only descent is to turn back. Settlements in high altitude areas tend to be few and far between; plan so as to ensure you have sufficient provisions as well as camping gear in case the altitude or weather means you aren't able to pedal as far as you'd been expecting each day.

There are two life-threatening conditions that can occur as a result of AMS. High Altitude Pulmonary Oedema (HAPE) is a fluid build-up on the lungs which reduces their effectiveness in an already oxygen-depleted environment; High Altitude Cerebral Oedema (HACE) is a similar condition involving swelling of the brain. If you begin to experience severe symptoms such as vomiting, increasing tiredness, confusion and a reduction in coordination you need to descend immediately. This is the best defence against altitude sickness, and symptoms can ease even if you drop only a small amount.

Some climbers and cyclists on short trips where every day is vital try to speed up their acclimatisation by taking Diamox (acetazolamide) prophylactically. Be wary of this option as it will encourage you to go higher while masking symptoms – by far the best solution is to go slow and acclimatise in the first place. Once acclimatised, riding at 4000m is not overly taxing, and although you'll certainly be out of breath at 5000m-plus, you'll be able to enjoy these passes and be well on the way to being hooked on getting high!

HYGIENE ISSUES

Cyclists do get pretty filthy, sweating and riding in dust all day and it's not always easy to give your clothes a proper wash, so you need to be vigilant for the downsides of poor hygiene inherent in a camping-cycling lifestyle. Carry a small bottle of alcohol to smear the dirt around and kill any bugs before meals.

Many a cyclist develops minor skin irritations on the road due to infrequent or inadequate washing. Aspire to have a good wash either in a stream, or if privacy or downstream villages are concerns, using a folding bowl such as Ortlieb's 5-litre job.

In men or women, 'crotch rot' is endemic to cycling, all the more so in tropical climates and not helped by irregular washing or if you're wearing skin-tight, synthetic cycling shorts. Choosing natural fibres such as cotton or merino wool next to your skin can help, as does washing or changing your shorts or underwear daily. Whereas you only need two sets of clothing with you it is worth having multiple sets of underwear, particularly for women where an extra pair of knickers adds very little weight. If water or other facilities are in short supply, then a wet-wipe wash works wonders. Avoid using antiseptic creams and wipes as these will kill the good as well as the bad bacteria. A rash in your nether regions – for cyclists, anyway – can be cured with better hygiene and exposure to sunlight and fresh air, but if a fungal infection has developed it may need a cream from the pharmacy.

Left: After a day on a dusty 'highway' in Bolivia. © Ellen van Drunen
Right: A helpful sign, Ladakh.

WOMEN'S HEALTH

It is particularly important for women to maintain hygiene whilst cycle touring. Poor hygiene can increase the chances of **vaginal thrush** – a condition where an imbalance of bacteria in the vagina causes discomfort, itchiness and discharge. Treatment in the form of creams, pessaries and tablets are available in most pharmacies worldwide.

A second common complaint amongst female cycle tourists is **Urinary Tract Infection** (UTI). Symptoms include pain or burning sensation whilst peeing, a need to urinate frequently and pain in the lower abdomen. By drinking large quantities of water it may go of its own accord but if it persists then you will need a course of antibiotics. A good way to help prevent UTI is to wait a few moments after having a **wild wee**, to ensure there are no lingering droplets of urine, and use foliage as a substitute for loo roll. Finding a good place to take a wee can sometimes prove difficult: tie a jacket around your waist to cover your behind and in many countries this will be enough of a hint to make people look the other way. Carrying a urine diverter such as a Shewee or pStyle will kill two birds with one stone as you can pee more discreetly standing up (beware: this does cause people to double-take) and you can also use it to clear away those stray droplets.

Cycle touring may change the intensity and regularity of your **period** and for some women it disappears altogether, especially if you're putting a lot of stress on your body. Feminine hygiene products, and in particular tampons, are difficult to get hold of in many parts of the world. You shouldn't bury these as they take a long time to decompose, and carrying a bag of used tampons/pads around with you isn't pleasant and may lead to you being chased by feral dogs. Consider taking a **menstrual cup** such as the Mooncup or DivaCup – one cup lasts for years, they are easy to use and environmentally friendly. Bury the contents with a clear conscience and then clean with a squeeze of your water bottle. Female riders will be weaker during their period, and some prefer to spend a few days off the bike entirely and so plan rest days in advance.

Contraceptives can also be hard to find on the road. If you use **oral contraceptives** try to stock up before you leave home and either carry them all with you, or ask any visiting friends or relatives to bring you extra supplies. Be aware that they do not work if you get travellers' diarrhoea. By getting a

contraceptive implant before you leave home you will not have to carry the pill around and won't have to think about contraception for 3 years; you'll also be protected when you have a runny tummy. Another added bonus is that it is common for an implant to stop your period altogether. If you are using **condoms**, it is worth investing in a brand you can trust, despite the fascinating pictures and names that may adorn any local brands.

LEARNING TO PACE YOURSELF

Cyclists' health troubles are sometimes caused by overdoing the riding and under-doing the washing, proper eating and resting. Sufferers in these instances are commonly mileage-obsessed lone males or riders caught up in the initial 'must crack on' stage of a long ride; riding long distances day after day runs down your body's reserves of energy and nutrients and makes you far more susceptible to illness. Allowing plenty of rest gives your body time to recover and, if necessary, produce extra muscle to cope with the increased work. It can take a few months to find your natural pace – but many of the happiest bike travellers are those who've learnt to keep a steady, relaxed pace, staying within their range and thus having a good reserve of stamina and health to fall back on when they really need it.

Muscle pains may subside as your body adapts but are a warning sign that should be heeded. Joint pains and soreness are indications of overuse, or postural problems; you may need to change your bike's set-up or lighten the gear you are lugging around in your panniers. Try to keep within a comfortable range of exertion in terms of daily duration as well as intensity. Stretched and relaxed muscles are more supple and less likely to suffer damage than weakened or exhausted muscles that are close to their elastic limit. Muscle tissue needs time to rest and recover; rest days and simple maintenance such as daily stretching exercises and an occasional massage will help you stay fit and strong. Never forget it's good to take plenty of time off the bike. Going hiking or sightseeing are great ways to get other muscles working, and will make your trip a richer and more varied experience.

Food and water

A HEALTHY DIET

One of the joys of cycle touring is the ability to eat vast quantities of food without putting on weight. In fact it is often a challenge to cram in enough calories, and many cyclists lose some weight on tour. With a constant calorie deficiency you will spend hours in the saddle daydreaming about food, and eating all the local specialities sold at the roadside is a real highlight of most people's tours.

In order to keep cycling day in, day out you need to stay healthy, and a good diet is the foundation of this. It is best to adopt a balanced diet of fruit and vegetables, lean proteins such as eggs, beans, pulses and chicken, and complex carbohydrates such as oats, bread, pasta, rice and quinoa. This allows for slow absorption of calories in line with a steady burning of those calories while riding. We have never felt so strong as when living off a dhal bhat diet of rice, vegetables and lentils, cycling through the Himalayan foothills.

Your body will probably have other ideas about keeping a good diet, and riders who never normally eat and drink sugary snacks suddenly find themselves craving chocolate and fizzy drinks. Whilst on the road you won't find energy bars but in many developing countries chocolate bars are very common and Coca Cola is ubiquitous. In regions with little selection in the shops these are your quick energy sources but where possible choose fruits, nuts, seeds and beans. Rely on multi-vitamin tablets only in situations where the local diet is really limited or inadequate. Try to eat a good-sized breakfast and eat soon after setting up camp in the evening, so that your weary body can absorb nutrients straight away.

Keeping hydrated is an important part of a healthy diet. There is no hard and fast rule about how much you should drink, as it varies from person to person, but keep an eye on the colour of your urine. If it is clear, you are drinking too much; if it is dark in colour then it's time to fill your water bottles; if it's straw coloured you're probably doing OK. A pan of powdered soup with your dinner is a great way to hydrate and take on extra salt; sachets of soup are available throughout the world.

In those regions where shop supplies are limited, your menu will soon begin to become monotonous. Packing some herbs and spices into small plastic containers can really help jazz up meal times!

FOOD HYGIENE

To improve your chances of not getting sick as a result of what you eat, maintain a high standard of hygiene. If you can't cook it, peel it or wash it in clean water you should be wary of it. Street food is usually a real treat – it may bring with it a risk of food poisoning, but you'll get the hang of hunting down freshly cooked goodies and heading to the places locals frequent.

PURIFYING WATER

Ensuring you drink clean water is an essential aspect of your trip. In many countries tap water needs treating before drinking and much of the time on tour you'll be taking water from rivers and streams, particularly in remote, adventurous regions. We've met too many parasite-plagued tourers to suggest you just drink water as you find it, 'like the locals do', and would highly recommend treating all water (see p96) you drink, unless you're absolutely sure it's safe. When filling up bottles from water courses, consider the possibility of contamination upstream from settlements and animals, but also from mines or industry. Your UV pen might zap bacteria, but it sure won't get far trying to remove those heavy metals. In some countries, buying water in plastic bottles may be unavoidable, but where possible take the more environmentally friendly approach of using a UV pen or a filter.

Staying safe

AVOIDING ACCIDENTS

You're weaving through the Kathmandu traffic, a motorbike whizzes past your right shoulder, an auto rickshaw past your left, a papaya seller's crossing the road up ahead, and sh*?%t! there's a monkey about to be squashed under your front wheel!

Being involved in a traffic accident is one of those disaster scenarios we all want to avoid on tour. Fortunately serious accidents are rare, but heed these recommendations and you'll further reduce your chances of having a prang and increase your chances of emerging from one intact:

● **Stay alert and ride defensively at all times**. In most of the world Might is Right and us cyclists are well down the pecking order. Always expect the unexpected and in manic destinations add a 100-decibel air horn to your handlebar gadgets.

● **Cycle on roads with little traffic**. Don't make the mistake of thinking that because you're abroad you're invincible – you wouldn't fly into Heathrow, reassemble your bike and head straight to the M25 (even if it was legal), so it's always puzzling hearing about cyclists doing the equivalent elsewhere, like arriving in Santiago de Chile and jumping on the multi-lane Pan-Am Highway.

● **Plan your arrival in larger cities**. Catching transport into and out of metropolises like Bogotá, Bangkok, Cairo or Tehran can be a sensible measure. If you do choose to tackle them by bike, find out beforehand which roads and neighbourhoods to avoid.

● **Don't cycle at night**. Not only are you less visible to drivers, you're also more vulnerable to theft.

● **Beware of sidewinds**. Being lifted off the road into a thorn bush is no fun; being pushed into the road and under a juggernaut is far worse.

● **Remember what side of the road to cycle on**. Though it might sound like an obvious thing to get correct, after a few days on traffic-free roads in Xinjiang, or boarding in San Francisco and unboxing in Sapporo, that automatic hard-shoulder homing instinct can sometimes go awry.

● **Maintain and check your bike regularly** to try and prevent brake failures or equally unlikely but catastrophic events like a loose front rack collapsing into your wheel as you're flying down a slope.

On the road in Myanmar. © Amaya Williams

● And lastly, **bright clothing, a mirror and a cycle helmet** are all a good idea, even if you might not always spot them in the photos in this book!

THEFT AND ROBBERY

Before you set off, friends and family are bound to ask whether what you're planning is safe. Travelling in developing countries often elicits visions of robberies by bandits and narco-trafficking abductions. Fortunately these things are extremely rare and outside certain hotspots which you'll want to avoid anyway (see Route Outlines section) you'd have to be incredibly unfortunate to be caught up in something like this. If you must ride through dodgy areas, keep a close eye on news reports, internet forums and travel advisory recommendations, and pay attention to the advice given by locals – they will be familiar with the sit-

A typical tourer's room – food, drying clothes, airing sleeping bag, bike.

uation on the ground and better able to differentiate between 'avoid it like the plague' and 'you'll probably squeak through'.

The world over, the risk of robbery is higher in cities, towns and tourist centres than it is in villages and the countryside. Keep your wits about you in urban areas and see p30 for some tips on keeping money and important documents safe. Wild camping safety tips can be found on p124.

DEALING WITH DOGS

It's easy to get anxious about the threat of dog attacks on the road and you will occasionally encounter aggressive dogs on a leash that could do a lot of damage if let loose. Short of carrying a sawn-off shotgun (or a pistol as Dervla Murphy did on her pioneering *Full Tilt* cycle to India in 1963) there's no fail-safe way to fend off big, aggressive dogs. Eastern Turkey and Tibet are places infamous for these, but most encounters are with much smaller mutts who are all bark and no bite.

The most effective, but least satisfying, way to deal with a barking dog is to stop pedalling, get off and walk; this normally sees them quickly lose interest. Even if you don't stop, slowing down is a good idea if a dog approaches from the front or side, as running over it is normally as bad news for you as it

---

SLEEPING WITH YOUR BIKE?

Most of the world has far lower bike-theft rates than London, but it is still a good idea to take basic precautions against your precious iron-horse being pinched in the night. If you're staying in a town or village, don't leave your bike out in the street while you sleep, even if it is locked up – there'll always be somewhere to leave it inside your hotel, ideally in the room itself.

When camping, unless you really are in the middle of nowhere, it makes sense to attach a cable lock round a tent pole and to your bike. It can also be useful to tie guy ropes around the bike – both from a peace-of-mind point of view, but also from a tent-anchoring perspective, if you're camping on hard ground and can't bang in those pegs.

PART 3 – ON THE ROAD

A BIKING SAMURAI

I'm surely not the only touring cyclist who sometimes thinks about being robbed while out on the road. Thankfully it has never happened to me, but just in case a situation should arise there is always some carefully plotted plan in my head. However, I started to doubt the effectiveness of my plan when I met Kokoro, a Japanese cyclist who'd been travelling the world for four years. We were in beautiful Cappadocia in Western Turkey, and I was heading east, where if recent reports were right, knife-wielding shepherds had developed a penchant for robbing defenceless touring cyclists while they slowly climbed the long hills.

Kokoro heard of this potential threat while in Iran and decided to prepare himself before crossing the border into Eastern Turkey. The plan was simple but effective: pose as a Japanese Samurai warrior. Old Kung Fu films are broadcast the world over, so he thought there would be a fairly good understanding of his powers. To back up his non-existent Kung Fu skills, Kokoro found a stick and carved it into a sword, before adding a covering of aluminium foil to imitate a blade. With a few dramatic swipes he would certainly drive off any would-be attackers. But would he be forced to use it...?

Sure enough, while he slowly climbed a hill not long after entering Turkey from Iran, a pair of shepherds high on the hillside noticed him and started to rush down towards the road. Although they had far to run, Kokoro's slow speed meant there would be only one outcome if he wanted to keep moving .

The shepherds, knives in hands, beckoned the small and stocky Japanese man to stop his bicycle, which he did slowly and carefully. Out came the wooden sword with a dramatic swipe! Kokoro stood solid with the wooden stick pointing at the shepherds' heads. And had we been there we would have heard the words 'I AM KOKORO ... JAPANESE SAMURAI WARRIOR!'

The plan worked perfectly and while the shepherds ran for their lives, Kokoro resumed his long journey east.

© Scott Richardson

Scott Richardson

is for the mutt. If a dog is still aggressive after you stop, facing it to show you're ready and alert, while looking away is the aggression-lowering posture. Never look small or submissive.

Dog charges, often when they're emboldened by a gang of doggy chums, are usually all bluff. By running at them, throwing stones, shouting, waving sticks and looking like you mean business, they should turn tail.

Slings are used by many shepherds for herding cattle and also scare the hell out of dogs but are inaccurate and dangerous to anyone standing nearby. Catapults are much more accurate and easy to find in many rural areas of Asia. Ultrasonic dazers get the thumbs up from some riders, but the Hound of the Baskervilles may only be further enraged by the irritating sound.

There is a very small chance you will meet an untethered savage dog – watch out near flocks of sheep and especially at night when these dogs may be on the loose. You may be able to hold the dog at bay by standing still behind your bike, for hours if necessary, till the beast loses interest. In time, all dogs will calm down and walk away, so play the long game and circle the wagons if challenged by a seriously aggressive dog. If you do get attacked, don't hold back. Predators often back off if they decide it's just not worth it.

If you get bitten

In the unfortunate event of being bitten, rinse (don't scrub) the wound thoroughly for 15 minutes with soap and water, and clean with iodine if available. If you're in a country where rabies is present you'll have the dilem-

Not all canines are out to get you. Some will stand guard by your tent all night.

ma of deciding whether you need to get yourself to the nearest clinic for some post-bite shots. Recommended advice is always that you should even if there's only a slight chance the animal is carrying the rabies virus as the disease is 100% fatal if you don't get your jabs in time. However, this can be easier said than done. It's an issue worth reading up on before a trip so you have an idea of the prevalence of the disease and availability of post-exposure vaccines in different countries. This, along with reliable local information will help you plan a course of action if a pooch sinks its fangs into your calf in a rural area and the nearest vaccines are hundreds of kilometres away.

Dirt-road (off-road) riding

If you're tiring of main, paved roads through insalubrious towns which share the same unlovable features the world over, consider heading out on quieter tracks to visit those smaller places which are often a better window into a country's real character.

BORDER OFFICIALS AND CORRUPTION

Crossing borders can be one of the most daunting aspects of travel, leaving behind a country you understand and have become familiar with to enter another which may be totally alien. Bike travel ensures you usually see changes slowly unfurling over hundreds of kilometres, though at certain borders, such as Sudan-Ethiopia, everything changes in a flash. Aside from rare examples such as this, officialdom at the border itself is the biggest unknown, and this has the capacity to be intimidating.

A bicycle makes things relatively straightforward – there's no bike-related bureaucracy, and unlike backpackers you have your own transport and don't need to rely on dodgy taxi drivers to get you away from the unsavoury types who hang out at border posts. In the Americas, crossing borders is hassle-free and corrupt practices rare. In Western and Central Africa, and certain parts of Asia, petty corruption and bribery at border posts or checkpoints are common-place. Remaining cheery and polite but firm, and being prepared to wait longer than the official is before getting bored are usually all good pieces of advice. Asking for a receipt for a suspect 'tax' or charge often makes it magically vanish.

For many adventure riders the most rewarding times, and most vivid memories after a tour, relate to days spent on routes in areas with wild scenery or passing through villages that rarely see a foreigner. These will typically be on unpaved roads, though increasingly the world's transport network, including many of the erstwhile 'classic routes', are being tarmacked, especially in areas where Chinese road-builders exert influence.

By their very nature, dirt roads are more challenging and require more effort to ride than their asphalt counterparts, so a change of mind-set is required. Expect to go slow and travel far fewer kilometres per day – this doesn't mean foregoing adventures though as you're likely to have more than you ever would on a busy paved route. When our tours transitioned from mainly-paved to mainly-unpaved, our average speed plummeted from 16kph to 10kph, and our daily odometer readings dropped from 80-100km to 50-60km. Recalibrating expectations was necessary to prevent the perceived lack of progress bothering us – a recognition that it's about the experience, not the distance covered.

On unpaved roads you need to reduce tyre pressure to improve traction and comfort – the ideal pressure depends on the surface, weight of bike and rider and width of tyres. It pays to gravitate towards the 'lightly loaded' end of the spectrum to compensate for the surface and terrain sapping that extra chunk of your energy. It'll be more enjoyable and more rideable with a lighter setup, not to mention that your bike components will last longer. If you spend

---

TOURING ON A FAT BIKE

Setting out on a fat bike is an excellent way to turn your tour into an expedition. It opens the flood gates for what is possible on a bicycle, as the restrictions become only your own. If you hanker for the path least pedalled, or want to turn away from traffic, pollution and pavement in search of beautiful dirt, grit and a true realness of overland travel: 'Go fat, far and wide!' I like to say.

The fatter tyres' main attribute is excellent buoyancy through sand, deep gravel and snow. They also supply extra traction and stability, not to mention cushy suspension –

Fat bike setup for a long tour. © Cass Gilbert

much the same reason a 4x4 or overlanding vehicle has meaty balloon tyres. Yes, they do weigh more and add rolling resistance, though this is overcome by spinning lower gears, making it not much more difficult, just slower. What is the rush to end an off-road gallivant anyway?

The benefits of a fat bike can best be felt from travelling as light as possible, and I find myself at times reduced to 'hike-a-bike' mode. Not having bulky panniers increases manoeuvrability and makes pushing much easier, and having lighter gear compensates for the slightly heavier bike and allows the tyres to really shine with their buoyancy and suspension. The biggest trade-off for taking only the real kit essentials is less off-the-bike comfort than many people are willing to withstand on a longer tour.

The more tours I've ridden, I've found that for the options a fat bike provides, over all sorts of terrain, no matter the time of year, this occasional hardship is a price worth paying for more enjoyable riding, particularly somewhere as sandy as Bolivia. The fat bike is now my rig of choice every time.

Kurt Sandiforth

your days rattling along on rocky or corrugated tracks you need bomb-proof racks, strong panniers and wheels and it's also necessary to check the bolts on your racks more frequently, as they'll be jolted loose quicker than on butter-smooth tarmac.

CORRUGATIONS

Bumping over Tanzanian washboard your bouncing brain will have plenty of time to ponder how these surfaces come about. The generally accepted

Sometimes pushing is the only way...

explanation is they're caused by the braking and acceleration forces of passing traffic or by the 'tramping' shock absorbers of heavy trucks. On a rigid touring bike your wrists will get more of a juddering than a day wielding a pneumatic drill, however sometimes there's an optimum speed for skimming over shallower corrugations with the minimum of jarring. On all but the worst of these roads, there'll be a flat strip which makes for more comfortable riding, though you'll discover it can flit from one side of the road to the other, meaning you'll be weaving all over the place to find the ideal line.

SAND

Regions such as the Bolivian altiplano and the Mongolian steppe are synonymous with sandy tracks that'll see you pushing or dragging your bike for hours; a slow and frustrating process. Pushing is hard work for those of us with zero upper body strength – it's useful rigging straps/harnesses attached to your waist and the bike, to help drag your bike through long sandy sections. Having fatter tyres and going light can make all the difference to the amount you are able to ride, and if your tour concentrates on sandy areas, it's worth going fat.

Reducing tyre pressure makes a larger footprint and gives the additional grip that is vital on sandy roads. Also key is concentration – zoning out and hitting a deeper section of sand will lead to a spill, and getting started again in soft sand is tricky to impossible. Getting in a low gear and spinning legs quickly works well if the sand isn't too deep.

MUD

In wet regions or season, mud will be your biggest dirt-road hindrance. You'll soon learn it comes in all kinds of viscosities; the worst type is sticky and clay-like and will clog your forks and drive chain and prevent your wheels from turning. Routes with long stretches like this are unrideable and impassable without a lot of bike carrying; it's probably time to tinker with your route.

4 ROUTE OUTLINES
EUROPE TO
ASIA &
AUSTRALASIA

Adventure touring is about independence and freedom and inevitably taking a little risk too. You can pick and mix your countries just as you can dip in and out of sections of this book. Although here we highlight the most common routes for riders headed out to the Far East or down Africa from western Europe, as well as along the Americas, don't feel you have to follow someone else's route. Adventures often begin when you first strike out off the beaten track and onto an unknown one; with a couple of days' food in your panniers, chances are you won't go far wrong. If you need to hit the fast-forward button and beat winter or get out of somewhere before your visa expires, just do it.

Many riders are drawn to the idea of an epic RTW or transcontinental ride; it's a lifetime's dream and drawing a line across the map is easy, but don't feel you have to stick to an ambitious plan once you're on the road. You may well find greater rewards from exploring one region intimately rather than having a series of distant destinations in mind and rushing through places in an attempt to 'do it all'. Some parts of the route might be just too tough, too boring or too dangerous to ride, while conversely you'll probably also find that places that get a bad rap in the western media are some of the most friendly and rewarding to cycle through.

This section aims to give you a broad overview of the adventure cycling world, to show some of the possibilities out there and give a sense of what it's like to cycle in each country or region. From this you can build your own plan using detailed maps, information from blogs, forums and guidebooks. A number of mountain roads, such as the Great Divide Mountain Bike Route in the US or the Pamir Highway in Tajikistan, are so well known as cycling routes that each is covered in some detail, but otherwise we believe that adventurers like to find their own road.

Europe

Many first biking adventures begin in Europe – for those of us based here it's the logical and easiest place to cut our 'adventure touring' teeth, building confidence, experience and strength in the comfort of cultures and languages we are more familiar with.

Europe is ideal for a shakedown or short practice tour to test the waters and see if you like the lifestyle. You only need a smartphone or a map, not a guidebook, it's visa-free for most, and any bike troubles can be easily solved with parts and mechanics readily available.

Most riders on a long trip across Asia or Africa are able to use Europe as the warm up, a place to adjust to the simplicity of the way of life and begin honing wild camping and bike-tinkering skills, but there are some really challenging two-wheeled adventures waiting as well. Places like Iceland (see box p126) and Albania are exciting, off the pedalled-track destinations.

READY-MADE ROUTES

The Asia- and East Africa-bound have almost unlimited route choice before being channelled through Turkey. The EuroVelo website (🖥 eurovelo.com) and Bristol-based Sustrans (🖥 sustrans.org.uk) are good places to start looking for European bike path inspiration – EuroVelo is a cycle network of 14 transnational routes across Europe which, when complete, will total over 70,000km and run as far east as Moscow.

For bikepacking inspiration, search for 'European Bikepacking Routes' at 🖥 gypsybytrade.wordpress.com.

TO THE CONTINENT

Getting to the continent with your bike from Britain is a piece of cake. The cheapest and most popular option is that favoured by the purists, of riding to a port, jumping on a ferry, and cycling off at the other end. If you decide to fly we'd recommended heading to one of Europe's smaller airports if you plan on riding away from it, to avoid getting snarled up by traffic. Alternatively you could take your bike on the Eurostar train to Paris, Lille or Brussels, though check the web for conditions. There's even a dedicated bus service (🖥 bike-express.co.uk) from the UK to destinations in France and northern Spain, which will carry your bike fully assembled.

The excitement of a new country is just too much for some.

EUROPE EN VÉLO – 1929

In 1929, American graduate **Jean Bell** *worked his sea passage across 'the Pond' to Europe, bought a bike, had a rack fitted and became a true cycle-touring pioneer.*

8 July 1929 – Arrival in Antwerp

We seem to have taken an extremely long time getting here but the seaman's pay which got us to Europe puts us quite a bit ahead of the game financially; the voyage finally ended, the crew paid off.

9 July 1929 – Buying bicycles

After breakfast, we set out in search of a bicycle shop. The call of the open road is strong and we're anxious to be on our way, really to begin our vagabonding abroad.

At first glance, Belgian bicycles look just like our bikes back home. Two wheels, two pedals, one chain, one seat, all that a cyclist needs for around-town riding; our plans for making a long-distance ride, however, require a luggage rack. We also would like to have a coaster brake and a tool kit which will permit us to make emergency roadside repairs. Obviously there is a need to upgrade our vélos for long-distance traveling. The salesman calls in the mechanic and we explain why we need a rack. We will probably be cycling to Paris, we tell them. The mechanic nods, 'Oui. C'est possible.' With a rack mounted over the rear wheel we now have a place to lash our 'carry-on' luggage.

Our next request. 'Can you install coaster brakes?' Here we foul out. What in the world is the French for 'coaster brake?' Eventually we drew a 'Pas possible,' followed by a vigorous shake of the head. We gather from his response that this technology apparently has not yet crossed the Atlantic from west to east. Brakes on these bikes consisted of a lever mounted on the handlebar which, when squeezed, activated a pad on the front wheel which served to slow down progress ... more or less. But the lack of coaster brakes, at that moment at least, did not seem worth wrestling for, so we skip to our next request: single [solid] tires.

Well, 'win some, lose some'. We would get the rack but struck out everything else. And, oh yes, the price. Would you believe it, their grand total selling price per bicycle,was 1100.25 Belgian francs ... the equivalent of US$25, all of which we recaptured when we sold them in Bulgaria some four months later. I don't know why the rims on the wheels of my bike are wooden; Amos's rims are metal. Some thousand miles later, the significance of this difference will become clear.

Weight and simplicity are significant factors in long-distance cruising. Our plans for the road are to wear blue jeans, blue work shirts and tennis shoes. Our baggage includes changes of shirt, underwear, socks and pyjamas, also a blue-knit 'UC' sweater. Add maps, camera and film, a water bottle ... the list grows with astonishing speed.

Ah yes, let me not forget to mention the $300 letter of credit Mom had tucked away with my passport and seaman's papers. Incidentally, this map mentioned above, is a Rand McNally pocket map of Europe and the Near East which I had bought in a New York drug store. This funny little map guided us all the way across Bulgaria and, eventually, to Jerusalem.

13 July 1929 – Amsterdam

I have one major goal in Amsterdam: to see the Rijksmuseum and that famous painting by Rembrandt, *The Night Watch*. All by itself the sight of this memorable canvas pays off the time and effort of getting there.

We decide to make an effort to end each day in a small town ... the smaller the better for a number of reasons: 1. The prices are more subject to bargaining. 2. The prices are usually lower. 3. Probably most important, your host is not so busy with other guests and an evening with him around the fire is a heartwarming experience. Some of our most interesting nights have been spent with the host and his wife. Their questions are exceedingly interesting and, hopefully, ours are too. Perhaps the best advice a traveler gets is 'Avoid stopping in big cities.'

23 July 1929 – Amiens

Noontime found us, like Goldilocks, lost in the woods outside Amiens. We were hungry, very hungry. Eventually we reached a promising peasant dwelling. An old lady in a black apron and white lace cap was feeding the chickens as we drew near. We told her we were hungry and wonder if she could sell us something to eat. What is outstanding in my memory of these strangers whom we approached with requests for favors such as this was their almost universal smiling and obliging aquiescence. Wiping her hands she said lunch had finished but if the messieurs would care to wait? We would! And while she podded peas and peeled potatoes for our three-course lunch we sat in her kitchen, spoke bad French and told her of our travels and of America. What a lunch!

With such experiences are the scrap-books of vagabonds filled. Nothing stereo-typed, nothing pre-arranged by a travel agency, nothing staged for its effect on tourist pocketbooks. Only a desire to please, a warm glow of friendship which steps across barriers of race and language. Such are the true joys of wandering.

16-28 September 1929 – Austria

What a lot of ground for two college boys to have covered in approximately two months!! Belgium, Holland, France, Germany! One thing about Amos and me, we are more than willing to 'dream big'.

7-14 October 1929 – Bulgaria

We expect to reach Svilengrad in three days. The map shows a 'very good road' most of the way. Seven days later we drag into Svilengrad cussing all Bulgarian road maps. We expected to find paved roads. We did! They were paved with a six-inch layer of yel-low dust which concealed rocks. Bicycling is evidently not the accepted mode of transport over lonely Bulgarian roads. We nearly cause a runaway or a smash-up each time we meet or pass an animal-drawn vehicle.

By mid-afternoon we have reached the foothills and begin what promises to be a long, steep climb. Suddenly there is a very loud bang and I find myself sprawling over the handlebars into the gravel. My wooden rim has shattered when my tire exploded and the inner tube is tangled in the chain. So ... here is our very first accident in all those long miles from Antwerp.

Have you ever tried pushing a loaded bicycle backwards **and** on one wheel? It seems that I have been pushing forever when we finally reach the small village of Razgrad. We eat our first meal since dining on bread and sausage the night before. That accom-plished, we show the waiter our bike. He is all smiles and indicates that we should follow him. About a block up the street we come upon a bicycle shop. To our great surprise we are greeted in very passable English. Here, in the middle of the Balkan Mountains, we have found a bike shop owner who had put in some 15 years as a waiter in Chicago and only recently returned home to retire. Our needs

When moving from one major metropolis to the next, we simply posted our city clothes on to await our arrival.

do not faze him. 'Of course I can get you a new wheel'. He will phone in the order and we should be ready to roll in two days. 'Two days?' I am very dubious. I had seen no phone lines; nor had we encountered either a UPS or Fed Ex van on the road.

Believe it or not, my damaged wheel is replaced and as good as new. We bid goodbye to all our friends (by this time it seems that we have become old friends with everybody in the village) and after three hours of steep hill climbing, we reach the pass. Some 3000ft below lies a broad valley through which the Maritza River flows gently, reminiscent of the Los Angeles River in late summer.

My nine-month trip around Europe, Asia and Africa cost a total of $265.67, almost all of which I managed to cover in various jobs along the way. Not as tourists, or states-men, or students but as *wandervogel* we 'did' the Old World on a minimum of cash and a maximum of exuberance.

Jean Bell continued to travel into his nineties, fre-quently visiting his son, Ross, in France. He died in California in 2009, aged 101. His autobiogra-phy, 'A 90-Year Journey Through the 20th Century' is available from 💻 www.amazon.com.

THE CALL OF THE ORIENT

Western Europe

France has a great road network for bikes, with a disproportionately high number of small D roads with little traffic. Biking in all its forms is well established, you'll get respect from motorists and the camping scene is excellent

---

WILD CAMPING

Wild camping can be an unnerving experience for novice tourers – parking up by the side of the road, wherever you happen to have reached that day, and rolling out your tent. Is it a safe or sensible thing to do? Done correctly, yes, and once you get over this initial anxiety, wild camping will become a highlight of life on the road.

After a few weeks on tour you'll soon develop an eye for discreet and secure camp spots, though the kinds of places you choose will vary for each country and type of terrain. In Western Europe the main priority will be to conceal yourself, as wild camping will likely be frowned upon and any attention may be unwanted. Woodlands are the best for free camping in Europe; just push your bike away from any footpath to avoid early-morning dog-walkers or mushroom-hunters and you'll be all alone. Asking for a place to camp will ensure you keep out of trouble so don't be bashful in countries or regions that are open to it. Wild camping generally gets easier as you move east in Europe: the French will point you towards the many municipal campgrounds, the Germans are more accepting of discreet overnight camping as long as you camp late and move on early, and east Europeans are most likely to suggest a place if you ask.

From the Middle East onwards, things really open up. Here one reason to pursue 'stealth' or discreet camping is that you may actually become overwhelmed by all the kind invites into people's homes! This tradition of hospitality is especially strong in Muslim countries where locals feel it's an obligation. Refusal can be awkward so think ahead; you will be faced with offers of tea from many, many kind people en route to China. If you do choose to camp near a community or household anywhere in the world it's always polite, and safer, to ask for permission.

An ideal camp spot is away from houses and dogs, unseen from the road, not in the line of vehicle headlights, close to water and with early morning sunlight to warm you and dry your tent. Pick a level spot – but not in a dip that may attract water – and one that is ant-free and with no signs of an impending visit from herds of sheep or goats. Among bushes is good and a place with plenty of firewood is even better, though make sure you are in a truly wild place and not farmland where locals may come and investigate. Fires are great in the mountains or remote places as long as you're not using someone's prized winter fuel and there's no risk of unwittingly starting a forest fire.

Avoid camping on the banks of a river (or dry river bed) for the obvious flash-flood risk; camping too close to a river has the added disadvantages of being colder and damper too. If your tent isn't strong, stick to more sheltered areas, but try to be at least a little in the open in order to get some moving air, which is needed for your tent to vent properly.

And as long as your chosen spot for the night meets all the other 'health and safety' criteria, such as avoiding exposed areas and ridges if a thunderstorm is likely, or making sure that you won't be caught out by high tide on a beach, camp where there's a great view; it's why you're there!

Wild camping in Bulgaria.

with good campgrounds in almost every town and many villages too. Go for the municipal two-star campgrounds which are generally the best value, with the necessaries but no frills and fewer caravans.

Wild camping in France can be a little tricky – leave it till late to pitch your tent and set off early in the morning as your presence is unlikely to be appreciated. If you're wild camping, and need the occasional wash, try a *camping à la ferm*e, which is usually the next-cheapest option to a night ensconced in some woods. Private *gîtes d'étape* offer relatively cheap overnight accommodation with meals but are beyond many budget travellers' means.

Bike paths abound in **Germany**, **Austria** and **Switzerland** (see 🖥 map.veloland.ch) and are often easily found on approaches to cities. Germany's bike trails are organised regionally, making planning a trip the length of the country a little tricky – for ideas, start at the interactive map at 🖥 germany.travel/en or at 🖥 radweit.de. Information on bike paths in **Italy** can be found at 🖥 italy-cycling-guide.info.

The **River Danube route** attracts lots of cyclists – not just long-distance tourers but day-trippers and commuters – so it can be crowded at weekends. The section from Germany to Hungary is most developed and provides over 1000km of almost traffic-free riding. There are campgrounds but you can also ask at boat clubs if you can camp on their lawns. The most beautiful and quiet section is the far west, where the Danube begins just below the Black Forest.

The Balkans

Before reaching Turkey there is some fascinating and satisfying touring in the Balkans. **Slovenia** is a delightful touring destination – the capital Ljubljana is a manageable size and the Julian Alps, which border Italy and Austria, are highly recommended. The north-western area of the country is home to Triglav National Park and Soca which has good hiking, kayaking and rafting as well as cycling. To the south, the *karst* formations of the Kras region offer laidback villages, forests good for camping, vineyards and rolling hills; while the south-east has rolling hills with spas, campsites on farms and easier riding.

Croatia has a beautiful coastline but you may prefer to ferry-hop and go via the islands to avoid the traffic on the busy coastal road. The Balkan countries have plenty of hilly riding – **Bosnia**, **Serbia** and **Montenegro** all have routes to entertain bikers, with quiet country roads where you'll be far from the tourist scene. In villages you'll see traditional farming techniques still practised; local people are very hospitable and you may get lucky and be offered food or a place to stay.

Mostly Muslim but a secular state, **Albania** is one of Europe's most adventurous cycling destinations. Lose yourself in the maze of mountainous army roads, built in communist times under Enver Hoxha, and try and get your head around why Mercedes Benz is such a common choice of car on the roads. Albania and **Macedonia** share

Exploring Albania's military mountain roads.

Lake Ohrid, which is well worth a visit, as is the town of the same name that lies on the Macedonian shore.

Bulgaria and **Romania** have little traffic and offer more superb touring, with mountain roads and a long coastline on the Black Sea. Horse-drawn carts are still seen in the countryside and there is an abundance of home-grown produce that villagers or farmers will happily sell you. Accommodation is often in private rooms, people's gardens, on farmer's land or even in churches. The wine-growing region near Melnik in south-western Bulgaria is a particular favourite. Island-hopping through **Greece** to reach Turkey is another good option, especially for those who are travelling in winter and wish to escape the chilly weather on mainland routes.

To avoid stumbling into Istanbul along the motorway, see box on p132.

TO WEST AFRICA VIA SPAIN

If you're heading down to West Africa from France, only **Spain** stands in your way. The Iberian Peninsula is less oriented than France to cycle touring but that only makes a cycle-tourist more of an exotic visitor and cycling down to the south coast is the best way to get an insight into rural life. The ferry from Algeciras in southern Spain to the tiny Spanish enclave of Ceuta, which abuts Morocco on the African continent, is the best option as it takes bikes for free and the Spanish-Moroccan border at Ceuta is relatively quiet compared to the crossing between Tarifa and bustling Tangier.

AN ADVENTURE IN ICELAND

I arrived in Iceland in February to experience riding a bike in winter. I wasn't well prepared and didn't have a plan – in fact I had no idea what I was getting myself into. Turns out they don't really turn the lights on here till early March, which is slightly inconvenient but makes for wonderful long nights in your tent, under the Northern Lights if you're lucky. The sight of the green, red, yellow and white lights dancing in the sky is enough to make you fall in love with this place.

By talking to locals and getting tips and ideas I ended up camping next to hot springs in the snow, sleeping in an ice cave inside a glacier and once in an igloo. People might seem reserved at first but I encountered some of the greatest hospitality in the world – one lady even knitted me a jumper specially!

Sure there is a lot of snow and ice and unique scenery to wow bikers, but if you're not careful to check the weather forecast, or where you pitch your tent, chances are you'll be blown away a little too literally. The wind can be brutal. Luckily there are lots of fjords to cycle round in both the West and the East, so at least half the distance you get a tailwind...

Research before you go and play and you will really be rewarded. I ended up staying longer than expected, by about 3 months, so I had the chance to explore a little of the interior too. Weather conditions mean most of the roads in the interior are closed about 10 months a year but when you do manage to get there the barren open volcanic moonscape, the midnight sun and black fumes of volcanoes erupting in the distance make it seem like magic.

Mirjam Wouters

View to the Icelandic fjords.
© Mirjam Wouters

THE NORTH SEA CYCLE ROUTE

Said to be the longest signposted cycle trail in the world and passing through seven countries, this 6000km-route follows the North Sea coast, mostly on protected cycle paths or minor roads, including unpaved roads in places. The route involves many ferries across seas and estuaries, though one flight is necessary, from Bergen to the Shetland Islands. This runs only twice a week and should be booked well in advance.

Expect wind and rain to be the biggest headaches and be prepared to camp for at least half the time, though there are some excellent wild camping opportunities in Norway, the wildest stretch. You will see very little traffic except on occasional short stretches of main road in Norway. The route isn't all villages; major cities passed through are Newcastle, Edinburgh, Aberdeen, Bergen, Gothenburg, Hamburg and The Hague. The German coastline is fairly crowded but cool and breezy – beware the institutional campgrounds from the old days of East Germany, though it's hard to find a free spot to wild camp along Germany's small and popular coastline. The North Sea Cycle Route can be cycled in either direction and a number of maps are needed to cover the whole route – Sustrans sell a selection. More details about the route can be found at 💻 northsea-cycle.com.

Mountain biking is a popular recreational activity in Spain and there are many signposted MTB routes in the Pyrenees and elsewhere. There are also the Vías Verdes, a network of disused railway lines (💻 viasverdes.com/en), which are good for getting into and out of cities without too much traffic trauma. Hopefully one day these routes will be combined to make one long off-highway route across Spain but until then the ancient pilgrimage routes to Santiago de Compostela, principally the main route between France and Santiago in the far north-west of Spain, or the Vía de la Plata, which runs between Gijón on the north coast, and Sevilla in Andalucía, (💻 rutadelapla ta.com/en) come the closest. Don't forget a helmet in Spain; it's the law.

Asia

For many, Asia is the epitome of adventure cycle touring: heading east for exotic lands to test your mettle on the Kazakh steppe, the passes of the Himalaya, or to ride across the roof of the world. It is still the most popular continent with Europeans for a long ride, although in recent years safety concerns on the southern route via Balochistan and visa hassles further north have complicated things. Sticks have been thrust between the spokes of classic routes such as the Lhasa to Kathmandu Friendship Highway and sections of the Karakoram Highway through Pakistan to Kashgar; but this has meant that adventure riders have begun shifting attentions elsewhere – to Myanmar and Mongolia, the dirt tracks of Kyrgyzstan, Tibetan areas in Qinghai and Sichuan, or circuits around little-known tropical Indonesian islands. It's a huge continent, and there will always be an unlimited number of biking adventures out there.

Asia MAIN TRANS-CONTINENTAL ROUTES

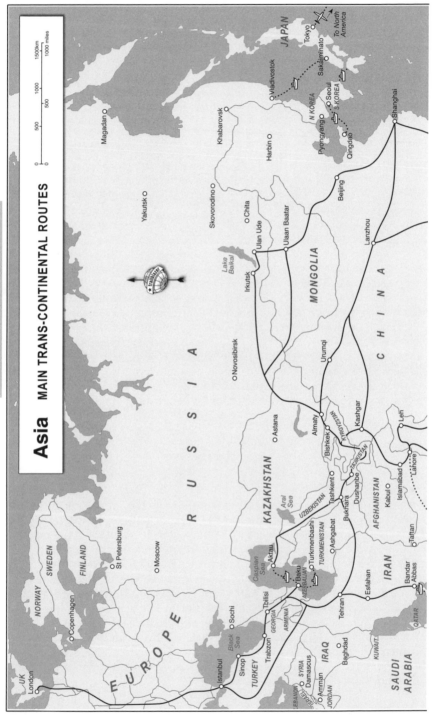

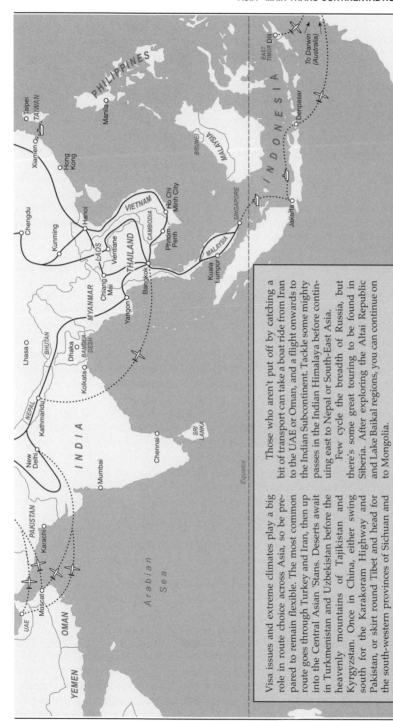

Visa issues and extreme climates play a big role in route choice across Asia, so be prepared to remain flexible. The most common route goes through Turkey and Iran, then up into the Central Asian 'Stans. Deserts await in Turkmenistan and Uzbekistan before the heavenly mountains of Tajikistan and Kyrgyzstan. Once in China, either swing south for the Karakoram Highway and Pakistan, or skirt round Tibet and head for the south-western provinces of Sichuan and Yunnan.

Those who aren't put off by catching a bit of transport can take a boat ride from Iran to the UAE or Oman, and a flight onwards to the Indian Subcontinent. Tackle some mighty passes in the Indian Himalaya before continuing east to Nepal or South-East Asia.

Few cycle the breadth of Russia, but there's some great touring to be found in Siberia. After exploring the Altai Republic and Lake Baikal regions, you can continue on to Mongolia.

Stormy skies and endless vistas over Tiger
Leaping Gorge in Yunnan, China.
© Amaya Williams

MAIN ROUTES

Traditionally there have been three main cycling routes that span Asia. The Southern Route crosses Turkey and Iran, to Pakistan then China or India. Security concerns currently preclude cycling between Iran and Pakistan, so many are opting to head to the subcontinent by air, often via the UAE or Oman. The situation regarding cycling through Myanmar is changing rapidly and continuing an eastwards ride from India to Thailand via Myanmar involves some tricky paperwork, though hopes are that this process may soon be simplified. It is currently easier to ride this part in reverse, from Thailand, through Myanmar to India (see p218).

The second route explores the Central Asian 'Stans, entering from Iran or via the Caucasus and ferry across the Caspian Sea; this route is still a classic and offers your best chance of riding an unbroken line from Europe to the Pacific.

Allowing a year from Istanbul to the South China Sea is enough time to avoid rushing either of these routes and includes contingencies for when visa situations change unexpectedly.

A more northerly route through Russia to China is quicker than the options above but has always been the least transited. It's becoming increasingly popular, however, to enter Russia from Kazakhstan and explore a bit of Siberia and Mongolia before reaching China.

For shorter, more concentrated trips, many areas hold great appeal. For mountains, head to Kyrgyzstan and Tajikistan, the Indian Himalaya or the south-western provinces of China; for easier riding, great food and smiles, check out South-East Asia. At present, Afghanistan, Balochistan and Tibet are the big stumbling blocks that riders must skirt round.

It's useful to bear in mind that many people don't ride the whole way across Asia. Accept the fact that though it's normally possible, it can be tricky to cycle every metre – visa complications, border crossings where biking no-man's land is not allowed, or unavoidable delays which mean you're unable to outrun the winter snows can all make it necessary to throw your bike onto transport. It's a continent that rewards flexibility and changing plans, so go with the flow; it's all part of the fun.

PRACTICALITIES

Seasons

A long ride across Asia will, in all likelihood, be an East-West (or West-East) affair, which makes itinerary creation tricky. January in Eastern Turkey is freezing, in Tajikistan it's perishing, in Mongolia the mercury regularly drops to -30C. In all those, a Siberian Yakut would be out in short sleeves. Conversely, summers are variously roasting, scorching, sweltering, stifling or mosquito-laden; but fear not, with good planning and some patience you can avoid travel in these extremes.

Those going via Central Asia will find early April is a good time to hit Eastern Turkey and means you can get through Iran and the deserts of Turkmenistan and Uzbekistan before it's too hot, then ride the mountain routes of Tajikistan and Kyrgyzstan in the summer months. Make it through Mongolia or western China before the winter chill descends, and you can spend December to February in South-East Asia's cooler dry season.

Snow still stacked high by the Rohtang La.

If you take the Southern Route, and are heading into the high Himalaya or Karakoram, note that passes usually open sometime in May and begin closing again from October.

Visas

Visa-collecting is a common and necessary pastime for tourers in many parts of Asia, so routes will need to incorporate large cities to visit embassies and deal with some baffling bureaucracy. It means it's vital to research beforehand which embassies are good for which visas, then hope the situation doesn't change before you get there; for some countries it changes surprisingly regularly. Heading east, visa hassles begin in Iran and Azerbaijan, and with a few exceptions, continue until the relative ease of South-East Asia.

Costs

Costs vary greatly between different nations – India, Nepal and China are among the places where it's possible to tour for under US$10 a day if you try. In Korea and Japan your daily average costs will be quite a bit higher.

Getting there

Most transcontinental riders' first sight of Asia will be across the Bosphorus from Istanbul, but there are many easily accessed airports which are frequently used by riders as the jumping off point for a tour: Tashkent, Bangkok, or Delhi, to name a few.

Language

Only a polymath would be capable of riding the length of Asia and be able to converse with local people the full length of the journey; in some countries the language changes by the state, or even by the valley. English is useful in many places, particularly in the subcontinent, while Turkish comes in handy not only in Turkey but in Azerbaijan and many of the 'Stans whose languages are Turkic. Having some command of Russian is invaluable in all the former Soviet Republics, as well as in Mongolia. If your tour concentrates on China, it's best to start those Mandarin classes now, buy a pointer book and get someone to write you a Magic Letter – see p180. A smartphone equipped with a good translation app always helps conversation too.

THE SOUTHERN ROUTE
Turkey

Emily Chappell

Pretty much all travel destinations claim to 'have it all', but Turkey is surely a better contender than most. Cyclists travelling west-to-east will find themselves funnelled through Istanbul like sand through an hourglass, and no matter where you've come from, or which route you're planning to take across Asia, this is a wonderful place to stop, relax, drink coffee, and compare notes with the dozens of other cyclists you're likely to run into.

And then – well, take your pick! To the south there are sunny beaches, secluded coves and ancient ruins; along the underexplored Black Sea coast you'll find lush green forests, rainy tea plantations and the world's oldest cherry orchards; in central Anatolia are long, quiet highways, surrounded by rippling golden prairies as far as the eye can see, plus the underground cities and bizarre natural rock sculptures of Cappadocia. Then there are the awe-inspiring mountain passes of Turkey's eastern highlands, coated in snow and ice for several months a year, leading you towards the glittering slopes of Mount Ararat, which sits at the junction of Turkey, Iran, and the Caucasus.

And Turkey is simply paradise for cyclists. Food is cheap, plentiful and delicious, the roads are broad and smooth, and you're now within the legendary Islamic hospitality zone of Western Asia – expect to be offered tea and

ENTERING ISTANBUL

Unless you're careful, your first encounter with this great city will involve inhaling fumes and dodging buses on a busy four-lane motorway, which cuts through 100km of urban sprawl, with almost no hard shoulder. This nightmare can be avoided by keeping south and hugging the Marmara coast, which has cycle paths most of the way to the centre of Istanbul. Heading east out of the city, many cyclists opt to take the ferry from Istanbul's central Kabataş dock to Yalova or Mudanya, rather than spend another day or three pedalling through the city's endless eastern suburbs. Istanbul is a good place to stock up on kit, with a cluster of outdoor shops in Beyoğlu, not far from cyclist-friendly Neverland Hostel. If you're in need of a bike shop, head over to Bisiklet Gezgini, which specialises in touring, stocks maps, and is the last Rohloff service centre until you get to Bangkok!

Leaving Istanbul on a quiet road north along the Bosphorus.

biscuits wherever you stop and prepare yourself for long sociable evenings in overheated living rooms, watching schmaltzy Turkish soap operas, wrestling with over-excited children and exchanging life stories in mutually incomprehensible languages with people you've only just met.

PRACTICALITIES

Visas

Most Europeans and North Americans can purchase a multiple-entry visa, valid for a maximum of 90 days, from the Turkish government's official e-visa website (🖳 www.evisa.gov.tr). It is currently also possible to buy a visa in cash on entry, though there are plans to phase this out in the near future. If you know you are likely to be in Turkey for longer than 90 days you should apply for a longer visa before leaving home, or for a residence permit from the local authorities in Turkey.

Eating and sleeping

A lot of people come to Turkey just for the food – a fantastic fusion of all that is best from Mediterranean, Middle Eastern and Central Asian cuisines. As well as the kebabs and mezes you'll already know from Turkish restaurants at home, you'll find that every region has its own specialities, that delicious fruit and veg are grown all over the country, and that Turkish people will be falling over themselves to share it all with you.

Turkish breakfasts are a real treat for a hungry cyclist: enormous spreads of cheese, eggs, yoghurt, honey, olives, sausage, tomatoes, and piles of fresh white bread to mop it all up. Pastry-wise, you'll find it hard to stay away from the shops selling *börek* (cheese, meat or veg wrapped in filo) and *baklava* (tiny sweet pastries filled with honey and nuts), and the pizza-like *pide* and *lahmacun* are excellent fuel for an afternoon on the bike.

Wild camping is easy enough in Turkey and half the time asking permission will lead to an invitation to stay with a family. Petrol stations can be a good bet as they often have a grassy picnic area, toilets (of varying standards), and sometimes even a shower.

Challenges and inconveniences

Communication is relatively straightforward – you'll find plenty of English speakers, especially in the western half of the country and the bigger cities (in the east they will be desperate to practise their English and will probably find you); German will also prove surprisingly useful.

The population is predominantly Muslim – in a laidback, cosmopolitan fashion in the west, and a more devout, traditional manner in the east – which means you'll be woken up by the melodious call to prayer from the local mosque no matter how far from civilisation you think you've managed to pitch your tent. Pay attention to whether you'll be travelling during Ramadan, as this will make a difference to how easily you can acquire food (see p138). Dress-code-wise, it's best to take your cue from those around you. Shorts and sleeveless tops won't raise any eyebrows in the beach resorts of the south-west or in the bigger cities, but you should at least keep your limbs covered in more rural or conservative areas. There's no obligation for women to cover their heads (except when visiting mosques) but some may prefer to blend in with what everyone else is wearing.

One of the first round-the-world cyclists, Frank Lenz, was murdered in Eastern Turkey in 1894, and for many years the area was considered lawless and unstable, controlled by Kurdish groups who weren't all that interested in being part of Turkey or that friendly to curious outsiders. Today's flashpoint is the southern border with Iraq and Syria. Until recently this region was known for its regular skirmishes between PKK separatists and the Turkish army – at the time of writing travellers were being advised to steer clear owing to the worsening conflict in Syria and Northern Iraq.

ROUTES

The most popular route for cyclists is straight across the middle. The Black Sea coast offers a milder (though also rainier) alternative, with a scenic coastal road. If you're in need of a bit of a rest or want to wait out Eastern Turkey's fearsomely cold winter, cycle down the west coast and take a break in Fethiye or Olympos, sit on beaches, explore ancient ruins, hike the Lycian Way and rekindle your enthusiasm for cycling. In high season these places are stuffed with tourists but pick your time wisely and they're the perfect place for a bit of R&R. Even in winter, the weather is rarely less than comfortably mild.

If you're heading east, be warned – most of this end of the country is well above 1000m, so you will effectively be riding uphill almost the whole way – except for some rather lovely descents from the various mountain passes. But you'll be rewarded with the stunning mountain scenery around Erzurum, and the chance to explore Lake Van, or the remote İshak Paşa palace, perched high in the mountains above Doğubeyazıt. Those heading to the Caucasus could investigate the Kaçkar Mountains en route to Georgia; strained relations mean the border with Armenia is firmly closed. The civil war in Syria means that it is not currently possible to cycle south from Turkey to Africa – see p236.

Turkish traffic is usually fairly manageable (with some notable exceptions – see box p132), and in Western Turkey there are enough decent roads that you can usually find one that's quiet and also well maintained. The route between Yalova and Ankara, via Lake İznik, Nallıhan and Beypazarı is a particular joy, with scenery reminiscent of Monument Valley, and next-to-no traffic. Further east, the main overland route is shared with a constant procession of trucks, so though there's plenty of space and drivers tend to be considerate, you may want to consider quieter alternatives.

TURKISH DOGS

It is a truth universally acknowledged that a dog, when presented with a moving bicycle, will chase it. You'll be used to this by now, if you've cycled through Europe to get to Turkey – but the ferocious hounds of Eastern Turkey are something else. Bred as guard dogs, they are trained to attack and are so dangerous that some cyclists have reported being offered escorts by concerned locals. Fortunately, various solutions are at hand. I made it safely through with a dog dazer (available in Istanbul's outdoor shops) kept close at hand in a pocket or bar bag, and met cyclists who had successfully used pepper spray to repel attacks. Others assure me they survived by shouting, throwing stones, or even just pretending to throw stones, since the dogs are apparently so accustomed to this line of defence that they'll flinch anyway. One Swiss cyclist proudly showed me his special thwacking stick, which had seen off canine attackers all the way across Anatolia.

CONTINUING TO IRAN

Turkey is the airlock where overlanders acclimatise between the easy familiarity of Europe and the dangers and mysteries of Iran. (Spoiler: once you've spent a week or so in Iran, it will seem just as easy and familiar as anywhere else.) Many find that their route through Turkey is partly shaped by the need to reach their nominated Iranian consulate before their visa authorisation code expires. Iran has four consulates in Turkey – in Istanbul, Ankara, Trabzon and Erzurum – and applicants generally specify where they wish to collect their visa. Since the bureaucracy can take a few weeks, it makes sense to nominate one further down the road and spend the intervening weeks riding towards it.

Leave time to withdraw enough currency to see you through your time in Iran (unless you're already carrying a lot), since, thanks to Western embargoes and sanctions your credit and debit cards won't work anywhere in the country. I found ATMs in Istanbul and Göreme that disburse dollars and euros (and recommend carrying both), and it's possible, with a little hassle, to sort things out at the last minute in the border town of Doğubeyazıt. Don't hang onto your Turkish lira though – they can only be changed at the border.

A long downhill near Mt Ararat.
© Scott Richardson

Iran

Emily Chappell

Ignore everything you've heard about Iran – unless of course you're talking to someone who's recently been there. The Islamic Republic formerly known as Persia has a bad reputation on the international stage but as every Iranian will tell you (and they *will* tell you, probably over a meal that they'll insist on paying for before dragging you back to their house to meet the family) there's a world of difference between ordinary people and the governments that claim to represent them.

Iranian friendliness is a big part of what makes this massive country such a joy to cycle through. Despite the many challenges that deserts, headwinds, speeding vehicles, lascivious gentlemen and tedious bureaucracy may throw at you, you can be sure that someone will be waiting to rescue you, to translate for you, or simply to cheer you up with a smile and a cup of tea.

PRACTICALITIES

Visas

Visas are a real headache, and though rules change, citizens of the USA and Canada currently have little chance of getting permission to tour independently in Iran. The most reliable way for British citizens to obtain a visa is via one of the numerous Iranian travel agencies – 🖥 iranianvisa.com and 🖥 lets-goiran.com are both popular, but it's a good idea to check traveller forums before you apply as agencies' success rates can vary from year to year. Most visa application processes will go something like this:

1 You fill in a form on the agency's website, giving all the usual personal details and nominating the embassy or consulate from which you wish to collect your visa.

2 The agency submits your application to the Ministry of Foreign Affairs, who will (all being well) issue a reference number to your nominated consulate. This will take anything from five days to twenty days, depending on your nationality.

3 Before they give you the reference number, the agency will ask you to pay their service fee, usually as an international bank transfer to a third party account in some other country, since it is not possible to transfer money into Iran directly. Once you have transferred the money, and sent them a copy of the receipt (as a scan or screenshot), they will release the reference number.

4 Hand in the reference number at the specified consulate, along with your passport, two passport photos (women must have their hair covered) and the visa fee. You will normally be invited to collect your passport (with visa) the following day.

Money

Iran's currency is the rial (IRR) and owing to numerous international sanctions the inflation rate is astronomical. For this reason you should avoid changing a lot of money in one go and get used to prices being quoted in the hundreds of thousands.

Most important to remember is that **foreign debit and credit cards do not work in Iran**. All the money you will need must be brought in with you, in US

DRESS CODE

All visitors to Iran are obliged by law to conform to the country's Islamic dress code, which for men means full-length trousers and sleeves, although the modesty squads will generally turn a blind eye to shorts and lycra if you are cycling. Women are also expected to cover their hair, arms and legs, and to wear a loose garment that comes down to at least mid-thigh. This could be a tunic, a long shirt or an Iranian *manteau* – a smart, mid-length coat, available all over Iran. If you are arriving from Pakistan or India it might be worth bringing along a couple of cheap *kurta* for this purpose. There's a lot of room for interpretation within the dress code – you'll see everything from young urban women in skin-tight manteau, with most of their hair showing, to devout matriarchs peering out through a letterbox of black fabric. Your own choice of hijab will depend on your personal standards of style and comfort. If you're the kind of woman who likes to accessorise, you'll have a lot of fun here!

A regular event on tour in Iran: posing for a photo with some friendly locals.
© Gayle Dickson

GENDER RELATIONS

Despite the liberal outlook of many of its citizens, the Iranian establishment enforces conservative gender roles and a much higher level of segregation than you may be used to. This affects men and women alike, albeit in different ways. Several foreign men I met complained that they had barely spoken to a woman in weeks, and felt like they were being shut out of half of society – whereas this was not a problem for me at all: as a solo woman I dealt with men as much as any other traveller, but was also regularly invited to spend evenings with the female members of a family, sitting cross-legged on carpets around the stove, eating sunflower seeds and exchanging lifestories. Male-female couples will often find, when dealing with officials, that people routinely speak to the man and ignore the woman. This can be frustrating for both, especially if the woman is usually the one who prefers to deal with bureaucracy. Both men and women may find themselves on the receiving end of sexual harassment, though women tend to bear the brunt of it, especially if they are travelling alone. Although it may be difficult at times, it is worth keeping an open mind about the people you meet. I once turned to glare at a driver who'd been crawling along just beside me for several minutes, only to see that he was grinning broadly and holding a packet of cakes out of the window.

dollars or euros, and converted in an exchange shop, at a bank or by a moneychanger.

Terrain and seasons

Although it doesn't feel like it when you're out in the middle of the desert, most of Iran is on a plateau almost 1000m above sea level (and much higher in some places), which includes several mountain ranges. This means that Iran's winters are much colder than you might expect, especially near the borders with Turkey and Iraq, whereas in the summer months it will be almost unbearably hot. Spring and autumn are the easiest seasons for cycling, although if you are canny about location, you can still cycle comfortably through (for example) the Zagros Mountains in summer or along the Persian Gulf coast in winter.

If you're heading west-to-east, you'll find the landscape levelling out as you go, which can be a blessing, and also a curse – fewer blistering climbs but worse headwinds, plus the tedium of pedalling through featureless desert day after day.

Eating and sleeping

Food in Iran isn't always the unadulterated pleasure you'd hope. Persian cuisine, when you can find it, is delicious, but in many places you'll be forced to subsist on burgers and pizzas – even Iran's succulent kebabs can get tiresome after a while and vegetarians may find themselves eating little more than rice. It's worth persisting though, as delicacies like *fesenjun* (chicken cooked with walnuts and pomegranate seeds) and *ash-e-reshteh* (green soup with tagliatelle, herbs and beans) are too good to miss – as are the freshly baked flatbreads that make up a typical Iranian breakfast (along with feta cheese, jam and

Alcohol-free beer, a ham-free burger and not having to brush your headscarf-covered hair for a week – just some of the idiosyncracies of touring in Iran.

RAMADAN

For one month every year, the Islamic world fasts between sunrise and sunset. For Muslims Ramadan is a time to reconnect with their spiritual beliefs – and with their family and friends – at the massive *iftari* banquets that take place every evening once the sun has set. But for non-Muslim cycle tourists the Holy Month can cause inconvenience, especially when, as for the next few years, it falls during the long days of summer.

Travellers (along with people who are ill, pregnant or menstruating) are not obliged to fast, but you may find it difficult or impos-

A hearty dinner with Iranian hosts.
© Gayle Dickson

sible to buy food during the day, and you should make an effort to eat in private – either between cities or in your tent. As well as food, Muslims are obliged to abstain from tobacco, chewing gum and even water, which despite their best efforts, can lead to bad breath and bad tempers. You might want to cut people a bit more slack than you normally would.

Opening hours change during Ramadan – shops and restaurants will often close during the afternoon and sometimes open later at night – so you should take this into account when planning your meals, and especially if you're in need of bike parts or anything else you can't do without.

As a general rule, the more secular a country, the easier it will be for non-Muslims to get by during Ramadan. In Western Turkey you'll usually find a few cafés open during the day – in Iran, forget about it!

And of course, the best bit of Ramadan is iftar – when everyone comes together to break their fast at sunset. Travelling in Muslim countries, you can expect to be invited to a few of these celebrations, held at mosques or in family homes, and to enjoy the curious contrast of fasting and feasting that characterises this most holy of months.

walnuts). It's easy enough to find a bakery first thing in the morning – just follow the smell. Dried fruit and nuts are abundantly available, and Iranian grocery stores offer all sorts of curiosities for the hungry tourist: carrot jam, Persian baked beans and even a local take on the digestive biscuit. Alcohol is strictly illegal but that hasn't deterred a generation of home brewers and private distilleries and, if you'd rather stay on the right side of the law, the local beer substitutes (fizzy malted drinks, flavoured with everything from pineapple to chocolate) are tasty and refreshing.

The bazaar in Esfahan is a visual treat.

Camping is straightforward and asking permission from a landowner will often result in an invitation to spend the night in his house. If you're disinclined to sleep outside, it's possible to stay in mosques – along the main highways, they seem to fulfil much the same purpose as a motel, with dozens of families setting up camp among the rich Persian carpets and graceful arches. Roadside ambulance stations also seem happy to host cyclists.

The only place cyclists might have trouble with accommodation is Zahedan, where the police will insist on checking you into the heavily guarded Zahedan Tourist Inn (US$50 per night) for your own safety. But you're unlikely to visit here unless the security situation in Balochistan improves.

Challenges and inconveniences

If you have come from Turkey, the most immediate change you'll notice is that Iran uses a different script. It's worth familiarising yourself with the Arabic alphabet and numeral system, and road signs tend to be bilingual so are a handy way of practising your Farsi. Generally, you'll be surprised by how many people speak English – it's a popular language in Iran.

Although Iranian people are overwhelmingly reasonable and tolerant, their government is not. Cyclists should avoid, as much as possible, any contact with the police or the army. Taking photos of government buildings and military installations can result in, at best, a telling off; at worst, arrest and detention, which is no laughing matter.

UAE & OMAN

With Balochistan off-limits, one option for continuing across Asia after Iran is south to the United Arab Emirates and Oman.

Tired after a long winter and with fond memories of living in Muscat, we chose to cycle south through Iran and catch the boat across the Straits of Hormuz (notorious for goat smuggling). Despite locals seeming to know nothing about it, there is a regular ferry service between Iran (Bandar Abbas and Bandar Langeh) and the UAE (Dubai and Sharjah). We cycled to the port just outside Bandar Abbas, bought our tickets and wheeled our bikes straight onto a surprisingly well-equipped ferry.

The contrast between Iran – a poor country isolated by international sanctions – and the UAE – home of decadence and the world's super rich – is striking. Oman is different again: a much calmer country with an abundance of culture, history and wilderness.

We pedalled the 500km from Dubai to Muscat, Oman's capital. The roads in both countries are super-smooth and although the UAE has some monstrous highways, there are a growing number of bike lanes, including a fantastic stretch out in the Dubai Desert. Oman's coastal road is busy but there are quieter parallel roads right next to it. Alternatively, the inland route via Nizwa is both quiet and beautiful.

Both countries are Muslim but are well accustomed to expats. Cycling in shorts and T-shirt is fine but wear trousers and long sleeves off the bike. Winters are warm (30s), summers are hot (40s or 50s). Outside cities, wild camping is incredibly easy. There are miles of pristine beach, stunningly jagged mountains and you can't beat cycling past camels in the desert for novelty. The food is amazing too – fresh fish, fruit juices and hummus to die for.

At the time of writing, the only way to get to India from the Middle East is by plane, as tourists are not allowed to enter the country by boat. Thankfully, flights from both Muscat and the UAE are cheap and frequent. Similarly, flights to northern Pakistan can easily be picked up from both hubs, for those attempting the Karakoram Highway.

It may be sad to miss out on Balochistan, but cycling in the Middle East is far from second best. In fact, it is pretty close to paradise.

Laura Moss

An Omani desert fort. © Laura Moss

ROUTES

If you're planning on continuing east from Iran, your route will be dictated by your decisions regarding The Trans-Asia Conundrum, which centres on the impossibility of riding through Afghanistan, and the increasing difficulty of even circumnavigating it. Previous generations of overlanders would pass through Pakistan on their way to or from India, but recent geopolitical tensions, a few high-profile kidnappings and the tightening of visa restrictions meant this option was extremely difficult and inadvisable at the time of writing.

One alternative is to follow a more northern route, via Tabriz, polluted Teheran with its crazy traffic, and devout Mashhad (or skirt around the Caspian Sea), and cross into Turkmenistan, perhaps making a worthwhile detour south (by bike or bus) to witness the delights of Esfahan and Shiraz.

If the situation improves, riders heading to Pakistan will generally cross the country in a south-easterly direction, passing through the ancient and picturesque cities of Esfahan, Yazd and Bam before crossing the border at Zahedan. A growing number of cyclists are now riding to Bandar Abbas on the south coast, taking a boat to Oman or the UAE, and continuing to India by plane.

Pakistan

Emily Chappell

Pakistan is hard work. But as you'll know by now, being a bicycle traveller, from hard work come great rewards, and it's no coincidence that many trans-Asia cyclists name this supposedly 'failed state' as one of their top countries.

As a cyclist you'll see a very different Pakistan from that portrayed by the Western media, which tends to focus on the problems threatening to tear Pakistan apart rather than the pride and resourcefulness that persistently hold it together. A lot of the Pakistanis you'll meet will be friendly, outgoing and highly educated, well aware of the pre-conceptions foreigners bring to their country and determined to disprove them. As in Iran, you'll quickly develop a sense of safety, knowing that, if anything were to go wrong, all of these kind and generous people would rally round to help. However, travelling in Pakistan does hold genuine risks – although the vast majority of Pakistanis are friendly, they will be powerless to protect you from the one or two who aren't.

For those who make the decision to visit Pakistan, a world of wonders awaits. The country stretches from the Arabian Sea to the Himalaya, from the rippling golden deserts of Balochistan, via the green and pleasant plains of Punjab, all the way to the snowy peaks and Alpine meadows of Gilgit-Baltistan.

PRACTICALITIES

Visas

The most important thing to remember about a Pakistani visa is that you have to **apply for it in your home country**. This can be a pain for people meandering across Asia from Western Europe, as it means they have to get into Pakistan within six months of obtaining their visa, and is even more of a headache for those travelling the other way. A few end up flying home to apply; others (especially those with multiple passports) trust their precious documents to international couriers.

Being aware that circumstances may suddenly change is a good rule of thumb for all of Pakistan, and applies especially to visas, so always confirm the current rules and requirements before applying.

Terrain and seasons

Pay attention to the seasons in Pakistan – the country endures extremes of heat and cold that are not only uncomfortable but might make cycling impossible. Between May and September anywhere south of Gilgit will be almost unbearably hot, with temperatures regularly topping 45°C. The Asian monsoon sweeps over the country from late June till early October, often leading to widespread floods and turning roads into quagmires.

Further north, the roads may be blocked by snowdrifts or washed away by the landslides that occur during the spring thaw. The Khunjerab Pass, Pakistan's only border crossing into China, is closed from 31st December to 1st May (and may open late in particularly snowy years), and the similarly lofty Babusar Pass, which links the Kaghan and Indus Valleys between Naran and Chilas, isn't usually cleared until June at the earliest. However, although the mountain summers are relatively short, this region still provides a welcome escape from the furnace of the plains, as well as some of the most beautiful mountain scenery in the world.

Eating and sleeping

Pakistan is a carnivore's paradise – if you have the purse and the appetite, you'll be able to stuff yourself with rich, meaty kebabs and curries at every turn. Vegetarians will not starve but may find themselves having to search a little more assiduously for proper sustenance, and occasionally politely eating around the chunks of meat served up by an enthusiastic host.

Hungry cyclists will be able to fill up on spicy samosas and parathas at roadside food stalls and special mention should be given to the Hunza cuisine north of Gilgit. Lighter and less spicy than the curries of Punjab and Peshawar, Hunza cookery is full of fresh organic vegetables and makes extensive use of the local apricot crop in both sweet and savoury dishes.

Alcohol is mostly prohibited in Pakistan, though if you're willing to jump through a few bureaucratic hoops and supply written proof of your non-Muslim status it can be found. Behind closed doors, of course, it's often a different matter, and Pakistan keeps very quiet about the Murree Brewery, founded by the British in 1860 and still producing beer, whisky and gin in the heart of Rawalpindi. Otherwise, you'll find yourself drinking countless cups of hot sweet *chai* and, if you're lucky, you'll get to sample the fragrant Peshawari *kahwa* (green tea), gently spiced and served with honey and crushed almonds.

You'll never want for somewhere to sleep in Pakistan. Hotels and guesthouses are generally cheap enough that (at least if you stay on the beaten track) there's no need to camp, and it's very common for cyclists to be taken in by friendly locals – and then put in touch with cousins, colleagues and school friends who'll put you up further along the road.

Challenges and inconveniences

The most challenging *and* inconvenient aspect of travelling in Pakistan is the number of limitations placed, officially and unofficially, by letter of law and by act of God, on where you can go and how you are allowed to get there. Some frustrated cyclists will find themselves spending more time on buses and in police jeeps than they do riding their bikes. With every year that passes more of the country seems to be closed to foreigners, and sometimes the police who stop you at roadblocks seem even less sure of the rules than you .

One of Pakistan's biggest selling points – its friendliness – can also prove one of its greatest trials. In populous areas like Punjab the constant attention can be overwhelming, especially for solo riders, and for females it can be difficult to differentiate between friendliness and lechery – too much of the latter and you'll begin to distrust the former.

ROUTES

Classic Route: The Karakoram Highway

The Karakoram Highway (KKH), which links Islamabad to the Central Asian hub of Kashgar, is one of the world's great adventure cycling routes. It's not an easy road, by any means. Passing through the seismically unstable collision zone of the Eurasian and Indian tectonic plates, the route is frequently disrupted by landslides – one of which, in 2010, blocked the Hunza Valley north of Karimabad, submerging 20km of the KKH and creating the Attabad Lake which is now navigable only by boat.

Starting from Islamabad (or officially in Havelian, a day's ride north), the KKH first passes through barren Indus Kohistan, an area known for centuries for its hostility towards outsiders. Many cyclists choose to err on the side of caution, travelling through this area by bus and buying themselves time to enjoy the safer and more picturesque stretches of road north of Gilgit. Others turn right at Mansehra and make a detour through the Kaghan Valley – which is notably greener and more friendly than the Indus Valley – and over the 4170m Babusar Pass to rejoin the KKH at Chilas.

North of Gilgit the KKH's mountain scenery is at its most spectacular. Until Pakistan's tourist industry died off, this area was highly popular with

climbers, trekkers and backpackers, and you'll still find some lovely hotels, such as the Diran Guesthouse in Minapin and almost anywhere in Karimabad, which are generally cheap enough for even the most penurious cycle traveller.

The Chinese insist that cyclists take the bus for 120km between the Khunjerab border and Tashkurgan, but the Pakistani authorities have no problem with cyclists riding up to Khunjerab to

View from the KKH near Passu.

bag the pass, and then back to Sost to get on the bus – usually a round trip of 2-3 days. There are no more towns or guesthouses after Sost but cyclists are generally given a warm welcome at the police posts of Bar Khun and Koksil and there are plenty of places to camp.

In Pakistani cities, Citibank and Standard Chartered ATMs are best for withdrawing cash, but note on the KKH you're unlikely to find a usable ATM anywhere north of Islamabad.

Other routes

Other popular cycling routes in Pakistan are now somewhat restricted by the region's shifting geopolitical tensions. Cyclists have long been prohibited from riding the Khyber Pass, and opportunities to continue your journey safely in Afghanistan are limited to the point of being non-

The chief Pakistani cheerleader at Wagah.

existent. Any bikers who manage to enter from Iran, via Balochistan, will almost certainly be obliged to travel by vehicle, usually with an armed escort (see box below), often as far as Multan.

There are a few good days' cycling to be had along the colourful Grand Trunk Road between Lahore and Rawalpindi, and *grimpeurs* will enjoy the blistering climb from Islamabad up to the hill station of Murree, with cool green pine forests and incongruous colonial architecture to reward you at the top.

It is still possible to cross into India by road – the cities of Lahore and Amritsar lie only 50km apart, separated by the Wagah border crossing. This hosts a daily Python-esque flag-lowering ceremony at 16:00, with turbaned and moustachioed soldiers from both sides high-kicking and goose-stepping in synchronisation, cheered on by rival stadia full of Indian and Pakistani daytrippers.

PART 4 – ROUTES – ASIA

SHOULD I GO?

A decision to tour in Pakistan should not be taken lightly. Whilst the vast majority of foreigners who travel, live and work in the country return home with happy memories, there are regular abductions and murders and cyclists have been specifically targeted in the past. Every traveller needs to weigh up the risks for themselves, thinking not only of their own safety but also that of the people among whom they will be living and travelling, who may be injured in attempting to protect them. Regions such as Balochistan and Peshawar are known to carry greater risks for foreign travellers but attacks have occurred in supposedly 'safe' areas, such as Islamabad and at the base camp of Nanga Parbat. The Foreign and Commonwealth Office website is a good place to start. Travellers' forums and local newspapers and websites also carry detailed and up-to-the-minute reports about events on the ground. Local contacts are invaluable, especially those in the travel industry, the military or the diplomatic service. Be aware that risk levels may vary considerably from place to place and even from day to day.

PART 4 – ROUTES – ASIA

India

Neil Pike

Incredible India! Colourful, energetic, exotic and fascinating, but also noisy, draining and exasperating, India can be one of the most challenging and rewarding countries to take on by bike. It's also one you're unlikely to forget for a long while – every day springs a new and wonderful surprise – so arrive with an open mind, a willingness to be sociable and forego privacy, and a good deal of patience; it may occasionally be tested.

Geography, population and bureaucracy make it a place where planning is really rewarded to ensure your tour avoids the Himalayan snows, those crazily busy stretches of road, or the heavily populated areas where it's difficult to get a moment's peace. This done, you'll be able to make the most of India's myriad of rewards for adventurous tourers: English is a national language so you can usually find someone to chat to in any region, particularly in the Himalaya and the south; local people tend to be curious, friendly and eager to assist any way they can; tasty food and street snacks are easy to find and there's ample opportunity to explore the varied terrain from quiet back roads which have more animal than vehicular traffic.

PRACTICALITIES

Bureaucratic fun

India's legendary officialdom is finally being simplified – for visas anyhow. Currently tourist visas must still be obtained in advance but the process is online and six-month visas are generally attainable – Brits should look at ⬛ in.vfsglobal.co.uk. At the time of writing, those coming to India from South-East Asia were finding six-month visas easier to get in Vientiane, Laos than in Bangkok.

In border areas with Pakistan and China, filling out forms so that your information can be copied into a ledger to be piled into a corner and never glanced at again is still the norm. Many of the areas closest to these disputed borders are not open to tourists, while for slightly less sensitive regions such as the Nubra Valley, Spiti and Sikkim, Inner Line Permits can be obtained locally in a day or two. Excitingly, it recently became possible to travel overland from Thailand to north-east India via Myanmar. Making this journey in the opposite direction is still a bureaucratic headache, but rules change fast so keep your ear to the ground.

Getting directions near Rishikesh, India. © Yoko Kai

Where and when to go

More a continent than a country, the diversity is such that you can experience and see almost anything without leaving India's borders; but some areas are far more bike-tourer friendly than others. Most popular are the Himalayan areas of Ladakh, Himachal Pradesh, Uttarakhand and Sikkim in the north for those seeking world-class mountainscapes and hilly riding; the south offers a wealth of ancient cultures, magnificent temples, sandy beaches and mouthwatering cuisine; ride through the deserts of Rajasthan in the west for majestic forts and palaces.

The northern plains in Uttar Pradesh and Bihar are home to many famous sites, like the Taj Mahal, Bodh Gaya, and the pilgrimage centre of Varanasi, but few riders enjoy cycling through these densely populated states with all the hassles of constant attention and heavy traffic – best to stick to the quieter and more relaxing areas described below.

At all times of year there is somewhere good to be riding on the Indian subcontinent. The high altitude areas of Ladakh, and the road through Spiti in Himachal Pradesh are only accessible in the summer, once the snows have melted or been cleared from the passes – generally June to mid-September. These areas are in the rain shadow and are not normally affected by the monsoon which sweeps across the rest of the country at this time, bringing daily rains and high humidity to add to the scorching temperatures.

After the monsoon can be an excellent time to ride in the Himalayan foothills, which tend to have their clearest weather from October to December, though in severe monsoon seasons roads will still be in the process of being patched up after landslides. In fact, after the rains end in September or October, nearly the entire country enjoys very sunny, dry and cool weather which is perfect for touring until the hot weather begins to arrive in February. The pre-monsoon period from March to June sees the plains roast in high temperatures; this is another time to head to those foothills and certainly avoid Rajasthan which will be unbearably hot at this time.

Eating and sleeping

Food hygiene standards might not be what you're used to back home, and with those ubiquitous tempting tasty eats at basic restaurants and *dhabas* (roadside food stalls) most people get the runs at some stage. Treating water is essential.

Except in the remote mountain areas in the north, there's little need to camp; in fact you will probably want to avoid it in most places as accommodation is cheap and plentiful, while it is a mission finding a quiet spot where your little tent won't be discovered. Costs are some of the lowest in the world, meaning you can stay in an en-suite room with 10 TV cricket channels to laze in front of for less than you'd pay at a basic European campground.

Delicious paratha and curd, from a roadside dhaba.

TRIP REPORT
HIMALAYA – INDIA & NEPAL

Name	Neil & Harriet Pike
Nationality	British
Year of birth	1979/1983
Occupation	Guidebook author / Patagonia travel consultant
Other bike travels	Istanbul-Oxford, Andes, Oxford-Scotland, Andes again
This trip	Himalaya – India and Nepal
Trip duration	3 months
Number in group	2
Total distance	4000km
Cost of trip	About US$12 pppd in country.

Longest day	112km – in the Uttarakhand hills. Ended after dark with a friendly guy on a scooter lighting our way – he led us to his family home to stay the night.
Best day	Making it up to the Kaksang La in Ladakh at the second attempt.
Worst day	Climbing to Manma on the Karnali Highway, West Nepal. Drive chain suffering in the dust and mud, hot temperatures, couldn't get any peace.
Favourite ride	Bikepacking the Hindustan-Tibet Byway in Kinnaur – on an old road far above the main highway.
Biggest headache	Restricted military areas and getting turned back at checkpoints.
Biggest mistake	Hoping we'd be able to cycle routes we'd found on Google Earth near the Chinese border.
Pleasant surprise	Meeting Prakash, an Indian cyclist, who helped us find the Old Hindustan-Tibet Byway.
Illnesses during trip	Nothing serious

Bike model	Surly Long Haul Truckers
Modifications	Fitted flat bars with Ergon Grips, replaced all worn out moving parts.
Wish you'd fitted	Electric feet warmers.
Tyres used	Schwalbe Marathon Extremes 2.0"
Punctures	None – love these tyres!
Bike problems	Headset bearings went – mechanic in Leh managed to bodge it well enough to last the rest of the tour.
Accidents	None, though nearly hit by rockfall.
Same bike again?	No – need something more off-roady
Any advice?	Whittling down your gear to the essentials opens up a whole new world of rideable roads.
Road philosophy	Take the quiet road… and some trekking kit to climb some hills.
What do you daydream about in the saddle?	Where that road on the other side of the valley goes…

Touring tips

With the variety and differing velocities of road users, from the buffalo-drawn cart to speeding 4x4s, a mirror is an essential inclusion on your packing list. If you go for one attached to your handlebars rather than your helmet, it'll also be appreciated by local children, who'll have one more bike gadget to fiddle with when you pull up for a rest.

Internet connections are generally good and with plenty of wi-fi you shouldn't have trouble staying in contact with the folks back home. 3G also tends to be good – though there is none in Ladakh and the rest of Jammu and Kashmir, where use of mobile phones is further complicated by needing to buy a region-specific SIM card.

Female cyclists often find themselves receiving unwanted attention from young Indian men. Even travelling with a male partner doesn't seem to lower the number of stares and requests for 'One snap' or to become Facebook friends, so be prepared to bat away unwelcome advances.

More than a third of the world's rabies deaths occur in India, so don't take any risks if you're scratched or bitten – get yourself to a clinic for some post-bite shots (see p31).

SOME ROUTES

Traversing the northern foothills

After the goose-stepping and silly stares at the Wagah border crossing, those entering from Pakistan will probably soon notice that it's all a bit more frenetic on the India side. A visit to the Golden Temple in Amritsar is a memorable experience, before the choice between riding south for Rajasthan (see below) or making your way into the Himalayan foothills of Himachal Pradesh and Uttarakhand.

A month or more rollercoasting through pine forest, crossing great tributaries of the Ganges and hanging out in hill stations with panoramic views, is time well spent – from Dalhousie in the west, through McLeod Ganj, Shimla and Gwaldam to Munsyari near the Nepal border. It's a perfect way to get an 'India-light' experience – wholesome food, friendly and inquisitive villagers, quiet roads through impressive landscapes, but enough action in towns for you to know you're on the subcontinent. The road through Munsyari is a high-

light but note there are no border crossings for foreigners in the hills – you can't head into Tibet, and to enter Nepal you must descend to the plains and Banbasa.

Funnelled out the eastern side of Nepal at Kakarvitta, you'll find yourself in West Bengal, where hanging a left will zone in on Darjeeling for some tea, cakes and Kangchenjunga views. Continuing northwards brings you to Sikkim, which only officially became part of India in 1975. This tiny state

Early morning in the hills of Uttarakhand.

PART 4 – ROUTES – ASIA

with a majority Nepali population is wedged between Nepal, Bhutan and Tibet, and is something of a dead end, as the only way out by land is back into West Bengal unless you can afford the vast expense of a visa for Bhutan. With an overwhelmingly Buddhist feel, famous gompas and a landscape studded with chortens it makes for a good tour – you'll need an Inner Line Permit, and be prepared for many steep climbs. The region is best avoided when being hammered by the monsoon. Laura Stone's *Himalaya by Bike*, also published by Trailblazer, is an invaluable guide to this state.

The North-East, and to Myanmar
Mike Roy

It's the same country, but another world. One of the most ethnically and linguistically diverse regions left on the planet, northeast India's 'Seven Sister' states are home to hundreds of different tribal peoples. Two generations ago, some of them still practised headhunting; now, children listen to Korean pop on their smartphones and speak perfect English thanks to the educational infrastructure built up by Christian missionaries. Separatist tensions and occasional militancy still affect the area, but travel restrictions have been lifted in all states except Arunachal Pradesh, so the area is open to roamers – provided you don't mind rough roads and endless mountains.

It's not exactly the land before time that a Google images search might lead you to expect. If you're really looking for a window into the past, you'd do well to avoid the capitals, stick to the dirt roads, and try to time your journey around the major festivals, for which villagers break out their traditional outfits (think loincloths and feather headdresses) and come together to celebrate and preserve all that culture that might vanish any day now. Even if you miss these, the region still differs enough from the rest of India to make for immensely interesting riding, and the rarity of cyclists makes it all the more rewarding.

Crossing the border from Tamu in Myanmar to Moreh in India's Manipur province isn't too difficult as long as you procure the necessary permits in advance in Yangon; crossing in the other direction is much trickier (see p218).

Ladakh, Spiti and Kinnaur
with Laura Stone

Widely regarded as one of the best bike touring regions in the world, Ladakh has it all if you enjoy climbing 5000m+ passes on a loaded bike. It has Tibetan Buddhist culture without the weight of oppression and Indian food without the heat – temperature heat, that is. And it's paved, to a degree. Spiti and Kinnaur are a bit more prone to landslides and hence the surfaces there are a bit rougher. Without breaks, you could ride through Ladakh, Spiti and Kinnaur in about a month, but a more sensible proposition if you don't have teachers' holidays is to do the classic Manali-Leh ride in around a three-week vacation, giving you time to acclimatise and some days in Leh at the end of the ride.

What has kept Ladakh free from the rampant development seen in much of India is the difficulty in getting there – it's snowed in for nine months of the year. Many riders have to make a special trip to get there as it's hard to line up the timing with a long ride through the region. It's easier to hit Ladakh in summer and then go to Pakistan for the KKH than it is to arrive late in the season for Ladakh and risk being cut off by early winter snows and forced to fly out. Inner Line Permits are needed if you go for some side trips such as to the Nubra Valley or Pangong Tso – an ILP is easily obtained in Manali or Leh.

If your tour focuses on this region, it's possible to travel the major routes without camping gear thanks to a good traveller infrastructure, though sometimes you may have to rough it at roadside truck stops known as

Parachute tents provide hot meals, shelter and accommodation along the Manali-Leh road. © Chris Scott

dhabas (bring a sleeping bag, mat and ear plugs for a good night's sleep). But camping enables you to get away from the road and enjoy sleeping out under star-studded skies. In summer, camping is the way to go, but in autumn you will be glad to huddle round a stove in a parachute tent.

Classic Route: Manali to Leh

Manali can be reached by bus from Delhi, or by riding from the Raj-era summer capital Shimla, a worthwhile tourist destination in itself. Only 500km of road separates Manali and Leh but there are two 5000m passes and the road climbs 2000m out of Manali to the Rohtang La in just 51km, so it pays to get fit before starting and acclimatise as best you can. Once over Rohtang La you can camp at around 3000m but the road heads quickly up to more dangerous altitudes, so take it easy and enjoy the culture and the views along the way. The second pass, Baralacha La, is at 4920m so you will be panting at the top and not much more comfortable camping near the tented camps of Sarchu at 4400m on the other side. The highest pass on the Manali-Leh run is Taglang La, which at 5330m is one of the highest paved (well, mostly) roads in the world.

Leh is another travellers' haven – good food, including spirited attempts at German bakeries, and cosy guesthouses await when you finally roll into town. It's a great place to put a bit of weight back on, take side trips to see monasteries, or just sit and take it all in.

North of Leh

A fantastic loop ride of around five days which can be undertaken from Leh is to head north towards the Nubra Valley. First, cross the Khardung La, which though not quite as high as the famous 'World's Highest Motorable Road – 18380ft (5602m)' sign at the top would have you believe, is still one of the world's

The sun! The sun! Things start to look up on the descent from Wari La.

THE WORLD'S HIGHEST MOTORABLE ROAD (ISN'T IT?!)

There's a roaring trade in Khardung La memorabilia done in Leh – hats and shell-suits proudly emblazoned with 'WHMR!' – and there's no denying it's a fun ride up from town. Sadly though, the calculators got their calculations wrong – it'd be so much easier if the highest rideable road in the world really was that accessible. On a 2012 tour, our GPS reading agreed with what others had already measured: that the 5602m sign should prob-ably be repainted with '5360m'. If you're looking for higher roads, they exist in Tibet (good luck getting to them), and others can be reached legally in the Andes, but there are a few in Ladakh too. Get your hands on an Inner Line Permit and head to Pangong Lake via the Chang La, which is probably slightly higher than the Khardung La; or to be sure of getting higher, climb to the Kaksang La, which at around 5430m, certainly is.

highest. When you reach the Shyok River, head east, and return back to the Indus Valley and Leh via the steep Wari La.

Alternatively, if you have a bit more time and would prefer to explore the Shyok and Nubra valleys further, you can head west upon reaching the Shyok River. Continuing along the Shyok is an adventurous ride – the most wester-ly villages are Muslim and you are allowed as far as Tyakshi, only 8km from Pakistan, before having to backtrack. If you branch off further north into the Nubra Valley, your ILP will give you access as far as Hargam – after this the military road continues on towards the Siachen Glacier, which is very much off limits.

To Srinagar or Zanskar

Leh is around halfway between Manali and Srinagar. If you are coming back to Leh after a ride down to Srinagar, consider leaving your camping gear in Leh as there is sufficient accommodation en route and camping is not recom-mended after Kargil. Kargil gives access to some much more ambitious riding than the main highway. To the south lies the region of Zanskar, reached by unpaved and rough roads. Road-building works are slowly pushing through to Padum in Zanskar from both the north and the south (see box opposite), but for now it's still relatively remote. The glacier views near Penzi La – the high-est point on the Kargil to Padum road – are some of the best in the Indian Himalaya.

Srinagar has lost its lustre since the outbreak of separatist and insurgent violence over the past few decades but the natural beauty is still there and the famous houseboats await and are as hungry as ever for business. Srinagar has an airport, though the nearest railhead is in Jammu, 293km away on a busy road. From Jammu it's only 219km to Amritsar and the Pakistani border.

Spiti and Kinnaur

The valleys of Spiti and Kinnaur can make a fantastic three-week circuit ride from Manali, or a horseshoe ride of around a fortnight from Shimla up to Manali. The passes are a touch lower than on the road to Leh but no easier, save for the lower altitude, and no less spectacular. Spiti is Tibetan Buddhist and the terrain is dry and exposed, whereas Kinnaur, to the south, is Hindu and the route follows the Sutlej River (which rises near Mt Kailash in Tibet), with dramatic tight valleys which funnel winds – mostly from the west. Because of this, it's probably better to go clockwise and have tailwinds on the very rough roads of Spiti and ride into the wind on the better roads of Kinnaur. Although the road is not too steep in the south, the towns of Kinnaur are all well above the river, and as there are virtually no wild camping spots in the narrow valley, be prepared for a climb at the end of most days. Kinnaur is definitely Indian –

Spiti is nearly all downhill when ridden north to south. © Stephen Lord

expect noise, traffic, road works, colourfully-dressed women and flies, even at 2000m.

Shimla makes a great start or end to the ride. It's the old summer capital of the British Raj and there are enough buildings from that era around the famous Mall, where memsahibs would stroll, to bring back a sense of it, though it's now smoky, noisy and overrun with monkeys. There are top-notch places to eat and stay as well as a steam train to Khalka from where fast trains run to Delhi.

The route from Spiti to Kinnaur runs very close to the Line of Control, ie the de facto border with China, and you need an Inner Line Permit, best obtained on the way as you pass through the towns of Kaza or Recong Peo, or in Manali or Shimla.

Rajasthan
Bill Weir

Rajasthan is the most romantic part of India and the state to ride in if you like tales of chivalry, clambering up impregnable hilltop forts, and admiring grandiose palaces and mansions. Close to New Delhi, Rajasthan's size means you could easily spend months looping around to all the sights. Jaipur is the capital with lots of grand buildings and streets encumbered with heavy and chaotic traffic. Wildlife parks in Rajasthan's east are worth seeking out if you'd like to see birds and maybe a tiger. Few travellers make it to the Shekhawati region in the north, but it's full of atmospheric little towns with

---

ZANSKAR

The Buddhist kingdom of Zanskar is tricky for bikers to reach. It's serviced by a single, dead-end road completed in the late '70s, although it still sports a rudimentary surface. This keeps motor traffic to a minimum, and at nil in the snowed-up winter months. To avoid backtracking the way you came in means walking out, with your bike on a horse if you wish, either south towards Keylong on the Manali to Leh Highway, or north towards the Indus Valley. But those bulldozers are coming, and in future years it may be possible to ride a rollercoaster loop through Zanskar, which will undoubtedly become an instant cycle-touring classic.

ornate mansions (*havelis*). Pushkar, near the centre, is famed for its sacred lake and temple; try to visit during the amazing Camel Fair (usually in November) when you'll see camels stretching to the horizon in every direction, as well as ongoing tribal life, and varied entertainment. Way out west, you'll get a thrill on seeing remote Jaisalmer Fort; this is also a good place for camel treks or cycling out to Sam to commune with giant sand dunes. Down south, Udaipur's lake and palaces will beguile you.

TAKING YOUR BICYCLE ON AN INDIAN TRAIN

You can cover vast distances by train fairly comfortably and even in luxury for a good price. You'll need your train ticket to book the bicycle as luggage, and the bicycle must go in a baggage van; there's a small fee and quite a bit of paperwork hassle, so it's a good idea to do this four hours or so before your departure. Hang on to receipts – you may need them to exit the station, as security is generally pretty tight. Not all trains have a baggage van and not all stops have baggage service, so check with the station's parcel office for advice – they are invariably more helpful to foreigners. It's best to take a train from the originating point to the terminus as your bicycle can go in a sealed van that's not opened until the terminus; this will be more secure and reduce the chance of damage. Transporting bikes between major cities on important fast trains is also not advised as the luggage vans are jammed to the maximum with freight and your bike is more likely to get damaged.

How the bicycle is packed will likely be left up to you but they prefer it partly covered to protect against scratches; then just wheel the bicycle up to the parcel office and check it in. A parcel-wrapping service may be available nearby that will use padding and jute bags. Try to arrange to have the bicycle travel on the same train as you but don't fret if the bicycle takes longer; sometimes there's a delay in opening a sealed baggage car or the bicycle may go on a later train and arrive days later. On arrival there's more paperwork; check baggage cars for your bicycle and, if not there, head for the Parcel Office – the bicycle may already be there. If you're not going to the final stop and the bike isn't in a sealed car, you may want to follow it onto the train so you know exactly where it will be when you get off. Head straight for the luggage van and make sure it comes off at your stop.

Local trains at non-peak hours are a good option for getting out of large cities such as Delhi and Mumbai without being bothered by traffic. As with other services, you pay a fee for the bicycle and then take it in the luggage compartment.

Don't forget buses for where the train doesn't run or when you're in a hurry, as they leave all the time and there's no paperwork needed, just a small fee and tips for the lads who will put the bike on top of, or under, the bus. Go for the deluxe 2x2 buses if possible as they are more comfortable and usually have enough interior baggage space for your bicycle. Very easy, but expect to pay a baggage fee. Taking a bike by air can also be straightforward but check airline companies' allowances and bike rules before buying a ticket.

Bill Weir

© Cass Gilbert

The South

For culture, ancient cities, mountain scenery and palm-fringed beaches, consider a ride in the southern states of Kerala, Tamil Nadu, Andhra Pradesh and Karnataka. All sorts of loops are possible; it just depends on your time and interests. The coastal plains have easy riding past beaches and many temples, but it's worth swinging into the mountains for the views, tea plantations and wildlife parks. Hindu religion remains strong in this region, as its relative isolation in ancient times prevented Muslim invaders from making major inroads. Kerala has a distinctive language and culture, along with some of India's best beaches. Canoes and motorboats will take you into the backwaters if you'd like time off the bike. The great temple cities in Tamil Nadu such as Madurai and Chidambaram have amazing interior stonework and entrancing ceremonies. Also in Tamil Nadu, Kanyakumari at India's extreme southern tip and Rameswaram on an island 'stepping stone' to Sri Lanka have major temples with an end-of-the-world feeling.

Nepal

Neil Pike

With the world's highest peaks, easy entry, low costs and fascinating Buddhist and Hindu cultures, on initial thought Nepal seems like a dream adventure cycle-touring destination. Standing in the way is the fact it doesn't have a surfeit of roads; the vertical terrain and annual monsoon pounding mean few rideable tracks have made it deep into the Himalaya here and those that have tend to sport the kind of challenging surface that'd have a Mars rover salivating. Added to this, discoveries of high altitude routes that can be ridden as a loop, rather than a 'there-and-back', are about as rare as sightings of rollerblading Yetis taking pet snow leopards for an evening stroll; we're not saying they don't happen, just probably not to you.

There are good rides, with great (particularly dirt-road) potential in the foothills between the lowland terai plains and the high mountains, but you have to search to find them. For a comfortable stay, avoid the heat of pre-monsoon season and the June to September monsoon itself when you're less likely to see a mountain than you are to be disrupted by landslides and road closures.

PRACTICALITIES

Arriving and travelling

Unless you come in on a guided tour from Tibet, land entry will be from India. As the pester-index plummets, you'll experience that 'aaaand relax' feeling and soon find yourself on the paved Mahendra Highway which crosses the terai east-west. This isn't the Nepal of adventure magazines – it's well populated and flat – but offers an enjoyable and more hassle-free option for continuing your trans-continental pilgrimage east than parallel routes south of the border. There's also the chance for a detour to Lord Buddha's birthplace at Lumbini.

Young shopkeeper, Nepal.

Touring tips

The tourist magnets of Kathmandu and Pokhara lie in the foothills north of this artery – both are places to stock up on camping gear and clothing with an array of international brands, local fakes and, pleasingly, an increasing number of decent quality local makes. Find Sonam at Dawn 'til Dusk in KTM for mountain bike parts and the low-down on local rides.

The pollution in the capital has to be seen (literally) and choked on to be believed, so unless you're waiting around for visas it makes sense to look after those lungs and hang out at Lakeside in Pokhara.

It also pays to count notes taken out of ATMs – it's the only country we've ever had issues with amounts being dispensed, and the bank error is never in your favour.

Fuel tends to be dirty and block multi-fuel stoves but gas canisters are found in tourist places and, anyway, with energy-loaded *dal bhat* power and cheap, basic accommodation available at every turn, few tourers find the need to cook or camp very often.

SOME ROUTE IDEAS

The volume of traffic on the main KTM-Pokhara highway precludes agreeable or safe cycling. Yep, plenty of people have done it, but it means relying on every bus driver diverting his attention from the Van Damme film blaring above him to the road for just long enough to spot you, and putting faith in the active ingredients of local Red Bull imitations to keep him awake if he's on the 20-hour shift from Birendranagar.

Fortunately there are serene dirt road options for linking the two cities further north, taking around five days and with distant Annapurna, Ganesh Himal and Langtang views. Travel light as there's loads of climbing and the usual dirt-surface gnarlyness.

If you're not averse to *a lot* of pushing, try tackling the Annapurna Circuit

Taking a noodle break on the road to Kathmandu.

trekking route – now jeep tracks have been forced up the valleys to the east and west of the massif, hardy bikepackers can complete the circumpedalation, staying in lodges the whole way to avoid carrying much gear. Suspension forks rather than a rigid touring bike are much better suited to this hike-a-bike route. After dipping their pedals into the country, many cyclists on heavy touring bikes choose to go off exploring on foot in order to really get in amongst the 8000ers.

The Caucasus

The fascinating Caucasus is a cradle of human civilisation. Arguably the historical location of the Biblical Garden of Eden, nowhere in the world has so much history, scenic variety, passion and political complexity crammed into such a tiny area. Since the collapse of the USSR in 1991 there are officially three independent countries in the south Caucasus: Georgia and Armenia are both ancient, Christian nations recovering from years of turmoil, while Azerbaijan is a low-key Islamic-Turkic nation whose capital Baku is undergoing a remarkable oil boom.

Since Armenia and Azerbaijan fought an unresolved war in the 1990s the borders between their territories have been firmly closed. The Armenian puppet state of Nagorno-Karabakh still occupies over 15% of Azerbaijan's land and is a de-facto country of its own. Landmines and ruined cities fill the no-man's land between Armenia/Nagorno-Karabakh and Azerbaijan so there's no earthly way to cycle across the borders whatever a map may suggest. You can pick up NK visas in Yerevan, but think carefully before you do that: visiting NK is classified as making an illegal entry to Azerbaijan and consequently you would be criminally liable should you later visit Baku.

For several years the borders between Russia and the South Caucasus republics have been closed to foreigners. As of 2014, however, foreigners with suitable visas have been allowed to cross between Azerbaijan and Russia, but you'll need to research the latest if you're considering going this route by bike. Russia and Georgia fought a summer war of 2008 which resulted in Russia recognising the independence of South Ossetia and Abkhazia, both of which had broken away from Georgia in the early 1990s. Unlike NK with Azerbaijan, visiting Abkhazia from Georgia is possible with an Abkhaz visa, and continuing into Russia would be a very adventurous choice – research locally for the current paperwork situation. Crossing from Russia to Georgia via Abkhazia is not allowed.

GEORGIA
Glorious Georgia, with its fabulous castles, Caucasian mountain tower villages, superb food and passion for wine (that many claim actually originated in Georgia 5000 years ago) is the obvious starting point when cycling east from Turkey. Visas are no longer required for most western nationals, there are lots of hostels in bigger towns and rural homestays can be a great way to experience the country.

Turkey to Tbilisi
There are two main routes from Turkey to Tbilisi, Georgia's delightful capital. The main route from Trabzon via Sarp takes you through Batumi, the surreal sub-tropical 'Las Vegas' of Georgia as well as historic Kutaisi whose airport is

The Mt'k'vari River in Tbilisi.

a handy option for off-beat budget flights. An alternative option that's also paved and much less heavily trafficked runs from the little alpine town of Posof via Akhaltsikhe whose hilltop fortress complex has recently been splendidly restored. On this route be sure to visit the Vardzia cave churches, the famous little spa town of Borjomi and Gori, where a museum remembers the town's (in)famous son Stalin. Tbilisi itself is one of the most appealing cities in Eastern Europe and well worth a few days' exploration. There are now countless hostels dotted throughout the old city with more around Marjanishvili metro.

Tbilisi to Azerbaijan

Crossing from Georgia to Azerbaijan is straightforward, though you'll need an Azerbaijani visa in advance. The main road goes from Tbilisi to Ganja via Krasny Most (Red Bridge) but the scenery is somewhat desolate and you'll end up in Azerbaijan's dreary central steppe (treeless plains).

FOUR REASONS TO TOUR IN GEORGIA

The people
The hospitality is astounding: we were invited to dozens of picnics, stayed with various families and were handed peaches and watermelon by the kilo on a daily basis. We really appreciated the openness and hospitality, and in Georgia you are sure to see a smiling face every day of your trip.

The camping
It's easy and safe to camp almost everywhere. There are plenty of rivers throughout the country and during our two months there we were able to swim nearly every sin-gle evening. The wonderful picnic culture means you will pass fire pits and free 'camping spots' daily, and since the locals are so friendly, you'll certainly be invited to join in picnics once you stop!

The wine
The sheer amount of wine Georgians consume may be overwhelming, but it's a 'must try' since it's nearly always homemade. The whole intricate drinking culture, involving special toasts before you down the whole cup in one go, is fascinating to see and partake in. As there are vineyards around every corner, you can also expect to eat more grapes than you could dream of if you go during September and October.

The mountains
They might not be as tall as the Himalaya, but the mountains in Georgia are peaceful and beautiful, especially in the hard-to-reach area of Omalo and in the more famous region of Mestia. There are many small dirt roads for the adventurous, as well as a nicely paved path to Kazbegi for those who want a more relaxing ride.

Shirine Taylor

Pushing up the steep road to Omalo.
© Kevin Dugan

Far nicer is to start off towards Georgia's wine-paradise region of Kakheti, and there are two main ways to do this. One crosses a mostly rural area of low wooded mountains via Gombori to attractive Telavi. The other is somewhat busier and passes close to Sighnaghi, a charming little hill town resort ringed by token fortress walls.

Whether you go via Telavi or Sighnaghi, you'll cross into Azerbaijan near Lagodekhi which has homestay-guesthouses and is a great place to spend a day hiking a network of well-marked National Park trails. The low-key border crossing is a few kilometres further and from there the road via Balakan and Sheki is beautiful and very varied for most of the way to Baku.

AZERBAIJAN

As you cross Azerbaijan the landscapes evolve from thick deciduous forests via rolling grasslands to deserts outside the cosmopolitan capital Baku. Curving round a bay on the Caspian Sea, Baku has many splendid century-old buildings and a UNESCO-listed walled old city. With a plethora of expat bars and Anglo-Irish pubs, it makes a great place to recharge the batteries if you're flush with cash (US$6 for a cappuccino!) but Azerbaijan is nowhere near as well set up for travellers as Georgia, and Baku prices are on average at least double those in Tbilisi.

You're likely to find fellow cyclists discussing the Caspian Ferry conundrum (see p171) if you stay at one of Baku's two small, central hostels (Caspian and Baku Old City). Neither are much more than local apartments turned into bunk rooms and prices seem high for what you get, so cyclists often seek out Warm Showers hosts (🖳 warmshowers.org).

Wherever you stay in Azerbaijan, a big issue is ensuring that you register your visa within three days of arrival. Most hotels will do it for you but if you're camping or staying in a homestay, you will need to get a local to help you whether by organising things through a local post office or by using the website 🖳 migration.gov.az – a major fiddle requiring the downloading, printing, scanning and uploading of numerous documents including a host's ID card.

Crossing Azerbaijan

The obvious cross-country route between Balakan and Baku is magnificently varied and well asphalted yet graciously quiet west of Qabala. You'll follow the base of Azerbaijan's stunning high Caucasus foothills on oak-lined avenues and there are appealing side trips, most notably to Sheki where there's a delightful old town, a renovated khan's palace and a sensibly-priced hotel in a superbly atmospheric old caravanserai.

Heading east

Azerbaijan-Russia land borders remain uncertain and little tested and heading north the only road route passes through potentially dangerous areas of Dagestan. You have two other main options from Baku. The best choice is to cycle south into Iran along an attractive but often thunderously busy and very rainy route through Iran's lush, rice-growing Caspian provinces. Visas for Iran are hard to arrange in Baku so it's better to come prepared.

The alternative is taking one of the 'floating vomitorium' ferries across the Caspian – a good proportion of cyclists get stranded waiting for these in Baku for days or even weeks. Whether from menacing Aktau or surreal Turkmenbashi, cycling onwards across Central Asia is not too visually exciting: there's endless dull steppe or the raging Karakum Desert to cross. However, both cities are railheads so you could zip across to more appealing parts of Central Asia fairly conveniently if you are not fixated on a punishing long-distance slog. In 2014, Kazakhstan decided to suspend visa requirements for many western nationalities (for stays of up to 15 days) so for now the Aktau route is bureaucratically the simpler of the two ferry routes, particularly as Turkmen visas are a severe pain to arrange in Baku where the consulate is open only two hours twice a week and is a mayhem of pleading crowds getting little joy.

Note that Azerbaijan is building a vast new seaport complex at Alat, over 50km south of Baku. At present there's a confusing situation where some ferries already use that facility, while others depart from Baku city. Do double-check.

ARMENIA
Tom Allen

Armenia is sometimes perceived as an unnecessarily mountainous alternative to Azerbaijan when it comes to getting from Georgia to Iran but it's actually a worthy cycling destination in its own right. Visas on arrival for most nationalities, stunning mountain landscapes, numerous scenic detours, a rich and tumultuous national heritage, and some of the best-preserved Soviet architecture around are all reasons you might choose to pay this little Caucasian republic a visit.

Routes through the country are more varied in the north, with multiple crossing points from Georgia and several options from there onwards. Maps indicate the beautiful road via Noyemberyan crosses Azeri territory, but with the border conflict a stalemate for decades it's rarely a problem to travel this route, though you'd be well advised not to venture into no-man's-land. The land borders between Armenia and both Azerbaijan and Turkey remain firmly shut, so overland routes are possible between Georgia and Iran only.

Up-and-coming Yerevan is worth a visit; the Genocide Museum sheds light on the country's historical woes. As well as possessing a small handful of bike shops and mechanics, it's also a reliable pick-up point for Iranian visas. If you don't want to lose an entire kilometre in altitude, you can bypass the city on a scenic route via the eastern shore of Lake Sevan and maybe spot an old Silk Road caravanserai or two on the way over from Martuni to Yeghegnadzor.

The route south to the Iranian border is fairly non-negotiable; only one through-route crosses this formidable territory. It's shared with the trickle of goods traffic to and from Iran as well as bus services between Yerevan and Tabriz/Tehran, so there are hitching opportunities if the climbs get too much. Expect to tackle five extremely long and challenging mountain passes, the biggest of which is a non-stop ascent from 700m to over 2500m in altitude.

Detours are usually worth taking. The minor roads are often in a state of disrepair but they're much quieter, and as ever it's here that the memorable and unexpected of Armenia is to be found: lush mountainside forests, naturally-carbonated mineral water springs and thermal baths, ancient monasteries perched on the most unlikely of precipices, and a rural welcome as warm as any you'll find in the Middle East.

Off-road in the Khosrov reserve near Yerevan. © Andrew Welch

If you've time, a side trip to the Mountainous Republic of Nagorno-Karabakh (or Artsakh in the local language) will unearth an isolated, time-warped version of Armenia proper; a de facto independent nation unacknowledged on any maps other than Armenia's own. Decades of fruitless territorial bickering have resulted in a stunning mountain landscape left to flourish with little in the way of modern development, and people even warmer and more receptive to tourists than those in Armenia itself. Watch where you camp; minefields do still exist and are marked as such.

Visas for Karabakh are easily procured at the country's sole embassy on Nairi Zaryan Street in Yerevan. Having any evidence of a visit to Karabakh in your passport will exclude you entirely from entry to Azerbaijan. Don't be tempted to try any route in or out of Karabakh other than the prescribed one between Goris and Stepanakert; at least not unless you fancy looking down the barrel of an Azeri-wielded Kalashnikov.

In terms of transport, Yerevan is now well-served by budget airlines from Europe, Dubai and various Russian airports. Minibus services – *mashrutkas* – can usually be persuaded to carry bicycles and run all over the nation from a variety of bus depots in Yerevan, as well as to neighbouring capital cities. The sleeper train between Tbilisi and Yerevan is an experience all of its own and relatively easy to wangle a bicycle onto too.

CENTRAL ASIA

John Burnham

This is quintessential Silk Road territory: desert, mountains and steppe. Central Asia played a significant role in the world's first international trade connecting Europe and Asia leading to one of the most remarkable exchanges of goods, knowledge, philosophy and culture in human history. Add to this melting pot the influence brought by Persian, Mongolian, Arab and Russian invasions over the centuries and you discover a unique flavour has evolved.

Collectively known as the 'Stans, these days Central Asia offers a little of everything for adventurous bicycle touring, from the fabulous ancient cities of the Silk Road and deserts of the west to the tough mountainous terrain of the Pamir Highway and Kyrgyzstan in the east.

You will find friendly, inquisitive and welcoming people in all of these countries, so brush up on your Russian small talk because sooner or later you're going to be sitting in someone's house or yurt or field and knowing only what '*Atkuda*?' means will just not be enough. Russian remains the lingua franca, so at least you can use the same phrases everywhere. If you know some Turkish you may be understood in Turkmenistan and Uzbekistan, while in Tajikistan a variant of Farsi is spoken. More and more youngsters are learning English, although outside of touristic places and the capitals it is still a rare find.

Descending the Ak-Baital Pass on the Pamir Highway in Tajikistan. © Gayle Dickson

BARMY BUREAUCRACY

The typical process for obtaining a Central Asian visa, outside your home country, goes something like this:

• Check online to see what documents are required to support your application. Ask at the consulate if Googling fails.

• Sometimes a Letter of Invitation (LOI) is required from a host, organisation or travel agency in the destination country. In most cases, this is something a travel agency can organise in advance – allow a month to request and pay for this service. Alternatively, a Letter of Recommendation (LOR) may be required from your embassy in the country in which you are applying. Embassies are used to such requests and usually have a standard letter for this purpose, but for Brits it's expensive.

• The application form at the consulate is usually submitted with: 1 or 2 passport photos plus a photocopy (sometimes in colour!) of your visa and/or entry stamp of the country in which you are applying, your passport photo page, plus any supporting documents like a LOI or LOR or just a covering letter saying why you want to visit.

• The application fee may have to be paid into a local bank first. The standard processing time is around one week, but can be double that. You may be able to get an 'express' service for an extra fee, but be aware that consulates have restricted opening times and like to take holidays. In some larger countries like Turkey and Iran you may be able to apply at one consulate and collect at another.

• If you've read this far, you'll realise you need patience, stamina, and to be prepared to spend time organising all this.

Tips: Most visas can only be applied for up to 3 months before entry so think very hard about the dates you plan to visit each country as the visa will have fixed dates. If you arrive 5 days after your 30-day visa began, you have only 25 days before you must leave. For transit visas, you must have a visa for the following country in your passport first. For an extra charge some countries offer double-entry or extended visas, which might be worth the extra money to allow some flexibility in your travel plans. Note that some consulates are very particular that US dollars be unmarked and unfolded.

PRACTICALITIES

Getting in

The biggest pain about travelling in Central Asia is sorting out visas. Most countries give fixed-date visas, which requires a bit of planning if you're travelling overland from Europe or East Asia as getting them on the road can be time-consuming and complicated. Kyrgyzstan is leading the tourist-friendly stakes, offering a 60-day stay without visa for North Americans and most EU countries.

The good news is that there's useful up-to-date information on the comprehensive website 💻 caravanistan.com about visas, border crossings and transport options.

All the 'Stans are bureaucratic and obtaining visas can be a logistical headache without careful planning (see box above for some advice). There are agencies out there that can help you for a fee, with Stantours, which is based in Kazakhstan, being well-established and recommended. It is a time-consuming alternative to do it yourself. Contemporary research on travellers' blogs and forums will be worthwhile as the requirements of consulates change regularly and can vary country by country and be dependent on nationality. If you are travelling overland you'll need to research the best location for an onward visa to Iran/Azerbaijan or China/Russia – the Caravanistan website is a good place to start.

TRIP REPORT
CENTRAL ASIA

Name	Elmar & Ellen van Drunen
Nationality	Dutch
Year of birth	1974/1975
Occupation	World cyclists at the moment! Formerly: bike mechanic / photographer and travel writer
Other bike travels	Europe (highlight: Iceland); India, China, Namibia, Canada, Alaska, Morocco, Malaysia, among others.
This trip	Central Asia: Kyrgyzstan & Tajikistan
Trip duration	2 months
Number in group	Two
Total distance	About 2500km
Cost of trip	US$5000 total for 2 people
Longest day	130km in the summer heat – fuelled by watermelons.
Best day	Testing ourselves mentally and physically on the muddy climb to Ak-Baital Pass between Kyrgyzstan and Tajikistan.
Worst day	A road the Chinese had just started work on and had covered with fresh sand. Cycling was impossible so we had to catch a ride for 50km.
Favourite ride	The traffic-free road to Bulunkul (Tajikistan) – like a mountain bike track snaking its way through colourful mountain scenery.
Biggest mistake	Not wild camping enough.
Pleasant surprise	The people! They were very friendly and helpful and left us in peace when we wanted it. We often couldn't understand a word, but a smile gets you a long way.
Illnesses during trip	Too many gut issues... Everybody gives you food, but hygiene is something else. We spent a lot of time on the open pit toilets.
Bike model	Santos Travelmaster 2.6
Baggage Setup	2 rear panniers, 2 front panniers, handlebar bag and tent in a dry sack on top of rear rack
Weight of kit	25kg
Wish you'd brought	Antibiotics
Wish you hadn't brought	Extra tyre – wasn't necessary
Recommendations	Bring a mirror and leave the handlebar bag at home – this gives you more control over steering.

Any advice?	Don't plan too much. Have time off the bike every now and then to keep your cycling spirits high!

When to ride

Timing is important for enjoying cycling in these parts. The summer months of June to August are better for the high passes of Kyrgyzstan and the Pamir Highway where snow lies until early summer; however, it's worth knowing that rain storms are most likely in June in the mountains. Temperatures in the deserts of Turkmenistan, Uzbekistan and west Kazakhstan are hottest in June and barely cool down in July and August, whereas April/May and September/October offer more bearable conditions. In the low-lying areas most cyclists find it easier to ride early mornings and late afternoons with a long siesta in between. Be aware that even in the desert the winters are harsh.

Where to go

It's fairly simple to incorporate all of the 'Stans into a west-east overland route. Alternatively a short tour could focus on Uzbekistan, Tajikistan and Kyrgyzstan which are undeniably the highlights of the region; Tashkent, Bishkek, Osh and Almaty all have decent international flight connections.

If you look closely at a map of the region you will see that the jigsaw-like borders don't always make sense – they're a relic from Soviet years. Not all border crossings are open to foreigners either, so check up-to-date sources to find which are open, bearing in mind that sometimes tensions between countries can lead to a crossing closing suddenly.

Sustenance

Let's face it – you don't come to the 'Stans for the food, but neither will you starve. Restaurants and teahouses (*chaikhanas*) are plentiful and invariably supply the same four or five staple dishes – all good fare for cycling but if you're vegetarian you'll probably want to self-cater at the local bazaars. The chaikhanas pop up everywhere along the main roads and usually have mutton *shashlyk* (barbecued chunks of meat on a skewer), *samsa* (a small mutton and onion pie), and *plov* or *osh* (a greasy rice pilaf dish with mutton and carrot). There are teabeds on which you eat and afterwards recline upon – handy for those siestas. Bread is the number one staple across the 'Stans and is treated with an almost religious respect. It's baked in a clay oven and is usually shaped like a dinner plate – wonderful when fresh and can be used as a frisbee when not. Outside of large towns you may sometimes struggle to find fresh food, especially in isolated mountain areas, but there are always basics like pasta, rice and instant noodles, condensed milk, tinned fish, biscuits and jam. In the countryside water taps are rare, so you'll probably get by collecting water from wells or pumps, like the locals.

Samsas make a great cyclists' lunch.
© Gayle Dickson

Sleeping

The standard of accommodation in Central Asia varies enormously and can sometimes seem over-priced for what you get compared to other parts of Asia, so haggle hard. There are homestay programmes in Tajikistan and Kyrgyzstan, developed to help local people in poorer areas, which are well worth supporting and where US$10 will usually get you a bed and two or three meals. You may also come across informal homestays in remote places.

Reise Know-How, Gizi and ITMB have decent maps covering the region. The driving standards are not great and you may begin to think you are invisible when you see overtaking vehicles bearing down on you; the better the road the faster the traffic – plus ça change. As anywhere, getting off the main roads will reward you with space and much more peace to enjoy the ride.

Petrol for your multi-fuel stove can be found everywhere – although lead-free is as rare as a happy camel. Screw-valve gas cartridges are available in outdoor shops in Almaty and Bishkek.

Turkmenistan

Renowned for being the most closed of the old Soviet republics, Turkmenistan suffered the weird personality cult of President Niyazov, who ruled with the name *Turkmenbashi*, 'leader of Turkmen', until his death in 2006. The country is rich in oil and gas reserves but the people live in relative poverty. North Korea comparisons might bear some truth, but at least you can cross Turkmenistan on a bicycle. Okay, the five-day transit visa is not such a good deal, especially if you're going north into the wind and the road is a bit shoddy, but you can't get lost if you're transiting between Sarakhs on the Iranian border, and Farab on the Uzbek border...unless you've deliberately ignored the transit visa requirements and hopped on the train to Ashgabat to check out the capital, anyway.

PRACTICALITIES

Arriving and travelling

Few cycle-tourists seek alternatives to the transit visa as tourist visas can only be obtained by hiring a guide to accompany you. This is an expensive option

---

OVERSTAYING YOUR TURKMEN TRANSIT VISA

If you are wondering what happens should you arrive at the border to exit Turkmenistan a day late, then check out Ollie and Dan's Supersized Adventure. These self-confessed Cornish cycle-touring bumblers could not get an Uzbek visa in Iran, possibly due to a misunderstanding. This meant that in May 2014 the only way they could transit Turkmenistan was to cross from Iran to Kazakhstan in the west of the country – a mere 800km in five days. Impossible, you say? Indeed it was, but our hapless and hilarious heroes were dealt with fairly by the border officials who gave them the choice: each pay a US$300 fine or face deportation and a two-year ban. Short of cash, the choice was easy. They were sent packing with food and drink for the onward journey.

at around US$140-200 per day, though it includes accommodation, guide, guide's transport and paperwork.

Camping isn't a problem if you make sure you have enough water, as there are some long stretches of road between settlements. From Mary to Turkmenabat you are close enough to the railway to hop on if you want, and ruin buffs might prefer to use the train to allow time in Mary to visit the World Heritage Site ruins of Merv. Another interesting variant would be to cross between Konye-Urgench and Ashgabat, passing the Darvasa gas crater, but it's unusual for such a route to be permitted on a transit visa. You could always ask…

Touring tips

There are no ATMs but you can change dollars with moneychangers at the borders or in shops – just check the black market rate published on the Lonely Planet website before you arrive.

Uzbekistan

Predominantly desert scenery, Uzbekistan might not be most cycle tourists' ideal destination, and yet it offers the best-preserved historical sites in the region. The country is home to some of the most hospitable people in Central Asia too, and asking folk for directions or a good place to camp often leads to an invite back to someone's home or into a *chaikhana* for food. Sooner or later a bottle of vodka will appear – Uzbeks are social drinkers.

Tashkent is the largest city in the region and a useful place to apply for onward visas, but the old Silk Road gems of Khiva, Bukhara and Samarkand are the outstanding places of interest. Following the break-up of the Mongol empire these cities were ruled as independent khanates; Samarkand thrived under Timur's reign, and many of the monuments have survived from this era. An undoubted highlight is the Registan but the real architectural gem is Timur's mausoleum – the Taj Mahal of Central Asia. The old town of Bukhara offers more in atmosphere and relaxing shady corners, whilst Khiva has arguably the best-preserved buildings. Don't be disappointed to find the mosques and madrasahs are no longer used for their original purpose – the communists put paid to that, but they did try to preserve the ancient buildings and even in the Soviet era Uzbekistan was open to foreign visitors. Cycling into one of the old cities you'll get a bit of a shock to find coachloads of tourists after passing through the unvisited countryside.

The Mir-i Arab Madrassah, Bukhara.
© Gayle Dickson

Simple but perfect camping in the Kyzylkum Desert, Uzbekistan. © Scott Richardson

PRACTICALITIES

Arriving and travelling

Tourists are supposed to stay in hotels registered for foreigners and receive slips from these to show to immigration when they leave. This is impractical for cyclists, so while you shouldn't worry about a slip for every single night in the country it is useful to get some hotel slips just in case you need to satisfy a bored policeman at a checkpoint in the middle of nowhere.

A good rail network connects the main cities but owing to political issues there are only international trains to neighbouring Kazakhstan. There's rarely a baggage wagon so you may need to negotiate your bike onto the train, and if there's more than one of you consider booking an extra berth on a sleeper to store the bikes.

Touring tips

Though there are ATMs in the cities that work with VISA, it's worth noting that at the time of writing the official bank rate was far lower than the black market rate. To change dollars ask at an upmarket hotel or in the shops near the bazaars – those selling imported goods may offer you better rates.

One thing the country lacks is any decent bike shop – local enthusiasts buy their stuff over the internet, so bring spares.

ROUTES

The classic routes from the west will bring you to Bukhara either from Turkmenistan or via Aktau-Beyneu-Nukus-Khiva from the Caspian Sea. From Bukhara you can continue east to Dushanbe, crossing the Tajik border close to Denau, or make the worthwhile detour up to Samarkand, though note that the Penjikent border with Tajikistan has been closed for some time now. Another option is to pedal north-eastwards to Tashkent and on to Kazakhstan; or enter the Fergana Valley to cross into northern Tajikistan or to Osh in Kyrgyzstan.

Tajikistan

The poorest of the old Soviet republics, Tajikistan is the one blessed with great landscapes, remote valleys and the Pamir Highway, one of the world's classic adventure cycle-touring routes.

PRACTICALITIES

Arriving and travelling

The Tajik government offers a 45-day visa as well as the normal 30-day one –

it's worth paying the extra because you'll probably find you want to stay longer than you originally thought. Note that there is a requirement to register with OVIR (the immigration authorities) if you stay longer than 30 days, something that is possible to do in Dushanbe, Khojand, Khorog and Murgab.

Dushanbe is a pleasant capital although it offers the cyclist little more than the chance to stock up on food supplies and collect onward visas; Russian tourist visas have even been known to be issued here.

You need a permit for the GBAO (Gorno Badakhshan Autonomous Oblast) region through which the Pamir Highway passes, and this is easiest to obtain at the same time as you get your visa. Failing this, pick it up in Dushanbe, usually in a day, for less than US$10. If you're coming from Osh an agent there will charge about US$50 to arrange the permit. Be aware that sometimes there are problems in the GBAO region, which is a drug-running conduit for opium from Afghanistan. Tourists are not targeted but there have been shoot-outs with the police and army followed by public protests and at these times the government stops issuing permits or allowing cyclists to enter the region, so keep an eye on the news.

Touring tips
Pleasingly, Dushanbe has a legendary Warm Showers host in the form of the wonderful French cyclist Veronique. She plans on staying here with her son until 2017 and they are well worth looking up for accommodation and friendly local knowledge.

There is no decent bike shop but if you're lucky you may find a spare Shimano part at VeloMoto on Abdulahab Kakharov Street, or a spare tube at Sultan Kaboni market.

ROUTES

To Dushanbe
Getting to Dushanbe from the west currently means coming in along a newly paved road from Denau in Uzbekistan. Approaching from the north can be trickier as it involves crossing the Anzob Pass via an old road that is plagued by avalanches, or through the infamous 5km-long 'Death Tunnel'. The tunnel is currently unfinished, is a nightmare for drivers, and very dangerous for cyclists too. If you don't drown in the water flooding it, disappear down a pothole or get crushed by a truck in the dark, then you'll probably die from asphyxiation! Cyclists have survived by pushing through, but the common sense approach is to hitch a ride. The Iranians, who are building the tunnel, have promised to complete construction in 2015 – don't hold your breath. No, do.

Classic Route – The Pamir Highway
The Pamir Highway was built by the Russians to connect Dushanbe with Osh in Kyrgyzstan, traversing the high mountains of the Pamirs through a region crossed by Marco Polo on his way to China. The route passes through isolated villages on ill-kept roads and combined with high altitudes this makes for challenging yet memorable cycle-touring. It's possible for seasoned cyclists to pedal from Dushanbe to Osh in about 16 days, but 25-30 days would give

more time for rests and for taking some of the alternative (read 'harder and slower') routes described below.

Leaving Dushanbe you have a choice. Either head east and then south to Tavildara before crossing the Sagirdasht Pass on the old road. This route is very scenic with a few river crossings, but the road is no longer maintained. The longer and busier alternative runs south via Kulab before the two meet at Kalaikhum and follow the fabulously dramatic Pyanj River to Khorog. This section is chewed up by Chinese trucks and the cycling can be slow and dusty, but it's a great ride with the added thrill of the sight of Afghans in their pretty villages over the river.

Before Khorog a tough route shoots off east from the main road, going to Vanj, then climbing the Bartang Valley and dropping back down to the main highway near Karakul. It's not for the novice but appeals to those who enjoy pushing their bike through remote wilderness.

Khorog is a good place for a rest, to catch up on route information from other cyclists and glean tips about the homestays, food and water points that lie ahead. Cyclists tend to stop at the Pamir Lodge which is run by a local Ismaili group. There are many Ismailis in this part of the world – a splinter group from Shia Islam who do not have mosques but use a meeting house (*jamatkhana*), do not observe Ramadan, and in which women are treated more equably. Their spiritual leader, the Aga Khan, raises funds to support many charitable projects here including the university in Khorog.

From Khorog come more choices. The main, asphalted highway climbs steadily to a high plateau all the way to Murgab. Just south of this is the lesser-visited Shokh Dara Valley which reconnects to the main highway via a dirt track. Further south a paved road continues from Khorog along the Pyanj River and turns eastwards towards the Wakhan Valley. The asphalt runs out soon after Ishkashim and the challenging route continues through remote villages on a sometimes sandy and gravel track before arcing back, via a 4300m pass, to rejoin the asphalt highway.

At Murgab, the only town of any size in the east, an asphalt road turns off to the Qolma Pass – a road which eventually meets the Karakoram Highway in China. Though only open to the Chinese and Tajiks at present, keep your ears open in case this exciting option opens up to foreign cyclists. Heading to

Osh you face a series of unpaved passes – the highest peaking at 4655m – as you pedal through a dry, barren, mountainous desert landscape. You certainly feel that you are crossing the Roof of the World. Be wary of the strong winds – one couple lost their tent here when it blew away as they were packing up one morning!

Once you enter Kyrgyzstan, you still have a few passes on the road to Osh, but the road is asphalted again and the going gets easier.

Camping on the Pamir Highway, Tajikistan.
© Yoko Kai

Kyrgyzstan

For a country with so much to offer it's a real boon that many nationalities can now enter Kyrgyzstan for a 60-day stay without a visa. Despite being the hardest of the 'Stans to spell, Kyrgyzstan is a wonderful place for cycling with great scenic variety and quiet back roads. It can be tough but the effort is always rewarded.

The two main cities, Bishkek and Osh, both lie in valleys surrounded by agricultural land, while between, and to the south, lie a series of mountainous regions where the heart of the people beats. The Kyrgyz are traditionally nomadic herders, very much like Mongolians; for half the year families and their herds of horses, cows and sheep head up to *jailoos*, the green pastures that appear when the winter snows have melted. Yurts abound throughout the country during summer months.

In the past Kyrgyzstan has lacked quality low-cost accommodation but now boasts two new places. *AT House* (8 Novosibirsk Street, round the corner from Gergert Sport) in Bishkek is Central Asia's only guesthouse specifically for cyclists. Run by cyclists Angie and Nathan, there's camping space and a kitchen and Nathan tries to keep a small stock of wheels and tyres for tourers in need. In Osh, the *Biy Ordo Guesthouse* (39 Salieva Street) is a calm oasis in the bustling city. Around Kyrgyzstan you'll find yurts and homestays run by Community Based Tourism (CBT) – which provide a great opportunity to engage with a local family.

Wild camping is not a problem, but sadly the same cannot be said for driving standards. Vodka, as in many other old Soviet Republics, is a bit of a curse so be wary of drunk drivers or morons who think driving close to cyclists to scare them is a sport. The good news is that away from the main roads traffic is very light and that Bishkek now boasts decent bike shops – Gergert Sport at 119 Gorky Street has SRAM parts, and a pair of shops on Toktogul Street have an eclectic Shimano mix.

ROUTES

The numerous possibilities for good adventure cycling make Kyrgyzstan possibly the best single destination in the region.

Entering in the south, from Kashgar in China, the Pamir Highway in Tajikistan, or the Fergana Valley in Uzbekistan, all roads lead to the lively old trading centre of Osh. You can head direct from Osh to Bishkek on the main highway via Toktogul Reservoir and two high passes, or turn off onto the back road to Kochkor along the way. A more exciting route veers eastwards at Jalalabad and into the central mountains, bringing the possibility of visiting Song Kol – a jewel of a lake surrounded by mountains – before continuing over to Kochkor and then Issyk Kol, the vast lake in the east of the country. A thrilling and beautiful ride can also be had over the Kegeti Pass between Kochkor and Bishkek.

Lapping Issyk Kol might seem a bit dull in comparison to other routes around the country but if you've brought your hiking boots there's great trekking up the valleys south of the lake. East of Issyk Kol is the back road into the south-east corner of Kazakhstan, open from mid-May to mid-October.

Frustratingly for purists, the border crossings into China require transport because the actual border posts are no longer at the international boundaries. The Chinese won't allow you to cycle between the border posts so you'll be forced into a lift – if you get lucky you may be able to hitch a ride. A taxi between the Irkeshtam border posts costs around US$35, but this is still far cheaper and easier than crossing the Torugart Pass south of Naryn which requires an agency to arrange transport at a cost of anywhere between US$130 and US$250 per person.

Don't forget to get your GBAO permit (see p167) in Osh if you're crossing into Tajikistan from Sary Tash, while if you're heading from Osh to Tajikistan through the Fergana Valley be sure to go around the Uzbek enclaves and also check that the Isfara/Batken border is open.

Kazakhstan

Unless you crave cycling through limitless flat steppe on arrow-straight roads, the largest of the 'Stans doesn't compete with its southern neighbours for great cycling and as such is used mainly for transiting by overlanders. In the south-eastern corner of the country is some tough off-road cycling that makes a good route into neighbouring Kyrgyzstan and if you're feeling really adventurous, explore the Altai region in the north-east. Kazakhstan is the most developed country in Central Asia but outside cities, typically, there is little sign of the wealth and prosperity that oil and gas has brought to some.

Certain nationalities are currently given a 15-day visa-free stay, and a 30-day visa is relatively easy to obtain. The only bureaucratic headache is having to register with the immigration police within five days of arrival, which can easily be done in Aktau or Almaty.

Almaty is the best city for cycle-touring services, with a couple of decent bicycle shops for spares (try Velo-Tour on the corner of Gogol Street and Kaldayakov Street, or EuroSport Service on the corner of Abai and Kurmangazy Street for SRAM parts) and *poste restante* to the central post office works , but only if you have a tracking number.

ROUTES

From the west, the ferry across the Caspian from Baku deposits you in Aktau. The most popular route from here is to head to Beyneu, then cut down to

THE CASPIAN SEA CHALLENGE

The Caspian Sea crossing is an adventure in itself: the one thing you are guaranteed is that nothing is guaranteed. The best way to approach the journey is to imagine you are going to watch a Samuel Beckett play at the National Theatre. You will need patience and time, a little bit of money, and you probably won't know what's going on or why for most of the time. The ferries have no timetable and only leave when they have a full load of cargo. Find the ticket office, leave them your number, phone them twice a day and call in each day. You can only buy a ticket on the day the ferry departs. The crossing between Baku and Aktau takes about 30 hours but expect delays because the boat usually has to wait before it can dock – sometimes for days. Avoid the Baku-Turkmenbashi ferry if you only have a transit visa for Turkmenistan because the unreliable timetable makes it probable you'll overstay your Turkmen transit visa. Take extra food, water and dollars just in case, and for updates check out Caravanistan's wonderfully detailed information: 🖥 caravanistan.com/transport/caspian-sea-ferry

Nukus in Uzbekistan. This is a hard, remote, desert stretch requiring research and planning, but there is basic food and water along the route so check out recent blogs for updates. If you're in a hurry there are trains from Aktau to Almaty, or to Kungrad in Uzbekistan.

In the centre you may cross between Tashkent and Shymkent and head east to Almaty, but why would you want to miss out on Kyrgyzstan? There's the main road between Almaty and Bishkek but the more exciting border crossing is at the eastern end of Kyrgyzstan's Lake Issyk Kol. Going this quieter way allows for a more interesting route to or from China, missing Almaty, as well as giving the option of an off-road adventure in the Charyn Canyon and crossing the beautiful Assy Plateau between Kegen and Almaty.

If you're into Steppe Aerobics and are Siberia-bound then the slog north of Almaty to the Russian border is for you. Alternatively squeeze your bike onto a train (literally, in the bit between carriages) to Barnaul and take a breather.

THE NORTHERN ROUTE
Russia

Gayle Dickson

Not many cycle-tourists head to Russia, dissuaded perhaps by its sheer size and images of endless forest, mozzies and the headaches of bureaucracy. But for those wanting to learn about the real Russia beyond Western media portrayals, and looking for a challenge in an untouristed part of the world, then cycling in the largest country on Earth will hold great appeal. It is now possible to cycle right across Russia – roughly 10,000km from Moscow to Vladivostok – and be on asphalt all the way.

With over 17 million square kilometres of land and a population of just 143 million, Russia is one of the world's most sparsely populated nations. You may imagine Russians to be a miserable bunch but bring your bike here and leave your misconceptions at home because you'll be pleasantly surprised. Most people live in European Russia, west of the Ural Mountains, where the cycling is not dissimilar to Eastern Europe – it's relatively developed, flat and with many route choices. Long-distance tourers wanting to visit Russia could bypass the European part and the monotony of the western section of the Trans-Siberian Highway by cycling from Western Europe via Turkey and Central Asia before exploring the more hilly Siberian terrain east of Novosibirsk. Areas that attract adventure tourers include the Lake Baikal region and the Altai and Tuva Republics.

PRACTICALITIES

Visas and visa registration

Almost everyone needs a visa for Russia and it is generally recommended that you apply for it in your home country. If you've pedalled a long way from home it may be possible to get your hands on a visa in Bishkek or Dushanbe in Central Asia, and also in Ulaanbaatar, but head to forums for the latest as Russian rules regularly change. Wherever you are, to get a 30-day tourist visa you'll need a Letter of Invitation, which can be easily and cheaply obtained using an agency such as Real Russia (🖥 realrussia.co.uk). The visa application form is available online at 🖥 visa.kdmid.ru and you must print it out and take it to the embassy with your LOI. Tourist visas are date specific, meaning you have to plan carefully, but those on the long haul across the country will be pleased to know that at the time of writing cyclists could arrange 90-day business visas even if cycle-touring is their only 'business'.

You must register at least once when you're in Russia and this must be done within 7 working days of arrival. The easiest way to do this is to spend your first night in a hotel and let them do the formalities – they will either stamp your immigration card or give you the stamp on a slip of paper. Don't even think about visiting UFMS (Federal Migration Service Organisation) yourself as this will entail a Kafkaesque process for both you and whoever you're staying with... and you may never get to ride your bike. When you leave the country you may be asked to show a registration slip. It doesn't matter if you have only one, just explain you've been cycling and camping. Check online and locally for the latest.

Long climb out of the Chulyshman Valley, Altai Republic, Siberia. © Gayle Dickson

Eating and sleeping

On the main roads you can find cheap accommodation, which is used by truckers, for around US$15 per person, but the big distances mean you'll still need to camp. Even small villages will have a shop but as it may not always be obvious, ask around for the *magazin*. Here you'll find basic provisions such as pasta, buckwheat, tinned fish, biscuits, chocolate and maybe some vegetables and seasonal fruit.

Swot up on your Cyrillic

All signposts and maps bought in Russia will be in Cyrillic, so it makes sense to learn this alphabet and some basic Russian phrases as not many people speak English. Various maps and road atlases of Russia are available in the country but most of those for sale outside Russia show the whole country at a scale too large to be used for anything but highway navigation. Exceptionally,

PART 4 – ROUTES – ASIA

CYRILLIC ALPHABET

Cyrillic letter	Roman equivalent	Pronunciation*	Cyrillic letter	Roman equiv	Pronunciation*
А а	a	<u>fa</u>ther	П п	p	<u>P</u>eter
Б б	b	<u>b</u>et	Р р	r	<u>R</u>ussia
В в	v	<u>v</u>odka	С с	s	<u>S</u>amarkand
Г г	g	<u>g</u>et	Т т	t	<u>t</u>ime
Д д	d	<u>d</u>og	У у	u, oo	f<u>oo</u>l
Е е	ye	<u>ye</u>t (unstressed: <u>ye</u>ar)	Ф ф	f, ph	<u>f</u>ast
			Х х	kh	lo<u>ch</u>
Ё ё	yo	<u>yo</u>ghurt	Ц ц	ts	lo<u>ts</u>
Ж ж	zh	trea<u>s</u>ure	Ч ч	ch	<u>ch</u>illy
З з	z	<u>z</u>ebra	Ш ш	sh	<u>sh</u>ow
И и	i, ee	s<u>ee</u>k, <u>ye</u>ar	Щ щ	shch	fre<u>sh ch</u>ips
Й й	y	bo<u>y</u>	Ы ы	y, i	d<u>i</u>d
К к	k	<u>k</u>it	ь		(softens preceding letter)
Л л	l	<u>l</u>ast	Э э	e	l<u>e</u>t
М м	m	<u>M</u>oscow	Ю ю	yu	<u>u</u>nion
Н н	n	<u>n</u>ever	Я я	ya	<u>ya</u>rd (unstressed: <u>ye</u>arn)
О о	o	t<u>o</u>re (unstressed: t<u>o</u>p)			

* pronunciation shown by underlined letter/s

Wild camping close to the Mongolian border.
© Gayle Dickson

Reise Know-How publishes four useful maps: West Russia, Urals to Lake Baikal, Lake Baikal and Lake Baikal to Vladivostok. The best available digital map is Open Street Map (🖥 openstreetmap.org) while the website 🖥 roads.ru/forum gives updates, in Russian, on the state of the roads.

Watch out for...

Despite the classic image of Siberian winters, the southern areas that most cyclists visit have a very warm summer from May to September. This is also when the mosquitoes, horseflies and ticks are most prevalent; the first two of these torment cyclists, particularly when camping, but they are more a nuisance than a hazard, and you can buy good repellents easily in towns. The ticks, however, are more serious and can carry tick-borne encephalitis and Lyme disease. Tuck in long trousers and keep arms covered if you walk in woods or long grass, and bring 'tick remover' tweezers in case that nightly body-check reveals unwanted squatters. By mid-August there are far fewer of these critters about.

You'll likely come across a fair bit of drunkenness in Siberia, especially in small, poor towns and you'll regularly be offered vodka which can be difficult to refuse, particularly for men. Saying you cannot drink and cycle sometimes works... If someone flicks or pinches their neck while looking at you they're not scratching last night's mozzie bites – this is an invitation to hit the sauce together. As Siberians like nothing more than heading into the countryside at the weekend armed with plenty of alcohol it's best to take extra care when finding a secluded place to camp. There are bears and even tigers in eastern Siberia, so ask locals as you go, but you're more likely to be bothered by harmless drunks and mozzies than by wild animals.

SOME SIBERIAN ROUTE IDEAS

European and Asian Russia can seem like two completely different countries and it is east of the Urals that the real adventure cycle touring begins. Siberia still feels like a frontier land with scope for exploration – even if at times there are not so many roads to choose from.

Early morning reflections from the Chuysky Tract, Altai Republic. © Gayle Dickson

The Altai Republic

One excellent option is a ride through the Altai Republic, which offers a worthwhile route for overlanding cyclists seeking an alternative to crossing the vast Xinjiang region in western China. The Altai is a little-visited part of western Siberia, lying at the very centre of Asia where

Kazakhstan, Mongolia, China and Russia meet. Most of the Altai is mountainous and includes Belukha, which at 4506m is Siberia's highest peak. The scenery is varied, ranging from typical Siberian *taiga* to alpine forest, narrow gorges, pretty river valleys and rocky peaks, with occasional small villages of wooden cottages. Further east towards Mongolia the landscape changes again to high steppe and semi-desert. With nearly 50% of the population being ethnic Altai and Kazakhs, the area can feel more Central Asian than Russian, and exudes a sense of being as yet undiscovered.

The main access point for the Altai Republic is the city of Barnaul, which can be reached by train, bus or plane – most easily from Novosibirsk or Almaty in Kazakhstan. Heading south from Barnaul it's a couple of days in the saddle to Biysk, from where the Chuysky Tract (M52) runs all the way to the Mongolian border at Tashanta. This is one of Russia's most beautiful rides with little traffic and gorgeous scenery as the road initially follows the Katun River, then the Chuya, before gradually climbing through the Altai Mountains to high steppe. One adventurous dirt road detour is to include Lake Teletskoe,

BIKING IN A SIBERIAN WINTER

In 2013, Helen Lloyd spent 3 months cycling through Siberia during the coldest months of winter. Here she explains some of the challenges.

There are different kinds of cold. There's the normal kind, which with the right clothing and equipment is great for cycle-touring. Then there's the Siberian 'What am I doing here?' kind, where average temperatures are minus 40°C, and the thermometer regularly plunges into the minus fifties at night. Touring in the Siberian cold is hard.

The difficulty is making progress. Everything takes much longer: packing up camp because of cold hands, having to melt snow for the day's water, cycling slowly in an effort to avoid sweating (because sweat makes your clothes damp and cools you down), fixing things that break (like plastic parts, which become brittle) or won't work (like fuel pumps and bike pumps because the seals become stiff and fail) or repairing punctures (because the inner tubes split easily).

Then, once you've finally overcome these obstacles, progress remains elusive with passing drivers stopping you to take photos, truckers offering you tea, and villagers inviting you to stay with them for the night or longer. To refuse would be to miss out on what is undoubtedly one of the highlights of travel in Siberia – the local hospitality.

Despite long distances between villages, finding food was no problem since many people gave me edible gifts, so much so that an entire pannier was always full of free food. One of the best is *salo* – cured pork fat. You need as many calories as you can get, and fat is excellent for helping fight off the cold. Another advantage is that it doesn't freeze, so it makes a tasty roadside snack to wash down with tea from the thermos.

Because of the long distances between villages, there are long periods without anything different to look at or interact with except snow, forest and the road. This can be very trying mentally, especially when your iPod stops working.

My final tip – avoid the vodka! Know that you'll never get away with just one; for if you drink one, you must have three – 'Russian tradition', they say.

Helen Lloyd

Winter touring in Siberia requires careful planning of equipment.
© Helen Lloyd

hitching a ride to the far end of the lake and cycling through the remote and beautiful Chulyshman Valley, before rejoining the Chuysky Tract at Aktash. Alternatively, with the right permits, you could also do a loop along the notoriously challenging Tuva Track, eventually rejoining the asphalt in either Kyzyl in the Tuva Republic or in Abakan a bit further north.

Lake Baikal Region

The main Trans-Siberian Highway passes through Irkutsk just before reaching Lake Baikal, the world's deepest lake. Those wishing to explore the Baikal region will find no road entirely circles the lake, but roads and tracks do exist around the southern and northern parts of the lake and you could use a combination of ferries and the Circumbaikal Railway to explore further by bike. Olkhon Island has no roads but makes for a wonderful off-road adventure. If you're prepared for extreme cold cycling, you could even visit the area in winter, when it's possible to cycle across the frozen lake. On the eastern side of Lake Baikal, and accessed by road from Ust-Barguzin, is the interesting Barguzin Valley, a stronghold of the indigenous Buryat people. The 250km road through the valley takes you up to an area of steppe and it's a fascinating place to learn more about Buryat culture.

At Ulan-Ude, to the south-east of Lake Baikal, comes the choice to continue onwards to Chita, or swing a right for the main route into Mongolia. The majority of cyclists who make it here take the road south towards Ulaanbaatar.

East to the Pacific Ocean

The brave few who continue on the Trans-Siberian Highway heading east pick up the Amur Highway from Chita and can follow this all the way to Vladivostok. A short distance after the town of Skovorodino, the Amur-Yakutsk Highway leads off north for 1150km to Yakutsk – see the useful ⌨ askyakutia.com and ⌨ yakutiatravel.com websites for more information.

Using studded tyres on a frozen Lake Baikal.
© Helen Lloyd

Opposite Yakutsk, on the eastern banks of the Lena River lies the town of Nizhny Bestyakh and the beginning of the famous 'Road of Bones' to Magadan and the Pacific. Named because the skeletons of forced labourers who died during its construction were used in the foundations, the road has become a bit of a 'rite of passage' for adventure motor-cyclists, and a couple of well-prepared, extreme cycle-tourers have tackled it too.

COLD WEATHER TOURING TIPS

1 Invest in winter tyres (eg. Schwalbe Ice Spiker Pro).
2 Invest in good quality winter boots and pogies (handlebar mittens) to keep your feet and hands warm.
3 Tape up / insulate any exposed metal you will touch, like brake levers and frame.
4 Glue one side of the outer tyres to the wheel rim to stop them slipping – this prevents loss of traction and ripping of the inner tube at the valve.
5 Avoid sweating as much as possible.
6 Cable ties and duct tape are useless – take metal wire and pliers for repairs.
7 If it is dry, consider bivvying out instead of putting up the tent. You will avoid cold hands from handling metal tent poles and can enjoy the starry night sky.
8 Use a petrol stove as gas is ineffective in cold temperatures.
9 Use a fire steel to light your stove as this is

© Helen Lloyd

much easier to use with gloves on than a lighter/matches.
10 Vapour Barrier Liner – use a water-tight liner inside your sleeping bag to prevent body moisture from saturating the bag as it will not dry until you next get indoors. Do the same with your feet/boots.

Helen Lloyd

PART 4 – ROUTES – ASIA

Mongolia

Gayle Dickson

The very name Mongolia conjures up dreams of adventures in remote mountains and a picture of nomadic herders and yak caravans wandering across the high plateau. Cycling in Mongolia gives you a real sense of the sheer size of the place – you and your bike will feel tiny in this land of big skies, grasslands, lakes and mountains. Wonderful wild camping opportunities are everywhere, total isolation and views to the far horizon are easy to find. It's a great place to ride a bike, especially if you're looking for a challenge and a bit of sand and wind don't put you off.

Traditionally Mongolians are nomads living in *gers* (yurts) on the rolling grasslands that take up most of Central Mongolia. There are high mountains and lakes, particularly in the north and west, while in the south lies the Gobi Desert. Driven by poverty, brought on in many cases by a

Cruising through the grasslands of Western Mongolia. © Gayle Dickson

SKY AND MOUNTAIN WORSHIP

One thing you'll see a lot of as you pedal through Mongolia are *ovoos* – piles of rocks and branches that look like cairns and are usually found on mountain passes. Used in the worship of mountains and the sky, as well as in Buddhist or Shamanist ceremonies, blue silk scarves called *khadags* are tied onto the ovoos and flutter ceaselessly, like Tibetan prayer flags. We were always happy to see these on reaching the tops of passes and rewarded our efforts for getting there by resting and listening to the scarves blowing in the wind.

series of severe winters, recent times have seen a huge migration to Ulaanbaatar (UB) where over 40% of Mongolians now live.

The first thing you notice when looking at a map of Mongolia is that there are not many roads...and even fewer paved roads. Only about 10% of Mongolia's 50,000km network of roads are asphalt – the rest are sand and gravel, making this heaven for those cyclists who get bored with tarmac and who are happy to jump off for a stretch of pushing every now and then. Most of the paving radiates out of UB and if you cross directly from Siberia to China via the capital you will be on tarmac all the way. Though more roads are being paved, nothing is happening fast.

PRACTICALITIES

Getting in

Americans get 90 days visa-free, and for EU passport holders Mongolia is currently visa-free for up to 30 days. As this is a trial that may not last, do your research well before turning up at a border. You can extend your stay by another 30 days easily in UB at the Immigration Agency out near the airport, but the visa extension can only be done here, not in other towns. Contrary to some information on the internet you do not, at the time of writing, need to do the extension within seven days of arrival in the country; nor do you need to register if you are there visa-free.

Spring in Mongolia can be dry, dusty and windy. Summer might therefore seem like a good season for a bike tour but, like in Siberia, this is also the time when you're most likely to be plagued by mosquitoes and ticks. Mongolia doesn't get much rain but when it does it mostly falls in summer. August up to early October is a good time to visit as days are long, bright, sunny and sometimes hot. Nights can be cold, occasionally very cold with ice and brief snow showers. Visiting in winter means snow, and average temperatures of minus 20°C. Recent severe winters with heavy snowfalls and freezing winds have brought disaster to many regions.

Sustenance

Away from UB, towns and villages are few and far between, but you can usually stock up quite well as even the smallest place will have a shop where you should be able to find bread, rice, pasta, semolina, tinned fish, biscuits, chocolate and the ubiquitous instant noodles. Petrol stations where you can get fuel for your stove are also to be found in these villages.

Occasionally as you're cycling along you'll find a café or a truck-stop where you can have a simple meal. Common foods include *khuushuur* – deep fried mutton pancakes (greasy but good), *buuz* – steamed meat dumplings similar to Chinese *jiaozi* and Central Asian *manti*. Another staple is *sholte khool* (which translates as 'soup with food'). You'll also likely be invited to drink tea by locals and this is a great opportunity to see inside a ger. *Suutei tsai* is the classic Mongolian milky tea with salt....if you try not to think of it as tea, it's fine.

Finding sufficient water can be a problem, especially in the arid, desert areas of western and southern Mongolia and more so at the end of summer – you may have to carry more liquid than you're used to at times. Each village has a pump house where villagers collect their drinking water. They're not always easy to find, so enquire in your very best Mongolian for the location of the *khudag* – if you just ask for water people will assume you want to buy it or point you to the nearest river.

Touring tips

There are ATMs in UB, the larger towns such as Tsetserleg and Kharkorin and at towns near borders.

The Cycling World (🖳 mongoliaprocycling.com) in UB, run by the Belgian Consul, is a reasonably good bike shop carrying some spare parts and renting and selling mountain bikes. There is virtually no shelter to be had out on the steppe so it's important to have a decent tent that can withstand strong winds.

There's not a lot of choice out there in terms of cartography, but Reise Know-How publishes a reasonable map of the whole country. The tracks that criss-cross Mongolia are marked on paper maps and will also appear on electronic maps, but accuracy and completeness leave something to be desired.

If the sand all becomes too much, fear not – it's not that difficult to take a ride. Public transport only really exists between the 'bigger' towns but if you're in a village and want a lift just ask around and there'll be someone willing to take you. Be prepared to haggle.

GPS – GER POSITIONING SYSTEM

If you find yourself disoriented and out of batteries while out on the steppe, an alternative to conventional satellite-based GPS navigation in Mongolia is the local variant: the Ger Positioning System. Low-tech but reliable, this: Mongolian gers (yurts) always have their doorways pointing south. Keep following the doorways, and you'll reach the Chinese border; head in the opposite direction, and it's only a matter of time before you're in Russia.

Edward Genochio

Getting wet feet in central Mongolia.
© Gayle Dickson

WHERE TO RIDE

Long distance cyclists cross Mongolia between Russia and China and as more borders open there are several trans-Mongolian options.

If you're allergic to sand you'll want to cross Mongolia north-south on the paving between Kyakhta (Russia)/Altanbulag and Zamyn-Uud/Erlian (China).

Coming into Mongolia from the west is a more demanding undertaking and there are only two open borders. One with Russia between Tsagaannuur (north of Olgii) and Tashanta in the Altai Republic, and a second between Bulgan and Takashiken (Xinjiang province, China). Continuing across Mongolia, the most northerly route passes through Moron and Ulangom and you could visit the beautiful Khovsgol Lake; the southern route goes through the Gobi Desert; and a more direct central route goes from Olgii to UB via Tosontsengel, Jargalant, Terkhiin Tsagaan Nuur, Tsetserleg and Kharkhorin.

Doing a loop within Mongolia and exploring one area is also a great idea – you could fly into UB, extend your visa (or your visa-free stay) if necessary and pedal off in any direction…soon you'll be out of the capital and feel like you're in the middle of nowhere.

Possible loops include cycling north-east from the city to visit both Gorkhi Terelj and Khan Kentii National Parks, or cycling north-west to Erdenet, Moron and on to Khovsgol Lake. The variations are endless: just grab some noodles, put on some wide tyres, and go.

MAGIC LETTERS

If you are cycling through a country where you don't speak the local language or even read the script, try and find someone to write out a letter explaining the purpose of your trip, which you can show to people you meet on the road. You'll be surprised how effective it can be in helping locals understand why on earth you just turned up on a bike in their town!

Phrasebooks, picture-pointing books and smartphone language apps all come in handy too, especially somewhere like China.

EAST ASIA
China

Bill Weir, with contributions from Mike Roy

China offers a vast range of touring opportunities, from historic city-hopping in the east to village-to-village explorations in the interior, to hard-core mountain and desert traverses in the west. A staggering 94% of the country's population lives in eastern China, which is crowded, intensively cultivated and relatively low-lying. Western China is virtually empty with vast ranges of grassland, desert, high mountains and plateaux.

If you want to see villages and teeming, modern, fast-changing cities, ride on good roads and find decent food and accommodation every day, head south and east. Camping here can be difficult because nearly all flat land is either under intensive cultivation, built on, or flooded – in any case it is hard to find a spot away from prying eyes and it's much easier learning how to find cheap places to stay than to live like a fugitive. Much of the adventure in these parts will come in immersing yourself in Chinese life – the eye-opening outdoor food markets, the whole aisles in supermarkets devoted to items you probably can't identify, and the joy of trying to communicate in villages which never see a *lǎowài* (foreigner).

If you're into more challenging terrain, go west, and though China is rapidly paving its roads, be prepared for some unpaved surfaces, more extreme conditions and, if you seek them out, long stretches with zero facilities – in other words, classic adventure-touring.

PRACTICALITIES

China is divided roughly 50-50 between endless plains and plateaux which can get dull to ride, and steep and rugged mountains, so start your pre-arrival planning with a good topographical map. For detailed route planning and on-the-bike navigation, you'll want to get hold of a Chinese road atlas (available from big-city bookshops such as the state-run Xin Hua), use a GPS, or else buy a cheap local SIM card at one of the ubiquitous mobile phone shops and use your smartphone. Though bureaucracy involved in getting hold of the SIM card can be a bit of a pain, it's easy to top up once you have one.

The massive peaks of Jade Tiger Snow Mountain are an awe-inspiring sight on the ride to Tiger Leaping Gorge.
© Amaya Williams

T R I P   R E P O R T
CHINA AND SOUTH-EAST ASIA

Name	Mike Roy
Nationality	USA
Year of birth	1984
Occupation	English teacher (in South Korea)
Other bike travels	Lots of commuting plus short trips in South Korea.
This trip	Korea, China, South-East Asia, Myanmar, India
Trip duration	Two and a half years so far
Number in group	Minimum of 1, maximum of 7, everything in between
Total distance	27,000km and still at it
Cost of trip	US$12 per day

Longest day	192km, 16 hours in Taiwan. Had injured my knee two days before and wanted to get to a friend's home to rest. Didn't cycle again for two weeks.
Best day	One of many: cycling along with a 13-year-old Laotian kid back to his village.
Worst day	One of few: over the 4200m Sela Pass, Arunachal Pradesh. 25km downhill in rain, fingers numb from cold. My companion's brake pads wore out, but he didn't notice until it carved a gash into his rear rim.
Favourite ride	Meghalaya, north-east India is great, particularly on 'Bandh' days when eco-terrorists have declared traffic bans and there's not a car or truck in sight.
Biggest headache	Visas, particularly India & Vietnam.
Biggest mistake	Not learning more about cleaning, maintenance and repairs before setting out.

Bike model	Merida Cross 650, secondhand, but good-as-new.
Modifications	Butterfly handlebars, fenders, flashlight mount above front wheel, DIY bamboo flagpole mount.
Tyres used	Schwalbe Marathon Tour Plus 32mm (15,000km), Schwalbe Marathon Mondial 35mm (12,000+km).
Baggage Setup	Four Ortlieb City Classic panniers, giant handlebar bag, 45 litre pack across the back rack.

Wish you'd brought	Usually wish I had less stuff.
Wish you hadn't brought	A stove: definitely not necessary in East Asia.
Bike problems	Broken racks & eyelets. Fixed by Indian mechanics with aluminium wire and strips of rubber, still holding.
Accidents?	Knocked off my bike by a (probably drunk) scooter driver on an empty road in Myanmar.
Same bike again	Maybe not. As much as I love the bike, the front suspension isn't really necessary and makes for an ugly front pannier setup.
Any advice?	Don't worry too much, everyone loves cycle tourists.

Bureaucracy

Disappointingly, in recent years the bureaucratic situation in China has deteriorated for cyclists, and some of the former classic rides in the west of the country, most notably in Tibet, are now off limits to independent travel. **Rules and restrictions change all the time**, so keep checking internet forums for the latest.

You'll probably find it difficult to get a long enough visa for a cross-China ride, which typically requires 3-6 months depending on the time you spend sightseeing and meandering. Having said this, China now issues ten-year multiple-entry visas to US citizens. Find out which Chinese embassies and consulates give the longest visas by asking other travellers and checking online, as success varies greatly depending on where you apply; Hong Kong is often a good place for Europeans to get hold of visas. Travel agencies can sometimes wangle longer visas than you can obtain on your own. Once in China, you can usually extend your visa once.

Accommodation

Hotels for budget travellers are plentiful and cheap, and getting into inexpensive digs is a matter of learning what to look for (see box p186). Good hotels can be found in cities, and it's worth knowing that any prices posted in hotel receptions usually only relate to holiday periods, so at other times it's possible to get a better price by asking nicely. Hotel rooms always come with a kettle, and usually wi-fi too. In big cities, youth hostels are popular with touring cyclists and can be good for obtaining information as they're often staffed with helpful English speakers. Outside the largest cities you should be able to find an acceptable room for US$5-10, although many owners will not have any experience in dealing with foreigners.

There is great wild camping in many mountain and desert areas, but be prepared for inquisitive visitors regardless of how remote you may think the location is. In the back-country it's possible to stay with local families if you're able to establish a good rapport. An experience like this can be a fascinating way to learn about how the local people live but it can also be very draining: you will definitely earn your keep by providing entertainment for the family and friends for the duration of your stay!

Food and drink

For the touring cyclist, Chinese food is cheap and delicious – you can eat very well for only US$5 a day. Breakfast in southern China usually consists of noodles, while in the north dumplings are the mainstay. Lunch can be with rice, noodles or dumplings. Vegetarians will have to be persistent in their no-meat requirement. Stating that you don't eat meat is like saying you don't breathe air – even if there is no visible meat, vegetables are often cooked in meat fat.

All running water in China must be treated before consumption, but almost all hotels and guesthouses will provide you with a large ther-

Baozi in Yunnan. © Mike Roy

THIS IS CHINA – GET STUCK IN!

I rode out into China. After the sterility of Japan my senses exploded into action. It was biting cold and windy, the streets were dirty and potholed and the traffic a whirlpool of hooting chaos. Taxis and buses raced among pedestrians weaving across the wide streets. Excitement welled as I rode into the pandemonium. Memories bubbled of the mad places in the world, the buzz of travel in unknown lands where every day is novel and every trivial task a hurdle. At the same time I thought nervously of how massive and foreign China was. My stomach churned through these emotions as I slipped unthinkingly from Japanese cycling mode (stay patiently in your lane, stop at traffic lights) into the riding mode that most of my favourite countries run on (ignore lanes, ignore traffic lights, ignore everything, get stuck in). I embraced the madness in those first few minutes, making snap comparisons and observations. 'Poorer than Japan... richer than Russia... driving worse than Mexico...' As I concentrated on surviving the hectic streets of Qingdao, my mind took in the grubby old apartment blocks, shiny skyscrapers, McDonald's, street stalls, foetid gutters, mediocre cars, clunking bicycles, rude drivers and potholes. The noise, the chaos. And I used to think Japan and China were pretty similar.

Excerpt from *Thunder & Sunshine* by
Alastair Humphreys

mos of boiling water or green tea for free as soon as you check in. Beer is incredibly cheap; 660ml bottles can be found for US$0.50.

Money

ATMs are easily found in Chinese cities and towns, though as it can sometimes be tricky to find machines that accept international cards, make sure your stash of emergency funds is kept well topped up on a tour here.

CYCLING ACROSS CHINA

So vast as to be a world unto itself, China offers amazingly varied experiences to those who cycle across the country. As Tibet has been closed to independent travellers for a number of years (see p191), adventure tourers coming in from Central Asia now ride across Xinjiang – either on a northern route through Urumqi, or the southern route via Hotan. This province is not without its officialdom hassles or difficulties for foreign cyclists either, with issues such as being banned from entering some towns, and gasoline proving extremely difficult to find in certain areas.

You can enjoy Tibetan culture and scenery without actually entering the Tibet Autonomous Region by cycling in southern Qinghai, south-western Gansu, western Sichuan and northern Yunnan. These areas were once part of Tibet and still have thriving Tibetan villages and monastery complexes amidst high-altitude splendour. Not all parts of these provinces are open to foreigners – generally the closer to Tibet you try to go, the less likely you are to get there – and a route that is open one month might not be the next, meaning you have to do your research and then keep your fingers crossed things don't change.

Beginning or ending your trans-China journey in the Beijing area is not recommended because you would have to cycle through dirty industrial areas. Coming in from the west and Xinjiang, most riders choose to swing south across the very scenic provinces of Sichuan and Yunnan, with detours possible to Guizhou, Guangxi and Chongqing.

CHINA'S SOUTH-WEST

Centuries ago, the Chinese lived mainly along the east coast and called the wild and mountainous territory to their south-west, the 'South-West'. Today the name lives on even though China has pushed its borders much further west and this region is geographically in the south-east. It comprises the five provinces hemmed in by Tibet and Myanmar to the west, Laos and Vietnam to the south, and the coastal plain provinces of Guangdong, Hunan, and Hubei to the east. For cyclists, the South-West offers incredible cultural diversity and scenic splendour. In Yunnan, for example, you can start in the tropical south inhabited by peoples of South-East Asian cultures, move north through regions populated by ancient highland cultures, then reach Tibetan areas amongst glacier-clad summits in the north-west – all in just one province! Each province has its own distinctive landscapes and peoples and you can drop into provincial capitals for good museums, spacious parks, and cultural life.

Try to get a regional guidebook for South-West China because the all-China guidebooks omit many interesting, out-of-the-way places. Spring (March to May) and autumn (September to October) generally have the best cycling weather in the region. Summer has the highest rainfall and can be very hot except at high elevations. Winter sees much of the region freezing, so avoid the high routes at this time, but southern Yunnan can be very pleasant; Guangxi is damp with 'rain dust' in March – rideable, but with little sun. Good flight and rail connections make it easy to reach your starting and ending points; all of the provincial capitals have flights to neighbouring countries, with Chengdu offering flights to Europe as well.

Sichuan

This vast province includes expanses of Tibetan plateau in the west and the fertile Sichuan Basin in the east where even bananas grow. For high adventures, head west into the Tibetan areas, perhaps extending the ride into Yunnan in the south or Qinghai or Gansu in the north. If you head west from the large and lively provincial capital of Chengdu you can be in the mountains within a day's ride, but take care to go slowly enough to acclimatise. One

Left: Friendly monks in Sichuan's scenic grasslands region welcome passing cyclists to pitch their tent for the night. © Amaya Williams.
Right: Screaming thighs and throbbing calves are par for the course when cycling the terraced fields of Yunnan Province. © Eric Schambion

ESSENTIAL CHINESE FOR BIKE TOURERS

China has its fair share of foreign teachers, backpackers, businessmen, and diplomats in the big cities, but once you get out into prime cycling territory, there's a good chance you won't run into any other *lǎowài* for … well, for as long as you're there.

The locals in remote areas see few foreign tourists and have little incentive to learn English, so a bit of linguistic preparation will take you a long way. Here are some words, characters and habits worth knowing:

Counting
Throughout China, locals have a delightful way of counting up to ten on one hand.

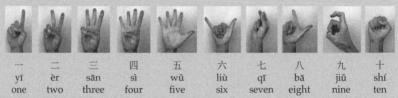

一	二	三	四	五	六	七	八	九	十
yī	èr	sān	sì	wǔ	liù	qī	bā	jiǔ	shí
one	two	three	four	five	six	seven	eight	nine	ten

Internet
Using internet cafés (网吧, wǎngbā) almost always requires a Chinese ID card; there are sometimes ways around it, but you'll probably need a decent command of Chinese to find them.

It's usually better to bring your own laptop or tablet and look for cafés or hotels with wi-fi (无线网络, wúxiànwǎngluò), ask a friendly Couchsurfing host, or use 3G on your phone.

The internet is heavily censored in China, so don't expect to be able to get onto Facebook, Gmail, or YouTube without using a work-around like a Virtual Private Network. VPNs are best set up before you arrive in China.

Sleeping
In general, the higher on this list, the better quality your room will be, and the more you'll pay for it. However, in many cases the choice of a name (is it a hotel? an inn? a lodge?) is entirely arbitrary, so your best bet will be to investigate the room yourself and haggle accordingly.

What to look for		What to expect
酒店	jiǔdiàn	**hotel** Establishments bearing this name tend to be big, well furnished, and more expensive.
青年旅舍	qīngniánlǚshè	**YHA (HI) hostel** Many major cities have branches of the Youth Hostel Association (🖥 www.yhachina.com). Great for meeting other international and domestic travellers, finding English speakers and getting information.
宾馆/住馆	bīnguǎn / zhùguǎn	**guesthouse** Quality not measured in stars, but still usually one of the nicer options.
客栈/客房	kèzhàn / kèfáng	**variable** Some of these are as nice as proper hotels, some are grosser than hostels and offer rooms by the hour. Wink, wink.
旅社 (or 旅馆, or 旅店)	lǚshè	**hostel** Often less than a dollar for a double, but you get what you pay for.

Eating
There are several different names for 'restaurants' but, as with accommodation, the differences are best ascertained by simply popping in the front door and having a look.

The following four common varieties are pretty much the same:

酒店	jiǔdiàn	'alcohol shop'		餐厅	cāntīng	'meal hall'
(same characters as for hotel)				菜馆	càiguǎn	'vegetable hall'
饭店	fàndiàn	'rice shop'				

Despite the lack of English, it's actually easier to order food in China than in many other countries since the restaurants often have large, glass-doored refrigerators showcasing whatever meat and vegetables they have in stock; ordering is as simple as pointing to your food of choice, then waiting to see what they decide to do with it.

If you want to be specific, you can ask to have your meal **stir-fried** (炒, chǎo) or **served in a soup** (汤, tang). Other eateries worth knowing include:

What to look for		What to expect
小吃	xiǎo chī	**'small eats'** China's version of a fast-food restaurant. Whips up quick versions of most of the stuff in the 'basics' list below.
自助餐	zìzhùcān	**buffet!** Dozens of different dishes laid out for you to pick from as you like. Sometimes a flat rate per plate, sometimes you pay by weight, sometimes it's just plain 'all you can eat'.
市场	shì chǎng	**market** For those who prefer to wander around and eat whatever appeals.
超市	chāoshì	**supermarket** For cookies, packet noodles, sauces and other goodies

Reading the menu

米饭	mǐfàn	plain, steamed white rice
炒饭	chǎofàn	fried rice
盖饭	gàifàn	steamed white rice with whatever vegetable or meat you want on top.
炒面	chǎomiàn	fried noodles ('chow mein')
米线	mǐxiàn	rice noodles in broth
包子	bāozi	fist-sized dumplings, stuffed with meat, veg or sweet bean paste
饺子	jiǎozi	small pot-sticker dumplings stuffed with meat/veg
火锅	huǒguō	hotpot soup
豆浆	dòujiāng	soy milk

肉	**ròu**	**meat**	鸡肉	**jīròu**	chicken
牛肉	**niúròu**	beef	鱼肉	**yúròu**	fish
猪肉	**zhūròu**	pork	鸡蛋	**jīdàn**	(chicken) egg

□菜		**cài**	**vegetable dishes (my recommendations)**
红烧茄子	**hóngshāoqiézi**	aubergine fried in a spicy red sauce	
西红柿炒鸡蛋	**xīhóngshìchǎojīdàn**	tomato and egg stir-fry	
土豆丝	**tǔdòusī**	fried julienned potatoes, sometimes with peppers and vinegar	
青菜香菇	**qīngcàixiānggū**	sautéed green vegetables and shiitake mushrooms	

素		**sù**	**vegetarianism**
我吃素	**wǒ chī sù**	'I (only) eat vegetarian food'	
不要放肉	**bú yào fàng ròu**	'Please don't put any meat in it.'	

Last but not least:

再来一个(x) **zài lái yī ge** (x) 'More (x) please!'   **Mike Roy**

Left: Six hungry cyclists. **Right**: A homestay breakfast. © Mike Roy

increasingly popular mountain route is to ride between Chengdu and Shangri-La (Zhongdian) in Yunnan, via Xiaojin, Yajiang, Litang and Xiang Cheng – a journey of 1200km which takes in numerous high passes up to 4750m. The challenging mountain terrain in southern Sichuan is populated by many minority groups as well as Han Chinese.

Yunnan

It's been said that if you only have time to see one province in China, head for Yunnan, which is extremely scenic from the rice terraces in the south to the icy Himalaya in the north. There's a price for this splendour – the province is overwhelmingly hilly, so slap on the low gearing and enjoy. Ethnic minorities comprise about half the population, and you'll find over half of China's 55 minority groups here. Many of those in the south practise the same Theravada Buddhism as neighbouring Laos, Thailand, and Myanmar. Five of Asia's major rivers cut deeply into rugged landscapes – the Nujiang (Salween), Mekong, Yangtze, Pearl and Red. Yunnan's most exciting ride is a grand tour the length of the province, taking 1-2 months. This could include a ride

DO THE TASTIEST CHICKENS GROW ON TREES?

When I told my friends in South Korea that I intended to buy a bicycle and ride it across China, they nodded their heads, unfazed; but when I told them that I planned on sticking to my vegetarian diet the whole way, I was promptly assaulted with doubt. 'There's no way,' said one, who had visited Beijing on a package tour the previous summer and had been traumatised by the sight of skewered scorpions. 'They put meat in everything,' said another, who had lived in China as a student, spoke the language fluently, and now worked as a translator. Their input discouraged me slightly, but then again most Koreans found it hard to believe I had been getting by (thriving, if you ask me) as a vegetarian in their country for several years.

It only took two hours off the ferry and wandering around a random market in Dalian, the starting point of my cycle journey, to convince me that they were completely, totally wrong. First it was the market full of mangos, mangosteens, and other fruits I recognised only because I had backpacked around South-East Asia a few years previous. Then it was the hamburger-sized cornbread dumplings stuffed with sautéed cabbage, on sale for 3 Yuan apiece. Next was an afternoon snack of peanuts, broad beans and beer with my cycling partner on the stairs in front of a supermarket while waiting for our Couchsurfing host. For dinner, Chinese-style burritos filled with our choice of stir-fried

veggies; the following night, home-cooked variations of the same, except with local cilantro and imported Old El Paso refried beans. And more, as we moved south: fresh soy milk and doughnuts from vendors who set up in the streets early each morning; crispy, griddle-fried leek pancakes; autumn-only 'moon cakes' packed with crushed nuts and diced dried fruits; sweet potatoes sold out of ovens on wheels, roasted until their insides turned the consistency of ice-cream. Not to mention the standard restaurant fare of rice, noodles, soups, tofu, and of course the classic point-and-pick vegetable stir-fry.

So it was that during my ten months on the Chinese landmass I hardly had any problems maintaining my diet of choice. Only twice did I run into any real trouble. First was the time an overly friendly host of the slightly pushy variety insisted – all generosity, face home to a beaming smile – I eat both lobes of the goat brain he had bought just for me. (Fearing souring our relations, I obliged; it tasted like mild tofu, and wasn't quite as repulsive as anticipated.) Second was just a few days before I crossed out of China and into Laos. Coming south from the Nujiang Valley at the east end of the Himalaya, the landscape grew more and more tropical by the day, precarious rice terraces being replaced with expansive paddies and pine groves giving way to banana plantations. In one restaurant, alongside the usual assort-

through rugged mountains in the far south near the Laos and Vietnam borders, connecting Laos or Jinghong with Kunming via Jiangsheng, Luchun, Yuanyang, Gejiu, Jianshui and Tonghai.

Central Yunnan has many traditional villages surrounding Dali that can inspire loop rides. A few days further north, you'll see icy peaks of the Himalaya from the extremely picturesque town of Lijiang. It gets even better as you continue north to Tiger Leaping Gorge, which you can cycle all the way through. From the east end of Tiger Leaping Gorge a very scenic road climbs into Tibetan country and leads to Shangri-La (Zhongdian), which has a large Tibetan temple complex and can be linked with Chengdu. If you really wish to get off the beaten track, head for the far west of Yunnan and follow roads that roughly parallel the Myanmar border all the way from Laos to the edge of Tibet, the last part up the increasingly spectacular Nujiang Valley.

The Mohan (China) – Boten (Laos) border crossing in the far south is very popular with cyclists, and it's only four cycling days through Laos to Thailand now that the Huay Xai – Boten road is fully paved. Further east, the Hekou (China) – Lao Cai (Vietnam) crossing is another popular option. Laos visas are

ment of vegetables in the display case, I spotted an odd purple, conical mass – the oft-overlooked flower of the banana plant – which I asked the chef to cook up for me in whatever vegetarian-friendly way he deemed appropriate. The result was a scramble of about one third red chillies, one third stringy white flesh, and one third pimply yellow rind. Not only did it look and taste exactly like chicken; it tasted rich, juicy, and succulent, like the best chicken I had ever eaten.

With each bite I grew more and more convinced that despite how smoothly the order had seemed to go, a mistake must have been made. I called over the chef's six-year-old son and asked him, 'This is chicken, right?'

'No, it's vegetarian.'

I took another few bites, but remained unconvinced, beckoning this time to his twelve year-old. 'You're saying this isn't chicken?'

'No, it's banana flower.'

He seemed sure of it, so I relented. Within another bite or two, though, the nagging doubt came back. More out of a desire to resolve the mystery than anything else, I grabbed my plate and walked around the corner into the kitchen. 'Are you sure this isn't chicken?', I said to the chef.

'No, it's this.' He pointed at another banana flower sitting there in the refrigerator case.

'But it looks and tastes just like chicken.'

'Nope, it's a banana flower. Here.' He grabbed the vegetable in question, slapped it down on a cutting board, and promptly chopped off a cross-section for me to investigate. At the base of the cone were small, light-coloured stalks, to be sautéed until they had turned the colour of flesh. Inside, beneath a few layers of purple sheathes, was the yellow heart that I had taken for chicken skin. Not an ounce of actual meat in sight.

I returned to my seat to polish off the rest of the plate, savouring every bite of the most delicious dish I had come across in China, and regretting only the fact that I'd be out of the country in less than a week, perhaps never to taste it again.

Mike Roy

The chef and his family. © Mike Roy

available at the border, but you must get a Vietnamese visa in advance from a consulate (the nearest is in Kunming).

Yunnan also has the only available China – Myanmar border crossing, located between Ruili and Muse. At the time of writing you still needed a special visa from the Myanmar consulate in Kunming (or a permit from Yangon if headed the other way) and help from a travel agent to do this (try Seven Diamond Express Travels in Yangon, see p218); however, it may well become simpler soon.

Chongqing

Chongqing straddles a section of the Yangtze east of Sichuan. The hilly terrain in the city of Chongqing deters most cyclists but you'll find many historic sites and museums here. Boat tours cruise the Yangtze River downstream if you'd like a few days off the bicycle. The Dazu area, 125km north-west of Chongqing, has dazzling Buddhist grotto art; worth a detour if you're in the area.

Guizhou

Picturesque minority villages spread across wildly scenic hills in the eastern part of this province. It's nearly all good riding, and if you enjoy cycling in the hills there's even a road to the top of Leigong Mountain (2180m). The scenery keeps on going in the west with some of China's best caves and waterfalls. Longgong Caves make a great daytrip from Anshun; trails and boat trips link

---

BORDER CROSSINGS IN WESTERN CHINA

In western China you'll probably follow one of the Silk Routes, passing ancient grotto temples, watchtowers, and fortifications. Adventurous cyclists have the option of crossing between China and three of the 'Stans – Pakistan, Kyrgyzstan and Kazakhstan. There's also a road into Tajikistan, but so far it has been restricted to locals for trade purposes only (see p169).

Most cyclists visit the old town and markets of Kashgar in the far west of China, from where you can access the spectacular Karakoram Highway which links Pakistan and China via the Khunjerab Pass – see p141.

Passes to Kyrgyzstan are also accessible from Kashgar – the Irkeshtam (see p170) crossing connects China with southern Kyrgyzstan and provides a quick way to Tajikistan's fabulous Pamirs, though you'll need to get a Tajik visa in Almaty or Bishkek before doing so. The Torugart Pass offers a shorter route between Kashgar and Kyrgyzstan's capital Bishkek, but requires advance transport arrangements (see p170) on the Chinese side through a travel agency in Kashgar. Fortunately many nationalities can now get into Kyrgyzstan and Kazakhstan without a visa, which is a real

bonus given that Kashgar lacks consulates; Ürümqi, in China's north-west, offers Kyrgyz and Kazazkh consulates, as well as flights to both countries.

You can cycle to Kazakhstan by heading west from Ürümqi to Korgas, fairly dull desert country most of the way – though you might spot herds of Bactrian camels – until you climb to beautiful Sayram Lake with vistas of snow-capped mountains. From here it's just a day's ride to Korgas with plenty of hotels, restaurants, and shops on the Chinese side. You may have to pay for a vehicle to carry you the silly kilometre between Chinese and Kazakh posts. The Kazakh side has no facilities but you'll find an ATM, bank, hotel, and food in Zharkent, the first sizeable town to the west. Two other border crossings further north between China and Kazakhstan have occasionally been used by cyclists transiting Kazakhstan between China and Russia – Tacheng and Jimunai. Be warned that bicycle theft is a major problem in Central Asia, so camp away from villages and always lock the bicycle to something solid.

To access western Mongolia from the Takashiken border post in Xinjiang, to the north-east of Urumqi, see p180.

PUTTING BIKES ON CHINESE TRAINS

● Find the train you need online (try 🖳 travelchinaguide.com) and buy your ticket at the station in advance, explaining that you have a bike. Note that the new High Speed trains (train numbers beginning C, D & G) don't carry bikes as they have no baggage wagons. Also, dedicated High Speed rail stations have no consignment facilities.

● Once you've bought your own travel ticket you'll be told to take the bike to the consignment hall, which is usually next to the station.

● At the consignment hall they'll help you fill in a form, which is in Chinese. Pay for your bike and get a receipt. The standard delivery time is three days, but you may be able to pay extra for a faster service. It may be possible for the bike to go on the same train as you – check when buying the bike ticket.

● It's recommended to remove pedals before handing over your bike, to prevent joy-riding.

● At your destination go to the consignment hall, show your receipt and pick up the bike.

John Burnham & Gayle Dickson

a long series of large and small caves. Zhijin Cave will amaze you for its vast chambers filled with ornate and highly varied cave features; it's near the town of Zhijin, a day's ride north of Anshun. Huangguoshu Falls, a day's ride south-west of Anshun, rank among Asia's largest.

Guangxi

Come here to experience those impossibly steep limestone pinnacles so often pictured on Chinese landscape paintings. The scenery is for real, and you can experience it by cycling on backroads near Yangshuo or on a Li River boat cruise. Minority villages just north of Guilin have spectacular rice terraces and intriguing wind-and-rain (covered) bridges; from here you might continue into eastern Guizhou to experience additional minority culture. The south of the province has a bit of coastline with beaches on the Gulf of Tonkin. Two border crossings connect Guangxi with Vietnam – on the coast at Dongxing and northeast of Hanoi at Pingxiang (Friendship Pass) – get your visa in advance at the consulate in Nanning. You could also reach Guangxi by cycling west across Guangdong Province from Hong Kong or, more easily, from Macau.

Tibet

Tibet is many cyclists' view of the ultimate in adventure touring – long, self-supported travels on the roof of the world, the kind of freedom that only cycling provides, all at high altitudes and sometimes on the roughest of roads. Where others fear to go, or might drive through with the windows of their Landcruisers shut tight to keep dust out, cyclists thrive. It's not just about riding at 5000m either: Tibet's traditional culture is like no other. Tibetan Buddhism is possibly even more colourful than the Buddhism you will see in the rest of Asia and it's very much a living religion among the vast majority of the population. Despite the harsh climate, Tibetans are some of the friendliest people you could hope to meet and have a great sense of humour. Much of the attraction of a trip to Tibet lies in meeting local people on the road or visiting *gompas* (monasteries).

Nomad camp in West Tibet.
© Dominique Kerhuel

Restrictions imposed since the riots of 2008 have sadly made independent cycle trips into Tibet all but impossible – the only way of visiting the country legally on two wheels is restricted to expensive guided tours on the Friendship Highway from Lhasa to Kathmandu. Even the time-honoured tactics employed by adventurous cyclists in previous years of travelling at night to dodge checkpoints, avoiding hotels, and camping very well hidden no longer work, as the PSB (Public Security Bureau) now picks up travellers on the road between checkpoints and the military also arrests bikers. Current Chinese policy for dealing with bikers who have somehow managed to sneak in seems to be a fine, followed by removal from Tibet to a neighbouring province, or even deportation out of China.

In the hope that the situation might change for the better and independent biking on major routes be allowed again during the lifetime of this book, here are a couple of tasters for epic rides that can be found onto (or off) the plateau:

ROUTES

The Friendship Highway – Lhasa to Kathmandu

One of the three original great cycling routes in the Himalaya, the Friendship Highway stands alongside the Manali-Leh road and the Karakoram Highway as a fantastic adventure through different cultures and among high peaks. It's around 950km from Lhasa (3650m) to Kathmandu (1300m), or 1150km if you include the recommended side trip to Everest Basecamp (EBC). The route includes five major passes, three of which are over 5000m, as well as one of the world's longest downhills: the descent from Yarlung Shan La into Nepal. The best time to ride is summer and autumn, and you should allow at least 18 cycling days, including the EBC sidetrip. The high altitudes and possibility of fierce storms and headwinds make it a challenging ride, but it's almost all paved these days and there are at least basic facilities on the route. Allow extra days for rests and visiting important sites along the way in Lhasa, Gyantse and Shigatse; see Laura Stone's *Himalaya by Bike* for more detail.

The Tibetan epic – Kashgar to Lhasa

One of the longest, highest and hardest routes in the world, the ride across west Tibet from Kashgar to Lhasa used to attract a handful of determined cyclists every summer. A west Tibet ride is all about the human spirit and whether you've got what it takes. Don't undertake this ride lightly, there are other, more pleasant routes in the region for carefree riding – the KKH (p142) is a cakewalk by comparison. But the rewards of travelling to such a remote place, under your own steam, self-supported with panniers jammed with food, and entirely exposed to nature, are immense. From Kashgar to Lhasa via the Aksai Chin plateau, Ali and the base of Mt Kailash, is 3000km. Most of the route is now paved but the 30 or so passes and extended periods at high altitudes mean that it takes most people seven to nine weeks to ride. Not for the novice.

Inside a Tibetan guesthouse. © Stephen Lord

Eastern Tibet – Lhasa to Markham

The beautiful eastern route between Lhasa and Sichuan is unlike western or central Tibet in terms of terrain and people, and it was often closed to foreign cyclists even before the blanket shutdown of 2008. It's a land of roller-coaster passes with huge climbs and descents that will exhaust any cyclist. Passing through farmland, you'll see new housebuilding in the Tibetan style, and seemingly every valley has its own unique style. Nomads are uncommon but every day in the autumn you will pass pilgrims walking to Lhasa, prostrating every step. Three of the world's great rivers are crossed in their upper reaches – the Yarlung Tsangpo/Brahmaputra, the Salween and the Mekong, and if you turn south at Markham you will cross the Yangtze close to Shangri-La (Zhongdian).

Taiwan

Amaya Williams

With extraordinary geographic diversity and an ever-expanding network of bike paths, Taiwan is finally starting to figure on the radar of international cyclists. From the spine of mountains running the length of the country, to the white sandy beaches and steamy jungles of the far south to the rocky eastern seaboard, the landscapes never disappoint.

It's a good choice for both a short bicycle tour or as part of a longer Asia trip and biking Taiwan can be as easy or as difficult as you want to make it. If you crave a challenge and are up for some lung-bursting climbs, hit the mountains and cycle one of the cross-island roads. For a more tranquil tour, stick to the flatter coastal roads.

PRACTICALITIES

Arriving and travelling

Taiwan can be cycled year round, with a climate that varies considerably depending on elevation and whether you're in the north or south. Autumn (September to November) and spring (March to May) are the best times to be

The entrance to Taiwan's Taroko Gorge.
© Amaya Williams

on the road, as you'll avoid the summer heat and the chilling winter cold; rain can fall at any time of year.

Most cyclists fly into Taipei, but you can now reach Taiwan by sea from mainland China. A comfortable overnight ferry travels between Xiamen and Keelung and costs around US$100 for a berth in a four-passenger cabin. Taiwan offers visa exemptions to many nationalities, the only catch being that strained relations with the mainland government mean there's nowhere to obtain or extend a Chinese visa in Taipei. Come to Taiwan only if you've already got a multiple-entry visa for China or if you're planning on flying out elsewhere afterwards.

Cycling in Taiwan poses few difficulties: you rarely go long distances without services, roads are in good condition and finding your way isn't tricky as most road signs are in both Chinese and English. Nearly everyone speaks at least some English and Taiwan is one of the best wired nations in the world so accessing online maps is never an issue.

Eating and sleeping

Taiwanese food, a delectable blend of Chinese, Japanese and Javanese flavours, is outstanding value and a saunter through the night market (every town's got one) is the perfect way to top off a taxing day in the saddle. You might also restore aching muscles with a prolonged soak in one of the many hot springs scattered around the country.

Camping is catching on in Taiwan and there are a growing number of mega-campsites along the southern beaches. Wild camping is an accepted practice and poses no particular security issues. Police stations often double as cyclist pit stops and friendly officers will top up your water and might even let you pitch your tent for the night. The local 7-11 convenience stores are another haven for touring cyclists as they offer cheap and convenient meals, clean restrooms, cold water and also keep tools and pumps on hand for the express use of cyclists.

SOME ROUTES

Circumnavigating Taiwan, a distance of around 1500km, is relatively easy and extraordinarily popular with local Taiwanese bicycle tourers. You'll roll through everything from colossal, cosmopolitan cities to tiny rural villages that take you back a step in time. On some stretches you'll cruise along on wide cycle paths and on other parts you'll be riding the highway, usually with a good shoulder.

Taiwan's west coast is the country's economic heartland and home to most of the population. Coastal highways here can be congested so it's best to stick to county roads further inland.

Cyclists thirsting for more adventure will want to tackle one of the three cross-island highways. The Northern Cross Island Highway, linking Taoyuan and Yilan counties, is less taxing than the central and southern options and offers the added bonus of passing through the forest of magnificent ancient cypress trees at Mingchi.

No matter which route you choose, don't miss Taroko Gorge. The road into the gorge is carved into the mountainside and you'll pass through a series of three-sided tunnels and over spectacular bridges as you meander past stunning limestone formations and temples shrouded in mist.

South Korea

Amaya Williams

In the mood for some pleasant, stress-free cycling and don't have the time or inclination to do a lot of planning? Korea's first-rate biking infrastructure is unrivalled in Asia, so it might just be the place for you.

The country's massive multi-million dollar Four Rivers Restoration project spawned 1745km of tranquil long-distance riverside bike paths, meaning criss-crossing this fascinating country couldn't be simpler. Beautiful parks line the riverbanks, dedicated bike tunnels cut out much of the climbing and the purpose-built paths jut out over the waterways at times, offering a magnificent cycling experience. If semi-tropical islands are more your style, hop on a ferry to Jeju and circle the island following serene coastal cycle paths.

Adventure addicts, don't despair. The Korean population is concentrated in major urban centres such as Seoul and Busan, leaving much of the countryside delightfully empty, and mountains cover 70% of the country's land mass. If you think cycle paths are for wimps, head to the far north and test your mettle on the switchbacks and steep climbs.

PRACTICALITIES

Visas
Most visitors to Korea receive a free 90-day stay upon arrival, and the best times to visit are autumn and spring. In September and October temperatures are cool but comfortable, skies are generally blue and autumn foliage is beautiful. By November, temperatures start dipping to freezing in the mountains but the southern provinces and Jeju Island are still pleasant. Spring brings cherry blossom and wildflowers. Korean winters are harsh, while summers tend to be unpleasantly hot and humid and can be quite rainy, especially in June.

Sleeping
With a reasonable budget, it is possible to cycle-tour in Korea without a tent as there are numerous motels and small guesthouses charging US$30-40 a night. Many local long-distance cyclists stay at Public Bath Houses, which may sound odd but it's a common form of family lodging in Korea. The accommodation is cheap (around US$7) but communal.

Daybreak in Korea, Land of the Morning Calm. © Amaya Williams

Camping is surprisingly easy and official campsites are springing up all over the country as pitching a tent catches on as a pastime. Many camp-sites are free, while others charge a minimal fee of around US$5. Wild camping is widely accepted, and most villages have a small gazebo-like structure on which you can put your tent; perfect for rainy days.

Touring tips

Unsurprisingly for a country in the throes of bicycle fever, every city has at least one well-stocked bike shop. In Seoul, local cyclists recommend **Plush Bikes**, **Storck-Watts bike shop** and **Biclo**. It's easy to take your machine on public transport too – some trains provide special bike carriages and on week-ends you can even take your bike on some subway lines.

Detailed road atlases are available but most are in Korean only. Luckily this isn't a big problem because you can teach yourself to read Korean script (Hangul) in under an hour – see 🖥 ryanestrada.com.

Onward travel to Japan is possible by comfortable overnight ferries from Busan to Fukuoka and Shimonoseki; there are also several sea links between Incheon and mainland China.

POSSIBLE ROUTES

The easiest way to discover Korea on two wheels is by following the 4 Rivers Bicycle Routes (🖥 riverguide.go.kr/eng). The most popular route is between Seoul and Busan following the Nakdonggang and Hanggang Rivers – the entire 640km ride is on dedicated cycle paths or quiet country roads.

Korea's most mountainous province, Gangwon in the far north, is 80% covered by woodlands, and is a mecca for mountain bikers and adventure enthusiasts. If you're up for a challenge, ride stunning Route 44 past craggy peaks and dense forest in Seoraksan, the country's most famous national park.

Other scenic mountain roads include:
• Route 56 between Yangyang and Nae-Myeon
• Route 460 between Hwacheon and Dong-Myeon
• Route 453 between Dong-Myeon and Buk-Myeon.

Japan

Rob Thomson

Traffic-free roads, sleepy fishing villages and some of the cheapest, most delicious food in the developed world – few would guess this is an honest-to-God description of Japan. Its reputation as a crowded, expensive country to travel in stems from so many visitors travelling by public transport and visiting only the most popular tourist destinations, which will entail expense and battles with the crowds. However, you're likely reading this book because you prefer to eschew the beaten track and forge your own adventures by bicycle, in which case you'll discover a refreshingly laid-back Japan: a developed country that certainly won't break the bank.

Note the emphasis on developed country here. Japan is worlds apart from many of its hectic developing neighbours on the Asian mainland. It is a land of order and poise. As such, it is the perfect destination for those keen to dip their toes into an 'oriental' culture for the first time.

Japan will offer everything you expect: sushi, shrines, and *shinkansen*, but seeing it by bike is a ticket to experiencing the true Japan: generous hospitality, respectful curiosity, and access to sights out of reach of public transport. And you'll find things you never expected too, like the grand outdoors, the wide open spaces and the potential for adventure.

PRACTICALITIES

Arriving in Japan
The ferries that run daily from Korea to southern Japanese ports are a stress-free way of getting from the mainland. If flying in, let yourself rest easy in the fact that you'll arrive in one of the safest societies on the planet. Don't sweat it if you forget your wallet full of freshly exchanged 10,000yen bills in the arrivals lounge – it'll still be there when you go and fetch it a day later.

Bicycles are generally free to carry onto domestic planes and trains, so long as they're packed properly. For trains, the front wheel must be removed and the whole bike wrapped (a cheap blue-sheet tarpaulin will suffice) or put into a bike bag. Bicycles can be rolled onto ferries, though a small extra fee is usually charged.

Finding your way
Grab a 'Touring Mapple' map book, available at most large bookstores – you'd be hard-pressed to find a

Bikes bagged and stowed on a train in rural Hokkaido. © Rob Thomson

Japanese cycle tourist without a tattered, well-used 'Touring Mapple' stuffed in a pannier. Sold in prefecture-by-prefecture volumes, it shows campgrounds, *onsen* (the ubiquitous natural hot-springs – learn that word!), dirt roads and scenic byways, giving a great overview of possible routes. It's all in Japanese, so stay with a Warm Showers host at the start of your tour and ask them to decipher the map symbols. Paired with an Open Street Map app on your smartphone you'll be set for some great self-directed off-the-beaten-track routes through spectacular countryside.

Accommodation

Campgrounds are fairly common and tend to range from free to around US$30 a night, but considering that many do not have showers, wild camping can be a better option. Luckily, Japan is hands-down the easiest country to wild camp that I've cycled in, and costs saved on paid accommodation offset the 500yen (US$4) for an *onsen* soak.

The Japanese can be notoriously reserved or extremely hospitable, which means wild camping in public parks, road-side parking areas, and at temples will result in either the best night's sleep you've ever had or a jovial late-night invitation to a BBQ party.

An option worth exploring for at least a few nights is a 'Riders' House', a type of accommodation that is cheap (from free to 1000yen) and exists solely for motorcyclists, cyclists, or other human-powered travellers. Especially common in Hokkaido, expect into-the-night discussions about the best routes, tall tales, and tips for places to see.

HAULING IN SHIKOKU SQUID FOR BREAKFAST

Like most nights on my quick two-week tour of Shikoku, I had pitched my tent under a pagoda next to a small fishing port. At the crack of dawn the next morning, I was jolted awake by someone shaking my tent. Outside was a jovial guy from the previous night – the one who had appeared out of the blue to hand me two chilled beers. It became clear he was a fisherman, and was now insisting that I help pull in his nets. Out on the water, the sun rising over the calm sea was magical.

Pulling up to his nets, he killed the engine and we started work in earnest. With him barking orders in a hard-to-decipher local dialect, I managed to help him haul in 10kg of squid over the next couple of hours. Reward for my efforts was joining him and a friend for a breakfast of boiled squid. Perhaps it was my hunger from early-morning effort, but that squid was delicious – less than 20 minutes out of the water, it was a delicacy. 'Consider it payment for the beers last night', said my new fisherman friend.

Rob Thomson

Supplies

For good quality fresh food, expect to pay no more than 700yen when eating out for a healthy lunch, and not much more for a dinner. Menus often come with pictures, and if all else fails, just point at one of the intricate wax models of the dishes in the storefront window.

You'll find fuel for multi-fuel or alcohol (which is sold at drug stores) stoves more easily than gas canisters. For cycling supplies, larger cities have shops stocking parts likely to be of interest to a touring cyclist.

Communicating

On the whole, English communication skills are in surprisingly short supply in Japan, and when chatting to locals you're likely to meet one of two types of people: 1) the enthusiastic communicator who, quite independent of any second language ability, will simply be enthralled with interacting with a foreign cyclist, and 2) the nervous type who just wants the interaction to be over as soon as possible. The latter isn't being rude – their behaviour is simply a reflection of the intense politeness of the Japanese culture, not wanting to put you in a situation where you are struggling to communicate. Learn a few Japanese phrases and you'll never hear the end of the compliments.

Foreign visitors will find a lack of public wi-fi, however the situation is improving and, as a last resort, you can usually access internet at public libraries for free. In larger cities, internet cafés can make for a cheap and convenient place to sleep for the night – shower included. As for Japan-specific SIM cards, it is a closed shop. Pre-paid SIM cards do not exist, leaving most people with the option of rental mobile phones or dongles, which aren't cheap.

ROUTES

'Gosh that was a flat country', is not something you'll ever hear said about cycling in Japan. There are of course plenty of flat areas, but they're typically crammed with buildings and people. In the great outdoors – the places worth spending days on end in the saddle – expect plenty of hill climbing, compact valleys and low passes opening out to more passes and valleys.

Hokkaido

Northern-most of Japan's large islands, Hokkaido has endless exploring options due to it being the least densely populated and most-recently colonised of the main islands. It is also Japan's most brown bear-infested island; Alaska-style bear precautions apply when wild-camping. For those willing to commit to the effort of getting to the start of the route by plane and train, I cannot recommend enough an across-Hokkaido sojourn that starts at Abashiri (from where you can see Russia) and ends in Sapporo, Hokkaido's capital. You'll cross swathes of uninhabited native forest, deep gorges, fertile farmland (think wide open dairy farms and corn-fields), and be offered the option of sampling some of the finest dirt roads the country has to offer. Temperatures in winter drop to -20°C in places, and Sapporo gets an average of six metres of snow a year, so for a holiday tour choose summer; for a well-planned expedition choose winter.

Honshu

Moving south is Honshu, the slender main island which is home to big cities such as Tokyo, Osaka, Kyoto, and Hiroshima. Many would call this the 'real' Japan – sandwiched between the industry and commerce are the paddy fields, shrines and temples, and a deep history. Don't overlook the majestic Japan Alps for getting away from the guidebook-toting crowds: on your way south from Tokyo, consider a (hefty) detour across Japan's highest paved road – on Mt Norikura – and marvel at the way such a massive population manages to fit into such a compact, and predominantly steeply-forested country.

Shikoku

Tucked in between Honshu and Kyushu, diminutive Shikoku is well worth the detour. The coastal climbs can be brutal, but the southern coastal scenery from Kochi to Matsuyama is breathtaking. Keep an eye out for white-clad pilgrims on their way around Japan's most popular 88-temple pilgrimage route, and consider visiting some temples yourself – many of them offer basic accommodation for walkers and cyclists.

Kyushu

If the short, sharp hills of the Shikoku coast run you down, there's always the option of jumping on a short ferry from Yawatahama to the southernmost island of Kyushu. Miyazaki Prefecture on Kyushu's eastern coast has some of the best beaches in Japan, which should bring some relief. Cut inland and you'll hit the land of the volcanoes: Mt Aso is Japan's largest active volcano with a caldera over 120km in circumference.

Mt. Rishiri on the remote, far-north Rishiri Island. © Rob Thomson

South-East Asia

Amaya Williams

South-East Asia serves up everything you'd wish for in a cycling adventure abroad: alluring landscapes, challenging terrain, delectable and diverse cuisines plus a fascinating mix of people, all set against a rich and abundant historical and cultural backdrop. Locals are friendly, prices reasonable (some

South East Asia
MAIN ROUTES

PART 4 – ROUTES – ASIA

An extremely easy region for riders, with plenty of open border crossings – Myanmar has the trickiest bureaucracy. Almost any rideable road is a good route and avoiding traffic is one of the main considerations. Bangkok or Singapore are probably the easi-est places in the region to fly to and begin a circular tour, though consider taking a bus or train to get out of Bangkok, beginning your ride on quieter rural roads. Note that getting from South-East Asia to Australia generally involves flying as there is no passenger ferry.

T R I P   R E P O R T
ROUND THE WORLD

Name	Lorenzo Rojo
Nationality	Born in the Basque Country
Year of birth	1961
Occupation	High School Teacher until 1997
Other bike travels	Houston-Quito

This trip	America (North, Central and South), Oceania, Asia, Europe, Middle East, Africa, the Americas again
Trip duration	Since June 1997
Number in group	One (most of the time)
Total distance	About 190,000km
Cost of trip	Around US$10 per day

Longest day	200km (being pushed by a rare wind in Patagonia).
Best day	Hopefully in front of me.
Worst day	Leaving Addis Ababa, Ethiopia.
Favourite ride	North Sudan (Nubia), Tibet, the Andes, West USA.
Biggest headache	The hours after a stone hit my head in Ethiopia (needed some stitches).
Biggest mistake	Telling my parents when I left that I would be back in six months.
Bribes paid	Nothing really big, neither very often. Less than US$10, once, to enter Equatorial Guinea.
Illnesses during trip	Nothing serious.

Bike model	Two chromoly bikes: first one, hybrid; current one, mountain bike.
New/used	Current one (since 2001): used.
Modifications	Painted it several times. Changed (cut and welded) the lowest part of the frame (where the bottom bracket goes in).
Tyres used	Schwalbe Marathon XR the last few years.
Baggage Setup	Front and rear Carradice panniers (tough), a small backpack, handlebar bag.
Wish you'd brought	A warmer sleeping bag, sometimes.
Wish you hadn't brought	A couple of useless fears.

Bike problems	Nothing unusual. Never got stranded on the road.
Accidents?	None with the bike.
Road philosophy	Be curious and respectful.

What do you daydream about in the saddle?	Sometimes I dream about impossibilities, endless roads; but in the late afternoons happiness is just a quiet camping spot and a big pot of spaghetti.

say ridiculously cheap) and bureaucracy minimal.

If you're new to cycle touring or haven't travelled abroad much, South-East Asia is a great place to gain experience and build confidence before dashing off to more daunting destinations like Central Asia, the Andes or Africa. Stick to the classic routes and you'll find plenty of perfectly paved roads, comfortable guesthouses and a good variety of restaurants without having to compromise on outstanding scenery or interesting rides.

An intricate network of quiet red-laterite roads criss-crosses Cambodia.
© Eric Schambion

Intrepid bicycle travellers who delight in dirt roads and discovering spots where stunned locals still stop to gawk at the sight of a sweaty tourist trundling along a rutted jungle track are equally well catered for. Throughout South-East Asia, you'll find it's surprisingly easy to access rugged and remote areas barely touched by tourism. Even in a country like Thailand that attracts 16 million foreign visitors a year, it's possible to cycle for weeks without seeing another foreign face.

PRACTICALITIES

Getting there
If you're flying in to the region the best transport hubs are Bangkok, Kuala Lumpur, Singapore and Bali. If beginning your trip in Thailand, check the possibility of flying into Chiang Mai: it's a much easier city to navigate than Bangkok. Kuala Lumpur's traffic is particularly perilous for cyclists so consider getting public transport out of the metropolitan area into more rural surroundings.

Climate
The region is generally hot and humid year round except in highland areas where the weather varies from warm and pleasant to decidedly cool. The wettest part of the year in most of the region is between June and October. Rain tends to fall fast and furious in South-East Asia and you'll want to duck for cover inside the nearest thatched hut, under a highway overpass or slip into a restaurant for a steaming bowl of noodle soup. The best time, weatherwise, to cycle the region is December to February which sees cooler temperatures. By early March things start heating up considerably and, after a sweltering day in the saddle, you might be more than willing to splurge on an air-conditioned room.

Costs and cash
By eating in local restaurants, camping some of the time and watching your beer and banana shake intake, careful budget cyclists can get by on around US$10 a day. Double that and you can travel comfortably without keeping a sharp eye on every Bhat and Kip that escapes from your handlebar bag. With a budget of

Rickety bridges and rough roads are
challenges you face when setting off on
the backroads through Laos.
© Eric Schambion

US$35-US$50/day you can easily enjoy mid-range hotels with en-suite facilities, treat yourself to the best restaurants and enjoy your fill of Beer Lao. ATMs are common all over South-East Asia so getting cash is rarely a problem.

Safety, hassles and minor annoyances

South-East Asia is one of the safest and most hassle-free regions in the world. Border procedures are, for the most part, straightforward; theft is no more a problem than in Europe or North America and, unless you're extremely unlucky, it's highly unlikely you'll fall prey to any scams or rip-offs targeting travellers. Overcharging is not commonplace outside of tourist areas, although it's always good practice to ask prices before ordering meals. Traffic noise on main roads and in urban areas can be a serious issue, particularly in coastal Vietnam and Indonesia.

The locals

Expect warm smiles and friendly greetings throughout the region. In off-the-beaten-path places curious crowds may gather to stare. You'll surely receive lots of thumbs-up as you tackle big climbs and spontaneous offers of cold drinks, snacks and even invitations home for a meal are common.

Staying connected

Internet cafés are slowly disappearing as more people have internet access at home. With the exception of Myanmar, wi-fi is widely available in hotels, guesthouses and restaurants throughout the region. It seems everyone – from the farmer out ploughing his field with a water buffalo to the businessman in the flashy SUV – has a mobile phone. 3G coverage is good and you'll have no problem setting yourself up with a SIM card and local telephone number for a very reasonable fee.

Maps

Cyclists are turning increasingly to GPS technology and online maps in South-East Asia, as these provide more detailed information on the countless minor roads connecting villages. The best paper maps are those made by Reise Know-How and Nelles, but even these are not 100% dependable.

Being such a popular touring destination, almost every corner of the region has been explored by bike at some point. Roam around ⌨crazyguy onabike.com or Google some obscure route and you're almost certain to come back with solid, up-to-date information.

Planes, trains and buses

With the advent of low-cost regional carriers such as Air Asia, cyclists are now flying within the region. We've heard more than one sad story of a cyclist turning up at the ticket counter with an unboxed bike and heavy gear and ending up paying many times the ticket price in excess baggage fees. Be sure to read the fine print before booking a flight.

Roads and driving standards

Chaotic. That's how many people would describe the traffic in South-East Asia. Scooters zip in and out, minibus drivers suddenly lurch to a halt, horns blare, cows wander across the highway, pedestrians weave their

Southern Thailand's white sandy beaches are the perfect place to rest and recuperate.
© Eric Schambion

way through traffic, cyclists roll along in the hectic mass of humanity. It's actually fun once you get the hang of it and not nearly as dangerous as it appears. Really. The trick to coming home unscathed is to go with the flow, make wild hand movements before executing any turns and use your bell liberally.

Overall, roads in the region are of a fairly high standard and drivers reasonably courteous. If you stick to the main highways, you could easily ride on skinny tyres, but as it's much more fun to do some dirt, we recommend tyres at least 1.75" wide.

Sleeping

Guesthouses and hotels are generally good value. The Couchsurfing and Warm Showers hospitality networks are catching on in the region and you can almost always find a host in larger cities. Blame it on the heat and humidity or the relatively high population density, but not many cyclists camp in South-East Asia. Of course it is possible to pitch your tent in off-the beaten-track areas and in rural areas, with Buddhist temples known to offer hospitality to passing two-wheeled travellers.

Staying energised and hydrated

There's no better place to indulge in some food devouring than South-East Asia. The region is known for its astonishing array of cheap and delicious eats. Whether it's *tom yum* in Thailand or *pho tio* in Vietnam you're guaranteed

PART 4 – ROUTES – ASIA

GOING ...

... ultra-light
Yes, it's possible. Guesthouses and roadside restaurants are so frequent many cyclists decide to ditch their camping and cooking gear and just cycle with the essentials. A lighter load means you'll be able to cover more kilometres, but not being self-sufficient may limit your route possibilities. It's a tricky trade-off.

... solo
If you've never toured solo before or are the type that prefers socialising to solitude, South-East Asia is the perfect place to set off unaccompanied. By planning your route around popular tourist haunts, you'll rarely find yourself in want of company. Set off on Highway 13 in Laos and you're guaranteed to cross paths with other cyclists every single day!

a satisfying meal after a day in the saddle. Top honours for cuisine go to Thailand, closely followed by Malaysia.

The climate in much of the region dictates that you'll probably need to down at least five litres of water per day. Tap water is not generally safe to drink so pack water-treatment solutions.

Communication
Malaysia and the Philippines are the only South-East Asian countries in which English is widely spoken. In other parts of the region you'll come across English speakers in large cities and areas that cater to tourists. When needed, creative sign language works well as people are generally very helpful and take time to understand the message you're trying to convey with your highly entertaining gestures.

ROUTES – INDOCHINA EXPRESS
With scores of possibilities, plotting a route through South-East Asia can be tricky. If you've got a couple of months, consider flying into Bangkok, heading east into Cambodia at the Poipet border and continuing to Siem Reap to take in the temples at Angkor Wat. Go south to Phnom Penh and follow the Mekong to the Vietnam border at Khanh Khua. Explore the delta region then start heading north past Ho Chi Minh City into the mountainous region around Dalat and on to Dien Bien Phu where you can cross into northern Laos. Ride to Oudomxay and take scenic Highway 13 all way to Vientiane. Cross back into Thailand at Nong Khai and follow the Mekong to Chiang Khan, head to the temples at Sukhothai and then return south to Bangkok, taking in the floating markets along the way.

Thailand

Most cyclists – particularly those who've just spent months roughing it on the overland trail through Central Asia – are quickly charmed by Thailand's many allures: excellent roads, scrumptious cuisine, comfortable guesthouses, flourishing temples and indubitably picturesque landscapes. Those who say it's too easy or too touristy need only to head north and explore the serpentine routes and misty mountains of Nan province. Beneath Thailand's modern veneer lies a deeply traditional country. Forty percent of the population farms for a living, women in wooden boats glide along narrow canals hawking fruits and vegetables and sinewy men haul in enormous nets overflowing with the day's catch. Being on a bike allows you to give the banana pancake trail a wide berth and discover little seen sides of the Land of Smiles.

PRACTICALITIES

Arriving and travelling
Bangkok is the most popular jumping off point for South-East Asia tours. If you don't feel up to fighting for a place on the road with the metropolitan

area's 8 million inhabitants, consider a bus or train to a less chaotic spot – the accommodating Thais make it easy to take bikes on public transport and you are not required to box them.

Many western nationals can obtain 30-day visas on arrival at airports and land borders.

Thailand boasts a mind-boggling number of quiet backroads, many of them paved, so this is one country where even technophobes should consider using a GPS or Google Maps to navigate. For a small fee, you can get hooked up with a SIM card and data usage plan at any of the ubiquitous 7-11 convenience stores.

Travel in Thailand is generally safe except for the southern provinces of Yala, Pattani, Narathiwat and Songkhla where separatist movements have caused unrest and violence.

Curious novice monks in Thailand surround a strange overloaded machine.
© Amaya Williams

Touring tips

If you're in need of a haven from the heat, stop by the local police station where officers welcome tourists with free wi-fi, ice-cold water, coffee and even cookies for particularly famished-looking riders.

If dusk is falling and there's no guesthouse in sight, drop into a temple and the kind monks will likely grant you permission to pitch your tent for the night. A small donation is always appreciated.

International ATMs can be found almost everywhere but all charge a hefty 180 Bhat (US$6) fee per transaction.

Thailand has the best bike shops in the region – even small towns will have a shop stocked with standard Shimano parts. In Bangkok, Bok Bok Bike, ProBike, Bike Zone and VeloThailand are all highly recommended.

ROUTES

The north is all about sweeping vistas and steep climbs served up on silky smooth tarmac. A strenuous but highly satisfying ride is a 650km loop from Chiang Mai, via Lampang – Phrae – Nan – Chiang Muan – Phayao – Wang Nua and Mae Kachan. Nan makes an excellent place to take a break and wander around the gorgeous temples – it's similar to Luang Prabang but with a fraction of the tourists.

Don't be put off by Central Thailand's tangle of superhighways – use your electronic maps to navigate along the intricate network of shady rural roads, many of which stretch along palm-lined canals. The provinces to the north-west of Bangkok are awash with magnificent temples and colourful floating markets.

South of Bangkok, en route to Malaysia, enjoy some relaxing days riding through the salt flats between Samut Songkhram and Cha-Am. Be sure to swing through Khao Sam Roi Yot National Park south of Hua Hin. A great gateway to Malaysia is via the Wang Kelian border crossing following the twisting mountainous road skirting Thale Ban National Park.

Cambodia

Spend some time delving deeper into Cambodia and you'll soon discover there's a lot more to this beguiling country than the famous temples of Angkor.

By bicycle is the best way to zip around the stunning temples of Angkor.
© Eric Schambion

Much of Cambodia is pancake flat, making this the best place in South-East Asia to challenge yourself to a 100-miles-in-a-day century ride, as you blaze through a succession of dusty provincial towns on your way to Siem Reap.

The red laterite roads of the forested Cardamom Mountains and the impenetrable jungle of Botum Sakor National Park are sure to satisfy even the most intrepid cyclists. Cambodia's infrastructure is improving at lightning speed and most major roads are now paved, with a wide shoulder. Dirt lovers don't despair; you will not be disappointed in the country once dubbed the Wild West of Asia. Singletracks and trails connecting neighbouring villages abound. The only limit to your explorations will be your tolerance for self-induced suffering. Count on spending a good deal of time bogged down in muck and mud or stuck in sand.

PRACTICALITIES
Visas are available on arrival for US$20. Budget accommodation is widely available but wild camping is possible in the countryside (though be aware that there are still landmines in some parts). You may also be able to pitch your tent at one of the many Buddhist temples.

ROUTES
The ride from Phnom-Penh to Pailin via the Koh Kong Conservation Corridor and Cardamom Mountains is both challenging and rewarding. You'll pass near three national parks (Kep, Bokor, and Botum Sakor) and enjoy diverse landscapes of thick mangrove-lined rivers, pristine rainforests and gleaming waterfalls. Possible side trips are to the golden-sand beaches of Sihanoukville or the Bokor hill station.

Don't miss the right turn north towards the Cardamom Mountains 10km before Tatai Bridge. It's a rough ride on tough mountain terrain with plenty of river crossings and many opportunities to jump in for a refreshing swim.

Vietnam

With its sun-toasted coast, sultry jungles, postcard-perfect mountains, fascinating mix of minority peoples and rich colonial heritage, Vietnam will appeal to just about any sort of cyclist. This is a country of movers and shakers and the pace can feel frenetic at times, but slip off the main roads and you'll quickly encounter sleepy villages and friendly folks ready to chat. The southern delta region is flat and offers plenty of opportunities to kick back and relax; up north your calves will be screaming for relief as you chug up the terraced mountainsides before flying down into emerald green valleys.

PRACTICALITIES

Seasons

Southern Vietnam is hot and steamy all year, but the north has distinct winter and summer seasons. The best time to bike the mountainous area around Sapa is during the dry season from October to late March. In December and January it can get downright cold, and in these cooler months heavy morning fog can obscure the views, but by afternoon the sun is usually shining brightly.

Prevailing winds blow from north to south, meaning cyclists pedalling south from Hanoi might suddenly believe they're ready to ride in the Tour de France while those heading north from Ho Chi Minh will be tempted by the first chicken bus that rolls past.

Arriving and travelling

Visas are not available at the border; you must obtain one in advance. Be sure to provide a date of entry on the application form or your 30-day visa will start running out from the date it is issued, not the date you enter Vietnam.

In such a densely populated and highly-populated land, wild camping can be tricky – it's next to impossible in the coastal areas but you'll have better luck in the highlands.

Some visitors to Vietnam report a high number of hassles, scams and outright rip-offs, mostly in heavily-touristed areas. Of course, not everyone will treat you like a walking ATM machine but be sure to negotiate all prices for meals, products and services in advance.

ROUTE SUGGESTIONS

Some love it, others loathe it – but there's no denying that iconic National Highway 1, running the length of this narrow country, is the most popular cycling route in Vietnam. While Highway 1 isn't exactly adventure cycling, it does have the advantage of passing major attractions such as the Hue monuments, My Son Sanctuary, the ancient town of Hoi An and the white sandy beaches of Nha Trang. Although traffic is heavy, there's a wide shoulder for cycling.

Alternatively, you could ride the Ho Chi Minh Highway (AKA Highway 14), which runs parallel to Highway 1, around 100 kilometres inland. You'll have mountains to contend with and some rough stretches of road, but the traffic will be lighter and you'll encounter far fewer tourists.

Dubbed the Vietnam Alps, the soaring mountains of north-west Vietnam are home to many colourfully-clothed highland minority people including Hmong, Meo Muong, Black Thai and White Thai. Visiting the bustling markets is an unmissable highlight.

It's possible to do a northern mountains loop of around 800km through challenging terrain, that takes at least 10 days. From Hanoi, head north-east to Lang Son on the border with China. Continue north-west to Cao Bang, and then head west to the border town of Lao Cai. You can continue on to Dien Bien Phu via Lai Chau and take route 6 back towards Hanoi. Alternatively, near the village of Mai Chau, approximately 100km south-west of Hanoi, you could turn south onto the Ho Chi Minh Highway.

Laos

Almost everyone loves cycling in laidback Laos. It can be hard work huffing and puffing it over the rollercoaster hills, down muddy jungle tracks and up the mist-shrouded mountains, but every iota of effort will be immensely rewarded. A ride through rural Laos is a step back in time. Village life remains resolutely traditional and you'll still find women cooking over smoky fires, weaving intricate baskets and spinning silk using old-fashioned looms. As you pedal along one of the country's many meandering rivers, you'll glimpse men and boys ploughing the fields with a team of oxen or heading off to hunt using ancient rifles, cross bows and even sling shots. Everywhere you pass, you'll be met by gleeful children welcoming you with a cascade of exuberant *sabaidees*. It's hard not to be happy in Laos.

PRACTICALITIES

Arriving and travelling
Visas are available on arrival at most land border crossings for approximately US$30. During the rainy season (late July to September) unsealed roads quickly turn into rivers of mud, so you'll be better off plying the paved roads, or combine cycling with a trip on a riverboat down the Mekong.

ATMs that accept foreign bank cards can be rare in remote northern areas so plan accordingly.

For bike repairs and parts in Vientiane try **Chongchareon Bicycle Shop** (ask for Willie, a French bike mechanic) or **Sonboon Bicycle Shop**.

Eating and sleeping
Tourism plays an increasingly large role in the Lao economy and food and accommodation standards are rising; even in small towns you'll find at least one guesthouse and a couple of restaurants.

Laos is less populated and has much more empty, uncultivated land than neighbouring countries, making it fairly easy to find serene spots to pitch your tent; but as unexploded ordnance still litters much of the countryside, always stick to well-trodden paths. It may be possible to stay at a temple or school in more remote areas.

ROUTES

The Royal Highway

Route 13 between Vientiane and Luang Prabang is arguably South-East Asia's most popular cycling route, and for good reason. In 437km you'll get a good dose of gut-bursting climbs through thickly forested mountains plus you'll pass by verdant rice paddies, traditional markets and villages of the Hmong people, the stunning karst peaks near Vang Vieng and the UNESCO temples in Luang Prabang.

For intrepid cyclists keen to strike out into more far-flung parts of the country, there are many options; just keep in mind that many secondary roads are poorly maintained and may be impassable after heavy rains.

Top to bottom

Taishang (border with Vietnam) to Veun Kham (border with Cambodia). Beginning in the remote northern highlands, follow the Nam Pot, Nam Phak and Nam Ko rivers through rolling hills to Oudomxay. South of Oudomxay, turn east towards the mountainous Phou Loei Conservation area (route 1C) before heading south to the mysterious Plain of Jars near Phonsavan. From there you can take Route 1D traversing Bolikhamsay Province as far as Nam Theun dam. Route 1D now becomes Route 1E, then 1F and finally 1G when it reaches Saravane (Salavan). From Saravane you can access Pakse on the Mekong via the Bolaven Plateau, famous for its coffee plantations. Route 13 will take you all the way to the Cambodia border. For some well-deserved relaxation, stop off on the Si Phan Don islands and spend some time swinging in a hammock, gazing out over the lazy Mekong.

Ultimate adventure

This is a seriously challenging route involving rough roads and steep climbs with gradients of 15-20%. Your reward will be experiencing some of the most remote and beautiful areas of Laos. Only attempt it in the dry season. From Luang Namtha, head to Muang Sing via Nam Ha National Park. Stay on Highway 17 (the Akha road) to reach Xieng Kok. Continue to Xieng Dao via a muddy 30km jungle track along the Mekong. Road conditions improve as you head south to Paklay across a succession of steep rolling hills and one big climb up to 1500m. Near Pakbeng you'll finally reach asphalt, but if you continue south, the hills don't let up until Sainyabouri.

Give us a push? A friendly band of followers in northern Laos. © Amaya Williams

Malaysia

Malaysia is a potpourri of jungle-clad hills, white sandy beaches, dense, dark rainforests and ultra-modern cities. An eclectic mix of Malay, Chinese and Indian influences permeate the country's culture and cuisine. Many cyclists rush through, put off by the daunting multi-lane highways, megamalls and sprawling housing developments, but those that travel at a less hurried pace often find themselves enchanted by the country and linger longer than anticipated.

PRACTICALITIES

Arriving and travelling

Most visitors will be granted a 90-day stay on arrival. Apart from the speed-demons who rule the roads near the capital, you won't run into any particular annoyances or hassles. Everybody speaks English and things function with an efficiency which may surprise seasoned overland cyclists.

Cycling is increasingly popular in Malaysia and you'll find quality bike shops in all cities; **Rodalink** is a popular chain offering a good selection of parts.

Eating and sleeping

Accommodation is slightly more costly than in other South-East Asian countries so you may want to camp in spite of the heat and humidity; some cyclists pitch their tent on east coast beaches.

Restaurants are excellent value, particularly the lunch buffets where you can consume copious quantities of delectable and diverse dishes for just a few dollars.

ROUTES

You've got three main choices for cycling the peninsula: the west coast, the central highlands and the east coast.

The **west coast route** passes near the colonial city of Penang and the UNESCO World Heritage sites of Georgetown and Malacca. You can also wander off on smaller routes to visit temples, ancient mosques and other cultural attractions.

Malaysia's **east coast** is the country's conservative heartland and more rural than the frenetic west coast. South of Kota Baru you'll roll through sleepy fishing villages, past palm-fringed beaches and traverse wide swathes of agricultural land. The bucolic beauty comes to an abrupt halt north of Johor Bahru where palm oil plantations reign supreme.

A straight shot down the **central highlands** will be the best option for those in search of mountain vistas and more serene surroundings. The trade-off for all that beauty is a smattering of killer climbs. Start off on the east-west highway at Gerik near the Temengor reservoir and travel 330km south to the Cameron Highlands.

From Johor Bahru you can reach **Singapore** via the causeway. The road can be hectic, but just follow the line of motorbikes and you'll make it through immigration and into calmer cycling conditions in Singapore.

Indonesia

If the rest of South-East Asia feels too tame for your tastes, jump on a ferry to Indonesia. Whether you pedal along the quiet palm-lined coastal roads of Sulawesi or Sumbawa, beside one of Sumatra's sparkling high-altitude lakes, through Lombok's sleepy fishing villages or bump along a rutted rural road in central Java, you'll experience some of the region's most dramatic land-scapes and come away with the distinct feeling of being well off the banana pancake trail.

Jagged coastlines, undulating landscapes and a land dominated by rumbling volcanoes are defining features of the archipelago's islands. Flat roads are about as common as blizzards on Bali, so come prepared for intense climbs. Indonesia, more so than most countries in the region, requires a certain amount of logistical planning. Navigating the smaller islands of Lombok, Sumbawa, Flores, and Timor isn't too tricky but you'll need to arm yourself with a GPS and detailed maps in order to steer clear of the hectic highways of densely-populated Java.

PRACTICALITIES

Getting there
From the Malaysian cities of Port Dickson, Port Klang and Malacca, there are daily ferry links with Dumai in central Sumatra. Another option is to take a short ferry ride from Singapore to nearby Batam island in Indonesia and from there catch the weekly Pelni ship to Jakarta, a 28-hour journey. Another economical option is a cheap flight to Bali.

Arriving and travelling
Travellers from most western countries are granted a 30-day visa on arrival. This visa cannot be extended (at least officially) and as Indonesia stretches for more than 5000km from Sumatra to West Timor, with such a short stay you can't see much more than a tiny sliver of the country. For longer stays you will need to apply for a Social Visa which grants you an initial 60 day stay and can then be extended four times for a period of 30

Cruising past one of Indonesia's 130 active volcanoes. © Amaya Williams

days each. *Voila*, six months in Indonesia! Just one caveat, you'll need a local sponsor for each visa extension. With a little luck, a sympathetic host from Warm Showers or Couchsurfing will vouch for you; otherwise a travel agent may act as your sponsor (for a small fee, naturally).

A detailed map such as the ones published by Nelles or Reise Know-How and a GPS are almost essential for venturing into those out-of-the-way spots that make cycling Indonesia so exciting.

Indonesia straddles the equator, which means hot, humid weather all year long at lower elevations. Cooler conditions prevail in the mountains of Java and Sumatra where you'll hit elevations of over 2000m and even the central highlands of Flores climb to well over 1000m.

Little English is spoken outside of large cities; fortunately, Indonesian is one of the world's easiest languages as there are no messy tones or complicated tenses, and even the linguistically challenged will master the basics within a few weeks.

The burgeoning 'bikepacker' (as bicycle touring is known locally) and bike-to-work movements in Indonesia mean the once-lowly cyclist is gaining new respect on the road. Quality bike shops are opening up all over the country so finding spare parts isn't the wild goose chase it once was. **Rodalink** has dozens of shops and sells top global brands as well as the local **Polygon** brand of parts.

Even small towns have ATMs that accept international bank cards so getting cash is never a problem. SIM cards are a real bargain and for less than US$1 you're set up with a phone number and enough credit to text mom and let her know you haven't been flattened by a *bemo*, Indonesia's infamous minibuses.

Sleeping

You'll find budget accommodation in most towns but it's a good idea to pack a tent when travelling to remote parts of Sumatra or Sulawesi. Indonesians are extraordinarily social people and exceedingly hospitable towards foreign visitors. Cyclists in remote areas will find themselves regularly invited to stay at strangers' homes and can always count on a warm welcome at the local school, health centre, police station or church if they're in a bind and in need of place to stay for the night.

Moving on

If you're heading to Australia after Indonesia, low-cost airlines offer good deals between Bali and Perth, Sydney or Darwin. If you're intent on island hopping all the way to East Timor, you can then catch a flight out of Dili to Darwin.

SUGGESTED RIDES

Sumatra

A vast series of mountain ranges stretches the length of Sumatra on its western side. Cycling from Banda Aceh in the far north to the southern tip of the island, you will traverse three national parks, pedal past multiple volcanoes and several high-altitude lakes, including magnificent Lake Toba. You'll cycle smack dab through both the Batak and Minangkabau heartlands, giving you a chance to witness these unique cultures close up. At times, the busy Trans-Sumatra highway will be your only option, but it's better to avoid it whenever possible and opt for the much calmer but more physically demanding secondary roads which wind their way through the mountains.

Java

Cycling Java, one of the most densely populated places on earth, poses a dilemma. Wanting to avoid this heaving concentration of humanity, your

Locals head to the fields as another day of cycling begins in southern Sumatra.
© Amaya Williams

first instinct may be to bypass the place altogether, but that would be a mistake. Java is home to numerous unique natural attractions – including Mount Bromo, Mount Kerinci and the Kawa Ijen plateau – and cultural attractions such as the Borobudur World Heritage site. Rest assured, with a little planning, you can experience the exceptional beauty of the land while avoiding the most congested areas.

The western half of Java from Merak to Yogyakarta is less interesting than the section further east. We suggest you follow one of two strategies cycling this section: either blast through on the hectic main highway cranking out the kilometres, or take it extra slow and chart a route following the network of tiny rural roads that criss-cross the heavily-cultivated Javanese countryside. Arm yourself with a GPS loaded with detailed maps and a good dose of patience.

The route between Yogyakarta and Banyuwangi, where the ferry departs for Bali, boasts untamed topography and a succession of spectacular attractions. First off are the ancient Buddhist temples of Borobudur and Prambanan, next you can cycle right past Merapi, glimpsing smoke drifting over the peak of Indonesia's most active volcano. Then it's on to Mount Bromo where it's possible to ride right up and across the sandy crater surface. After, you can continue to Mount Semeru National Park before arriving on the Ijen Plateau, famous for its traditional sulphur mining techniques. From Ijen it's a steep, rough ride down towards Banyuwangi and the pier.

Bali

Take the less busy northern coastal route to Singaraja, then head to the highlands passing through the Ubud region before catching the ferry to Lombok at Padangbai.

Lombok

Lombok is something of a scaled down and more cyclist-friendly version of Bali. There's excellent coastal cycling on fairly quiet roads once you escape the touristy Mataram-Senggigi area. Follow the coastal route north as far as Kaliputih. If you're up for an adventure, turn right and take the mountain road that passes between Mount Rinjani and Mount Nangi to reach Labuhan Lombok. Alternatively just continue on the coastal road to Labuhan Lombok where you can catch the ferry to Sumbawa.

PART 4 – ROUTES – ASIA

BACK TO SCHOOL

A tiny hand snatched my cycling jersey and began beating it furiously against a rock. Giggles rose from a growing circle of onlookers. I could only guess what they were thinking: this strange lady on her heavy bike may be able to ride around the world but she doesn't know the first thing about washing clothes in an Indonesian river. The kids took over with expert precision. A confident girl of 7 or 8 submerged our embarrassingly smelly cycling attire in the fast flowing water, and passed the items off to a little tyke who doused the clothing with detergent. Next, a capable girl of middle-school age did the tough job of beating the clothes and getting the dirt out. Finally, the youngest kids took over for the rinsing and wringing.

Our washing work completed, we trundled along a forest track back to the rural school where my husband and I had set up camp for the night. Stomachs grumbling after a hard day battling Sulawesi's unrelenting hills, it was time to fire up the stove for dinner. The crowd of curious observers grew as villagers returned from the fields. The men admired the power of the compact cooker while the ladies squatted on their haunches craning to see what I'd manage to concoct for a meal. The boldest woman took me up on my offer to have a taste and awarded my vegetable coconut curry an enthusiastic thumbs up. As soon as the cooking show concluded, our audience scattered.

Later, there was a tentative knock on the school door. I looked out to find my band of merry washing assistants clutching their English books and holding out a plate of cookies and tropical fruits. After an hour or more of language practice, my courteous pupils bid me farewell with a kind, "goodnight teacher, and sweet dreams."

In the morning, the whole village turned out to see us off to big waves and warm wishes of *Selamat Jalan!*   **Amaya Williams**

Sumbawa

Sumbawa is less developed and more traditional than the other big islands, with just one main road that hugs the coast and then cuts inland over the mountains to Sape and the ferry to Flores. For a really far-flung adventure, take a tour around the Tambora Peninsula – be ready for a bumpy ride on sandy surfaces.

Flores

Flores, with its striking Catholic churches and mountainous interior, is a long-running favourite with travellers. From Labuan Bajo to Larantuka it is 700km of torture as the route cascades through a series of diabolical climbs. Take a well-deserved break in Moni village and explore the coloured crater lakes in nearby Kelimutu National Park.

Timor

Brace yourself for the jam-packed overnight ferry to Timor and arrive very early to secure a spot on deck. You will definitely turn heads as you pedal through the dusty villages, since the few foreigners that make it to this out-of-the-way island are usually aid workers. If you're heading to Timor Este, be sure to apply for a visa in Kupang as the paperwork cannot be processed at the border.

Sulawesi

If it weren't so hard to get to, Sulawesi would surely be one of the top cycling destinations in the region. Rugged mountains clad in dense tropical jungle rise up from the coast. The oddly shaped island is home to many unique cultures including the seafaring Bugis as well as the Torajans and their mystifying burial practices. A suggested ride beginning in Makassar is to head east across the mountains to reach Sinjai, passing by the Malino hill resort. Then turn north to reach the highlands of Tana Toraja region, stopping for a few days to explore the fascinating burial culture. Continue north to reach Lake Poso. From there you can either continue on to Palu via the main road or set off on what is sure to be a really big adventure by following dirt tracks through the Bada and Besoa valleys in the Lore Lindu National Park. From Palu the northern route hugs the coast all the way to Manado passing through quaint villages and offering jaw-dropping views out over the sea.

Borneo

Mythical Borneo is a place of impenetrable rainforest, rushing rivers, teeming wildlife and exotic tribe people. In reality, you'll find colossal palm-oil plantations, mega oil refineries and rampant deforestation. Borneo's pockets of great beauty are mostly quite far off the beaten track and better accessed by boat than bicycle. That said, Sabah offers some spectacular rides, particularly from Sipitang to Ranau via Keningau. East and West Kalimantan, the Indonesian parts of the island, are less developed, so be prepared for rough roads and limited services.

Philippines

There's much more to the Philippines than the tired fun-in-the sun clichés put forth in advertisements for holiday resorts. It may take some extra planning to get to the Philippines, but your efforts will be richly rewarded.

PRACTICALITIES

While you probably won't run into any problems, keep in mind that the Philippines is less safe than other countries in the region and wild camping is not generally recommended. That doesn't mean you'll have to go to a hotel every night – Filipinos are highly hospitable and cyclists are often invited to stay at the local church or community hall; just ask to speak with the Barangay (neighbourhood) Captain to arrange things. Filipinos love to chat and almost all speak at least basic English so this is one country where you'll never feel lonely.

Visas on arrival grant you a 30-day stay, but they are time-consuming and costly to extend. A better alternative for longer stays is to apply in advance for a 58-day stay. Consider flying in and out of Cebu as it is much less hectic than Manila.

POSSIBLE ROUTES

If you're up for some climbs and ready to face seas of mud masquerading as roads, then head on up to the Cordillera in northern Luzon. This area is home to the Ifugao rice terraces and several more World Heritage sites including the colonial towns of Vigan, Santa Maria and San Augustin. Mindoro Occidental's west coast road offers quiet riding through tribal areas with the ocean crashing in on one side and craggy mountains rising up on the other.

Don't miss Palawan, an almost undiscovered bicycle touring paradise. The sparsely populated, jungle-covered, mountainous island has just one 600km highway, but numerous tracks branching off from the main road just beg to be explored.

Myanmar

Amaya Williams

Those who have biked Burma rave about the kindness of the people, the beauty of the landscapes, and the sense of adventure pedalling through a place where the 21st-century world has barely intruded. Horse carts remain a common form of transport and locals have yet to trade in their skirt-like *longyis* for the humdrum shorts and t-shirts so common in the rest of South-East Asia. Women and children slather on *thanakha*, a facial paste made from ground bark, and almost everyone partakes in the country's national pastime: chewing wads of blood-red betel nut. Myanmar has a deep culture of hospitality and openness and you're guaranteed to be greeted by wide smiles and hearty hellos. After five decades under a repressive military regime, the Burmese are enjoying their newfound freedoms and are eager to connect with foreign visitors.

PRACTICALITIES

Things are changing, mostly for the better, at breakneck speed in Myanmar. Old rules and restrictions are being relaxed and the country is becoming a much more tourist-friendly destination. Be sure to check the latest info online before travelling.

Arriving

If arriving by air, use Myanmar's e-Visa service to obtain a single-entry tourist visa for US$50. If arriving overland, a tourist visa valid for 90 days, which permits a 28-day stay in Myanmar, can be obtained with minimal hassle in Bangkok, Kuala Lumpur or Vientiane. The easiest way to enter Myanmar is via Thailand at the Mae Sot-Myawaddy (Kayin State) crossing, where you do not need a special permit, only a valid Myanmar visa.

Special permits are required when entering (or exiting) Myanmar via India at the Tamu (Chin State) – Moreh crossing or via China at Muse (Shan State) – Ruili. These Special Permits can be obtained in Yangon (try the Seven Diamond Travel Agency for a fee of US$100 or at Exotic Tours for just US$50). The permits can take up to ten days to be issued but can be received by email and then printed out so you don't have to waste precious visa time waiting in Yangon. If coming from China, you can obtain the Special Permit at the Myanmar consulate in Kunming. At the time of writing, entering Myanmar from India is tricky to organise as you must obtain the Special Permit in advance, however there are signs the process may soon become easier.

Travelling

Myanmar has three seasons: the hot season from March to April; the cooler rainy season from May to October when the country is subject to torrential downpours and mud can be a serious issue; and the ideal November to February period when the warm weather isn't stifling.

Gone are the days when you had to arrive in Myanmar with bundles of pristine US dollars. ATMs now accept foreign cards but in remote areas coverage is sparse, so it's still a good idea to bring pristine US dollars or euros. You can get a good exchange rate at banks and official money exchanges, so there's no need to change money with dodgy black market dealers. These days SIM cards are available cheaply, though in rural areas 3G access is often patchy and the internet is almost always distressingly slow.

Officials are unfailingly polite at the many police checkpoints throughout the country and it's usually just a question of taking down your passport details.

Sleeping and eating

Since opening up in 2011, visitor numbers have skyrocketed, resulting in some serious tourism teething pains. The main problem is the lack of budget hotel rooms authorised to accept tourists, a particular issue if you arrive late in the day as most cyclists do. Demand in tourist hotspots far outstrips supply during the high season, meaning prices have soared – a US$10 room in Thailand might cost US$30 in Myanmar.

It'll take a little planning to bike Burma on a budget, but don't worry, it is possible. Keep in mind that, officially, locals are not allowed to host foreigners in their home, though in practice cyclists are often lucky enough to be invited to stay with families and most come away with an overwhelmingly positive experience. Many cyclists stay at monasteries, although solo women may not be welcomed. Camping, though technically illegal, is another option, but be sure to find a well-hidden spot because if local authorities catch you, you'll probably be packed on a bus and moved to a guesthouse. Remember, it's important to keep a low profile when bending the rules. If you're unable to reach a town with an authorised guesthouse, your best bet may be to come clean to the local police and let them sort out a solution.

Among the many culinary joys of a ride through Myanmar, don't miss the cold draught beer available in

The map said there would be a bridge...
© Mike Roy

almost every sizeable town. Look for signs advertising Myanmar, Mandalay, Dagon, or ABC – perfect for passing those hot afternoon hours.

ROUTES

With the opening of its land borders, Myanmar is set to become a key link in the Asia-Europe overland route, and you can cycle via Myanmar between Thailand and India's Manipur State or China's Yunnan Province.

The 1700km route from the Thai border to Myawaddy – Hpa-An – Yangon – Pyay – Bagan – Gangaw – Kalemyo – Tamu and into India has been ridden by some intrepid bikers (see p311). Expect mixed conditions with perfectly paved portions and other stretches of pure potholes. For added challenge you can take a detour through mountainous Chin State. Most tourists stick to the well-worn route of Bagan, Mandalay, Inle Lake, leaving much of Myanmar largely unexplored.

Setting off on less-travelled roads is guaranteed to be highly rewarding and usually poses only minor difficulties. You're sure to pique the curiosity of local authorities and don't be surprised if a not-so-secret plain-clothes police-man follows along on his motorbike. These cops are generally harmless and can even be quite helpful with providing directions and tips on where to find the best stop for lunch. Authorities in remote areas will also help arrange a stay at a monastery.

Colour section (following pages)
● **C1** (Opposite) **Top**: Indonesia – Experience rural life as you meander through isolated villages and simple family farms in Sulawesi. (© Amaya Williams). **Bottom**: Some friendly lads in Sikkim. (© Mike Howarth).
● **C2 Main picture**: Looking across to Afghanistan from the Pamir Highway. (© Gayle Dickson). **Bottom**: Cycling the Pamir Highway in Tajikistan. (© Gayle Dickson).
● **C3** Riding past glaciers in Zanskar.
● **C4 Main picture**: Morning in Myanmar. (© Amaya Williams). **Bottom left**: Taking a shortcut in the hills of Nepal. **Bottom right**: On the way from Kathmandu to Pokhara, Nepal. (© Yoko Kai).
● **C5 Top**: Riding the Canning Stock Route, Western Australia. (© Agnieszka Waligóra). **Bottom**: Beware of crocs! Approaching the Pentecost River crossing, Gibb River Road, Western Australia. (© Scott Richardson).

C3

AUSTRALASIA
Australia

Alia Parker

Wide clear skies, long lonely Outback roads, curious kangaroos and quiet beaches, Australia is the perfect continent to ride following a trip through bustling Asia. The world's sixth largest country by landmass, and the only one to have its own continent, there is so much space out here that you can quite literally spend months cycling the same road.

All that space is populated by just 23 million people, of which 80% nest along the eastern seaboard, namely in two cities: Sydney and Melbourne. This creates an anomaly for cycle travellers as you'll spend much of your time becoming acquainted with a remote side of Australia that most urbanites never see.

Life in the bush is chalk and cheese to the hipster scene, trendy bars and restaurants of the cities – particularly in the Outback where you'll largely survive on greasy roadhouse burgers, frozen bread and powdered soup. Outback Australia has more natural wonders to dazzle you than you can poke a stick at; duck into the local town's Tourist Information Centre or pull up to the bar at the pub and you'll soon know the locals' favourite spots, and all the town gossip too!

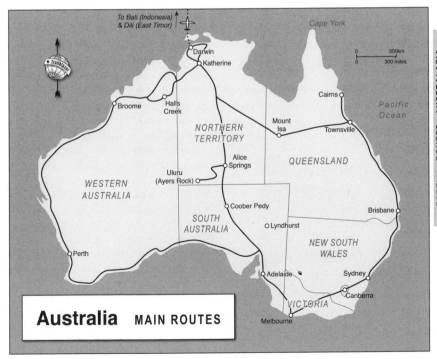

Australia MAIN ROUTES

A FEW BASICS

- **Law**: helmets are compulsory in Australia and the cops will fine you if they've got nothing better to do.
- **Public transport**: you can wheel your bike onto local train networks but you'll need to box them and pay a fee if you take them on intercity routes. Taking bikes on buses varies depending on the company.
- **Fuel**: you can stock up on butane at camping stores in large towns and cities, but it will be hard to find elsewhere. In remote regions, stick to multi-fuel stoves that take petrol,

white gas or kerosene, which is available at service stations. Alternatively, almost all towns have a free gas hotplate BBQ at the local park.
- **Post**: you can receive parcels at most Australia Post offices; in remote areas where no post office exists, roadhouses or pubs sometimes handle the mail. Always call ahead to check how each place would like you to address the package because if they're not expecting it, they may not accept it.

In between these two extremes sit the many farming regions that produce some of the world's best fruits and vegetables, meats, honey, dairy and seafood – often sold right from the farm gate. Check out gourmet regions like Queensland's Scenic Rim and South Australia's Fleurieu Peninsula, or Tasmania for its delicious cheeses. And then there's the highly acclaimed Aussie wine, of which the best is always found at the cellar doors throughout hamlets like the Barossa, Clare and Hunter Valleys, and Margaret River – all idyllic places to cycle.

PRACTICALITIES

Finding your way

Traffic near the cities tends to get uncomfortably heavy, so make your ride easier by looking up the bike paths via local council websites. Sydney is the trickiest city to navigate without a cycling map, but you'll retain your sanity by visiting 🖳 sydneycycleways.net.

For regional Australia, pick up good old fashioned paper maps, available from most bookstores, newsagents and information centres, preferably while in a city as it can be hit-and-miss in small towns. Hema maps are often the most useful, particularly those in the 4x4 (SUV) series, because they include more back roads as well as handy info on campsites and water sources. Hema maps can also be downloaded and there are others in the digital sphere as well, like Mud Map; however, these GPS versions may not be as detailed as the paper series.

A few things about Aussie maps: most of those rivers, creeks and lakes will be dry much of the year, especially away from the coast in the dry season; there are many historical towns that appear on maps but are nowhere to be found in the real world; and all those 'towns' marked in inverted commas are actually private cattle stations.

A long way between services on the Gibb River Road in Western Australia.
© Scott Richardson

So always chat to a local about what's ahead before you set off with just one litre of water and your lunch, and you'll avoid becoming another one of the many stories told by Grey Nomads (retired folk that roam the country in caravans) and police about rescuing dehydrated cyclists with heatstroke.

You can find more detailed info on cycling routes through Australia on my website ⌨ cycletraveller.com.au or at ⌨ cycletrailsaustralia.com, as well as ⌨ railtrails.org.au.

When to ride

The Australian continent has a split personality when it comes to the weather. Areas north of the Tropic of Capricorn have two seasons: The Wet (October – April) and The Dry (May to September). South of the Tropic weather patterns begin to fall back into autumn (March to May), winter (June to August), spring (September to November) and summer (December to February). As a general rule, the ideal time to cycle in the north of the country is right in the middle of The Dry season – it's cooler, although still hotter than a European summer, and there are fewer flies. Many roads in the north are closed in The Wet due to torrential rain and cyclones; besides, it gets ridiculously hot and the flies will cover you like a second layer of skin.

Summer in Australia is hot all over, but you can find cooler retreats in beautiful Tasmania as well as up in the elevated parts of the Great Dividing Range, such as the Victorian Highlands and the Snowy Mountains – that's right, contrary to popular belief, it does snow Downunder, so be wary of these areas in winter. Winter in the southern parts gets chilly; even out in the desert the thermometer can drop below zero at night, so take some woollies. The Bureau of Meteorology (BOM) website ⌨ bom.gov.au is a good source for weather as well as prevailing wind directions, which can be strong and change greatly over the seasons and from region to region.

Cost of living

The bad news first: things in Australia are pretty expensive. Food prices are high and you're lucky to find a basic motel room or cabin for less than AUD$100 a night. An unpowered site at a caravan park averages around AUD$25.

The good news: there are many free campsites around the country, most of which are listed on phone apps like WikiCamps or Campee. They're often nothing more than a highway rest area shared with a half dozen Grey Nomads and a few backpackers crammed into a Combi van, so don't expect a shower, but they're great if you're on a tight budget. You can score a shower at most roadhouses, often costing a few dollars, and sometimes at sports fields. Small towns without a caravan park often have a free or cheap campground with showers at the local showground. Other times you may stumble across a pub in the middle of nowhere where you can camp for free in exchange for your presence at the bar. Free bush camping is generally permitted on State Forest land or on official stock route rest areas, and many National Parks have cheap designated campsites.

Technically, it's illegal to camp by the side of the road, other than in the designated rest areas. However, if you can't make it into a town and pull well off into the bushes, authorities are likely to understand (well, at least, no one

Riding the straight, straight road to
Cape York. © Alia Parker

will see you) – just make sure you're
not on private land.

Supplies and communications

The downside to having a big country
with a small population is that it's hard
to get things out in the bush and food
selection and services are limited in
small towns. There'll be enough for
you to get by, but if you're in need of
speciality items – especially bike parts
– stock up in the cities or large regional centres.

Mobile phone and internet connections are patchy at best in the bush and
some tiny towns have no mobile coverage whatsoever. Telstra has the widest
coverage by far outside the main cities, which is why they charge so much more.

For those concerned about riding through remote areas with no means of
calling for help, get yourself a small UHF radio with a decent signal strength.
All the cattle stations, road train drivers and even some Grey Nomads communicate via UHF radio and most of the time at least one of the above will be
within radio reach.

Road trains

Australia has the biggest road trains in the world, pulling as many as four
trailers and weighing up to 200 tonnes. All road users, not just cyclists, are
required to jump off the road if necessary and give way to these beasts if they
can't safely overtake you. They can be extremely dangerous, are difficult to
drive and can take up to 300 metres to come to a stop.

POPULAR ROUTES

Red Centre: Darwin to Melbourne via Alice Springs

Welcome to Australia's untamed north – home of Crocodile Dundee – where
rusty red gorges and mountains shaped over millions of years take centre
stage alongside the rich cultures of Australia's indigenous peoples.
Juxtaposed against that is the Stuart Highway, the only sealed road through
the centre, with its road trains and roadhouses which serve up greasy burgers
and an assortment of tacky souvenirs. You'll feel like you've entered an entirely different world by the time you jump off the highway to cruise through
South Australia's wine regions and the small city of Adelaide. From there it's
on to the Great Ocean Road, where the wild waters carve a spectacular coastline that leads you to the cosmopolitan city of Melbourne. It's easy to see why
this route is a favourite with world cycle travellers.

This is a challenging ride, mostly due to wind, long lonely distances
between stops and the occasional frustration of sharing the road with trucks.
The route is a minimum of 4000km and an extra 1000km (return) on sealed
roads from Erldunda to see Uluru, Kata Tjuta and Kings Canyon. There is an
alternate dirt route to these via the Mereenie Loop but prepare well because
it's often bumpy, sandy and very slow going. Whatever you do, don't contin-

ue down the highway without seeing these sights – if you don't feel up to pedalling there, pick up a budget three-day tour in Alice Springs (it's a side trip, so it won't be considered cheating).

West Coast: Darwin to Adelaide
This ride will take you down past the jaw-dropping Bungle Bungle Ranges, near to gigantic whale sharks at Ningaloo Reef, across open plains, through Perth and into the acclaimed pro surf and wine region of Margaret River before hooking down to the scenic southern coast around Albany and across the notorious Nullarbor toward Adelaide. All up, about 7200km if you stick to the highway. It's another popular option for global cycle tourers but don't underestimate it – parts are quite exposed and windy and Western Australia is big, so big it alone could swallow up the entire UK ten times and still have room for dessert – and desert!

The Nullarbor Plain
Cycling The Nullarbor – a vast and arid expanse that spans the Great Australian Bight in Western and South Australia – has emerged as the ultimate challenge for cyclists. Once you leave the small town of Norseman in Western Australia, you won't hit another until 1200km later in Ceduna, South Australia. You will, however, come across a number of roadhouses spaced out at 1-2 day intervals, providing much needed water stops (although you may need to pay for this scarce resource). You can stay at these roadhouses, at free rest stops, or hide in the bushes along the road itself.

KANGAROO ENCOUNTERS

There's nothing worse than spotting a kangaroo by the side of the road on a nice downhill run. I'm well into the descent nearing the dip when I see him, a big one, and he's looking straight back at me. I check my speedo; 58km/h, and way too late to slam on the brakes. Besides, if I keep my speed up, I might just get past him. Time slows, my eyes fixed on his every move, anticipating what will unfold over the next few split seconds. Don't get me wrong, I adore kangaroos, but they've never quite figured out how roads work. I've got a small chance this fella will jump away, but a much bigger one of him sending me flying into the rocks strewn at the bottom of the causeway.

I start angling toward the middle of the road in case he goes for me, and yep, he does, right at the last second. Kangaroos make up the vast majority of road-kill I come across, and it's always worse during dry spells when the greener grass by the side of the road draws them out of the bush. He's still looking me straight in the eye and I can't for the life of me figure out what's going through his head because we're both going to get hurt. Remember to roll, I tell myself. Some excuse for a scream escapes me, and instantly, he flinches and attempts to change directions, twisting his body like a liquorice stick. But his feet skid out from under him and he's now sliding across the road. It has however, bought me a vital second and my bike flies past missing him by mere centimetres. Phwarr!

Keep a look out for kangaroos, near the Flinders Ranges in South Australia.
© Alia Parker

The Nullarbor is arid, but not as 'plain' as many expect, with coastal trees, rolling terrain and plenty of wildlife. Even so, it may feel like the longest 1200km you've ever cycled if you get hit in the face by the powerful wind that whips up from the Southern Ocean. On the other hand, if it's behind you, get ready to set a new personal best speed record. You'll have the best chance of surfing a tailwind if you ride from west to east in the winter between June and August – just be prepared for the cold, and for the wind to change its mind.

Tasmania

Tasmania is a real little gem and a favourite cycling destination among locals. This green southern island has stunning coastline and craggy mountains, historic convict settlements, and a flourishing gourmet farmers' market community. Cool all year round and particularly chilly in winter, it's the place to escape the summer heat on the mainland. The popular way to cycle Tassie is to circumnavigate it, which is roughly 1000km. Most roads are good for cycling, although try to avoid the main inland highway between Launceston and Hobart. The east side of the island is more populated, but still quiet and sleepy, and the west is enchantingly rugged. And then there are many lovely country roads that meander inland. Highlights include Cradle Mountain, Wineglass Bay, the Bay of Fires, the Styx Valley of the Giants, Port Arthur and Hobart's Museum of Old and New Art.

East Coast: Melbourne to Cairns via Sydney

There are plenty of roads to choose from along the east coast, so make good use of them rather than sticking to the highways. A good way to mix up your east-coast experience is to travel north out of Melbourne up through the Victorian Highlands – a popular cycling region with some good rail trails such as the Murray to the Mountains and the Great Victorian Rail Trail. Head up to Australia's highest mountain, Mount Kosciuszko and then down to Sydney via the capital Canberra. The best route into Sydney is via the industrial city of Wollongong, along the engineering marvel that is the Sea Cliff Bridge and the Royal National Park. A ferry takes you from Bundeena to Cronulla, from where you can follow bike paths right up to the Harbour Bridge. Scoot north along the coast to Brisbane to sample some of the country's most popular swimming beaches, then escape the traffic by heading Outback and along the Great Dividing Range to Cairns, from where you can visit the Great Barrier Reef.

Heading off the beaten track

Australia has a marvellous network of dirt roads that cover much of the continent. Some of these routes have become quite popular with hard-core cyclists, including the trip up to Cape York, QLD, the Gibb River Road and the Munda Biddi Trail (the longest custom-built bicycle trail in the world) in WA, the Mereenie Loop in the NT, the Mawson Trail and the Oodnadatta Track in SA, and the Tasmanian Trail. There are also routes that run through deserts as well as epic old stock routes, like the Canning Stock Route. Some of these tracks may be rough or sandy and better suited to mountain bikes or even fat bikes. Do your research before heading off on any remote dirt track because you'll need to carefully plan your gear and supplies. *Outback Survival* by Bob Cooper is a good book to read before attempting these types of expeditions.

New Zealand

Jonathan Kennett

New Zealand is a small country with huge variety: of terrain, of weather, of roads and trails. Consequently, experiences range from fantastic to horrible. A poorly informed cycle tourer will often feel like they are cycling through purgatory, whereas a well informed one will enjoy great scenery on quiet country roads and purpose-built cycle trails and paths. The best months for touring are January to April, when most days will be calm and clear, but New Zealand's variable weather means you'll still need to be prepared for the occasional storm.

ROUTES

In 2010, the government started pouring millions of dollars into building the **New Zealand Cycle Trail** network and the result has transformed trips, leading to a local boom in cycle touring. This network consists of 23 Great Rides (similar to the famous Great Walks), which are predominantly off-road and pass through stunning landscapes. The Great Rides are connected by the safest and most enjoyable country roads available; construction should be complete in 2016. They range from very easy rail trails to tough mountain bike tracks, so you need to choose carefully to ensure you get the riding you'll enjoy most.

Traditional cycle tourists may be tempted to ride the main highways in New Zealand but this is not a good idea as the volume of traffic, especially large trucks, has significantly increased over the last few decades. Now much better alternatives exist, so the only reason to ride highways is that they provide the shortest possible route from A to B.

New Zealand is a diverse country where the landscape changes with every few hours of pedalling; and it's hilly, so the less gear you take, the happier you will be. In many ways, it's ideal for the new bikepacking breed because the rough stuff is where the best scenery is to be found. From spectacular snowy mountains to vivid blue coasts, steaming volcanoes, lush green forests, rushing rivers and, of course, plenty of rolling farmland. There are even a few flat areas.

The South Island has better scenery and a much smaller population, but the North Island is not to be overlooked as it is home to half of the New Zealand Cycle Trail network. The Great Rides are the gems, but the on-road cycle routes connecting them are both quiet and pass through beautiful landscapes.

Plenty of options exist for a fabulous tour and the best website for information on trails is 🖳 www.nzcycletrail.com. No website yet shows the full network, so we recommend you take the guidebook *Classic New Zealand Cycle Trails* which details all the best cycle routes and has become the bikepackers' bible.

Mavora Lakes, Southland. © Jonathan Kennett

SOUTH POLE, ANTARCTICA

Name	Maria Leijerstam
Nationality	British
Year of birth	1978
Occupation	Sport Events Business Owner
Other bike travels	New Zealand, Siberia, Portugal, Ireland, Coast to Coast England, Coast to Coast Scotland
This trip	World's first cycle to the South Pole, Antarctica
Trip duration	1 month on the continent, actual journey 10 days, 14 hours and 56 minutes.
Number in group	I was the only one cycling but there were three others on the expedition (2 drivers and 1 cameraman).
Total distance	638km
Cost of trip	Huge!!
Longest day	17 hours
Best day	The first day setting off, waving goodbye to the expedition crew and finally beginning a journey that had taken 4 years to plan.
Worst day	Christmas Day because I was cold, had a bad knee and missed my family back home.
Biggest mistake	Not taking more knee precautions early on.
Pleasant surprise	The weather was incredibly good – I was very lucky.
Illnesses during trip	Altitude sickness during the climb of the Leverett Glacier – sea level to 3000m in just 90km.
Bike model	Polar Cycle – only one in the world!
Modifications	It was made especially for the expedition based on user requirements that I had drawn up from experience of winter cycling.
Wish you'd fitted	Fewer wheels. On the polar plateau where the snow was deep, I had three tracks to break instead of one – which made for really tough going.
Tyres used	Surly 5"
Punctures	Two – both from valves bursting in the morning as I got going.
Baggage Setup	All on the rack at the back of the Polar Cycle. It can carry up to 90kg. I had 55kg when I started.
Wish you'd brought	Different boots. My feet froze in minus 100 degree boots. Not sure what I'd change them to though, I think there is a gap in the market here!
Wish you hadn't brought	My iPod with only 20 songs on it...
Accidents?	No crevasse falls luckily but I did see a number of them open up around me.
Where's next?	Mongolia possibly...

ROUTE OUTLINES
AFRICA

5

Peter Gostelow with contributions from Steve Halton

Africa remains the ultimate destination for those who crave adventure more than comfort on tour. News of political instability, disease, poverty and conflict often ends up miring the entire continent as a dangerous place to travel, but Africa is made up of over 50 countries and, for those that do visit, the reality is quite different.

Bicycles provide the mainstay of rural transport for people in many countries, leaving plenty of roads blissfully quiet and safe to cycle. People are also amongst the friendliest you're likely to meet – the waves and wide smiles of curious children at the roadside will become a familiar sight throughout your ride.

Beyond a few notable tourist spots, the majority of Africa sees very few foreign cyclists, particularly if you venture onto the smaller roads, something which is definitely recommended. Whether you find yourself sipping tea in the Sahara with a Mauritanian villager, crossing a river in a dugout canoe in Liberia or camping beside a village chief's hut in northern Mozambique, cycling through Africa offers an unrivalled experience in adventure touring.

MAIN ROUTES

The classic Cairo to Cape Town ride is a far more popular north-south route than the more adventurous option down West Africa. Trouble spots in Central Africa mean very few traverse from east to west, except in the southern part of the continent. Note that pedalling to Egypt on two wheels from Europe is currently not possible; you'll be taking a plane (see p236). To access Morocco and the western route down Africa from Spain, just jump on a ferry from Algeciras (or Tarifa – see p126).

Although some people race down in 90 days, a minimum of 6 months is really required to cycle between Cairo and Cape Town and get an appreciation for the continent; 9-12 months would allow time for exploring more of the lesser-ridden routes. The distance from Morocco to Cape Town is greater, as are the chances of

Long distance Africa trips tend to be down either the eastern or western sides. The western route is the longer and more challenging of the two.

Africa   MAIN OVERLAND ROUTES

delay, so 9-12 months is recommended as a minimum time-frame; it takes most people considerably longer.

PRACTICALITIES

Seasons
Summer months (May to September) in North Africa are uncomfortably hot, with daytime temperatures above 40°C. People do cross the Sahara and cycle through Morocco, Mauritania, Egypt and Sudan (with a lot of water!) at this time, but October to April is much more agreeable.

Three on a bike in Mozambique. Cycling is *the* way to travel through rural Africa.
© Peter Gostelow

At the other end of the continent, the southern hemisphere winter means some places, in particular the Highveld of South Africa and Lesotho, can be cold between May and October, when temperatures drop to freezing and below at night.

The rest of Africa is within the tropics, and any time of year is fine to tour. Rain typically falls hard and fast, but rarely for many days on end. While dry seasons can be dusty and hot, rain makes landscapes greener and more scenic. It also provides a refreshing coolness from the heat as you huddle under a tin-roofed shelter and make friends with a group of bewildered strangers. Unless riding specifically on dirt tracks, cycling through a rainy season, whether it be in Cameroon or Malawi, shouldn't make a massive difference to a tour, provided you are patient – something which always helps in Africa!

The majority of cyclists in Africa tour from north to south, simply because they are European and begin riding from home. In terms of the actual cycling, the intense heat of the Saharan summer is the main issue to consider, along with the fact that prevailing winds on both the eastern and western Saharan routes are from the north.

Visas
Visa situations change and are dependent on your nationality and where you apply, so it's always worth checking online before starting out, and again during your trip. As a general rule, East and Southern Africa present far less of a problem for obtaining visas than West and Central Africa. UK passport holders receive free entry on arrival for South Africa, Lesotho, Swaziland, Namibia, Botswana and Malawi; while Zimbabwe, Mozambique, Tanzania, Uganda, Kenya, Rwanda and Burundi charge between US$30-50 for visas of 30 or 90 days. Most major border immigration offices provide visas on arrival, but it is always best to research beforehand. US$ are the desired currency for visa payments and extensions are usually possible at least once while inside the country.

Ethiopian visas are available on arrival by plane but if crossing by land you will need to arrange a visa at an embassy in a neighbouring country. Sudan also requires you to obtain a visa before the border and, if coming from the north, the Sudanese consulate in Aswan in Egypt is reputedly a cheaper and easier option than applying in Cairo. Sometimes a letter of invitation is required, depending on where you apply.

Visas in West and Central Africa are more expensive and less commonly available at land borders. Morocco, Senegal and The Gambia provide free entry with a UK passport but are the only countries which do so. Nigerian and Angolan consulates in Africa and elsewhere often require added paperwork such as invitations or hotel bookings. Visas are sometimes issued on the same day you apply, for which there may be an extra fee, or they can take 2-3 working days, which means a considerable wait if you apply late in the week.

FIVE AFRICA MYTHS DEBUNKED

1 Africa is a dangerous place and its people are inherently violent.

Although there certainly are pockets of violence and no-go areas on the continent, cycling in rural Africa is as safe as cycling in rural areas in Europe or North America. In most places, you can leave your bike outside shops, have a stroll around the village and even hike up to see a waterfall and when you return your bike and belongings will still be there. Some African mega-cities such as Dakar, Johannesburg and Lagos live up to their reputations as dangerous places and you certainly wouldn't want to arrange a tour through conflict zones such as Darfur or Libya. Fortunately, with a little planning these places are easily circumnavigated. In most African capitals, keeping your wits about you will enable you to stay out of harm's way. During the two years I spent cycling around the continent, most Africans I encountered were gentle, humble and hospitable. They warmly welcomed me into their villages and shared generously of all they possessed.

2 African roads are so bad they're impossible to cycle on.

While it is true that Africa lacks a comprehensive paved highway network, that's part of the fun. Bouncing along on a narrow track waving at giggling toddlers, exchanging greetings with kids trudging off to school, stopping to chat with villagers on their way to the fields – the back roads are the best way to discover the real heart of Africa. Roads can be rough, especially after heavy rains, so you may not be able to cover as much distance in a day as you would in other parts of the world. With a little practice though, you'll soon become a pro at cycling through seas of sand, navigating rock-strewn roads and steering a course through muddy, rutted tracks. And for those of you with overly-sensitive bums, don't despair: you can now cycle all the way from Cairo to Cape Town on tarmac.

3 Africa is very corrupt and I will have to pay many bribes.

I never encountered any type of corruption in East or Southern Africa. Minor corruption in West and Central Africa is, however, quite common. I was regularly asked to pay miscellaneous 'processing fees' at border crossings and police checkpoints and sometimes asked to make a contribution towards a beer, soft drink or fuel for the generator. By standing firm, remaining friendly and being patient I never ended up paying any bribes or extra fees except on one occasion.

4 I will have trouble finding food if I cycle through Africa.

Food shortages do occur in Africa, but as a cyclist with money to spend you are unlikely to be affected by them. Even in some of the very remote stretches where most of the local population was living off food relief provided by international aid agencies, I was always able to buy food locally. Markets may not be overflowing, but you'll find enough staples to get by.

5 Africa is too hot for cycling.

The African continent stretches 30 degrees north and south of the equator and thus varies greatly in terms of climate. The only region where it's really hot and sweltering all year round is the narrow band of lowland tropics that straddles the equator. Cycling through Namibia in July (the southern hemisphere winter) will mean frost on the tent, you'll encounter snow on the high passes in Lesotho in August and the highlands of Ethiopia are refreshingly cool all year round.

Amaya Williams

Online resources

Up-to-date online information can be sought from either the Lonely Planet's Thorn Tree forum or the Sub Saharan Africa forum at Horizons Unlimited: 🖳 horizonsunlimited.com/hubb/sub-saharan-africa.

Budgets, food and accommodation

Country costs vary but Africa is not the cheapest continent to tour through, unless you camp wild most of the time and survive on a very limited local diet. A plate of rice, beans and meat can be bought for US$1-2 on the roadside in many countries but western food is more likely to cost US$5-10 for a meal, and the hardships of travel means you'll need it once in a while. Roadside stalls selling seasonal fruit and veg for passing traffic are commonly found throughout Africa, and in the evenings grilled or fried chicken, beef and goat meat, and chips or plantain are a frequent sight in small towns.

Good budget accommodation can be hard to find in capital cities for less than US$15, although there are cheaper camping options at some hostels.

On the whole West Africa tends to be more expensive than East Africa when it comes to accommodation, while Southern Africa is more expensive again. In South Africa, Lesotho, Swaziland, Namibia, Zimbabwe, Botswana and Zambia, expect a minimum average budget of US$20 per day. In Tanzania, Malawi, Uganda and

Foreign cyclists are of great curiosity for children throughout Africa.
© Peter Gostelow

Kenya, US$15 per day is possible. In villages where there is no official accommodation it is rarely a problem to pitch a tent for free, so long as you seek permission from an authority. Camping in villages where there is access to water means you can have a proper wash at night, rather than roughing it in the bush. The only downside to this is that you may well be the entertainment for the night, so forget any privacy until zipping up the tent and wishing your audience goodnight.

Money and communications

ATMs accepting international VISA cards exist in most capital cities and major towns though it's best to carry two cards from different card issuers. It's always worth having some reserve cash (crisp clean US$ dominate in East and Southern Africa, followed by euros, while euros followed by US$ are best in West and North Africa) for changing in banks, bureaux de change and when need be at border crossings. Never change large amounts at the latter as there are various scams and the atmosphere can be unsettling.

Mobile technology has advanced dramatically throughout Africa in recent years and the sight of mobile masts is very common in many towns, even if electricity remains absent. An unlocked smartphone allows you to swap SIM cards – which are very cheap and widely available – in each country and connect to the internet with relative ease. Speeds and costs vary but unless cycling

An eclectic mix of parts at a Zambian bike shop. © Logan Watts

on remote roads, accessing the internet isn't a problem. Most countries offer more than one mobile provider so it's sometimes worth buying SIM cards from two different networks as coverage varies depending on location. Wi-fi also exists in major hotels and tourist lodges, or you can just tether your smartphone to act as a dongle when the signal is strong enough.

Gear tips and break-downs

Outside of Southern Africa, bike shops stocking such items as Presta valve tubes or quick-release mechanisms are hard to find. The same goes for camping shops – they're rare – so if you're serious about a long tour through Africa it's best to come fully equipped. Wide tyres (1.75" minimum) will handle sandy roads better, and strong racks will ensure there's less likelihood of needing a welder. Carrying a spare foldable tyre is also recommended.

Bicycles are ubiquitous in many African countries, so it's never hard to find a local mechanic to fix a puncture or true a wheel, and if you were to decide to buy a bicycle here you might be lucky and find a reasonable second-hand import donated by a charity.

Seriously consider using a free-standing tent, preferably with plenty of inner ventilation. It's sometimes more comfortable pitching the tent on the floor of a guest-house room than suffering a sleepless night on a hollow bed with gaping holes in the mosquito net.

Waterproof jackets are ineffective in heavy rain but it's definitely worth packing a light one for higher altitudes when temperatures drop. A multi-fuel stove, rather than one requiring camping gas, is also highly recommended and if you're using a smartphone for both internet and mapping on the road then an external battery pack with a few USB ports will be very helpful.

Maps and road conditions

The best large-scale road maps of the continent remain those produced by Michelin (*Africa: North and West*, *Africa: North-East Arabia*, and *Africa: Central and South Madagascar*). These are great for pre-trip planning and also worth having on tour, but they lack the minor roads and detail provided by country maps (of which Reise produce some good waterproof ones). Outside of South Africa good road maps, like those mentioned, are hard to find. Smartphones and pre-loaded GPS devices using software such as Tracks4Africa are increasingly popular, and detail for Southern and East Africa is improving all the time, as are road conditions.

While there remain plenty of unpaved roads, it's possible to stay on tarred roads from Cairo to Cape Town, as well as through much of West Africa. Roads in the Democratic Republic of Congo are a different matter, although it's worth noting that a long tour through Africa without taking the time to explore the quieter rough roads wouldn't be quite the same African experience.

NORTH AFRICA AND THE SAHARA

Long before the Arab Spring of 2011 rewrote the routes map, tourism in the region had become restricted due to the threats and activities of Islamist terror networks. Even then the vast distances in the central Sahara were always marginal on a bicycle, while the often-imagined circumnavigation of the Mediterranean coast is today less accessible than ever.

Unless you have good local contacts, cycle touring in Algeria requires an escort which is impractical and expensive. Tunisia may lack Morocco's diversity and be a dead end, but can be rewarding. Distances are small, back roads are quiet and basic accommodation exists away from the coastal and desert resorts. For a year or two after Gadhafi's fall a handful undertook transits of northern Libya between Tunisia and Egypt, but now even that's considered too dangerous and the south is way off limits.

Which brings you back to Morocco and Egypt – both worthwhile destinations in their own right. The all-sealed Atlantic Route to Mauritania and West Africa is a pitiless 2000-km slog while the Nile Route to Sudan is less desolate but hotter. Either of these Saharan transits are something to consider only in the middle of winter, but you can still expect the UV to be relentless and temperatures to exceed 30°C as you head south.

Muslim customs and etiquette

Islam in North Africa is far less strict than that of the indigenous Arab countries further east. Nevertheless, depending on where you are it's good form to cover up with baggy rather than skin-tight clothing.

Muslims regard other religions with much respect but claiming atheism is not appreciated. During Ramadan, when Muslims don't eat, drink or smoke during the day, it's considerate to do likewise in public, though as a traveller (and a non-Muslim) you are exempt.

On the road

Roads in the region can be the usual mixture of glistening asphalt on its way to becoming a craterscape of spoke-snapping potholes. African drivers don't have a great reputation and cycling in cities like Cairo is an adventure on its own, though no worse than Western Europe. Where you have a choice, head for backroads where traffic is light. Unpaved tracks are hard work on a loaded bike – expect water and energy consumption to soar and average speeds to shrink.

Some visitors are driven crazy by the hassle in the tourist hotspots of Morocco and Egypt. The general advice is to politely not engage. Away from the tourist enclaves you'll be reassured by the hospitality of normal rural folk, and during your trip you'll almost certainly be invited to have tea, a meal or even stay at someone's house. When this is the case, a little gift in the form of some tea, sugar, sweets or a present for the kids will always be appreciated.

Desert cycling

Even on the all-sealed Atlantic or Nile Routes, cycling across the Sahara requires a realistic knowledge of your physical limits. In winter you'll still need 5-10 litres of water a day, with 100km or more possible on tarmac with a tail wind. Conversely, pushing through soft sand into a headwind will reduce that distance by 90%. The prevailing wind in the Sahara is from the north-east but don't rely on this.

Once in the desert, save your strength and resources: rest in the shade during the hottest hours of the day, sip your water continually rather than drinking every few hours, and ensure you replenish salts.

Chris Scott

Health tips

By taking some sensible precautions, it's possible to spend years travelling in Africa and suffer from no more than a few bouts of diarrhoea. Make sure you are well vaccinated before arriving (see p30 and note a Yellow Fever certificate is mandatory in many countries), and take malaria prophylactics in high-risk areas. A rabies vaccination is recommended, even though south of the Sahara dogs don't seem to find chasing cyclists that enjoyable.

Most people touring in Africa fall ill when their immune system is weak, usually from over-exertion and weight loss, so take plenty of rest days and stay well hydrated. Bottled water is relatively cheap and available in many small shops. Bore-hole water (not open wells!) in rural areas is also often safe; if in doubt, purify. Pharmacies in major cities stock most essential first-aid goods, but decent-branded sun cream and mosquito repellent are better brought with you. Even when the sky is covered in clouds the equatorial sun will burn fair skin.

Language

In East and Southern Africa, English will suffice for communication in towns and cities, except in Mozambique and Angola where Portuguese is spoken. Learning greetings and the basics in some of the more common local languages, such as Kiswahili which is spoken in Kenya, Tanzania, Burundi and northern Mozambique, will go a long way in terms of how you are received. It will also give the impression that you are more familiar with the country, thereby reducing the chances of being over-charged.

In West and Central Africa, French is more dominant and, although by no means a necessity, the more you know the better. Once again, picking up greetings and some of the basics in other native languages will win new friends.

The Nile Route

Steve Halton

It is not currently possible to cycle overland from Europe to Egypt due to the situation in Syria. In addition, political instability in Egypt has affected shipping in the area to the extent that the on-off commercial passenger ferries from Iskenderun and Mersin in Turkey to Port Said are not running. As such the easiest, cheapest and most reliable option is to fly directly into Cairo before continuing south.

Alternatives include flying to Tel Aviv in Israel, then either cycling south to Eilat and entering Egypt at Taba, or heading across the West Bank and into Jordan via the King Hussein bridge. However, though the Israelis don't stamp your passport as a matter of course these days, you'd still have a time gap which might have to be explained, and cause immigration problems, further south. It's preferable to fly direct to Amman, cycle south through Jordan, then take the ferry from Aqaba to Nuweiba in Egypt.

At the time of writing, authorities would not let tourists cross Sinai via St Catherine's Monastery due to security concerns; the Suez Canal therefore has to be reached by continuing south to Sharm el Sheikh before heading north. Information in this whole area is especially subject to change, so it's always worth checking out the current security situation before starting out.

ARABIC NUMERALS										
0	1	2	3	4	5	6	7	8	9	10
٠	١	٢	٣	٤	٥	٦	٧	٨	٩	١٠

EGYPT

Cycling in Egypt varies immensely from the manic driving and chaotic hustle and bustle of Cairo and Suez, to the deathly quiet roads of the Eastern Desert. Between tourist resorts, which now stand eerily deserted in the Post Arab Spring world, there are spots of ephemeral beauty and easy camping. Waking to watch pastel hues of sunrise beyond the azure blue of the sea is an inspiring way to begin your day.

There are some wonderful encounters to be had with the local people in Egypt, be it chatting about Islam and traditional family life at a desert outpost, or an invite into a home for dinner, a bed and if you are very lucky some freshly laundered clothes. Having said this, I found the people of Egypt a mixed bag and the lack of tourist activity in recent times seems to have inspired some alarming behaviour. Riding down the Nile can attract the attention of mildly aggressive teenagers persistently hassling and shoving from their mopeds, while further south the pestering of hawkers in places like Luxor and Aswan is well documented.

All things considered, pedalling the extra miles through the Western Desert between Bawiti and Kharga is very well worth considering, especially as you should benefit from favourable winds.

Previously, the only possible border crossing from Egypt to Sudan was the ferry from Aswan to Wadi Halfa. However, in late 2014 the new Qustul – Ashkeet land border opened, which shortens the ferry ride across Lake Nasser. Information is still sketchy as to how this new route works in practice for cyclists, though from Aswan escorts or a bus ride may be required to reach the port at Abu Simbel. A ferry takes you to the eastern shore and Qustul, from where it's a short ride to the Sudanese border near Wadi Halfa.

SUDAN

If the trials and tribulations of Egypt were getting you down, Sudan will bring welcome relief. Overwhelmingly honest, gentle and generous, you won't travel far without meeting Sudanese hospitality, be it offers of water, sweet chai, *foul* (fava beans and oil) or somewhere to stay. Off the bike in Khartoum, don't miss the Whirling Dervishes .

Like many of the friendliest places on earth, Sudan is a sanctioned country; as such it is not possible to access cash from ATMs in the usual way. If you're

A chai lady in Sudan. © Steve Halton

TRIP REPORT
ROUND THE WORLD

Name	Loretta Henderson
Nationality	Canadian
Year of birth	1972
Occupation	Author, Speaker, Woman Adventurer
Other bike travels	Zero prior experience.
This trip	Africa, Asia, Middle East, South America, Europe, Oceania
Trip duration	5 years
Total distance	Never been good at math, uncounted.
Cost of trip	Under US$10 a day.
Longest day	Chased by a Sahara sandstorm for 220km.
Best day	Almost every one of them.
Worst day	Ran out of food for 3 days when lost in Bolivia.
Favourite ride	Karakoram Highway, Pakistan.
Biggest headache	Being mistaken for a porn star (though this was flattering and funny!)
Biggest mistake	Not realising the world would take 5 years to cycle.
Pleasant surprise	I love cycling with camels, elephants, zebras **and** giraffes.
Illnesses during trip	Ate too much felafel – ended up in an Iranian hospital, barfing on my headscarf.
Bike model	Thorn Raven Tour
New/used	Pandemic The Magic Bicycle was purchased new.
Tyres used	Schwalbe Marathon Plus Tour, 4 sets.
Punctures	No idea but not a lot – great tyres.
Baggage Setup	I'm equipped for 4 season touring, but travel light with only 3 panniers on the back. I found I didn't need the extra gear or weight on the front wheel.
Wish you'd brought	More lipbalm and ziplock bags.
Wish you hadn't brought	My water filter – sent it home.
Bike problems	Almost none, love my Rohloff!
Accidents	Hit by a bus which was going 64mph when touring Patagonia in the winter.
Same bike again	Oh yeah, Pandemic is 100% trustworthy
Recommendations	No more planning, just go!

Any advice?	Anybody can get on a bike and go just about any-where.
Road philosophy	Live simply, be nice to people, eat everything.
What do you daydream about in the saddle?	Dervla Murphy and other women on wheels.

heading to Sudan it is recommended that you carry enough dollars to exchange once there. Don't panic if you run out, money can be transferred in via Western Union although the commission tends to make this a more expensive way of accessing funds.

Perfect tarmac through the Nubian Desert.
© Steve Halton

You can now cycle across Sudan on paved roads, but this doesn't detract from the rugged beauty and challenge of the Nubian Desert. The terrain is predominantly flat but the heat is relentless and the dead animals littering the roadside are a constant reminder that you are passing through a place where life is fragile. Water can be found in large ceramic pots along some of the more barren sections of the route such as the 375km stretch between Al Dabbah and Khartoum. Meandering south along the Blue Nile to Wad Medani, surroundings begin to get greener and villages more abundant, with trees offering dozing opportunities. Desert dawns and dusks and open-air camping under the brilliant night sky are highlights which will stay with you a lifetime.

CHAIN GANG, SUDANESE STYLE

As I rode into Sudan it became increasingly obvious that my chain was not going to survive much longer. It had been snapping with increasing frequency since crossing the border at Metema and I had to keep repairing it using links from old chains. With a long way to cycle to a shop with a chain that would fit my cassette, I decided to order spares to be shipped over while I waited in Khartoum.

A week later nothing had arrived, so I redirected my chains north to Dongola while I set out across the desert, on my broken bike, to meet them. After four days battling the blistering heat and wind the twinkling lights of Dongola came into view. All I now had to do was find the DHL store.

An English speaking local, Seed Ahmed, whom I'd asked for directions, sprung into action. He owned a car which was the vehicular equivalent of my chain – it was done for but somehow, like with everything in Africa, could always be patched up and coaxed a little further. Before long we were driving round town looking for DHL, with Seed canvassing opinion on where the shop might be as we went. Soon we had a whole car-full of advisors, each proffering an opinion more loudly than the last.

Despite my task force, DHL was proving elusive, so I suggested checking the internet. A net café owner was found and he was happy to open his shop just for me. While I searched online, the guys embarked on plan B: finding me a new chain. As expected, no such replacement could be found, but a bike repair man asked to take a closer look at the problem chain. With nothing to lose, I agreed.

I have no idea what he did, but the chain stayed intact all the way to Wadi Halfa. When I asked him 'how much', he shook his head and waved me away; my friend in the internet café wouldn't take money either. In fact not one of the people who assisted me that day in Dongola would accept payment for anything.

Seed insisted I spend the night at his house and his wife and sisters cooked up a delicious meal. The following morning I rode north feeling high on the knowledge that wherever you go in this world, there will always be someone to help you out, especially in Sudan.

Steve Halton

CYCLE ETHIOPIA – IT ROCKS

The infamous Ethiopia is in sight. The border is a medley of mayhem, merchants, touts, money-changers and self-appointed guides. The wonderful thing about a magic bicycle is it also serves as a getaway vehicle; a remarkably easy way to politely turn down the hassles that surround the business-minded beggars and crowds of folks ready to pounce on an obvious tourist dollar. The 'official immigration' procedure is fast and quite pleasant; the officer laughs at my tactics as I skid to a halt at the door of the immigration building, completely ignoring the overly helpful, shouting crowd of self-appointed guides.

I receive my entry stamp and off I go through the gates into Ethiopia. A country that is so renowned for its challenges that many, including myself, attempt to avoid it altogether by travelling through Uganda and Rwanda. Tackling Ethiopia's stone- and stick-wielding children, roads with hill gradients built by sadistic lunatics and an extremely high petty theft rate, never seems to rate too high on the must-cycle list. Traversing Ethiopia was my second choice until the Uganda, Rwanda via Sudan option

Making friends in Ethiopia.
© Loretta Henderson

became impossible due to politics and ferry boat cancellations. However, actual violent crime in Ethiopia is rare and almost unheard of against tourists, and the country is proudly brimming with a far lower crime rate than many North American cities.

Three days later sticks are flying and stones bounce off the insanely hilly ground. Children hold *Pandemic The Magic Bicycle*'s back rack and attempt to take anything that they can lodge free. Everything flying my way I pick up and take with me. I now have a stick on the front handlebars and a dung ball strapped to the back rack. I do not blame the children or the general mistrust on the part of the public; in many ways, Ethiopia has been destroyed by foreign aid swooping in with very short, well-funded, non-sustainable projects.

I have been asked for my shirt, my shoes, my braided hair, pens, medical supplies and many people are begging for food and water. A people rich with wounded pride now accustomed to foreigners giving out non-sustainable solutions, teaching a misguided, failed, altruistic message of 'we know best, you can't take care of yourself, you need our help'. A brief band-aid solution leaving many angry without community-based sustainable solutions to problems that persist for far longer than the provided funding period of a couple of grants.

However, deep within these challenges of cycling in a country so hilly that at times even my super-low Rohloff gearing system is defeated, leaving me pushing up hills, lies a beauty. Amongst the folks in the villages that dot the hillsides there's a quiet kindness and politeness to be found.

Many children and young adults just peer at me with their devilish smiles, as I stop my bicycle and offer to shake hand after rock- and stick-wielding hand along the roadside. I simply figure if they are going to throw things anyway, I might as well stop and try offering some attention instead. Shaking the hand of a might-be beggar or stone-throwing child is pretty effective thus far. So this solo female bicycle tourist is sticking to what rocks, and enjoying the hidden beauty of Ethiopia.

Loretta Henderson

ETHIOPIA

As soon as you set foot over the border at Metema, things change dramatically. People are everywhere, polite becomes plucky, calm becomes chaos, hot becomes cool, flat becomes steep and barren becomes lush. Ethiopia is notorious among cyclists as a difficult country to cycle because it is relentless. Bored kids, steep hills and a culture of begging mean that often it is impossible to get away from the shouts of 'You, you, you ...'. Stopping yields crowds of gawkers, campsites are inevitably discovered and disturbed, and occasionally a few little stones will come your way.

Crossing the Omo River in Ethiopia. © Steve Halton

Ethiopia, however, is surely amongst the most original places in the world – the people, the religion (Ethiopian Orthodox), the food, the music, the coffee, even the mentality. It is possible to love Ethiopia, but it takes a little effort. Playing with pestering kids can suddenly bring smiles and giggles, learning a few words in Amharic can help break barriers, and chatting with English-speaking locals both in towns and rurally really does provide an insight into the best side of Ethiopia. If all that fails, keep your MP3 charged up.

The adventurous will want to head in the direction of the Omo Valley and ride/push/drag their bike through some of the most ancient tribal lands on Earth. It's exciting, challenging and not for the faint-hearted, but provides a rare insight into a world which may soon be extinct. The security situation over the border in Kenya can be extremely volatile, so it's worth checking out the latest before you exit Ethiopia.

East and Southern Africa

East and Southern Africa contain the sights and attractions that tempt most people to the continent. A cycling tour through these parts provides the opportunity to admire the snow-capped peaks of Kilimanjaro or Mt Kenya, gaze over Victoria Falls, encounter the Big Five on safari, swim and dive off palm-fringed white beaches and much, much more. Aside from ticking off mainstream tourist attractions, it's the interaction with people out on the road that usually provide the most memorable experiences for cyclists. The region offers a good mix of paved and unpaved roads and, thanks mostly to the Rift Valley, varied topography and some spectacular natural scenery. There's a good chance of meeting a few other tourers on the road but numbers remain few and by exploring some of the secondary roads the challenge and level of adventure remain high.

WILD ANIMALS AND SAFARI CYCLING

These days most large wild animals no longer roam the continent as freely as they once did. In West and Central Africa, conflicts and political instability have left most National Parks poorly managed and bereft of animals. Fortunately East and Southern Africa provide more opportunities to encounter wildlife, and it's by no means a necessity to be in a safari vehicle to encounter them.

Cycling through a National Park in Africa might sound like a suicide mission, which is why most of the larger and more famous of them don't allow any two-wheeled transport. However, there remain many lesser known parks, reserves and protected areas where access by bicycle is not only freely permitted at times, but which provide a very real chance of seeing animals, and plenty of birdlife – something other tourists would pay hundreds of dollars to view.

Here is a selection:
Botswana Nxai Pan National Park
Burkina Faso Nazinga Game Ranch
Ghana Mole National Park
Kenya Hells Gate National Park; Sibiloi National Park
Malawi Kuti Wildlife Reserve
Mauritania Diawling National Park
Mozambique Gorongosa National Park
Namibia Caprivi Game Park
Nigeria Yankari National Park:
Rwanda Nuungwe Forest National Park
Tanzania Biharamulo Game Reserve; Katavi National Park; Kitulo National Park; Mikumi National Park; Saadani National Park
Uganda Bwindi Impenetrable National Park; Queen Elizabeth National Park
Zambia Kafue National Park
Zimbabwe Matopo National Park; Victoria Falls National Park

KENYA

Northern Kenya, with its hot and harsh climate, rough roads and nomadic tribes has an altogether more remote feel than the south of the country. Sandy tracks around Lake Turkana are hard going, but provide an alternative route into and out of Ethiopia to the Moyale – Isiolo road, which has long been prone to incidents of banditry and is best avoided unless the security situation changes. The same remains true for coastal areas close to Somalia and anywhere else in the far east.

Cycling through the cool green Rift Valley in south-western Kenya feels more like Europe at times, if you overlook the zebra on the roadside between Nakuru and Naivasha, that is. Jungle Junction in Nairobi is a popular overlanders hangout, and if the rough roads have had the better of your bicycle, the ever-welcoming David Kinjah and his team at 🖳 safarisimbaz.com will help out with repairs.

A heavy load in Uganda.
© Peter Gostelow

UGANDA

Boasting verdantly green rolling hills and roadsides lined with tropical fruit and smiling faces, Uganda is one of the continent's most welcoming places to cycle. The south-west of the country contains swim-friendly crater lakes, one of Africa's few remaining primeval forests in Bwindi, free access to pedal through Queen Elizabeth National Park, and plenty of challenging climbs such as that between Kabale and Kisoro.

In order to escape the heavy cross-border traffic heading to Kenya, it's well worth the effort to push north to Mbale and loop over the top of Mt Elgon National Park. Camping in front of the Sipi Falls along the way is recommended, but the Suam River border crossing can be muddy during heavy rains.

RWANDA

Within minutes of entering Rwanda you'll see why the country is dubbed the Land of a Thousand Hills. Flat land is scarce, but most roads are paved and there are no big distances between towns. One challenging but spectacular rough ride is to follow the Congo Nile Trail from Gisenyi to Cyangugu, following the shore of Lake Kivu. The views down to the lake and across to the DRC are some of the best in East Africa. Alternatively stay on tarmac and head for Ngungwe Forest, which offers another great opportunity to experience the kind of dense vegetation that once covered so much of equatorial Africa.

BURUNDI

Burundi is as green, mountainous, challenging and friendly to cycle through as Rwanda, but far less visited. Roads are well paved and blissfully free of traffic. The steep descent into Bujumbura coming from the Kayanza border with Rwanda is possibly the most exciting entry into any African capital.

Riding along the shores of Lake Tanganyika provides pleasant respite from the hills, with a number of places to cool off and swim in the World's second deepest lake. As so few foreigners travel here the degree of curiosity is greater than elsewhere in East Africa. A three-day transit visa is available at borders and can be extended in Bujumbura. One-week and one-month visas need to be arranged in advance and can usually be obtained on the same day in Kigali or at the Burundian consulate in Kigoma, Tanzania.

TANZANIA

Tanzania offers a bit of everything. The opportunity to cycle around the base of Kilimanjaro with its varying climatic zones is definitely recommended, as are the National Parks that allow entry on a bicycle (see box opposite). The back roads through the Pare and Usambara mountains in the north of the country offer a great route towards the coastal town of Tanga. Here it will be hot and humid, but Zanzibar and Pemba are wonderful to explore on two wheels.

The Dar-es-Salaam to Mbeya road offers one route onwards to Malawi and Zambia, but a lot of trucks also use this highway. Better and more adventurous alternatives exist in western Tanzania, south from Kigoma, and also in southern Tanzania below the Selous Game Reserve. It is also possible to load a bike onto the Tazara Train, connecting Dar-es-Salaam with Mbeya. From here you can explore the remote and wonderfully scenic Livingstone Mountains that rise from the eastern shores of Lake Nyasa. From Mbamba Bay there are boat services across the Lake to Malawi, or north to Itungi Port to remain within Tanzania.

The roads around Lake Victoria in the north of the country remain relatively free of traffic and the frequent ferry service between Mwanza and Bukoba provides a great alternative to road travel, as does the *MV Liemba* further south on Lake Tanganyika that connects Kigoma with Mpulungu in northern Zambia.

TRIP REPORT
SOUTHERN AFRICA

Name	Lars Bengtsson
Nationality	Swedish
Year of birth	1977
Occupation	One year this, the next year that.
Other bike travels	88 countries on six continents including places like Pakistan, Yemen, Sierra Leone, El Salvador, China, Paraguay and Scandinavia.
This trip	Around the Kalahari Desert, Southern Africa
Trip duration	5 months
Total distance	6500km
Cost of trip	Around US$20 a day, excluding visas and plane tickets. Almost all the money goes on food and drink...
Longest day	138km from the bush to Victoria Falls in Zimbabwe
Best day	Any day in the Namibian bush
Worst day	Boring highways in eastern South Africa
Favourite ride	Across Namib Rand Nature Reserve in Namibia
Biggest headache	Where are all the big game that once roamed Africa?
Biggest mistake	I didn't bring enough tyre patches to Lesotho...
Pleasant surprise	Swaziland!
Illnesses during trip	None
Bike model	Surly LHT frame and the rest is custom made
New/used	The frame and racks have done almost 70,000km
Tyres used	Schwalbe Marathon Mondial Travelstar
Baggage Setup	Two small (front) panniers in the back and a local rice bag with my tent above them. A bag with clothes on the front rack and a front bag.
Wish you'd brought	Nothing really – nowadays I know what I need and what I don't need.
Wish you hadn't brought	No one checked my yellow fever certificate – but you are in trouble that day when someone asks for it and you don't have it.
Recommendations	Don't burn yourself out: rest before you get too tired, eat before you get too hungry, drink before you get too thirsty.
Any advice?	Bring a tent to Africa – even if you don't like the bush (never met anyone who doesn't), it's possible to camp in many hostels.
Road philosophy	Go remote, cycle slowly, eat and drink a lot.

MALAWI

Another contender for Africa's friend-liest country, as long as you can han-dle the occasional child asking for money. Small, compact, and dominat-ed by a huge lake, it's hard not to enjoy cycling along the mostly paved and traffic-free roads here. If you can climb the steep rocky switchback bends leading up to the cool mountain air around Livingstonia, then you can tackle most roads on the continent.

Wildlife in Nyika National Park, Malawi.
© Logan Watts

Lake Malawi's shoreline offers some great places to pitch a tent, swim and relax for a few days. Nkhata Bay and Cape Maclear are two popular spots, and if the *MV Ilala* is operating on the lake it's another chance to rest the legs and experience some rare colonial era transport.

MOZAMBIQUE

If Africa hasn't lived up to your adventurous expectations thus far, then north-ern Mozambique just might. Hot sandy coastal roads, remote villages and long white beaches divide the Tanzanian border with the must-visit former capital that is Mozambique Island. The fact few people travel here is evi-denced by the level of curiosity when pitching a tent in a village. Inland, the air slowly cools and the tea-growing hills around Gurue are well worth ven-turing through if headed to Malawi.

ZIMBABWE

If wild animals on the roadside have remained elusive in the rest of the region, there's a good chance of encountering some in Zimbabwe. Matopos National Park is well worth cycling through for a day or two, for its distinctive granite *kopjes* and wonderful birds. Further north the well-paved Bulawayo-Victoria Falls road passes the outskirts of Hwange National Park, so don't be surprised if more than fresh elephant dung appears on the road in front of you. Victoria Falls National Park, aside from the main attrac-tion, contains plenty of wild animals as does the road west to the Botswana border.

ZAMBIA

It's a long way west from the borders of Tanzania and Malawi to reach the capital, Lusaka, and fur-ther still to Livingstone and the highlight that is Victoria Falls. Fortunately main routes are well paved and there is plenty of opportunity for wild camping. If you're not crossing the border at

You might be sharing remote roads in Northern Mozambique with non-vehicular traffic.
© Peter Gostelow

Livingstone into Zimbabwe you can continue along the banks of the Zambezi and cross into Botswana or Namibia. Prices in Zambia reflect those further south, so coming from East Africa you'll really notice the hike in accommodation and food prices.

NAMIBIA

For solitude on the road, dramatic desert scenery, stunning sunsets and starlit nights, Namibia is the place to head. Here it's possible to cycle for hours or even days and not see more than a soul or two. With that in mind, carrying plenty of water (6 litres or more) is a must as distances between settlements are longer than almost anywhere else on the continent. Good paved roads link the Caprivi Strip in the north with Windhoek much further south, but the best of Namibia is seen from the great network of well-graded gravel roads.

Opuwo, famous for its Himba tribeswomen, provides an interesting starting point to head south via Palmwag and Khorixas, then onward to Mt Brandberg, the country's highest peak. Elsewhere the sweeping panoramic views from the top of the Spreetshoogte Pass en route to the famous dunes at Sossusvlei, as well as the scenery surrounding the Fish River Canyon in the far south, make great destinations.

THOSE EMPTY AREAS

I love those empty areas. Maybe you know what I mean? Those areas you spend hours in front of a computer to research, and still you don't find anything useful at all. But the lack of information only triggers the urge to get there. The western part of Gaza province in Mozambique and around Gonarezhou National Park just over the border in Zimbabwe are such areas. According to my Michelin map the border to Zimbabwe is closed and the road through the area is under construction. Besides this, you don't know if you can cross the national park on a bicycle. Will the rangers let you pass? And if

they do – what kind of animals will you encounter...?

The road was indeed under construction, but more than I expected was tarred. On my left side the Limpopo forest went on all the way to South Africa's Kruger National Park. I liked the road and my only concern was the supposedly-closed border. I reached the border village after six days and was invited to stay in a hotel owned by an ex-farmer from Zimbabwe. He wasn't sure if I would be allowed to cross the Gonarezhou on a bicycle – but he had good news: the border was open! I stamped into Zimbabwe at the friendly border post; no-one stopped me from continuing into the park. By the time I reached the other side some hours later, I had seen giraffes, several antelopes, and elephant footprints.

A day later I tried to enter the park once again, this time from the north-west, but a ranger stopped me. Instead I went north on a small road that became a track and then disappeared. I pushed my bike down to the Runde River and carried it over with water up to my hips. A while later I arrived in an area called the Hippo Valley – and civilisation. It had been a great week. Sometimes you really have to give those empty areas a go!

Lars Bengtsson

Climbing up the northern side of the Runde River, Zimbabwe. © Lars Bengtsson

BOTSWANA

Botswana provides a similar solitude and sense of space out on the road as Namibia and what it lacks in terms of dramatic desert landscapes it certainly makes up for with opportunities to observe wild animals. Within minutes of entering the country at Kasane I rolled into a service station whose only other customer was an elephant nonchalantly walking through the forecourt! Like in Namibia, distances between villages are long, so fill up those water bottles.

SOUTH AFRICA

South Africa boasts some superb natural scenery and cycling opportunities. Most trans-continental journeys start or end in Cape Town, and it's definitely worth riding out to the Cape of Good Hope for some fantastic coastal views at the start or end of your big trip.

Main roads tend to be busy and dangerous as traffic moves fast, so where possible plan a route using the many smaller roads. Throughout much of the country landowners often fence roadsides, which makes finding wild camping spots much harder than on the rest of the continent. Fortunately campsites are plentiful and asking permission elsewhere is much the safest option. If you don't get invited to at least one *braai* (barbecue) as you pedal across the country, you've been very unlucky. Despite its crime problem, South Africa offers some of the most welcoming hospitality you're likely to find anywhere, even if most people will tell you how dangerous it is to be cycling through their country. The reality is that as long as you avoid cycling at night (as you should in all parts of the continent), you'd be unfortunate to have a problem.

LESOTHO

A strong contender for Africa's most scenic country, the Kingdom of Mountains is a must for those who enjoy wild open landscapes, as well as a challenging climb or two. Between May and September you'll need winter clothing as temperatures plummet to below freezing in many places and, as snow covers higher ground, camping is only for the hardy.

A good paved road with little traffic connects Maseru with Thaba-Tseka to the east, before dirt tracks and what will have become the familiar sight of shepherd boys wrapped in woollen blankets on the hillsides, escort you towards the stunning Sani Pass (2876m). The view and descent down to South Africa is one of the best on the continent.

SWAZILAND

Sleepy Swaziland, with its quiet roads, gentle rolling hills and friendly smiles, presents a welcome change from surrounding South Africa. A sign on the roadside as you enter Hlane Royal National Park reads 'Beware Lion and Elephant', but it's more likely you'll see giraffe, baboons and plenty of birds.

Both Lesotho and Swaziland match their currency to the South African rand and provide free entry for many passport holders, so crossing into either country poses few bureaucratic problems.

West and Central Africa

Traversing West and Central Africa presents a greater challenge than anywhere else on the continent. Bribe-demanding officials, bad roads, problematic visas, security concerns, limited food options; there are many reasons to deter visitors. But, collectively speaking, this region provides arguably a greater cultural experience than many of the well-trodden overland routes in East and Southern Africa. Tourists are few and far between and on back roads

WILD DOG CHASE IN THE SAHARA

There were exactly ten of them that followed me out of the petrol station forecourt. They'd been lying in its shade when I arrived 15 minutes earlier, seemingly oblivious to my presence as I sat quenching my thirst with a Coke – something to break the endless monotony of the western Sahara.

Where their sudden energy came from as I stood up and wheeled my bike back towards the road I don't know. Leaping up in unison they broke into an angry cacophony of barking – the movement of my feet on the pedals bringing them closer to the bike as I prepared to cycle back into the desert.

These dogs had no owners – wild but fit and healthy-looking mongrels, upon whose territory I'd encroached. I'd dealt with wild dogs before in places like Turkey and Tibet by stopping to pick up stones – the action often halted the dogs' approach before the stone had even been thrown. Here, however, I was clearly outnumbered by a working pack.

I resolved myself to walking alongside the bike, which seemed to be the only way to lessen the barking and dangerous baring of white teeth, in the hope that after a kilometre or two they'd lose interest and return to defending their territory. I was wrong.

The road was empty, but eventually I spotted a car coming from the direction of the forecourt. It slowed and pulled up alongside as I frantically waved for help. The passenger window opened, releasing a cloud of marijuana-scented smoke. A white-faced and blood-shot eyed passenger with long dreadlocks looked up at me. 'Un problème, oui?' I looked over at the driver, who I guessed to be Moroccan. He signalled for me to hold onto the roof rack. With my left hand holding the handlebars I grabbed the rack firmly with my right hand. We slowly increased in speed as I kept check on the road; the dogs excitedly crisscrossed in front of us. Glancing down at my bike computer reading of 35kph, I thought this would be a speed at which the dogs would soon give up chase. But they were happily running alongside, getting increasingly excited as the driver swerved from side to side to avoid hitting them.

Soon my right arm started to tire as I watched the speed increase. The driver seemed to have lost patience and the wind made it impossible for me to tell him I was losing my balance. Faster and faster we went – 40kph, 42, 45 – as I leaned into the car and felt the bicycle wheels moving away from me. Two dogs were still running alongside as I briefly looked down at the computer reading: 58kph. 'This is it', I thought. My mind flashed with a vision of hitting the road and being mauled by two ravenous dogs.

No longer able to hold on, I let go, miraculously managing to regain my balance as I shifted into top gear and pedalled as fast as I could. Ahead, the car disappeared with the French dope-head waving out of the window; the two dogs were still 50 metres behind me. For the next two kilometres I pedalled like crazy, managing to keep up a speed of 40kph into the wind, glancing over my shoulder with great relief to see the dogs give up the chase at last.

It had been a wild dog encounter like no other: had I gone down at full speed, my long journey through Africa would certainly have come to a premature end.   **Peter Gostelow**

in places like rural Nigeria and the DRC you're quite likely to be the first foreign face people have seen for a very long time. Whether you stick close to the rugged but welcoming shores of the Atlantic or head inland on hot dusty tracks, a journey through West and Central Africa is an adventure certain to provide plenty of unique stories.

MOROCCO

If all countries offered as much as Morocco, Africa would take many years to cycle through. Boasting four diverse mountain ranges in the form of the Rif, Mid-Atlas, High Atlas, and Anti-Atlas, ancient towns bursting with colourful markets and culture such as Chefchaouen, Fez and Marrakesh, plus endless kilometres of beach and Saharan landscapes, it's hard to rush through what might just be Africa's premier cycling destination. The Michelin map of Morocco provides excellent detail of the numerous roads and tracks out there.

If you're headed south to Mauritania then plan to be here from October onwards when temperatures are cooler. Passes in the High Atlas may have some snow on them from December, but with a few winter clothes you'll appreciate the last of this weather before the sun becomes your enemy south of Agadir. This is where the Sahara begins in earnest. Winds predominantly blow from the north during winter months so tailwinds should push you through Western Sahara towards the Mauritanian border. Visas for Mauritania are issued in Rabat, and not on the border, so come prepared. Make sure you carry plenty of water too, though there are well spaced service stations throughout the Sahara, and the road is in good condition.

Chris Scott's *Morocco Overland*, also by Trailblazer, is a great resource for cyclists, with all 10,000km of routes evaluated for cycling.

MAURITANIA

Cycling options are limited in a country dominated by the Sahara. You either follow the coastal road connecting Nouadhibou with the capital Nouakchott, or hop aboard the iron-ore train from Noaudhibou for an uncomfortable yet adventurous journey inland to Choum, from where a connecting road heads south to Atar. Most overland traffic crosses into Senegal at Rosso, a border post notorious for hassle; a far better option is to head west on a rough road and cycle towards the Diama border. The track follows the banks of the Senegal River and cuts through Diawling National Park.

Mind the mines in Western Sahara. A short section of the roadside close to Mauritania isn't a sensible place to wild camp. © Peter Gostelow

MALI

One of West Africa's most popular destinations, this vast landlocked country has been blessed with some outstanding geographical features to break up the monotony of the flat plains and scruffy bush. The Niger River runs through Mali for 1300km and the sheer mesas and craggy formations around Hombori have been compared to

PART 5 – ROUTES – AFRICA

TRIP REPORT
MOROCCO

Name	Logan Watts and Virginia Krabill
Nationality	USA
Year of birth	1973 / 1974
Occupation	Web designer / Nurse
Other bike travels	South Africa to Tanzania, Mexico to Panama, various off-road bikepacking trips.
This trip	Bikepacking in Morocco
Trip duration	6 weeks
Number in group	2
Total distance	~1000km
Cost of trip	US$20 pppd in-country spend.

Longest day	120km – coming out of the Atlas Mountains.
Best day	Third day in the Atlas Mountains – topped a pass, weather cleared, became a mesmerising ride over beautiful dirt tracks through an amazing landscape.
Worst day	Finding a dying kitten on the road.

Biggest headache	Buying alcohol to burn in our Trangia stove. Moroccans frown on alcohol in general and even though it's not for drinking it's hard to come by.
Biggest mistake	Only carrying a handful of spare tubes and several patches into the Sahara Desert. Everything is out to pop your tyres there – a series of flats forced us to catch a lift to a nearby town.
Pleasant surprise	A dirt road that looked like a beautiful downhill in the Anti-Atlas mountains ended up being a dead end, where we met a family who had us for a long lazy lunch. They showed us a goat path down a cliff where the road was meant to go; we had to hike it.
Illnesses during trip	Traveller's diarrhoea in the desert…. ouch.

Bike model	Surly ECR
Modifications	Rohloff / Tubus rack / Salsa Minimalist front rack / Selle Anatomica Saddle.
Tyres used	Surly Knard 127 TPI
Punctures	4
Baggage Setup	DIY waxed canvas longflap saddlebag / DIY frame bag / Big Agnes UL 3 tent / various dry bags / Crumpler Kashgar camera bag.
Weight of kit	About 12kg
Wish you'd brought	More tyre patches / tubeless setup.

Road philosophy	Stay off the paved roads, and travel lightly… you learn to live with a minimal kit and it makes riding that much more fun.

Utah's Monument Valley. The walled villages along the river are in the Sudanic style, moulded from the grey clay of the surrounding flood plain.

Mali can be a challenging country for cyclists owing to the heat, dust, long distances between settlements and the often monotonous landscapes, but in terms of culture it is one of Africa's richest.

Police road block in Sierra Leone. Be patient and courteous and African police won't be as threatening as their road block might suggest.
© Peter Gostelow

SENEGAL AND THE GAMBIA

Senegal provides a welcome introduction to Francophone Africa, just as tiny Gambia greets Anglophones with wide sandy beaches and cool Atlantic breezes. St Louis, the former capital of French West Africa, is worth stopping in, and the ever-popular Zebrabar, just 18km further south, is a favourite stop-off for overlanders to exchange travel advice and stories. You can cycle across The Gambia in less than a day, or take time to explore the interior by riding up the banks of the River Gambia then crossing on one of the ferries further upstream.

GUINEA BISSAU

Guinea Bissau is where West Africa starts to get interesting. Crumbing colonial Portuguese towns break up the steamy lush countryside of mangroves and cashew nut trees. A cheap one-week transit visa, easily available further north, is plenty of time to cycle through the country, and if you head east to the border with Guinea, it's more or less smooth tarmac all the way.

GUINEA *

The rolling green highlands of the Fouta Djallon region in northern Guinea are an adventure cyclist's paradise, with rough roads, and villages which have a remote wildness. Learn a few greetings in Fulani and the hospitality will be as memorable as the scenery. The cool climate and view overlooking Senegal from the hill-top town of Mali-ville is worth the climb. The political situations in Guinea and Guinea Bissau have been fragile in recent years so stay alert.

SIERRA LEONE *

Long overlooked as a cycling destination due to its civil war, Sierra Leone has some of Africa's best beaches and friendliest people. An excellent paved road connects Freetown with nearby beaches to the south, as well as much further afield to Kenema near the Liberian border. There is also a good network of unpaved roads linking small towns in the interior and some spectacular karst

* EBOLA

At the time of going to press, the Foreign and Commonwealth Office was still advising against all but essential travel to Guinea, Sierra Leone and Liberia owing to the Ebola outbreak of 2014. Check online for the current situation before planning a tour here.

DESERT RIDING TIPS

• The wind, not the sun, could well be your worst enemy. You don't want headwinds across a country like Mauritania, so do some research into the wind direction before the trip.
• Plan your day around how the wind blows. Headwind during daytime? Get up early and cycle during the usually-calm hours right after dawn. Tailwind in the afternoon? Why not enjoy a good lie-in and save your energy for harder times? The wind can be furious at night too, so secure your tent and try to pitch it behind a dune, rock or anything that provides protection.
• If wind is not so much of an issue, leave early before the heat, and rest in the middle part of the day.

The Sahara Desert in northern Sudan. This used to be one of the hardest parts of a Cairo to Cape Town ride; nowadays it's paved. © Lars Bengtsson

• Protect yourself from the sun. A hat, sunglasses and suncream are essential. I have toured in desert areas in shorts and T-shirt, but you might prefer to cover up. Bring at least something with long sleeves and legs.
• Bring a buff. It works as sun protection, fly protection and dust protection. Or use it as a head scarf during cold nights.
• It's definitely more painful to be without water than it is to carry some extra liquid – if I think I'll need ten litres, I take twelve. Make sure you have a reliable way of carrying the water.
• Sand will get everywhere. Literally. Seal things up if you don't fancy sand in your morning coffee. Or in your camera.
• Some desert areas, like Africa's Sahel, are extremely thorny. If you push your bike from the road into the bush to pitch your tent for the night you'll get flat tyres. Sometimes I carry my bike to my chosen camp spot.
• Wide tyres are much better on sandy roads, and remember you are way slower on sandy roads than on paving.
• You can navigate with a paper map or paper map and a GPS; don't go out on a long trip with only a GPS. If you plan to go seriously remote, bring a GPS, but you don't need one if you stick to ordinary roads.
• Don't forget to watch the stars – night skies in deserts are amazing!

Lars Bengtsson

scenery rising up from the rolling green hills between Kabala and Makeni.

Try to avoid the rainy season in July and August, as these parts record the highest levels of rainfall anywhere in Africa.

LIBERIA*

Liberia (*see p251) shares Sierra Leone's troubled past but the people are equally welcoming. Aside from the good paved road connecting the Sierra Leonean border to Monrovia, as well as upcountry to Ganta, the road network is limited. The ghostly and dramatic coastal town of Harper, close to the border with Ivory Coast, is reached by an adventurous dirt track through areas of dense rainforest.

IVORY COAST

The paved Southern coastal road provides the most convenient way to cross the country, although expect more scenery consisting of palm oil and rubber tree plantations than views of the sea. Roads and traffic in Abidjan can be busy but it's a useful place to pick up a Ghanaian visa and enjoy one of Francophone

(Opposite) Hot hard roads in northern Mozambique. (© Peter Gostelow).
(Overleaf) Bikes strapped to a pirogue on the Lulua River in DR Congo. (© Archie Leeming).

Left: Beach cycling in Ghana. When the tide is low sometimes the beach provides an alternative route. **Right**: Church camping in Nigeria. A free standing tent is a great advantage in Africa as you never know where you might find a pitch. Both © Peter Gostelow

Africa's biggest cities. East from Abidjan it's possible to avoid the city traffic by following the road out of Cocody then making use of a small passenger boat service heading to the former colonial capital of Grand Bassam, from where it's a short hop to the Ghanaian border.

GHANA

One of West Africa's few stable countries, Ghana provides some respite from the hardships of travel elsewhere in the region. Towering slave forts line the palm-fringed coast, where liquid refreshment from roadside coconut sellers is never far away. Inland, a journey from Akosombo across Lake Volta to Kete-Krachi offers an interesting alternative to road travel and a springboard into eastern Ghana. It's worth stopping at Wli Waterfalls, West Africa's biggest, before crossing into, and through, the small nations of **Togo** and **Benin**.

NIGERIA

Travel here is not for the faint-hearted. Main roads are usually busy and dangerous due to the sheer amount of traffic. Police check-posts are common, and what appear like small towns on a map end up being large, over-populated jungles of chaos. There is rarely a moment of peace cycling in Nigeria, so intense is the experience and interest generated by a foreigner on a bicycle. In recent times cyclists have also reported being suspected as Boko Haram terrorists, such is the hysteria and tension surrounding the issue. For this reason venturing into the Muslim-dominated north is not recommended.

That said, Nigeria is an incredibly diverse country and for the most part Nigerians smile broadly and go out of their way to help you. Small dirt tracks in rural Nigeria feel like a world apart from the urban hustle and bustle, and it's certainly worth taking time to explore them. The Hotel Sheraton in Abuja provides an oasis of peace by allowing overlanders to camp for free out the back. There are plenty of embassies in Abuja so it's a good choice for securing onward visas to places like Cameroon.

CAMEROON

Northern Cameroon presents some serious climbs and dramatic scenery near Bamenda and the tea-growing slopes that surround it. The Baptist Mission

(Opposite) Top: Village camping in Lesotho. (© Logan Watts).
Bottom: A warm welcome, on the road in Malawi. (© Logan Watts).

Resthouse here provides a welcome break before continuing south. The old Anglophone coastal town of Limbe, with its volcanic black beaches overlooked by Mt Cameroon, might be the last place you'll see the Atlantic for a while. It's worth watching the sunset with a few cold beers before tackling the real challenges of Central Africa which await.

DEMOCRATIC REPUBLIC OF CONGO

If you survived and thrived in Nigeria then you can probably handle the DRC. Nothing is relaxing or easy about travelling here so you're on your own when it comes to making it through.

In many ways a bicycle is the ideal mode of transport to navigate the numerous narrow and overgrown forest tracks. You're rarely alone, as bicycles provide the main mode of transporting goods in rural parts of the country. On a daily basis I met men with upwards of 100kg of goods on their single speed Chinese bicycles, often pedalling and pushing them for many days so that they could sell their load for a small profit, before returning home.

Aside from a dense network of forest tracks, the River Congo and its many tributaries provide a lifeline and transport system for the country's population. Congo barges travel between Kinshasa and Kisangani, a journey of over 1000km that can take many weeks. With a bit of luck and patience it's possible to jump aboard and give your legs a rest.

Jungle Highway in DRC, where the main roads are often just tracks through dense forest. © Peter Gostelow

Security situations change and it's sometimes hard to get up-to-date information for a place few people travel. There remain many Christian Missions throughout the DRC, which not only provide a safe and calm place to sleep if you ask politely, but can often advise on local security situations. The same can be said for some of the few NGOs working in the country. If you're looking at crossing the DRC from west to east, or heading in a southeasterly direction towards Zambia, it's wise to get a 3-month visa. The DRC is a place where delays are sure to happen, but you can be assured that your time here will probably be the most memorable of the trip.

ANGOLA

Securing a visa seems to be one of the hardest challenges of travelling to Angola, so as always check forums for the latest about how and where to apply. For those fortunate enough to make it here, their experience often turns out to be a real treat. Once you accept that daily costs are likely to be significantly higher than anywhere else in Africa – Luanda rates as the world's most expensive capital city thanks to oil money – Angola and Angolans might just become the highlight of your tour. The view down from the top of the dramatic Leba Pass is not to be missed.

ROUTE OUTLINES THE AMERICAS

6

Neil Pike

In recent years, Alaska to Tierra del Fuego has become *the* classic transcontinental adventure cycle-tour. The PanAm's appeal is clear: the opportunity to pedal the entire length (well, almost – see p276) of the Americas, the longest land mass on Earth. And for once, tracing a line on a map from the comfort of your own sofa, cup of tea in hand, can be put into reality on the ground. Bureaucracy worries are few as obtaining entry stamps is generally a breeze and restrictions on where you can visit are limited to a few hotspots which are easily, and best, avoided anyway. The geography of the route runs along lines of longitude meaning you can migrate with the birds, and, provided you plan well, stay in the best season for most of the time.

If you're in it for the long haul from Prudhoe Bay to Ushuaia, count on taking at least 18 months over the epic ride, much more if you become addict-ed to circling through the

Chasing llamas to Sajama, Bolivia.

Andes on unpaved back roads. Starting in the north and heading down has an aesthetic appeal, but also a practical one – it means beginning with a more familiar language and culture in countries where bike shops and parts are easily obtained – and builds up to the most challenging, and for many the most exciting, riding in South America. It also has the added benefit of avoiding beginning your tour with the infamous winds of Patagonia in your face; save them as tail- and side-winds (OK, and some headwinds) when you're a toughened tourer at the end of your ride.

You'll soon find you want to avoid many sections of the Pan American Highway itself and head out on smaller roads away from traffic. Mountain lovers in particular will be in dreamland, pedalling through the Rockies, then the Sierra Madres and onwards to the mighty Andes.

Still not sold on this continent for your big ride? Well maybe here's the clincher. Leafing through this book, you'll have already picked up on the joy of interactions with local people in those in-between towns and nondescript villages which rarely see a tourist. Put in the effort to add Spanish to your language repertoire, and from Tijuana to Tolhuin you'll be able to continue those roadside chats you'd been having with all and sundry between Anchorage and Antelope Wells.

NORTH AMERICA
USA & Canada

With such a familiar culture it would be possible to overlook North America as an adventure cycling destination, but those who revel in wilderness and off-road riding would do well to give it their full attention. With little difficulty it's possible to find many exciting rides and there are some meaty long-distance challenges, including the Great Divide Mountain Bike Route (GDMBR), the longest mapped off-road route in the world.

Those on Round the World trips will likely find themselves pedalling across the US from west to east or vice versa. Beginning on the Pacific Coast takes advantage of prevailing winds, and there are as many routes across the continent as there are roads, the smallest of which are traffic free.

Riding south from the Arctic to the Mexican border and beyond is the migration favoured by PanAm riders – from Alaska, through the Yukon, British Columbia and the American West. Ninety per cent of Canada's population live within 100 miles of the US border; north of that you have all the forests, rivers, distances and summer insects of Siberia, but without the checkpoints – in other words adventure riding at its finest.

The best paved and dirt road routes in the US have been mapped by the

Riding the Redwoods in Northern California.
© James Butcher

Adventure Cycling Association (💻 adventurecycling.org), who supply route guides for their entire network, which at present stretches over 42,000 miles (67,000km). The bikepacking scene which has sprung up in North America in recent years means that documented and GPS-mapped routes are the most extensive anywhere. See box p267 and check out 💻 bikepacking.net or 💻 pedalingnowhere.com for ideas about some of these gnarly multi-day off-road and singletrack rides.

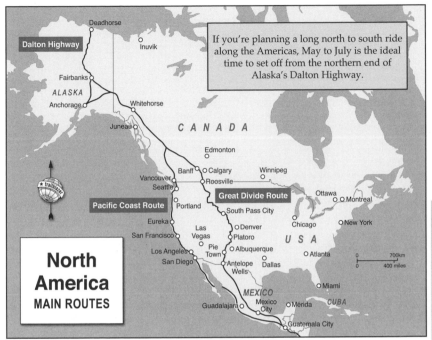

Here we concentrate on the best options available to those on lengthy north-south rides from Alaska, focussing on the GDMBR, the toughest and, for adventure riders, probably the most satisfying trail in North America; and the Pacific Coast Route, the most commonly travelled route between Canada and Mexico.

PRACTICALITIES

Timings and seasons

Cold and snow means that May is the earliest you can realistically begin riding south on the Dalton Highway from Deadhorse, near Prudhoe Bay (or from Inuvik at the north end of Canada's Dempster Highway). From May until July is an ideal time to set off if you're on your way to Tierra del Fuego, as it enables you to avoid the cold in the northern and southern extremes, as well as catch the dry seasons in the tropics in Central and South America. If you're heading in the opposite direction, you'll probably want to reach the most-northerly Arctic outposts by the end of September, before the real chill sets in, unless you're set up for extreme cold and snow riding.

The GDMBR takes about three months, and heading southwards it's best to leave Banff between mid-June and August. For most riders, it's unfeasible to begin at Deadhorse and fit in the GDMBR in the same season; as a result the majority choose either to begin in Alaska and cycle a faster route through the Lower 48, such as the Pacific Coast, or to begin further south and swing via the GDMBR en route to Latin America.

HASSLE-FREE RETURN TO THE USA?

It is paramount that you hand in your I-94 Arrival-Departure Card, usually stapled to a page in your passport, when you leave the country, otherwise the US authorities might think you've overstayed your visa. While this might sound like a simple procedure, at many of the Mexican border towns it is unclear just where you should perform this duty. Quite often, you'll find yourself off American soil, smelling the barbecue chicken and preparing yourself for the entourage of taxi touts, when you realise you are still in possession of this official piece of paper that must be handed in before you leave. If in doubt, ask one of the US immigration authorities to point you in the right direction. Sometimes handing it in through the wired gate is sufficient to get it into the right hands.

If you are passing through Canada between Alaska and Seattle, it may not be necessary to part with your I-94 card, but to be on the safe side check all your documents with officials before leaving.

You cannot take citrus fruits into the USA.

Sonya Spry

Visas

The US Department of Homeland Security currently requires travellers from Visa Waiver Program (VWP) countries (including the UK, Australia and New Zealand) to obtain approval through the Electronic System for Travel Authorisation (ESTA) prior to travelling to the United States. VWP enables eligible citizens to travel to the USA for tourism or business for stays of up to 90 days without obtaining a visa – you must apply (at a cost of $14) for travel authorisation via the ESTA website at 🖥 esta.cbp.dhs.gov. The 90 days starts when you enter the United States, and includes any time spent in Canada, Mexico and adjacent islands. The VWP permit cannot be extended, and you can only ask for a re-entry on the VWP if you leave the continent altogether.

If you are planning a ride from Alaska, through Canada and the Contiguous United States to Mexico, you'll almost certainly find that 90 days is not sufficient time, meaning you'll have to apply for a six-month tourist visa. At present this process requires an interview at your US Embassy, which can take time to arrange. Regulations are subject to change so it pays to do proper research well ahead of your planned departure date.

PanAm route ideas

RIDING ALASKA TO THE LOWER 48
Nathan Haley

Whether you get your buzz from big distances on paved roads or hard fought remote riding, you'll likely fall for Alaska and the routes and trails of the Americas' northern-most reaches. The dramatic seasonal changes make for almost perpetual sunlight during the riding season, from May to September, and perfect cycling temperatures. However, temperatures can fluctuate so cold weather gear is a must. Alaskan riding is more often than not accompanied by awe-inspiring mountain views, but aside from Atigun Pass over the northern Brooks Range, the cycle routes rarely involve more than rolling climbs. If you're just beginning a long Americas tour, you'll appreciate this, given that distances between supply points can be large and your panniers are often heavy with food. Unlike food, water is readily available, but always requires thorough treating due to the widespread presence of giardia.

Start a trans-Americas ride with a bang on Alaska's Dalton Highway. © Nathan Haley

The headline threats are black and brown (grizzly) bears which live throughout Alaska and western Canada. Their presence necessitates various precautions (see box p263) but should not distract riders from other potential threats such as moose, which are more numerous and statistically more likely to hurt you. Perhaps the biggest threat to an enjoyable tour in the northern wilderness, however, are the famous Alaskan mosquitoes. Often touted as the worst in the world, this bitey menace can be tamed with a head-net, bug spray and smoke repellents.

The Dalton Highway: Prudhoe Bay to Fairbanks

Alaska's roads congregate almost exclusively in the south-east corner of the state, making most of its nearly 1.5m square kilometres inaccessible to cyclists. The one exception is the James Dalton Highway (aka Haul Road) that sprouts north all the way to the Arctic Ocean. The Dalton Highway magnificently routes 415 miles (668km) through lonely Alaskan wilderness south from the town of Deadhorse, deep in the Arctic Circle. Originally constructed in 1974 to link Fairbanks with the oil fields of Prudhoe Bay, it runs across the Arctic tundra of the coastal plain, up the north slope, over the Brooks mountain range and down into thick forest before eventually linking up with the paved Elliot Highway north of Fairbanks. Despite the slow creep of pavement, the Dalton is still ostensibly a single lane gravel road (25% is pavement) almost completely devoid of services. The only notable stopping point is close to halfway where the Coldfoot truck-stop offers an all-you-can-eat buffet. As a unique opportunity to ride alone and remote amongst wild bears, moose, muskoxen, wolves and caribou, the Dalton Highway is considered by many to be one of the Holy Grails of bicycle touring.

Aside from an 8- to 12-day bicycle ride from Fairbanks, there are two ways to access Deadhorse; either fly from Anchorage or Fairbanks, or take the twice-weekly Dalton Highway Express bus (16 hours, June to the end of August) from Fairbanks. Hitching may offer a third option but for insurance reasons the numerous lorries won't pick you up. Unfortunately it is not possible to venture the additional few miles from Deadhorse to Prudhoe Bay and the Beaufort Sea (Arctic Ocean) by bicycle. Anyone who fancies a dip in the icy Arctic waters will need to register in advance with photo ID (the day before is usually fine) and pay for a tour of the oilfields.

Visit ⌨ alaskageographic.org for free downloadable Bureau of Land Management visitors' guides to Alaska.

TRIP REPORT
NORTH AMERICA

Name	Anna McNuff
Nationality	British
Year of birth	1984
Occupation	Part-time marketing consultant, part-time adventurer
Other bike travels	Wales, Scotland, the Alps
This trip	The 50 US States (plus one Canadian province)
Trip duration	7 months
Total distance	11,000 miles (17,700km)
Cost of trip	US$11,000 total ($40 per day on the road)
Longest day	130 miles (210km)
Best day	Riding through Denali National Park, Alaska, and seeing my first grizzly bear (I wet my pants).
Worst day	Iowa. Setting out to ride 100 miles in freezing cold rain and 30mph crosswinds. I ended up soaked to the skin, verging on hypothermic and looking for a motel within 20 miles.
Favourite ride	The week crossing route 50 in Nevada – great views and a heap of Wild West history.
Biggest headache	Rumble strips being put in the shoulder.
Biggest mistake	Riding into Denver, missing the cycle path and winding up on a busy highway, in the dark and pouring rain. I've never been honked at so much in my life.
Pleasant surprise	Utah. A truly incredible state with mind-bending landscapes.
Bike model	Santos Travelmaster Alu, 700cc wheels.
New/used	Brand shiny new, and a Pink custom frame (oh yeaaaahh).
Modifications	Swapped on a Brooks saddle, of course.
Wish you'd fitted	Side mirrors to spot the big ugly trucks a-comin'.
Tyres used	35mm Schwalbe Marathon (plus one emergency Walmart tyre for 300 miles).
Punctures	11
Baggage Setup	4 x Ortlieb Bike Packer panniers + Sea to Summit waterproof bag strapped over with tent in it.
Wish you'd brought	A high viz vest (I got one halfway through)
Wish you hadn't brought	So many clothes.
Accidents?	Only throwing myself onto the forecourt of a gas station while riding in over ice. Embarrassing.
Same bike again?	Absolutely. Although would reconsider the Magura rim brakes – which are hard to get hold of and wear fast in rain and grit.
Recommendations	Comfort is king! All else is supplementary.

The Dempster Highway

A comparable experience to the Dalton Highway can be found on the Dempster Highway in the Yukon Territory of northern Canada. The Dempster begins just east of Dawson City, and ends nearly 750km further north in Inuvik on the Arctic Ocean. Inuvik is most easily accessed by plane from numerous destinations in Canada; alternatively MGM Buses offer an on-demand (and more expensive) overland option.

South from Fairbanks

At the southern end of the Dalton Highway lies Fairbanks, a melting-pot of artists, students and military personnel that can provide a fascinating and well deserved break. From Alaska's third largest city, the remote, rolling Richardson Highway runs south-east to Delta Junction. Here it joins the Alaska Highway (aka ALCAN highway) to the Canadian border, about a six-day ride from Fairbanks.

Alternatively, lovers of dirt roads, big landscapes and wildlife should consider leaving Fairbanks south-west on the George Parks Highway (aka Parks Highway). Down this route is Denali National Park and Preserve, home to Mount Denali (aka McKinley), North America's highest peak. Unrivalled views of the mountain come with an exhilarating ride down the unpaved and traffic-free track that is the Park Road (see p334).

If unforgettable views of the Alaska Range aren't a temptation, then another tasty unpaved morsel forges east from Cantwell, south of the National Park entrance. The mostly gravel Denali Highway offers tourists unable to venture onto the Dalton Highway a more accessible taste of unpaved Alaskan wilderness. For an easier paved adventure carry on down the Parks highway its full length to Anchorage before turning east onto the Glenn Highway to Canada. Mountain bike enthusiasts would do well to continue south of Alaska's largest city to explore the extensive mountain bike trails of the Kenai Peninsula.

The Yukon and British Columbia

Whitehorse, the charming capital of the Yukon Territory, lies on the shores of the Yukon River, nearly 500km from the Alaskan border. If riding a couple of days down to Skagway and taking the ferry through the Inside Passage to Vancouver can be resisted, there are two routes south from here. While most motorised traffic continues on the ALCAN Highway down to Dawson Creek, cyclists generally prefer the quieter, more westerly, Stewart Cassiar Highway.

Snaking elegantly through magnificent forest and the impressive snow-dusted mountains of British Columbia, the Cassiar Highway is another bike touring gem. With widely spaced supply points, sizeable unpaved sections, an abundance of black bears and little

Riding the Icefields Parkway.
© Nathan Haley

traffic, the Cassiar offers an easy step into adventure. Tacking on a cheeky side trip west to watch the bears feed at Fish Creek can put the icing on the cake of this stunning ride. Gambling with the weather with an autumn (early September) ride may also offer colourful rewards.

To the Great Divide or Pacific Coast Route

Perhaps the most iconic route in the whole of Canada is the Icefields Parkway between Jasper and Banff. This paved jaunt through the stunning Canadian Rockies will satisfy mountain bikers just as much as roadies. A feast of dramatically jagged snow-capped peaks, sublime forest campsites, vibrant-coloured lakes and rolling glaciers, the Parkway offers the perfect segue onto the GDMBR. During the swinging summer season the road can be thick with traffic and campsites full, so riding on the shoulders of peak season is advisable. As with all the routes described here, services are minimal so it's best to stock up for the five-day ride in either Jasper or Banff.

For tourers intent on reaching Vancouver for a ride down the Pacific Coast, the Sea-to-Sky highway provides an unbeatable way into the city. This hilly spin meanders over the demanding Lillooet Mountain range, through the ski town of Whistler and adventure capital of Squamish before skirting Howe Sound on the way into west Vancouver. The Sea-to-Sky highway can hold its head high in the company of the region's other jewels; the Dalton, Dempster, Cassiar and Denali highways, and the Icefields Parkway.

A BEAR ENCOUNTER

We were approaching the Yukon-Northwest Territories border and I was casually chatting to Julien. Patagonian plains, Mongolian steppe, the new openness of the tundra around us ... our talk was flying over borders, from place to place, when an unexpected vision took my breath away and made me come down from the clouds. I stopped the bike. "Look, Look!" I said to my friend. Some 50 metres away, looking at us from a small rise by the road, was a grizzly bear, over two metres high – a big hairy giant, standing upright on his hind legs, gazing at us, smelling us. He wanted to know who we were, who were these strange creatures

entering his territory?

The following happened very quickly. The bear lowered his front legs, turned and fled. He galloped, as if running from the smell of hell. Onwards and onwards, not stopping for a minute. What good runners bears can be! We were surprised how far he went, moving fast through the vast, green, beautiful tundra plain. Further and further, growing smaller and smaller. In the end, when we could see no more than a tiny brown speck, he stopped and began to walk quietly here and there. Now, in his own new kingdom, there was no-one going to bother him.

That bear, there, standing upright in front of us, smelling us ... it was a thrilling moment, one of those that remain engraved forever in the memory and in the eyes. And then the running away ... We really scared the poor bear! "Humans stink!", he probably thought. And it's not surprising. I do not think anyone would have thought different if you had come close to us in those days – there are not many opportunities to shower while cycling the Arctic roads.

Lorenzo Rojo

CAMPING IN NORTH AMERICA

In bear country

Bear attacks in the wild are extremely rare, but you still need to make sure you swot up before beginning a tour in bear country. Wherever you choose to stop for the night, you have to be cautious about storing food, as well as toiletries with any scent – it makes sense to buy bear bags (heavy duty Ziploc bags that seal in odours) which are available from many outdoor stores. Campgrounds will often have bear-proof food lockers available or, if not, try stashing your food bags in the back of the metal bin lockers. Food caches accomplish the same thing for wild campers – this necessitates hauling food bags on a line up over a tree branch, ideally a hundred metres or so from camp. If camping in a tree-less area, such as the Arctic tundra you'll find in northern Alaska, stash your food well away from camp, down-wind under some heavy rocks. Eating away from where you sleep is another essential precaution – when planning a wild camp, it's not a bad idea to stop and cook, then carry on a few more kilometres before putting up your tent.

Knowing your black bear from your grizzly, and how to react should you encounter either, should form an essential part of your trip planning. Most cyclists also carry bear spray as a further precaution – in reality it might not save you in the unlikely event of an attack, but the comfort it provides will probably help you sleep better!

Campgrounds and wild camping

Campgrounds are common in the USA and Canada, and wild camping can also be a pleasurable experience, but you must be aware of where you are allowed to camp. The USA has an amazing amount of unspoiled natural scenery – almost a third of the country is publicly-owned land – which makes for great camping. Planning your route through these areas is easy if you visit the National Park Service's website at ⌨ nps.gov; the State Park information site at ⌨ stateparks.com; and the US National Forest Campground Guide at ⌨ forestcamping.com.

In the USA, wild camping on Bureau of Land Management (BLM) land is generally allowed, and it is also legal to camp on National Forest land so long as you are out of sight of trail heads. National Forest lands often border National Parks where camping rules are incredibly strict. Park officials will think nothing of giving you a hefty fine should they find your tent pitched outside designated areas, so being aware of the boundaries is very useful.

Crown Land (public land) accounts for 86% of Canadian territory and is open to wild camping. There are also hundreds of free camp and recreation areas with benches and long-drop toilets. Read up on the permits required to camp in Provincial and National Parks – like in the USA you'll be punished for incorrect permits, whether backcountry or in campgrounds.

Forest fires regularly devastate the North American wilderness so fire bans must be respected – stoves are mandatory for cooking in certain parts.

PART 6 – ROUTES – AMERICAS

PACIFIC COAST ROUTE

If you're crossing the US north-south between Canada and Mexico, the quickest and most popular option is the Pacific Coast Route from Vancouver to San Diego. Coastal panoramas, charming towns, sea cliffs and pristine beaches all help make it a beautiful ride, and if you choose to start here it's the perfect introduction to a longer PanAm tour. Though rarely flat, it's all paved (unless you take some of the off-road detour options), camping is cheap and plentiful, and supermarket supplies are easy to come by. It's a sociable route too, and the many hiker-biker campsites along the way mean you'll never be short of a fellow tourer to chat with by the campfire at the end of the day. Most riders go north to south so, if you do as well, you're likely to be camping by the same new friends night after night.

Despite romantic images of peaceful coastal roads, the main downside of the PCR is that Highways 1 and in particular 101 are in reality busy main roads, regularly passing through long urban drags a fair distance from the coast.

Respect from some drivers won't be as great as you'd like, and there are sections with no hard shoulder, so make sure you wear bright clothing and bring along your helmet. If you're keen to take alternatives to the main highway, it pays to keep your eyes open for quieter detour routes along the coast; these are always worth it and offer some great wild camping (see box opposite for ideas).

Navigation
The route is clearly signposted, so navigating is possible using the free state-highway maps which can be picked up at the many tourist offices in Washington, Oregon and California.

The Adventure Cycling Association (ACA) has details of the route on their website ⌨ adventurecycling.org, and also produces five maps which cover the whole route – these provide loads of useful information and handy tips, including elevation charts.

Other helpful websites for planning include the Oregon State website (⌨ oregon.gov) which has an informative Oregon Coast Bike Route Map in pdf, as well as bike touring maps; while the Washington State Department of Transportation (⌨ wsdot.wa.gov) has helpful Highway Maps.

When to go
Most riders tackle the route between April and November, and for a comfortable trip, **allow 6-8 weeks** for the full ride. Spring and autumn are the best periods as they avoid the heaviest of the summer traffic. Expect rain and the greenest landscapes in spring, and northerly winds in summer – the hottest months are July and August. At any time of year, there'll be some days with dense fogs which are part of the coastal microclimate in which redwoods and many wildflowers flourish.

Sleeping
When it comes to **camping** facilities, the Pacific Coast is a cyclist's dream. You won't have to stress about finding a place to put your tent as the sun goes down, because State Parks conveniently dot the entire length of coastline and offer specially set-aside 'primitive' camp areas for hikers and bikers. These sites are good value – Oregon State Parks charge $5pppn, in California the price is $5-10 while in Washington it's $12 per tent. A complete list of hiker-biker sites along the Pacific Coast Route can be found at ⌨ tour.tk/country-information/usa.htm, but be aware that if you can't find a site with hiker-biker rates, ordinary camping is likely to set you back over $30 per pitch.

Hiker-biker camping at Mackerricher State Park, Northern California. © James Butcher

RIDING THE GREAT DIVIDE
Scott Morris

Created in 1997 by the ACA, the Great Divide Mountain Bike Route (GDMBR) is the world's longest mapped off-road touring route, an unpaved 2800-mile (4500km) network of graded dirt roads and 4x4 roads,

SOME PACIFIC COAST ROUTE HIGHLIGHTS AND DETOUR IDEAS

● San Juan Islands, Washington – blissful biking and camping on almost traffic-free islands; take the ferry from Anacortes, south of Bellingham.

● Portland, Oregon – a cool, cycling-centric city.

● Jedediah Smith Redwoods State Park, N California – an interesting alternative to the tourist trap 'Avenue of the Giants' further south, with great camping and some peaceful and secluded dirt roads to ride amongst the redwoods.

● Prairie Creek Redwoods State Park, N California – worth a look for mountain bike trails and unpaved roads.

● Lost Coast – a good stretch of wilderness in N California, south of Ferndale and through the King Range.

● Yosemite, California – for some neck-craning at El Cap and Half Dome, leave the PCR near San Francisco and swing east.

● The southern section of the PCR channels bikers through Los Angeles and then San Diego. To avoid this whole area head inland near San Luis Obispo, and maybe take in some of the big-name National Parks – Sequoia, Death Valley, Mojave, Joshua Tree. If you're heading for Baja, you can still drop in via Tecate or Mexicali, or else keep heading east for Arizona, New Mexico and the northern Mexican mainland states.

James Butcher

with the odd section of rougher mountain-biking thrown in. It follows the Rockies from Banff National Park in Canada, into Montana, through a corner of Idaho, then Wyoming, Colorado and New Mexico, ending at Antelope Wells on the Mexican border. Over that distance you'll clock up over 200,000ft (60,000m) of total elevation – nearly seven Everests.

The Great Divide is a fabulous unending treat that will take three months – a blissful summer of riding and camping each night in a remote, off-highway setting. It's sometimes possible to ride from town to town, but perhaps the greatest appeal of this route is the chance it gives you to camp for free on public lands, passing through towns only for lunch and provisions.

The ACA sells the maps and a book that make this trip a doddle, though the latter is not strictly necessary. You can also download GPS data for the trip. The route itself is unmarked, it's the map that shows the way so you'll need an accurately calibrated bike computer so that when the map says 'turn left at 3.5 miles', you hit the mark.

Terrain

The scenery is mostly 'Big Sky country' rather than closed-in valleys and you'll be continuously exposed to the power of nature and mountain weather on the Great Divide. A mix of ranchland and forest, the route strays no more than 60 miles either side of the Continental Divide. Gradients are on average 5% – almost perfect mountain-biking country, giving you long, easy downhills. There are only one or two short sections where almost everyone will have to push their bike for a half mile or less. See 🖳 adventurecycling.org and my website 🖳 topofusion.com/divide for more stats and detail.

Although there's almost no traffic, there's plenty of washboard, rocks and loose gravel and you'll easily get through two sets of tyres. The weather is typical of the high country: snow is always possible, high winds from any direction, thunderstorms are a certainty towards the south, but more often than not it will be brilliantly sunny and very dry.

A rare singletrack section of the GDMBR, in Montana. © Scott Morris

When to go

The best season for biking the Great Divide depends on which direction you ride. Most riders go south where the earliest possible start dates are typically mid-June. Snow can linger on the high passes in northern Montana until July, but the route itself is usually clear earlier. Another consideration is the seasonal rainstorms in New Mexico; several portions of the route become impassable after hard rain, so it is best to travel through New Mexico in late August or early September. Northbound riders should start in late May to avoid the heat, but it's not advisable to start too early or you'll encounter snowed-over passes in southern Colorado.

Gear considerations

You will see a lot of BoB Yak trailers (see p68) on this ride, towed behind full-suss bikes; Glacier Cyclery in Whitefish sells and rents them. A BoB makes for less rattling than a pannier set-up – if you go with panniers, use the strongest you can get and check bolts daily. Front suspension will greatly reduce fatigue and increase your comfort, and your spine will thank you for a suspension seatpost too, however each year plenty ride the route on rigid touring bikes.

Due largely to the influence of Tour Divide, the annual gentleman's race held on the route, ultra-light bikepacking setups (see p71) are also quite common. With a sufficiently light kit, it's not impractical for very fit riders to cover 100 miles some days. The downside is less comfortable camping, and a greater reliance on towns.

A petrol stove is the best choice. If you cannot find small cans of white gas, outdoors shops will often refill your fuel bottles cheaply. Outside towns, mobile phone coverage is poor throughout the route. Carrying a bear spray (easily bought there) will give some peace of mind in Montana.

Route highlights

Starting in Banff National Park, the views are legendary as the route traces the shoreline of Spray Lake. It continues to wind its way around large lakes and even bigger forested mountains. The road surface tends to be pretty rough, and there are three major passes to climb before reaching the US border. A long descent to the border results in the lowest elevation of the entire route. Whitefish is the first decent-sized town with a bike shop and camping shops; well worth a stopover. At Holland Lake, a simple US Forest Service campground backs on to Holland Lake Lodge, which has a bar, restaurant and sauna that is usually open to non-residents. Lincoln is your next stop with a campground, then a long ride across country to Montana state capital Helena where the museum is a must-see. The old copper-mining city of Butte is a few days south and is also worth a tour. The route moves into more open country, briefly crossing a deserted corner of Idaho into Wyoming.

The trail runs into strikingly beautiful country near the Grand Teton mountains. This is a good spot for a detour to the town of Jackson for some R&R, cunningly avoiding the first major pass in the process. Towards the Great Basin, an enormous bowl in the Continental Divide from which no water escapes, the land becomes more barren and treeless. The ACA advises carrying three gallons (11 litres) of water for the Great Basin, but that seems excessive for an overnight bivouac or two. There are also a few reliable sources of water out there, surprisingly.

From Rawlins you begin climbing into Colorado. The landscape changes drastically from wind-blown deserts to cool pine forests. If you aren't a climber, you'll sure be one after riding through Colorado. Fortunately, most of the climbs are on firm, non-technical dirt roads. After crossing the Colorado River at the ghost town of Radium, you'll climb several more high passes before reaching the most urbanised area of the route, Silverthorne. The hordes of bustling tourists and shoppers will seem out of place, but the area is host to world-class mountain biking trails and is worth the stop.

ULTRALIGHT SINGLETRACK TOUR IDEAS

The western United States is a hotbed for long-distance singletrack hiking trails. In the last decade, bikepackers have been lightening their kits and venturing out to thru-ride and explore them, combining adventure touring and mountain biking. Below are a few of the most classic and ridden bikepacking routes. Taken together, the three are considered the 'Triple Crown of bikepacking'.

Arizona Trail

Designed from the ground up as a multi-use trail, the Arizona National Scenic Trail (AZT) welcomes mountain bikers and bikepackers. It's a rugged footpath that traverses the diverse landscapes of the Grand Canyon state – from harsh deserts to giant forests and from Mexico to Utah. Ultralight setups are preferred due to the demanding terrain and fre-

quency of hike-a-bike sections. The trail culminates in the ultimate hike-a-bike – the Grand Canyon, where bikepackers are allowed to carry, but not ride, their bikes from one side to the other.

Colorado Trail

With an average elevation above 9000 feet (2750m), the Colorado Trail (CT) is a high-altitude affair. Stretching some 500 miles (800km) from Denver to Durango, the trail is well established, well signed and well constructed. The long climbs and lack of oxygen will force extended sessions of bike pushing. Some of the highest sections are above the treeline, where the alpine scenery and abundance of wildflowers are a highlight.

The Continental Divide Trail

Running parallel to the Great Divide Mountain Bike Route is a singletrack route named the Continental Divide National Scenic Trail (CDT). The CDT is unfinished as yet, but some sections can be tied in beautifully as singletrack alternates on the GDMBR. Else tackle the entire CDT, a journey that will require solid map-reading skills, copious amounts of hike-a-bike and a good chunk of a year. It's over 3000 miles (4800km) long and some sections are difficult enough that covering 25 miles (40km) is a good day.

For more information on these and other singletrack routes, visit 🖳 bikepacking.net/bikepacking-routes.

Scott Morris

Great riding on the CDT in Colorado.
© Eszter Horanyi

HOMAGE TO REPACK ROAD

If you fancy some dirt riding, Marin County, north of San Francisco Bay, is the birthplace of mountain biking and many early brands and models were named after local features. It was here in the late 1970s that Gary Fisher and Joe Breeze tested their fat-tyred hybrids down the famous Repack Road (a turn-off on the Pine Mountain loop) – so-called because they had to repack the wheel bearings of their old hub-braked bikes after each descent. Local bike shops have info and maps.

Other dirt excursions in the Bay Area

There are many easier but just as scenic off-highway routes in the area. Generally, only doubletracks are open to bikes and they are serious about enforcing their 15mph speed limits; rangers patrol with radar guns, fining cyclists on the spot.

Mt Tamalpais (2500ft) is another great ride. Don't be put off by fog – ride through it to win fantastic views of the clouds below, perhaps punctured by the top of the Golden Gate Bridge or the skyscrapers in downtown San Francisco.

Samuel P Taylor State Park is hidden away amongst redwood trees, and to the south of 'Mt Tam' is the Marin Headlands Hostel, set in a rugged location far from towns (stock up on food first, you'll want a couple of days here). It's the kind of scenery and location Kerouac wrote about in Dharma Bums, isolated and surrounded by hills. A tunnel saves you some legwork if you want to get through the hills to Sausalito, or to the bike trail that runs from Mill Valley into San Francisco.

South of San Francisco and less than five miles short of Santa Cruz, Wilder Ranch State Park is well worth a stop for mountain biking on the thirty-odd miles of mixed-use trails in and out of forest overlooking the Pacific.

Stephen Lord

From Del Norte, Colorado, the route begins its longest and highest climb to Indiana Pass, just shy of 12,000 feet (3650m). The reward for the climb is sweet; on the far side lies a wonderland of high-alpine scenery that'll have you reaching for your camera. Not long after the tundra and alpine meadows the route travels through a Superfund cleanup site and Summitville, where the impacts from mining are profound.

In New Mexico the climbs are almost as big as Colorado, but the riding becomes more challenging. However, by the time you're there you'll be ready for it. The route in New Mexico is more remote, less travelled, and easily as beautiful as any other portion of the route. Be ready for some rough riding and lack of services. Towns are further apart and water becomes a serious concern.

The obligatory 'bike leaned up against pass sign' shot, on the GDMBR in Colorado.
© Cass Gilbert

After descending out of the pine- and fir-covered Jemez mountains into the town of Cuba, the route traverses a remote stretch of desert BLM land featuring deeply eroded *arroyos* (gullies), tall cliffs and interesting rock formations. You're unlikely to see anyone, apart from another Great Divide rider, on this section. Eventually, after climbing back into the ponderosa pine forests of Mt Taylor, you'll have a blast of a descent into the town of Grants on the historic Route 66.

Grants was once a booming mine town but as with many towns on the Trail it has metamorphosed into a service-based economy after the bust that inevitably followed the boom. You'll find more than enough services to stock up on supplies for a long stretch of service-less riding; the next major city is Silver City, some 250 miles (400km) away.

The route now traverses El Malpais (The Badlands) south of Grants. Cinder cones erupted in this area, covering the plains with black volcanic rock. It's rather beautiful and makes for some pleasant cycling. Before reaching Silver City you will run into a place whose name says it all: Pie Town. Eat as much as you can.

The Geronimo Trail follows a narrow corridor between the Aldo Leopold and Gila wilderness areas. An off-route hike (no bikes in the wilderness) here leads to some stunning vistas. After riding on the Continental Divide itself for a few miles, the route drops to the Mimbres River Valley where a hefty off-route climb leads to the impressive Gila cliff dwelling national monument.

Silver City is another large mining town long since bust and picking up the pieces. But it offers everything the touring cyclist needs after a few days in the wilderness. The 120 miles (200km) from Silver City to the Mexican border at Antelope Wells features typical Chihuahuan desert terrain, treeless and desolate with a unique, quiet beauty. If there isn't a headwind, you'll glide the last miles of road to the border station with ease.

Mexico and Central America

Anna Kortschak

What is it that makes cyclists so interested in visiting Mexico and Central America despite their well-publicised dark sides? Simple! The region has a fascinating history from pre-Columbian to contemporary times; the landscape is lush and varied; the area is dotted with striking and mysterious ruins and is inhabited by a diverse collection of indigenous cultural groups; the jungles and wetlands are teeming with exotic wildlife, and the coastal regions boast glorious beaches and extensive coral reefs. So you'll find plenty of things to do out of the saddle and, similarly, while on your bike, the riding also offers a multitude of options. If you prefer pavement you could stick to the PanAm, but head off road for more rewarding adventures. One word of warning, though – don't expect much of the terrain to be flat.

There is no denying that Mexico and Central America come burdened with a reputation – a bevy of recent civil wars, endemic gang violence and a burgeoning narco-trafficking industry, against a background of grinding poverty, provide plenty of material for narratives of lurid violence. What is overlooked by a sensational media industry and travel advisory warnings is that the violence in Mexico and Central America is mostly targeted at known actors within rival political, criminal and social/ethnic groups. It follows a heinous but mostly predictable pattern.

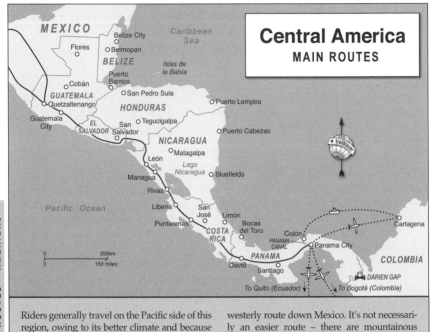

Riders generally travel on the Pacific side of this region, owing to its better climate and because most bikers are heading south and have taken a westerly route down Mexico. It's not necessarily an easier route – there are mountainous roads and 4000m peaks in western Guatemala.

The vast majority of people are friendly, honest, hardworking and are cheerfully getting on with making a go of things, despite various difficulties that affect their lives far more seriously than they do those of passing tourers. People in Mexico and Central America are far more likely to astonish you with their kindness and hospitality than rip you off when you are paying for tacos or – much less – threaten you or your belongings.

PRACTICALITIES

Safety

So let's take a deep breath and think calmly about safety. An effort to educate yourself is one of the most important basic precautions you can take. From every point of view it will improve your experience if you understand a little of the history, cultures, languages and economic conditions of the place that you are in. And once you have a clue, just let common sense be your guide.

Muggings and crime of course do occur in Mexico and Central America, but take it as read that large cities are more dangerous than towns and big towns are more dangerous than villages. It is worth remembering too that weapons, and firearms in particular, are more common in the Americas than in Europe or Asia.

Most big cities in the region don't have that much to attract the passing cyclist anyway and are probably best avoided. If you do choose to ride into larger towns and cities it is sensible to arrive early in the day so that you can negotiate any less salubrious neighbourhoods and find accommodation in daylight. Another approach is to take a bus in and while this has some advantages, it means becoming just one more overloaded backpacker, with the additional burden of a bike. Also, bus stations are often located in fairly dodgy areas.

Keep an eye on popular travel information networks, like the PanAm Riders Google Group, to stay up to date on specific trouble spots or incidents.

Anecdote suggests that travelling on bigger, more heavily trafficked,

Urique, at the bottom of Mexico's Copper Canyon. © Anna Kortschak

highways puts you at greater risk, not only from traffic, but also of potentially dangerous encounters with people. On back roads, the majority of your fellow travellers are likely to be local residents going about their daily business. On highways, people travelling fast by car or motorbike have a far greater range and anonymity.

Listen to local advice but be aware that it will contain a certain amount of cultural bias and that most locals consider travel as inherently dangerous.

Climate
In Mexico and Central America think broadly in terms of wet and dry. Wet runs from May to October but the further south you go the more extended the rains are, potentially running all the way into December by the time you reach Panama. Dry is what's left over. That said, there is plenty of variation and micro-climates – the climate on the Pacific side of the continent is quite distinct from the Atlantic side – but overall it gets warmer the further south you get. While low-lying regions in Central America are sweltering for most of the year, in Mexico temperatures are much more comfortable from November to May. If you cycle in the mountains it can get quite chilly in these months as it's winter which, confusingly, the locals will call summer because it's dry season.

Visas and fees
Visas aren't required in Mexico and Central America for those from the EU and North America. The length of stay varies from country to country: Mexico offers a generous 180 days, while Guatemala, El Salvador, Honduras and

---

HOSPITALITY

The hospitality of strangers in most of the world is truly heart-warming and travelling by bike you'll be amazed by all the kind offers of accommodation you'll receive. Pedalling around makes you appear more human and breaks down all kinds of barriers, meaning you are more approachable to local people in areas you're travelling through. In Latin America, the *bomberos* (fire-fighters) are often open to putting cyclists up for a night or two, and in Central America churches and schools can also be surprisingly hospitable. However, on routes where cycle touring is becoming more and more popular, these alternative forms of accommodation can come under increasing pressure. Please remember that hospitality is just that – an act of generosity and kindness, not a right automatically granted to you by your chosen mode of transport.

C4 BORDERS

The most straightforward way to renew your C4 visa is by crossing any border outside the C4 area, but it is worth noting that the C4 agreement is rather unevenly enacted. Guatemala allows for renewals from within its borders, while El Salvador takes a dim view of this practice.

I was threatened with fines and expulsion from the entire C4 area by immigration officials as I left El Salvador, on account of a shoddily performed visa renewal at the Guatemala/Mexico border. But the Honduran immigration officials, on the other side of this supposedly non-existent C4 divide, laughed uproariously, said something unprintable about Salvadorans, and put a nice new stamp, granting me another three months, in my passport right next to the aggressively scrawled, '3 days to leave'!

Nicaragua have a joint visa agreement – known as the C4 – which means, in theory, that you have only 90 days to explore all four countries. You could burn through the C4 in far less than 90 days but there are plenty of reasons to linger if you are inclined to a more leisurely tour.

Belize grants a 30-day visa and charges an exit fee of US$20, while various of the other Central American countries charge small entrance and/or exit fees depending on your nationality; none of these fees exceeded US$10 at the time of writing. It is worth checking for recent information as you approach a border since unscrupulous border officials sometimes try to charge 'fees' that don't exist.

Food

Eating in Mexico and Central America won't disappoint and there is plenty to discover besides the nutritious basics of tortillas, rice and beans.

You'll find an astonishing array of colourful exotic fruits – often sold on the street, pre-cut, with a refreshing dressing of chilli, salt and lime juice. Fresh juices are also commonly available at markets and street stalls and ice-cream shops sell locally made confections featuring the same wide range of fruity goodness. Young coconut for sale on the roadside makes for a delicious ultra-hydrating drink and snack combination.

In most areas, villages and settlements are frequent enough that you don't need to carry much more than a day's worth of food. Produce markets are widespread but there are also plenty of economical restaurants to choose from if you don't care to cook. Lunch tends to be the main meal of the day.

Vegetarians will find their options far more limited than omnivores and frustratingly meat products are often used as flavouring in otherwise vegetarian fare such as the ubiquitous *frijoles* (beans). Strict vegetarians might have to stick largely to self-catering.

All water should be treated in Mexico and Central America and keep in mind, too, that those delicious salsas might have been sitting on the table for some time.

Accommodation

Warm Showers and Couch Surfing are popular with the more sophisticated population of Mexico's cities and larger towns but pretty thin on the ground elsewhere. Hotels in Mexico are often set up for larger family groups and can be quite a good deal if you are travelling in company.

Use your judgement to work out when it is sensible to wild camp and when it would be better to ask a friendly looking family if you can camp under their protection. Most people are at home in bed at night but there are areas where people can be out and about and, possibly, up to no good after dark. Border areas in particular see various sorts of illicit traffic, while people may be poaching for wildlife or timber in forest areas.

MEXICO

Highlights Mexico has rugged mountains and canyons, arid deserts, glorious beaches and extensive wetlands. Wildlife spectacles include the Monarch butterfly over-wintering colonies in Michoacán, whale migrations and giant tortoise breeding sites on the Pacific coast, flocks of flamingos and other water birds in the wetlands, jungles echoing with the throbbing roar of howler monkeys while toucans and trogons flit from tree to tree. On the cultural front there are countless fascinating festivals such as the famous Day of the Dead.

Food tips The food is definitely not going to get any better further south – so eat up big, here in Mexico. It's a diverse country with distinct regional differences that are reflected in a complex cuisine that is unquestionably the pinnacle of eating in the Americas. Most cyclists don't need encouraging, but

MEXICO CITY

Mexico City is the one major city in this region that is well worth visiting. Known by the locals as 'DF' (*Distrito Federal*), the city has an absorbing history and is jam-packed with enough ruins, museums, galleries, cultural events, bookshops, markets, restaurants and bars to satisfy any interest.

Of particular note is the National Museum of Anthropology with an incredible permanent collection of pre-Columbian artefacts. If pre-Columbian ruins are your special thing don't miss the Aztec ruins beneath the cathedral facing the *zócalo*, the huge central plaza. If you are more interested in contemporary art, culture and history you'll want to visit Diego Rivera's murals in various central public buildings, the Frida Kahlo Museum and the Trotsky Museum.

And for those of you that live for cycling there is the Sunday *Ciclovía* – a weekly event in which the city's major avenues are closed to motorised traffic and given over to human powered wheels. Amongst the crowd of everyday weekenders, an incredible array of bike groups takes to the streets, to pedal their various messages and missions.

In fact, bike culture is so strong in DF that you will find plenty of support to negotiate the labyrinthine freeway snarls. It was

possible, I discovered, to find a cyclist willing to meet me at the outskirts of the city and guide me to the door of where I planned to stay. Bicitekas (🖳 bicitekas.org) is the DF-based cycle activist group that made this possible. Among other things Bicitekas provide a community access bike workshop (🖳 bicitekas.org/casa-biciteka).

About 500km to the west of DF, Guadalajara is another place worth mentioning; it's a lively university town with an active bike culture and a Casa de Ciclistas 🖳 gdlenbici.org/casa-ciclista (see p291).

The Ciclovía attracts all types of cyclists.
© Anna Kortschak

Mexico is a country where it's worth being adventurous and fully investigating the food scene.

Route tips

The most popular route through Mexico is via Baja California and the coast, with two main border posts to choose from – San Diego/Tijuana, or Mexicali, a little further inland. Both posts have a reputation for being busy and a little rough around the edges, so stay alert and take your pick. These busy crossings see a lot of daily traffic and the officials expect people to know the ropes. Heading southwards there won't be people flagging you down, so it's up to you to make sure you get your passport processed appropriately (see p258). For a more laid-back entry to Mexico, cross on relatively quiet roads at the small town of Tecate, which lies between the two busier posts.

Baja highlights include desert landscapes and beautiful beaches and at some stage you will cross the Gulf of California, aka the Sea of Cortez, which is the most bio-diverse sea on the planet, famous for whale watching and other marine wildlife encounters. But keep in mind that these joys can be tempered by stiff winds, soaring temperatures, the need to carry quantities of food and water, busy roads with no shoulder and galloping gringofication.

There are two ferry options from La Paz, in Baja, to the mainland: a 6-hour trip will take you to Topolobampo, or an 18-hour journey will carry you to Mazatlán, 400km further down the coast. Check the Baja Ferry website (🖳 en.bajaferries.com.mx) for schedules and fares.

On the mainland coast, too, dreams of lounging on perfect beaches sipping cool drinks while admiring sunsets may be shattered by a less romantic reality. The ocean is often out of sight and the 'coastal' road is surprising steep in a rolling kind of way. You have to contend with heat, high humidity and insects. The traffic can be heavy and the narrow winding road does not have a hard shoulder in many places. Coastal areas are popular destinations with local and international tourists and wild camping on the beach is best approached with caution as robberies and assaults are not unknown.

Mexico's mountainous interior is a viable and increasingly popular alternative to the coastal route. People who follow the Great Divide Mountain Bike Route in the US are particularly well placed to enter Mexico in Chihuahua and continue riding the high country. The Antelope Wells border posts (there are two) are quiet and safe. Route options through Chihuahua, Durango and Zacatecas are diverse and range from smooth paved highway to rough dirt roads.

The Copper Canyon area in Chihuahua is one of the highlights of Mexico's Sierra Madre but exploring it by bike is not for the faint-hearted. It's a 2000-metre drop from top to bottom and the quality of the roads make the climb out the other side memorable. There is some excellent walking to be

Yaxchilán, one of the lesser known ruins in Chiapas, southern Mexico. © Anna Kortschak done in the area if you fancy some time off the bike – **Entre Amigos Hostel** in Urique makes a great base.

Your best resource for finding a route through the Sierra Madre are cyclist blogs and for those wanting to branch away from the main roads, more or less reliable maps – on a state by state basis – can be obtained from the *Secretaría de Comunicaciones y Transportes* in any state capital.

To Guatemala
Whether following the coast or the mountains, most people converge around Oaxaca, to delve deeply into Mexican cuisine and then find their way to San Cristóbal in Chiapas to investigate the complexity of Mexican indigenous culture and politics. Chiapas is the beginning of Central America and has more in common with Guatemala than the rest of Mexico.

From San Cristóbal the choice is to either follow the PanAm Highway to the Ciudad Cuauhtémoc border post, or take the more roundabout and adventurous route that skirts the border between Mexico and Guatemala, running through lush wildlife- and ruin-filled jungle. If you take the latter you'll find several options for crossing the border by boat into the department of Petén.

YUCATÁN PENINSULA / BELIZE

Highlights The Yucatán peninsula is way off the classic route but cheap flights in and out of Cancún make it a possible start or finish point as well as a convenient jumping off point for flights to Cuba (see p278). Inland, the peninsula's cycling is hot and flat, but persevere and you'll find some of America's most intriguing pre-Columbian ruins, limpid cenotes, gorgeous beaches and coastal wetlands with astonishingly prolific bird life.

Safety tip Leaving the Yucatán, if you find yourself passing through Belize it's worth taking a few extra precautions. Belize City and the Hummingbird Highway have a nasty reputation for violence, robbery and sexual assault.

GUATEMALA
Guatemala is another fascinating country with particularly colourful and diverse indigenous cultures. For many adventure cycle tourers it is the highlight of Central America, with a range of good routes to chew on in the Guatemalan Highlands.

Highlights Tikal, a Mayan archaeological site close to the picturesque Lago Petén, is one of Guatemala's biggest draw-cards, rivalled only by the dramatic volcano-ringed Lago Atitlán. Semuc Champey's aqua-blue natural pools and intriguing caves reward hardy souls willing to brave the steep mountain route to reach them. Quetzaltenango (Xela) is a great base for those wanting to do an intensive Spanish course and/or get

School girls in the Guatemalan Highlands.
© Anna Kortschak

involved in 'volunteer tourism' with one of the many NGOs there. Volcano treks out of Xela make for exciting excursions.

Stopping off for a stint as a volunteer at Maya Pedal (⌨ mayapedal.org), an organisation that recycles bikes and bike parts into useful pedal-powered machines, is a popular break for cycle tourists in San Andrés, near Antigua.

HONDURAS

Highlights Diving on the Bay Islands. The Copán Ruins. Or, for the extreme experience – if you feel like forgoing roads altogether – find your way across La Moskitia.

A Maya Pedal pedal-powered blender. © Anna Kortschak

Safety tip Honduras (along with Belize) has the worst reputation in Central America for violence and crime. The big cities are well worth avoiding and extra care needs to be taken around other population centres.

CROSSING THE

There are loads of options for jumping the Darien Gap – the roadless section between Panama and Colombia – but all of them present challenges and difficulties.

1 Plane

The easiest and most predictable way is to fly, whereby the challenge is confined to finding a bike box and packing your bike. This may forgo continuity and accrue a heavier carbon footprint than is fashionable but it is fast and efficient and you can pick your destination in South America as you please.

2 Sailing boat

This will get you from either Panama City, Colón or Portobelo in Panama to Cartagena, Colombia via San Blas, and is a pretty expensive option these days. It can vary between the trip of a lifetime – think snorkelling crystalline waters with hammerhead sharks and manta rays, dining on lobster, relaxing on deserted islands while palm trees paint the sky – and a totally wretched and life-threatening experience – think sea-sickness, drunk captains, a three-berth boat packed with 12 twenty-something backpackers in the mood to pa-a-arty, or even, in the worst case scenario, shipwreck. Do your research.

There is also a similar motorboat tour called the *Darien Gapster* which is somewhat cheaper than sail.

3 Speed boat (*lancha*)

Local *lancha* is cheaper than sailing but unpredictable and notoriously uncomfortable. Bad weather will makes things much worse.

You need to have enough Spanish to negotiate your passage at your port of choice. The options include Colón, Portobelo or Miramar on the Caribbean side. Colón is famously edgy, Portobelo shows a slightly softer face to tourists, Miramar is the port of last resort and has zero infrastructure to make your life easy.

From any of those points of origin you'll end up in Puerto Obaldia where you exit Panama by taking another lancha to Capurganá, the entry point for Colombia, before getting yet another lancha to Turbo. Expect an overnight stay in Capurganá – which has a well developed tourist infrastructure – as the ongoing lancha leaves in the morning. The lancha from Capurganá is a set price and you will be charged per kilo for your bike and baggage. Turbo is a rough port

NICARAGUA

Highlights The colonial towns of León and Granada. Ometepe.

Route tip To avoid the PanAm, take a ferry to Lake Nicaragua's twin peaked island of Ometepe where you can cycle on quiet roads, climb volcanoes and investigate 'permaculture' tourism.

Border info From Ometepe, a ferry trip will allow you to exit Nicaragua at San Carlos and enter Costa Rica (on another ferry) at Los Chiles so that you don't have to compete with crowded buses and other heavy traffic at the hectic Peñas Blancas border crossing on the PanAm.

COSTA RICA

Highlights An extensive national park system and loads of wildlife. Visit the Nicoya Peninsula for yoga retreats and surf camps; Arenal is the name of both a picturesque lake and an active lava-spewing volcano.

Food tips *Gallo pinto* is not chicken – it's a delicious vegetarian mix of beans and rice. Black beans and rice will form the basis of most meals in Costa Rica.

Budget tip Costa Rica (and Panama) are potentially expensive if you want to

---

DARIEN GAP

town where you probably won't want to hang around.

It is also possible to take a lancha on the Pacific side between Jaque and Bahía Solano but this is less commonly attempted and anecdotes imply a greater degree of unpredictability and risk.

4 Cargo boat.
This option requires reasonable Spanish skills and a lot of legwork in Colón to negotiate a passage. Departure times are unreliable, it is increasingly expensive and incredibly slow, as the boats make many, many extended stops to load and unload cargo. Smaller and often less sea-worthy cargo boats also leave from Miramar.

5 Canoe
Some adventurous souls have canoed from Panama to Colombia. This is hard on your bike due to unavoidable exposure to sea water and perhaps not advisable unless you have some serious open-water canoeing experience under your belt as conditions will be tough. Be aware also that getting hold of a canoe isn't going to be cheap. And no, a pack raft isn't an appropriate choice of craft for the crossing.

6 Ferry
After a few false hopes, in late 2014 a ferry service finally began operating between Bocas del Toro, Colón and Colombia, for around US$100 per person and the same again per bike. For those of you with pets in your panniers, cats and small animals are carried for a bargain US$20! More information, some of it in truly baffling English, can be found at 🖳 ferryxpress.net.

If this service continues to defy the expectations of cynics, the days of the dreaded 'gap' may be over.

Crossing the Darien Gap in a small unseaworthy cargo boat. © Anna Kortschak

eat at restaurants or stay in hostels in popular tourist areas, but if you camp and buy and prepare your own food, prices aren't much different from the rest of Central America.

Border info If you're on a roll down the PanAm you'll cross the border into Panama at Paso Canoas. Expect crowded buses, long waits, bag searches, stress and hassle. Head to the Atlantic coast, and you'll cross the rickety bridge from Sixaola in Costa Rica to Guabito in Panama which is a far more chilled-out experience. Panama's rather strictly enforced entry requirement of proof of onward travel is usually satisfied by the presence of a bike, or even (I discovered on a flying retrograde trip to Costa Rica for emergency repairs) a solitary wheel.

PANAMA

Highlights Bocas del Toro on the Atlantic coast, a group of lovely Caribbean islands not yet entirely spoiled by rampant tourism. A side-trip to Santa Catalina on the Pacific side for excellent surfing or diving. The Panama Canal.

CUBA

On world maps, Cuba appears as a tiny dot in the Atlantic Ocean, but looks are deceiving. The island is 1200km long and you'll need a good three months to see all of its mountains, beaches, sugar cane fields and historic cities from the seat of a bicycle. Our time was far more limited so we spent an autumn hunched over maps, trying to select the best routes for a one-month tour.

With the help of *Bicycling Cuba* – an ageing but still useful guidebook – and the *Guía Carretera* road atlas, we settled on a route west out of Havana, through the nature reserves around Las Terrazas and onwards to the cities of Pinar del Rio and Viñales. We then put our bikes on a bus to central Cuba and rode clockwise through the Colonial cities of Cienfuegos, Santa Clara, Remedios, Sancti Spiritus and Trinidad. This last section, from Sancti Spiritus to Trinidad, turned out to be delightful: oceans to our left, mountains to the right and vendors selling fresh sugar cane juice every few kilometres. It was, without a doubt, the cycling highlight of the trip.

We timed our journey over Christmas and New Year. The July to November hurricane season had passed, the days were sunny

Taking a Cuban bike for a test ride. © Andrew Grant

and temperatures a moderate 20-25°C. It was also high tourist season and beach resorts were booked solid but as wandering cyclists we had no trouble finding a room in a *casa particular* or Cuban B&B. When our first choice was full, the owner always called around until he found us another spot.

The front porches of our many casas turned out to be the ideal spot for absorbing Cuba's fascinating bike culture: vegetable sellers, bakers and families on their way to school regularly pedalled by on bicycles cobbled together from whatever parts are available.

Food was another big advantage of casa life. It was never fancy but was served up in portions generous enough to satisfy even the hungriest bike tourist. Our typical dinner consisted of beans, rice and a big plate of meat or fish but first we always tried to find an enterprising Cuban mixing cocktails on the street for just pennies. We usually succeeded. Eating options were more limited in the countryside, though roadside pizza stands were fairly common and we also regularly found *batidos* (milk and fruit smoothies), bananas or sweet pastries for sale.

Friedel Grant

Food tips Fresh fish and *patacones* (fried plantain chips).

Route tip There are two bridges across Panama's famous canal. If you have no desire to visit Panama City, don't cross the Bridge of the Americas (which is officially forbidden to bicycles anyway), opt for the Centennial Bridge which puts you on route towards Colón without the need to negotiate any of Panama City's dodgier neighbourhoods.

South America

Neil Pike
with contributions from **James Butcher, Sarah Bedford and Laura Mottram**

As an adventurous touring destination, South America's case for being the most exciting and varied continent on the planet is strong. Extremes of environment and topography: the longest mountain range, the biggest rainforest, the highest waterfall, driest desert and largest salt flat; glaciers you can pedal past and ice caps you can walk to. If you're after remote roads, or wild spaces, it has plenty of them too – a vast network of dirt trails to head out and investigate. Did I mention the best steaks and biggest road climbs in the world? (Not into climbs? I meant descents! Biggest descents!)

Complementing all this are mystical ancient ruins, fascinating and rich cultures, and as much as the range of scenery your tour will be built around interactions with friendly locals and a great freedom brought about by a lack of bureaucracy or wranglings with officialdom.

PRACTICALITIES

Seasons

Seasons, seasons, seasons. We've banged on about them all book, and South America is no different. Though the continent has been affected by El Niño and La Niña in recent years, with unusual and out-of-season weather patterns, you'll still benefit hugely from being in places at the right time. This means **dry season in the mountains** of Colombia (December to March), Ecuador (June to September), Peru (May to September) and Bolivia (May to October), and the summer in Andean Chile and Argentina (October to March). See individual country sections for best times if you'd rather stick to the Peruvian coast and the low areas in the northern halves of Argentina and Chile.

Those lucky enough to have **a year** to cycle the length of the continent will find that setting off from the Caribbean coast in the early months of

Cycling the Huascarán Circuit, Peru.

South America
MAIN ROUTES

Almost all riders stick to the Andes, on the west side of the continent. From Colombia to Bolivia plan your trip to avoid rainy seasons, whilst in Patagonia in the south it's best to visit from late spring to early autumn (October to March), even though the winds are stronger then.

For information about touring in South America, see:
- andesbybike.com
- elpedalero.com
- bicyclenomad.com
- whileoutriding.com

the year is best; February is ideal. If you need to leave in October or November for a 12-month trip, it's better to cycle northbound from Ushuaia. Leaving from either extreme from June to August is a bad idea – better to start off somewhere in the middle, ride one half, then fly back to ride the remainder.

A rough year-long schedule that would work well for mountain lovers is: Colombia (2 months), Ecuador (1), Peru (3), Bolivia (2), Argentina/Chile (4). If you're not such a fan of the climbs or unpaved roads, factor in more time in Argentina and Chile, and less in Peru and Bolivia.

Visas
The rest of the world might seem like it's determined to make it harder for you to get in, but don't worry, South America isn't. For most Europeans the continent is visa-heaven, meaning you won't have to detour from your preferred route to visit embassies in capital cities. Turn up at a border, whip out your passport, see it stamped for free (usually with '90 días'), swing your leg back over the crossbar and continue pedalling. Non-EUvians need to investigate more closely but rules are usually still generous. US citizens have to get their wallets out for Bolivia and Argentina and apply online before arrival in Argentina. Extensions aren't available in every country but, where they're not, you can often cross into a neighbouring country for a day, then return.

Costs
US$10-20 is an achievable daily spend on the road in South America. Chile is the most 'developed' and expensive Andean nation, and you'll struggle to survive on US$15 a day there, particularly in Patagonia, unless you wild camp. Brazil and French Guiana are expensive too, but few bikers make it that far east. Bolivia is the cheapest of the popular countries, where a bed for the night and three meals can still yield change from a US$10 bill.

Main routes
Almost all riders crossing the continent attach themselves to the western, Andean side where paradise biking routes abound: Colombia to Ecuador, across Peru into Bolivia, then down through Chile and Argentina. The variety and mountain grandeur rarely abate the length of the Cordillera, meaning that those on shorter, more focussed trips are well catered for too. Each of these countries has outstanding routes and scenery, and dishes up varying cultures and cuisine. Heading east of the Andes is unusual as Brazil's vast and stifling interior or Argentina's seas of unbroken, flat pampa don't hold the same appeal; but for some bike, jungle and boating fun in Venezuela and the Guianas, turn to p308.

Getting there from Europe or North America
Quito, Lima, Santiago and Bogotá are all places people regularly fly into to start a tour. From Europe it's often cheaper to reach Sao Paulo or Buenos Aires, but that leaves you with a further flight, a long bus journey, or a very long warm-up ride to reach the Andes.

Those riding down from North or Central America usually arrive by boat in Turbo or Cartagena in Colombia (see p276), while the hardy bunch beginning in Ushuaia are best off flying or bussing it there via Buenos Aires or Santiago.

Safety
Safety issues and South America tend to go hand in hand in western news reports, but in reality you'd have to be unlucky to have a serious problem. It

T R I P   R E P O R T
SOUTH AMERICA

Name	James & Jane Hall
Nationality	British
Year of birth	1967/1966
Occupation	Consultant Urological Surgeon / Teacher
Other bike travels	2-week trips in UK, France and Spain.

This trip	Cusco to Ushuaia then Cartagena to Central Peru.
Trip duration	9 months
Total distance	13,000km
Cost of trip	US$25pppd on the road.

Longest day	161km El Calafate to Rio Gallegos (nice Patagonian tailwinds)
Shortest full day	33km Rio Grande to Julaca, Bolivia; grit storm leading to retreat into tent at 10am till next day.
Best day	So many. Cycling onto then sleeping out on the Salar de Uyuni probably the winner.
Worst day	Just before crossing to Tierra del Fuego. Sidewinds, fast lorries and no shoulder to cycle on.
Favourite ride	Paso Sico crossing – 5 days, all dirt, challenging weather, felt remote.
Biggest headache	Dogs, f**king dogs.
Biggest mistake	Not doing this decades ago. Not investing in a good spec trailer tyre.
Pleasant surprise	Northern Peru – fun, kind people, great biking and lots of positive surprises.
Illnesses during trip	2 bouts of D+V close together in Colombia.
Bike model	On-One Inbred frame, then we built them up with mainly Deore spec. Rigid forks. 26" wheels.

Wish you'd fitted	Machine gun for the dogs!
Tyres used	Schwalbe Marathon Plus Tour 2.0"
Punctures	1 penetrating puncture all trip – between us.
Baggage Setup	Bar bag and 2 rear panniers each, and a BOB Yak for James.
Weight of kit	40kg between us (~25/15kg split)
Bike problems	Rear disc vibration led to spokes tightening and 1 snapping each day for a week till we worked out the problem.
Same bike again	Yes
Recommendations	Ignore the 1001 reasons not to do it and JFDI, now! If you're a couple, agree before you leave that it's OK to take an hour, a day, or longer, apart every now and then: 24/7 for months on end isn't normal.
Any advice?	Avoid timescales. Use transport if it's not working for you and get to somewhere it does.

pays to avoid dodgy *barrios* (neighbourhoods) in larger cities and keep your wits about you in tourist centres, while you need to be aware of certain areas of the Colombian jungle and northern Peru coast to stay clear of too. But most riders concentrate on scenic routes through smaller towns and villages, where keeping your camera battery charged will be the biggest concern.

Stop for a minute in Colombia and you'll draw a friendly crowd. © Sarah Bedford

Language in Latin America

Though English is spoken by some in larger cities and tourist places, learning Spanish is the most worthwhile way to spend your time either before or at the start of a trip in Latin America. Those conversations with Argentinian gauchos won't be nearly as rich if your Spanish doesn't stretch beyond '*me gusta asado*', and you'll be slightly more cash-rich too, as the gringo taxes fall away with fluency. If you make it to an altiplano village where only Aymara is spoken, or an Ancash *caserio* where Quechua rules, you'll have to start signing, but at least you'll know you've found a truly adventurous route!

On a shorter trip you can make do with school Spanish and a smartphone app, but for a longer tour consider taking an intensive course as early as possible in your trip. The Spanish from Mexico to Bolivia is beautifully clear, and courses in these countries will be cheaper than in Chile and Argentina, where the accent, speed of delivery, and use of slang makes the language more difficult to understand anyway.

COLOMBIA
James Butcher and **Sarah Bedford**

'The only risk is wanting to stay' proclaims the Colombian tourist board's slogan, and for once it's not just hyperbole. Forget any lingering preconceptions you may have – with its geographical variety, incredible hospitality and genetic passion for cycling, Colombia is the perfect gateway to adventure cycle touring in South America.

SAFETY IN COLOMBIA

If your mum is having kittens at the prospect of you cycling into Marxist ambushes deep in the Colombian jungle, then you can tell her to relax. The security situation in Colombia has improved dramatically in recent years and the likelihood is that during your time here you will face no more than the usual risks of petty crime you find anywhere.

Having said that, there are still isolated areas which remain *zonas calientes* ('hot zones') and where you may find a heavy military presence. The situation here is complex and fast-moving, so keep an eye on travel warnings and ask the police or military for local advice if you feel at all uncomfortable. Colombians are generally very protective towards tourists, and chances are locals will warn you long before you pedal into anything dangerous.

For an excellent introduction to modern Colombia, read Tom Feiling's *Short Walks from Bogotá: Journeys in the New Colombia* (💻 tomfeiling.com).

MAIL AND COURIER SERVICES IN LATIN AMERICA

Receiving mail and packages in Latin America can be something of a vexed business, but those on long rides usually find it necessary at some point.

For smaller or less valuable items it can be easier to use the standard post than couriers. It's useful having a local address to get the package sent to, though if street addresses in the area are vague you might be better off getting stuff posted to the post office (*correos*). If you do this, check how to get the parcel addressed (in some countries it's to '*Lista de Correos*') and make sure the name matches your ID documents – it doesn't matter if all your friends know you as Princess Lollipop Pitter Patter, if it's not on your passport it's not going to roll. Whether or not it arrives in a timely fashion is pretty hit and miss so don't get anything really important

sent on a totally inflexible time-schedule – you may end up like me, riding in circles for six weeks in Costa Rica waiting for a new debit card.

International courier services are reasonably reliable but packages have a habit of getting caught up in customs, and duties that can seem quite unreasonable are often levied. If the parcel's tracking status online doesn't seem to be changing, it pays to be proactive and get on the phone to the courier (in Spanish) to find out where it is. Often things grind to a halt if documentation like a passport photocopy is needed, but nothing will happen unless you get in contact. Having parcels sent to the shipping office in a larger town, or to a Warm Showers host, is normally the most hassle-free way to go.

Anna Kortschak

Modern Colombia is a vibrant and diverse country emerging from decades of brutal civil war. Sociable, loquacious and fun-loving, Colombians live to eat, drink, dance – and talk. You'll quickly learn the art of climbing a muddy pass while chatting with a curious Colombian hanging off the side of a motorbike, and before long you will be invited inside for a friendly interrogation. "What do you think of Colombia?" they'll ask as they offer you a freshly squeezed *jugo* (juice), a plate of *patacónes* (fried plantain slices) or even a bed for the night. "Now go and tell the rest of the world what Colombia is really like!", they'll urge as they send you on your way.

And so whether you choose to spend your time on pristine Caribbean beaches in Santa Marta, inching your way through the Andean foothills in Boayacá or perfecting your salsa moves in Cali, chances are that it will be this proud hospitality and infectious lust for life which become the lasting impressions of your time in Colombia. Expect to stay for longer than you think – this is an addictive country whose warm embrace is very hard to leave.

Before you go

Most visitors receive a three month tourist stamp on arrival, which for most is enough to cross the country; if you need longer it's possible to extend at an Immigration Office.

National Geographic's *Colombia Adventure Map* is probably the best paper map of Colombia to buy before you go, and will be sufficient if you're sticking to major routes on paved roads. If you're seeking dirt-road adventures, then

Colour section (following pages)
- **C1** (Opposite) **Top**: Sampling burritos from a road side food stall in Chihuahua, Mexico. (© Anna Kortschak). **Bottom**: Rainy season in Nicaragua. (© Sarah Bedford).
- **C2** Looking down on Lagunas Verde and Blanca, from high in Chile.
- **C3** Flying down from a 5000m pass in Peru. (© Mike Howarth).
- **C4** Salar de Uyuni, the ultimate campsite. (© Anna Kortschak).

C1

C3

C4

the Agustín Codazzi Geographical Institute in major Colombian cities offers a good range of regional and departmental maps. You can find their interactive maps at ⌨ igac.gov.co.

On the road

Colombia's cycling culture means that most towns will have a bike shop and a decent mechanic, and in the cities you'll find a range of quality parts. If you're on a long PanAm adventure, this is a good place to give your bike some TLC, as further south good parts become harder to find.

Decent unleaded fuel for your stove is available everywhere, although watch out near the Venezuelan border for the poorer quality contraband stuff. Food supplies are rarely more than a day's ride away and while cuisine generally follows the South American pattern of low on

Jugo de papaya – tropical fruit is a Colombian highlight.
© James Butcher

flavour and high on carbs, there are some highlights (see box).

Accommodation in *hospedajes* is plentiful and reasonably priced. Finding a quiet spot to camp is usually easy, especially in the highlands – although probably best avoided if you find yourself in a *zona caliente* (see box p283). Come prepared for all weathers – you might find yourself digging out your thermals in freezing rain up on the páramo moorland at 2000m and sweating down by the Río Magdalena all in the same day.

Colombia is a country that loves to party, so take in as many fiestas as you can – see ⌨ colombiafestiva.com for dates.

Cordillera-hopping

Consider this your Andean warm-up, where things get a little *columpio* (lumpy). Colombia is split down the middle by the Andean chain, whose three fingers – the western, central and eastern *cordilleras* (ranges) – converge at the Ecuadorian border. Between these lie the steamy valleys of the Magdalena and Cauca rivers. To the west lies the Pacific coastal region, and to the east the *llanos* (plains) stretch towards Venezuela and the Amazon.

COLOMBIAN FOOD HIGHLIGHTS

Set lunches Crispy *chicharrón* (pork crackling), hearty *cazuela* (bean stew) or the gut-busting Antioquian *bandeja paisa*.

Tropical fruits Try *pitahaya*, *granadilla* and *guanábana*, or order a *jugo* (juice) of *maracuyá*, *lulo* or *tomate de arbol*.

Drinks Ice-cold Pony Malta; hot *agua de panela* (sugar water), served with fresh cheese for dunking; or frothy hot chocolate.

Coffee Try sweet shots of tinto from roadside vendors, or if you're a serious caffeine hound, visit a *finca* in the *Eje Cafetero* to follow the whole process from bean to cup.

Snacks *Buñuelos* (deep-fried cheese balls) – best served fresh with tinto; *arepas* (maize flatbreads) stuffed with cheese, chorizo and more.

(Opposite) Top: In Patagonia. (© Cass Gilbert). **Bottom left**: Descending through the cloud in Bolivia. (© Joe Cruz). **Bottom right**: Little and large. (© Cass Gilbert).

Riding with new friends in Colombia.
© James Butcher

Most cyclists take one of two routes from north to south through the mountainous central third of Colombia: either a western route which tracks the central cordillera through Medellín and Cali or an eastern route following the eastern cordillera through Bogotá. Both have their highlights as well as some tedium, so if time allows then a mix and match, zig-zag approach will involve cordillera-crossing at least once but will provide a taste of almost everything Colombia has to offer.

Arriving from Panama

If you've taken a boat from Panama, your first challenge is to cross the dull and sweaty coastal plains towards the foothills, without prematurely ending your Colombian adventure squished like a *patacón* under a truck load of bananas. Instead, avoid the arterial routes and head south-east across the beautiful Magdalena delta towards Bucaramanga, with a stopover at Simón Bolívar's favourite sleepy backwater town of Mompox.

Eastern route

From Bucaramanga, the temperature drops and the pace of life slows as you climb into the eastern cordillera and the departments of Santander, Boyacá and Cundinamarca. Take the rollercoaster back roads to discover tranquil highland villages and test yourself where cycling heroes like Nairo Quintana learned to climb. El Cocuy National Park offers fantastic high-altitude hiking – but check trail status first at 🖥 parquesnacionales.gov.co and 🖥 pnncocuy.com as the flagship seven-day circuit has been known to close for long periods.

Bogotá offers the usual capital city conveniences and stresses. If you're looking to head west towards Manizales and the *Eje Cafetero* coffee region you can do so here – either via the legendary 83km, 3200m paved climb to Alto de Letras or via a dirt route through Los Nevados National Park.

Otherwise, push south for the archeological zones of Tierradentro and San Agustín via the tiny Tatacoa Desert. All that remains is Colombia's dirt swansong: the 'Trampoline of Death' from Mocoa to Pasto. Named for its erratic profile and the regularity with which drivers topple over its near-vertical ledges, on a bike it's a much more appealing proposition. If you can't face the Trampoline, there is a jungle escape route from Mocoa into Ecuador at San Miguel/Lago Agrio.

Western route

Staying west takes you from the coastal lowlands on a winding climb up into the central cordillera to Medellín. If your legs and bike need an overhaul, take a break at Manuel and Martha's friendly *Casa de Ciclistas* in nearby San Antonio del Prado (🖥 casadeciclistasdemedellin.blogspot.com).

From Medellín, plot a back roads route through beautiful Antioquian villages such as Jérico and Jardín, and towards the Eje Cafetero. If your hips are

A NEW COLOMBIAN ADVENTURE

The world bicycle touring map is in a constant state of flux, and no place ever stays the same for long; as one territory closes another invariably opens elsewhere. Exciting changes that as bicycle tourists we're free to explore like no one else.

Developments in Colombia are some of the most welcome of recent times. In the past decade it has quietly evolved away from its lingering reputation for violence, drug war and kidnappings, transforming from a 'place to avoid' into an adventure cycling gold mine. In the process Colombians have cemented a reputation for incredible warmth and bicycle obsession.

Keen to find new routes, in late 2013 I took my tour of northern Colombia deep into the department of Norte de Santander, on the border with Venezuela. Map research revealed a rich bounty of dirt roads crawling through tight valleys and hopping over sharp passes. Exactly the kind of landscape I love to explore. However, with pockets of paramilitaries still hiding in the mountains and ongoing terrorist activity, from the outside it looked like a no-go.

But experience has taught me to explore the gap between reputation and reality. A constant dialogue with locals and a heavy dose of common sense can totally transform the perception of danger. So I ventured into Norte de Santander and discovered nothing but kindness. Privileged to be the first cycle tourist to ride through many of the villages, I unearthed a fascinating dichotomy of military bunkers, warmth and friendship. The reward for my curiosity was a rare glimpse into cut-off communities and enlightening encounters with excited youngsters and interested elders.

Nathan Haley

restless and you are set on salsa in Cali then keep south, but be prepared for some tedious pavement en-route. Otherwise, jump cordilleras from Manizales to pick up the archaeological highlights of the eastern route.

After Cali, it's hard to avoid the final haul on pavement to Pasto, with only the so-called 'white' (but actually rather grey) city of Popayán offering brief respite. Just before Popayán is your final chance to cross the high *páramo* to the eastern cordillera.

Crossing to Ecuador

Both routes converge in Pasto, just a day's ride from the Ecuadorian border at Ipiales. This is the perfect place to toast your last night in Colombia over roast *cuy* (guinea pig) – and unless you're confident in your rat identification skills, it's worth paying a little more.

ECUADOR

James Butcher and **Sarah Bedford**

If Colombia is South America's *café longo* then Ecuador is its *espresso corto*: rich, intense, and – if you're not careful – gone before you've really had a chance to savour it. This may be the smallest country you pedal through in South America but don't dismiss it – what Ecuador lacks in sheer size it more than makes up for in intensity and variety of experience.

Ride precipitous, cobbled roads over the equator and along Ecuador's chain of volcanoes to mighty Chimborazo, the furthest point from the centre of the Earth. Pause to refuel on *hornado* (roast pork) and stock up on multi-coloured llama-wool leggings at remote indigenous markets. And if all the climbing becomes too much, freewheel your way down to the Amazon, head for the beach or even take a detour to the Galapagos.

Impromptu roadside geography lesson.
© James Butcher

You might be able to blast through Ecuador in just a couple of weeks but with all those tantalising side trips to be had, why on earth would you want to?

Practicalities

Cobbled, steep, climbs aside, Ecuador is an easy country to cycle through; its compactness and variety also make it the perfect candidate for a short stand-alone tour. If you stick to the highlands of the Sierra and dabble with a few dirt detours as most riders do, expect to spend four to six weeks here. National Geographic's *Ecuador Adventure Map* covers all but the smallest dirt roads and includes those all-important contours.

Accommodation is cheap and plentiful, and the *bomberos* are often welcoming. Even the smallest villages have a market, where for a couple of dollars you'll find hearty set lunches of delicious *sopas* followed by *fritada* (fried pork) with *mote* (boiled corn) or *llapingachos* (fried potato balls). Make sure you try *ceviche*, especially if you're near the coast.

Route inspiration

Ecuador divides neatly into three regions – the *Costa* (coast), *Sierra* (highlands) and *Oriente* (Amazon) – but most focus on the central spine of the Sierra. If you're tempted by a side trip to the Amazon or the coast but are put off by the long pedal back up to the Sierra, putting your bike on a bus is cheap and easy.

Stick to the PanAm for too long and you won't see much through the belching bus smoke and your descending red mist. Instead, take to Ecuador's tough but rewarding network of dirt roads wherever possible.

From the Colombian border at Tulcán, don't miss the other-worldly dirt ride across the Páramo El Ángel, through swathes of triffid-like *frailejónes*. Pick up a new woolly hat at the touristy market in Otavalo before tackling the steep but beautiful cobbled climb to the Lagunas de Mojanda.

En-route to Quito you'll suddenly find yourself in the Southern Hemisphere. Follow the magnetic pull to Santiago's legendary Casa de Ciclistas

Selling traditional fedora hats, Simiátug, Ecuador. © James Butcher

15km outside the city in Tumbaco – where two nights easily becomes two weeks. Quito itself is best avoided by bike but consider a short bus ride to visit the historic centre and the stunning museum of Quechuan painter Guayasamín – not to mention blowing your kit budget on that must-have down jacket at outdoor store Tattoo.

For one of Ecuador's best rides, take the dirt rollercoaster past the volcanoes of Cotopaxi and Chimborazo – but if you'd rather stick to pavement

RIDE THE VOLCANIC ROLLERCOASTER

If you have an appetite for steep dirt and cobbled roads, then why not join the snow-capped dots of two of Ecuador's most majestic volcanoes – Cotopaxi and Chimborazo – in one epic dirt rollercoaster:

• From Sangolquí, take the cobbled route to Cotopaxi via Rumipamba. Wild camp under the glow of Cotopaxi, or ride up to the refugio.

• Cross the PanAm at Lasso onto the high altitude Quilotoa loop, catching your breath at the turquoise crater lake and the lively Saturday market in Zumbahua.

• Follow the back roads towards Chimborazo via the market in Simiátug and the chocolate co-op in Salinas.

• Take the paved loop around Chimborazo or the boggy off-road route between Chimborazo and Carihuairazo.

• Reward yourself with *hornado* in the laid back town of Riobamba.

For more information on this route visit 💻 whileoutriding.com/ecuador.

then Leo's Casa de Ciclistas in Ambato will offer welcome respite. From Riobamba there are a multitude of options depending on your style and Peruvian plans. The colonial city of Cuenca makes for a stylish stopover, as well as offering the first escape route towards the coastal deserts of northern Peru at Huaquillas.

Instead, many prefer a more easterly route via the Lagunas de Atillo, into the sticky lowlands of the Oriente at Macas and on to Loja. Here there's a last chance for a PanAm dash to Peru at Macará – but we'd highly recommend heading for Zumba, pausing to admire the pickled gringos at Vilcabamba. This lumpy but tranquil route will set you up perfectly for the unmissable Incan ruins and dirt roads of Chachapoyas.

PERU
Neil Pike

Among cyclists, Peru polarises passions unlike anywhere else in the Americas. Some hate it, put off by the Cordillera's whopping climbs or the coma-inducing boredom of the PanAm – 'Wake up! there's a tree in 100km, and a bend the day after!'. But we'll let you into a rapidly escaping secret: for lovers of dirt mountain roads the opportunities in the vertical Inca heartland are virtually unrivalled in the adventure cycle-touring world.

A decade of strong economic growth based, as for centuries, on mineral wealth, has brought infrastructure investment and a burgeoning road network which expands faster than you can turn those cranks up the hills. To every mine and two-llama town, past glacier-etched peaks and into the deepest canyons, roads cut through one of the most geographically diverse countries on earth. As you chug up one side of a valley in deepest darkest Ayacucho, stopping occasionally to compliment a *campesina* on her fabulous hat, a faint zigzagging track appears opposite. But even if it's only 10km away as the condor whirrs, can you summon the energy to cruise down, then saunter up the other side to investigate?

Throughout the mountains and along the coast, impressive archaeological sites pepper the landscape. The visiting masses converge on the wonders of Machu Picchu, but with your own wheels other more ancient marvels like Kuelap, Choquequirao or Chan-Chan become readily accessible.

I need how long?

With so much choice, few riders lay down identical GPX tracks through Peru, but it's still possible to categorise the main ways from north to south. Either stick to the tarmacked highway near the coast; take the established, and almost all paved, 'Mountain Route' through Huaraz, Huánuco and Cusco; or else head onto the rough stuff for the challenging 'Peru's Great Divide' route along the Atlantic-Pacific watershed. As numerous roads cut east from the coast, most people mix and match the three, tailoring the terrain to fluctuating energy levels and priorities.

It's easy to underestimate the size of the country or the effort required to pedal through. Sticking to the PanAm, Tumbes to Tacna is over 2500km and takes in excess of a month. Head into the hills for some kicks, as most riders do at some stage, and even if you remain on the blacktop you'll need over double that. Begin yo-yoing through the sierra on dirt roads, your altitude profile soon pogoes like the output from some out-of-control seismograph, and if you brave it this way for the long haul to Titicaca there's a half-century of 4000m passes to tackle before you emerge, euphoric or broken, and more than three months older, onto Bolivia's alienly-flat altiplano. Luckily, many can get six month visas on arrival, so there's no reason to race through it all; not that you could if you tried.

Getting your seasons right

Dry season in the Peruvian mountains is May to September and if hills are what you bike for it's worth planning your whole Andean jaunt to coincide with this. During wet times you'll at least be able to get through if you stick to paving, though you can guarantee there'll be plenty of misery, and days curtailed by electrical storms. Venturing out on high dirt routes in wet season is a whole different undertaking and means accepting the additional inconvenience of being slowed, or turned back, by mud and snow, particularly in the wettest months of December to March. If you're headed south bask in the lack of wind: as sure as *lomo saltado* follows *sopa*, it won't last.

In contrast, the coast is often windy, generally blowing from the south, and though cycling at any time of year is possible, it gets hot in the north in the summer months from December to April. East of the Andes, dirt routes rapidly become mud baths in rainy season.

On the road

Paper maps will suffice if you're sticking to major roads but they're next to useless for dirt road enlightenment – it'd be like trying to navigate Britain's

---

CHEAP PERUVIAN EATS

The food is a pleasant surprise in Peru, even in villages and non-touristy towns. As elsewhere in the Andean world, chicken- and chip-guzzling rivals football as the most popular pastime, but look out too for *chifas* (Chinese restaurants) and menu restaurants. The former can be relied upon for cyclist-sized portions, while at the latter you'll be able to tuck into a two-course set meal for a couple of dollars. *Sopa* (soup) then *segundo* (main course) is standard – favourites include *ají de gallina*, *lomo saltado* and *trucha frita*. Along the coast, fish and seafood are a highlight.

CASAS DE CICLISTAS

The Casas de Ciclistas are a Latin American institution and we were keen to visit as many as possible during our trip, hoping for an insight into the local culture and customs not available when cycling across other continents. The casas offer the long-haul cyclist a place to sleep, rest up and relax after months on the road and are often a welcome respite from the rigours of the desert, Andes, altiplano or myriad other landscapes that make cycling in the region so popular.

The original casa was founded in 1985 when Lucho began inviting passing cyclists back to his home in Trujillo, on the northwest coast of Peru. The family has since moved out but the building still contains Lucho's workshop, where it's not uncommon to find him working away until the early hours of the morning, surrounded by decades of memorabilia.

Lucho and the casa have played host to over 2000 grateful cyclists, something attested to by the pile of eight thick guestbooks full of stories, sketches, photos and hand-drawn maps: annotated in every conceivable language and dating back thirty years.

More casas have opened since then, their locations passed on by word of mouth as cyclists cross paths over the continent. These days, lists can be found on the internet, and the casas themselves are spread around the whole region, from Baja Mexico to the Carretera Austral.

Like Lucho, the founders of other casas are often professional bike mechanics, meaning they're ideal places to get bikes repaired after a long time on the road, and better than the local bike shops for locating touring-specific parts. If it's not possible to source something locally, their experience and contacts often fashion a suitable alternative, like a hack for a handlebar bag mount or welding up a new steel rack.

Santiago and family have been taking in cyclists for over twenty years and are now based in Tumbaco, outside Quito. Another busy bike mechanic, Santiago operates his business from the courtyard of their home, which is a hub for the local cycling and outdoor community. They drop by most evenings to share stories around the kitchen table over hot chocolate and a communal supper and are a fantastic source of local knowledge and a wonderful resource for the road ahead.

The Casa de Ciclistas in La Paz, Bolivia, occupies a small city-centre apartment, which, depending on the season, can have cyclists sleeping in every corner. It's a great place for exchanging maps and information with those heading in the opposite direction or catching up with friends you last saw a continent ago.

Although each very different, the casas and their hosts all share two deeply engrained Latin American traits: a love of cycling and socialising, and it is this that has ensured their longevity and success, making a visit to at least one a worthwhile feature of any ride through the Americas.

Andy Peat

Lucho and his wife Aracelly in the Casa de Ciclistas in Trujillo. © Andy Peat

footpaths using a motorway map. Much better are the downloadable electronic maps from the Ministerio de Transportes y Comunicaciones: 🖥 mtc.gob.pe/portal/transportes/red_vial/mapas_redvial.htm, or use a smartphone app. Ask around on the ground, though, as any mapping errors could lose you a day or two. See 🖥 perut.org and 🖥 viajerosmapas.com for invaluable GPX data for download.

To save energy on the climbs and make the mountains a more enjoyable experience, consider making use of bus companies' *encomienda* (cargo) systems. Going light opens up a whole world of new route possibilities, with

HIGH ALTITUDE RIDING TIPS

● Put thought into planning. Many high altitude areas are remote and there's unlikely to be much in the way of help if you encounter difficulties.

● Check the weather forecast before setting off.

● Take it easy and don't over-exert, particularly to begin with.

● Aim to sleep no more than 300-500m higher than the previous night.

● Lower your daily mileage expectations initially; as you acclimatise you'll be able to increase these a little, but 40km can still be a good day in some regions.

● Take a strong tent, warm sleeping bag and sufficient kit to survive the elements, but try not to burden yourself with too heavy a bike.

● Cooking at altitude requires more fuel, so increase the daily amount you carry.

● Adjust your menu plan: rice and some pastas don't cook well and end up a mushy mess, as the boiling point of water falls as altitude increases.

● Buy a BIC or other quality(!) lighter. Many cheaper ones don't work at altitude.

● Likewise certain electronics, including some smartphones and MP3 players, stop working above a certain height.

● Ladies: loosen your bra to make breathing easier.

● Muffle up on the pass – descents are usually bracing!

An exaggerated Chilean pass sign.

● Don't forget high factor sun cream and sun glasses.

● High altitude rides are usually cold, so you may need to heed some of the tips on p177 too.

---

roads which would have meant torturous hours of pushing suddenly becoming a rewarding challenge. Whatever you do, make sure you keep good waterproofs and heavy-duty gloves with you for when that rainy descent from a lofty pass just won't end.

For many, Peru still elicits visions of the Shining Path (*Sendero Luminoso*) and banditry, and raises the question 'but is it safe?' In recent years the country has become far safer and though there are occasional reports of robberies in lowland coastal areas in the north and you need to take the usual precautions in large cities, you're more likely to find poor driving standards and dogs with anti-cyclist tendencies the real annoyance. On main roads, riders often become frustrated by children and some adults shouting '*gringo*' as they ride by. It's rarely used as an insult, so it's best to treat these encounters with a smile and an '*hola Peruano*' or else to stick to minor routes where 'gringo' shouts are much more infrequent than being stopped by a kindly campesino wanting a natter.

A portaledge might seem a sensible addition to your kit in some areas, but wild camping on quiet roads in the Cordillera is generally easy and memorable. A night indoors won't break the bank, and even in small villages there's often a bed to be found if you ask around. The wide availability of clean white gas (*bencina blanca*) ensures you won't be spending time cursing your dirty malfunctioning stove; save that for Bolivia. Lima has the best selection of spares, but places with mountain biking scenes, such as Huaraz and Cusco, have plenty of parts too. Reassuringly, even if you're in, say, Challhuahuacho and it feels like the back of beyond, as long as there's a bus service, and you've got internet, enough Spanish and know what you want, it should be possible to arrange for that Shimano essential to be *encomienda*-d up from a bike shop in the capital.

Peru currently holds the dubious distinction of 'counterfeit dollar capital of the world', and lots of fake Nuevo Soles, the local currency, are produced too. It always pays to check notes, like the locals do, to avoid being lumbered with a worthless wad of bills.

Getting to Peru, and route inspiration

Peru makes an excellent stand-alone tour, but if you fly into Lima, do yourself a favour and don't try and ride out of town. Better to jump on a bus and start your ride somewhere *más tranquilo* and with fewer than 10 million inhabitants.

Coming from Ecuador

A number of crossings link Ecuador and Peru. *Pista* (tarmac) tourers usually enter at Macará and make their way through the desert towards the Chan Chan ruins and Casa de Ciclistas (see p291) in Trujillo. Watch out in the vicinity of Paiján, just north of Trujillo – it's notorious for an armed gang who took a fancy to robbing cyclists. Local police escort tourers through the danger area but make sure you read up for the latest beforehand.

The quieter, unpaved route across the border at La Balsa, between Loja and Jaén, opens up a myriad of interesting possibilities for progressing south towards Cajamarca. This part of Peru is little known in the mass tourism world – it's too much effort to get to on public transport – and there's some exciting, adventurous riding to be found. Possibilities include pedalling via Chachapoyas, the magical ruined fort at Kuelap and eerie mummy museum at Leymebamba, then tackling the famous road down to and up from the Río Marañón.

Cajamarca is an engaging city steeped in history – the place where the conquistadores' cunning and deceit put paid to the Inca Atahualpa, and whole rooms were filled with a ransom of silver and gold. Put some planning into your ride south to the Cordillera Blanca while you're here as there are various enticing small roads to pick from.

THE BIGGEST PAVED CLIMB IN THE WORLD?

From the coast at Lima, the Carretera Central climbs into the mountains. If you decide to begin crawling up this on day 2 of your trip, as did our French friend Jean-Marc, after a few days and 150km of continuous climbing you'll find yourself above 4800m on Abra de Anticona, with a sure case of AMS. The ascent might be high on many (an acclimatised) tourer's wish-list were it not for the fact the highway is narrow and absolutely rammed with bus and truck traffic heading to the cities in Peru's interior. As it is, you're better off avoiding this highway and sticking to some of the country's more relaxing slopes.

Cordilleras Blanca and Huayhuash

Nearing Punta Olímpica, the highest point on the Circuit.

Few can resist the temptations of these two neighbouring ranges, which offer some gob-smacking mountain scenery. For those who've PanAm-ed to this point it'll be the first foray into the peerless Peruvian Cordillera, and the excitement of the meeting is heightened by entry through the Cañón del Pato's many tunnels, and the views of Huascarán, Peru's highest peak. If you've made it this far through the mountains, Huaraz's tourist comforts will come as a relief – pizza and craft beers anyone? In season there are always other grizzled tourers to chew the coca with and, if they're headed in the opposite direction, spin outrageously exaggerated yarns about the colossal climbs that await. Once your energy's returned, aided possibly with a cheeky Inca Kola or two, make sure you set aside a week to pedal the Huascarán Circuit – it's one of the continent's classic rides.

Classic Ride – The Huascarán Circuit

The 300km circuit of Huascarán provides a visual and cultural treat to all intrepid cyclists willing to accept the challenge. The loop through some of the most spectacular natural beauty in the Andes crosses the spine of the Cordillera twice, at Punta Olímpica (4890m) and Portachuelo de Llanganuco (4710m), passes cut through rocky ridges in the 1980s for roads which soar high among glaciers and are towered over by the Blanca's largest peaks.

We think this region has some of the best hiking and biking in the world, so for more detailed route inspiration and information buy yourself a copy of our *Peru's Cordilleras Blanca & Huayhuash: the Hiking & Biking Guide*, also from Trailblazer.

South to Cusco

From Huaraz the 'Mountain Route' marches south; the gradients aren't steep, but the climbs are enormous. The oft repeated '4000-2000, 4000-2000' mantra touted in cycling circles is based on fact, and altitude that'll take a day or two to climb will be lost in a flash. The drive to pave this route through the Cordillera's largest cities has meant frustrating roadworks in recent years but

---

THAT'S IMPOSSIBLE

If you head out into remote regions anywhere in the world, asking for information about the route locally often leads to the reply: "By bike? Impossible!"

It's usually worth digging deeper – "impossible" can mean "I've never been there before", "I've never heard of anyone cycling there before", "there might be a bit of pushing", or "I have no idea, but it's safer to just say you can't get there". Other times of course it means the road you'd hoped to take descends 30km into a canyon, and the bridge over the raging, 100m-wide river still hasn't been built. In which case, short of going for a risky swim, then it really is impossible.

ACCESSING MACHU PICCHU

An entry ticket to Machu Picchu costs the best part of a week's budget for many bikers, and the train ticket is the same or more again, so choosing to eschew PeruRail but still visit the ruins is a popular option. There's no quick and easy method of doing this – the best being to make your way via Santa Maria and Santa Teresa to Hidroeléctrica by bike or public transport. Bikes aren't allowed past the hydro plant, so walk the 15km along the railway tracks to Aguas Calientes, stay the night and wander up to the ruins in the morning.

Machu Picchu gazing. © James Butcher

the Andes' master roadbuilders are finally getting there. Passing through Huánuco, Huancayo and Ayacucho en route to Cusco, this isn't a tranquil mountain road but there are opportunities to take quieter parallel alternatives.

Embarking on a 'Peru's Great Divide' route south from Huaraz is a far more demanding option, linking up a network of remote mining roads. It's not one for the heavily loaded, with high altitudes, steep sections, bad surfaces and a vertical kilometre to climb every day, but you reap the rewards in spades with spectacularly varied scenery, welcoming villagers and deserted roads. The route's topography makes it blindingly obvious why Pachacuti and pals never invented the wheel.

If your will to climb hills has waned and you're thinking of continuing south on the PanAm, be aware that the interest level (outside of shopping and sampling some *novoandina* cuisine in Lima) remains low until you reach the department of Ica, which boasts Paracas and the Nazca Lines. From Nazca a pleasant paved road rolls over a few high passes toward Cusco to rejoin the inland routes.

Cusco and the Sacred Valley

Iconic Machu Picchu and the Inca capital of Cusco are the reason the vast majority of foreigners visit Peru. Both are a must for most cyclists too and despite the circus that surrounds MP, few leave disappointed, or unmoved by its mysticism. Unfortunately, despite valiant recent attempts, it's not actually possible to reach the site by bike; however, there is still excellent riding to be had in and around the Sacred Valley. See the box above for how to visit MP without burning a hole in your wallet so deep that you can no longer afford to make it past Uspallata though you'd planned on Ushuaia. In Cusco, Hostal Estrellita (Av. Tullumayo 445) is central and welcoming and has been a favourite with cyclists for years.

Into Bolivia, Chile or even Brazil

The most popular cross-border route south is to head straight from Cusco to La Paz via Puno and the western shore of Lake Titicaca, from where there are distant Cordillera Real views. An increasingly popular alternative is to take

DON'T BRING...

On vertical Andean routes and other challenging terrain, what you don't bring is almost as important as what you do end up packing. What I bring is a reflection of what I can and can't let go of. I don't pretend that mine is the lightest conceivable load—it is certainly not—but it is an expression of an attitude toward touring where covering ground and having a bicycle configured for all terrain are paramount.

I don't bring: a laptop, tablet computer, GPS or compass (smartphones perform all of these functions); a DSLR; a spare tyre, or much by way of replacement parts at all; any merely small comfort – tempting items include some way to make 'real coffee,' a pair of speakers, a micro pillow, extra underwear, a journal, something to sit on, jeans, a book, or an extra t-shirt.

Food is an enormous part of weight, plus it requires space that in turn requires larger bags which are themselves heavier. I typically do not carry more than snacks, two breakfasts and two dinners, unless I absolutely positively know that I will not have a resupply opportunity. I *never* have food 'just in case.' Yes, this has meant that I have gone a day or sometimes two without eating. As long as I am hydrated, it is not an issue. I prefer to eat with locals when possible, so cooking is only ever a forced choice and therefore doesn't need to be gourmet; I carry no spices or oils or flavourings.

This said, having the right attitude is infinitely more important than having the right make, model, or amount of gear. In rural Peru I met Angus and Emilio, two twenty-something friends whose kit included snorkeling fins and a boogie board. Their only food was oatmeal that they would prepare with cold water because they didn't have a stove. Their easy laughter and relaxed shrugs hinted they were having the time of their lives.   **Joe Cruz**

the quiet roads round the eastern shore of South America's largest lake – this requires more planning, with a detour for an exit stamp in Puno.

Venturing into the Brazilian Amazon is rare but possible in dry season by taking the Puerto Maldonado road from Urcos, just south of Cusco; much more common is to cross the only border post with Chile, between Tacna and Arica.

BOLIVIA

Aboard a bike, adventure is never far away in land-locked Bolivia. The whole western side of the country is altiplano, a high altitude plateau lying above 3500m and housing many of the country's most famous biking treats. In the south-west lies the fabled Salar de Uyuni, scene of a million perspective-warping bike shots, and the lofty Lagunas route through the Sud Lipez to San Pedro de Atacama in Chile. Other highlights include bobbing through the Cordillera Real, pedalling past 6000m volcanoes and freewheeling into hectic La Paz.

As the poorest Andean nation, Bolivia's road network is correspondingly in worse shape than neighbouring countries', so expect to rattle over corrugations and flounder in sand, clog to a halt in mud and crunch over rocks. Much of it is real fat bike territory and many seasoned riders report it has some of the most challenging offerings around. Despite this there are some real route gems to be found. If you're mentally prepared and expect to travel slow, sure as titty calendar and depiction of the Last Supper share your altiplano restaurant wall, you'll soon collect a wealth of story material to tell the grandkids.

Practicalities

The dry season in Bolivia runs from May to October and is the optimal cycling time, with sunny days but cold altiplano night-time temperatures. Camping out in the department of Potosí, you can expect the mercury to fall below -10°C most nights, and occasionally to plummet under -20°C in the Sud Lipez. You might want to get a fleecy sleeping bag liner made up in the market and invest in a down jacket, a new *chullo* (Andean woolly hat) to slip under your cycling helmet, and some alpaca leg warmers to keep those ankles toasty. Pick campsites for early morning sun, otherwise it's hard to drag yourself out of your cocoon before half the day has elapsed. The altiplano gets windy, so having a sturdy tent helps.

The wet season is warmer but mud wreaks havoc with unpaved roads, particularly in the transitional Yungas area between Andes and Amazon and in the low-lying eastern regions; December to March are the soggiest months. Humidity, insects and downpours will add to the challenge in these areas and you may find at this time of year it's easier to swap bike for boat. These months are also storm season on the altiplano, and the Salar de Uyuni is usually flooded and unrideable for a few months – the exact timings of which change each year.

Staying on track and other challenges

Smartphones and GPSs have revolutionised altiplano route finding and navigation, superseding paper maps which could never portray the meanderings of sandy jeep tracks with any degree of accuracy. Be careful to check your batteries have sufficient power to last the long distances between power sockets, and take a compass (and dodgy paper map!) as backup. The country map at 🖳 abc.gob.bo gives an overview of the road network but if you're straying from main roads it's useful to have downloaded GPX tracks from the web, because signposts are at a premium.

When it comes to fuel, Bolivia is a country where it pays to know how to strip down your multi-fuel stove. With white gas extremely difficult to find, unless you use an alcohol stove you'll be reliant on low quality, dirty petrol. Some stuff is worse than others, so if you happen to get a bottle's worth of really bad petrol, consider disposing of it and filling up at the next petrol station you encounter.

Life on the altiplano is tough, as many a weathered face will attest. The altiplano's wildness, paucity of cultivable land and severe lack of water makes for few villages, so plan well as you'll need to carry a few days' worth (or more) of supplies at times. Village shops are less well

A 'shortcut' on the Bolivian altiplano might not save you much time.

BLIND IN BOLIVIA

I woke to a searing pain in my eyes. This pain was immense but worse still was the fear. Have I blinded myself? Any attempt to open my eyes resulted in unbearable agony and in the fleeting moments I managed to, the world was a complete blur. Alone, in an abandoned house, in a tiny village, in an extremely remote region of Bolivia, hours passed as I fought to stave off sheer panic. That was the longest night of my life.

The fault was entirely my own. Enjoying arguably the most magical landscape on a continent full of spellbinding scenery, I had ridden for three hours on the Salar de Uyuni without sunglasses. The result? I was blind for three days before slowly regaining my vision. A simple bit of plastic to shield my eyes from the powerful UV rays would have prevented this but on my third day riding the Salar I neglected to wear my shades.

Don't leave those shades off too long!
© Matt McDonald

On this occasion I was lucky. I phoned a Bolivia-based friend who knew someone locally that was able to come and help me recuperate. I spent three days in a dark room being brought food and water before catching the once weekly bus back to my friend's place in Potosí.   **Matt McDonald**

stocked than in other Andean countries and there's a dearth of fresh fruit and veg, making it difficult to maintain a good diet. Those with a weird penchant for alpaca steaks and *chuño* (freeze dried potato) will be in food nirvana, but for the majority it's a place to grin and bear it, force down some calories and stuff panniers with tasty treats whenever a larger town presents. Accommodation offerings are more basic than in other countries but bikers' cost of living is also low.

The indigenous Aymara people who inhabit the northern parts of the alti-plano tend to be reserved on first meeting, but crack a terrible joke to break the ice and conversation usually begins to flow. As in Peru, strikes by villagers and townsfolk protesting about the government or exploitation by multina-tional mining or logging companies are commonplace. These often manifest in road blocks, which cyclists are normally allowed to circumvent, but always make sure you ask before doing so – it's not a good idea to incur the wrath of an angry mob.

Some route ideas

From Peru

Whichever of the three routes you choose, it's only a day or two to La Paz, Bolivia's de facto capital. The Desaguadero route passes the pre-Inca ruins at Tiwanaku, the most important in Bolivia; however, pedalling via Copacabana, with idyllic location on the shores of Lake Titicaca, is more scenic and offers the chance to visit Inca sites on Isla del Sol. Via Puerto Acosta on the east side of the lake is also a beautiful ride (see p295).

La Paz

A first view of La Paz from El Alto is forever imprinted on my mind and for many a tourer it ranks high on the 'favourite cities in the Americas' list, despite the roads' perpetually gridlocked state and steep gradients meaning it's hardly Copenhagen in the cycle-friendly stakes. But what it lacks in bike lanes it makes up for in vibrancy, colour, fascinating markets and a spectacular setting, climbing the sides of a steep bowl chiselled from the flat plateau. For tourers it's a sociable place too, with the haven of Cristian's Casa de Ciclistas (see p291) usually chock-a-block with tourers and their steeds in various states of disrepair after the poundings of thousands of Andean kilometres. To extend visas head to the immigration office on Av Camacho. If you're migrating southwards it might be your last chance of decent food until you reach Chile or Argentina, so take the wise precaution of fattening up. Those beginning a trip here need to spend time in town acclimatising, as the centre lies at 3600m and all routes out involve climbing to even higher altitudes.

Head east for some greenery...

The really keen can day-ride up to the old ski station at Chacaltaya (see box p300), or you could head onto exciting dirt roads in the Cordillera Real east of town. If you've been too long in a landscape bereft of trees, consider heading over La Cumbre into the Yungas to reacquaint yourself with those unfamiliar leafy things. It's possible to loop northwards on a tough route to Sorata, via the old North Yungas road – which under the guise of 'World's Most Dangerous Road' is still the most famous section of road on the continent. In 2006 a new paved alternative opened up, meaning the old way has lost its traffic, but none of its narrowness or beauty; the drops haven't diminished either, so try not to fall off. Else head south-east after La Cumbre, through extremely hilly terrain towards Cochabamba.

If you fancy a taster of the lowlands or some jungle head even further east – but time it well to avoid the suffocating heat and game-ending mud.

Heading south and west

The main road south, and route of least resistance to La Quiaca in Argentina, is via Potosí and the Wild West-like scenery near Tupiza. This route begins on Ruta Nacional 1 but we wouldn't wish cycling the first part to Oruro on anyone. *Asfalto* is a rare commodity in Bolivia, and as incomes and car ownership rise, these kilometres are busy; if the need for speed forces your hand, please avoid being added to the prominent 'Scoreboard' near the toll booth outside La Paz. Assuming you reach Oruro unscathed, there are options to head to Uyuni, or go a hilly route via colonial Sucre (the judicial capital) to Potosí, whose mines on Cerro Rico, which can be visited today, once supplied the Spanish Empire with enormous quantities of silver.

Perched on the edge of the 'World's Most Dangerous Road'.

A safer route out of La Paz is to head west via Bolivia's highest peak in Parque Nacional Sajama, before honing in on the salars.

The Salars

Coming from the north-west, your first salt riding will be found on the Salar de Coipasa. Languishing in the shadow of its more famous big brother, chances are you'll be lucky and get the whole dreamy place to yourself. Bolivia's biggest draw, the vast salty sea of the Salar de Uyuni, soon follows, and it's the stuff of bike-touring dreams; the kind of place where 'should I have packed in that stable job' doubts just melt away…

Caffeine withdrawal on the Salar de Uyuni.
© James Butcher

Pedalling across tens of kilometres of dazzling salt flat is a mind-bending experience, but whatever you do, wear dark sunglasses and high factor sun cream – the brutal altiplano rays and their bounced reflections send UV indices off the scale, and you don't want to end up like Matt (see box p298).

Those destined for the Lagunas Route may find a resupplying trip to Uyuni town is called for – it's a dismal place that won't encourage a long stay, so hang around just long enough to suck up the tourist facilities before continuing.

The Classic Lagunas Route

The high altitude, barren Sud Lipez has been attracting adventurous riders for years, drawn to its otherworldly colourful lakes, salt flats and weird rock formations. The 'Classic Lagunas Route' heads from the Salar de Uyuni (or Uyuni town) through San Juan to Laguna Hedionda, Laguna Colorada and Laguna Blanca before whizzing down to San Pedro de Atacama in Chile. Allow around 7-10 days from Uyuni to San Pedro, and expect bad surfaces with corrugations and sand, cold weather and wind. You'll have to carry plenty of supplies too because the selection in villages and refugios is limited; planning for water is needed due to the long distances between habitations and because most lakes are salty or volcanically poisoned. There's a fantastic downloadable free guide to routes in South-West Bolivia at 💻 tour.tk. The Classic Route is uber-popular with backpackers on jeep tours, so if you choose to go that way

---

I'LL TAKE THE HIGH ROAD – CHACALTAYA, ACOTANGO AND UTURUNCU

The old ski station at Chacaltaya makes a long but worthwhile day trip from La Paz. The road end at 5250m gives bird's-eye views of town and the surface isn't too bad either (remember, everything is relative). Don't expect to be carving turns through the powder at the top – there's no skiing these days as the glaciers have retreated and slopes are snow-free.

Far less accessible but much higher roads lie on the volcanoes of Acotango and Uturuncu in the west of the country. Both can lay claim to be among the highest tracks ever forged and at 5700m there's only 50% of the oxygen at sea level. The steep sections are real lungbursters, making acclimatising in the Sud Lipez or Peru beforehand a must.

expect to be coated with dust at certain times of day – but at least there'll be people on hand to help if something goes wrong. Information on quieter alternative tracks can be found at 🖳 andesbybike.com.

CHILE AND ARGENTINA

These two most southerly South American countries are favourites among the band of touring riders. Whether you're a *ripio-* (gravel-) worshipping gnarletarian, or someone who prefers cruising between pleasant towns, nattering with locals, sipping good wine and puzzling over how to eat steaks the size of bricks, there are routes and riding for everyone. Sharing an extensive Andean border, most riders hop the watershed more frequently than a car parts-smuggling Argentine taxi

The long and winding road to Chacaltaya.

driver, in an attempt to lap up the best of each side's natural wonders. Darting between San Pedro de Atacama and the Quebrada Calchaquis, or Cerro FitzRoy and Torres del Paine, offers a far more visually exciting tour than electing to stay solely on one flank. Both nations have famous routes of which they are justifiably proud: Chile's south is traversed by the Carretera Austral, while much of the western side of Argentina could be run on Ruta 40.

Unlike in the northern half of the continent, the most popular biking areas see wind rather than vertical ascent as the biggest challenge. Parts of Patagonia are infamous for winds which hound cyclists and the same applies in the equally wild and arguably more adventurous northern region of the Puna, but in both it's focussed in certain areas and by no means blows a gale every day. It helps having a decent tent, but even then you'll become a dab hand at spotting the only Puna rock on a 10km stretch which offers any kind of camping protection, and will soon slip into thinking that laying out your sleeping mat in Patagonian storm drains, rodeo stadiums or bus stops is perfectly normal behaviour.

When and which way?

October to March is the time to visit if you like mountains, though the lowlands from Mendoza north are baked at this time by the strong summer sun. Outside these months weather in Patagonia and the high altitude northern areas becomes chillier and wilder, and facilities and access begin shutting down. Many border crossings between Chile and Argentina are closed by snow in winter and though busy crossings such as Mendoza – Santiago are usually cleared within a few days, others remain firmly shut for months. It pays to scour the 🖳 www.gendarmeria.gob.ar/pasos-fronterizos or 🖳 difrol.cl websites (or follow them on Twitter) for updates before heading to the hills.

In the windy parts of Patagonia and the Puna, airs are generally from the west/north-west. Ushuaia lies southeast of the Carretera Austral meaning it's easier to transit Patagonia from north to south, while on the Puna crossings are usually less effort when going from Chile to Argentina. Those on shorter trips to these regions should plan accordingly, but if you're undertaking a

Leaving El Calafate with a tail wind.
© James Butcher

transcontinental ride no-one's yet managed to be blown along by tailwinds the whole way; as anywhere you'll get more hindrance than help from the wind, so it's more important to get your seasons right. Having said this, be warned that unless you can train in a wind tunnel pre-departure or have the mental strength of an emperor penguin, choosing Ushuaia as a start point isn't ideal for inexperienced northbound riders. It's not unknown for the westerly blasts to unhinge hitherto sane bikers well before making it off Tierra del Fuego.

On the road

Developed-world bonuses include decent accommodation options and good food hygiene standards. Among the downsides are higher prices, meaning most bikers find themselves camping regularly and finding nourishment from supermarkets. Costs of transportation dictate that prices increase the further south you delve into Patagonia.

Putting bikes on public transport is not as simple as in the less developed nations to the north. Often, coach companies insist you dismantle or box your steed and, particularly in holiday season, double decker coaches with smaller *bodegas* (luggage compartments) may simply not have room for bikes, with all the rucksacks and mandatory musical instruments local tourists have stuffed in there. The increasing number of cyclists who end a tour in Ushuaia and need transport out of town means it can take a day or two to find bike room on a northbound coach – don't forget you can fly out, try to hitch, or, with a lot of luck, find a boat heading to some far shore.

A decent range of spares can be found in bike shops in larger cities, though high import taxes mean quality gear isn't cheap. Chilean outdoor brand Doite makes good camping gear and their gas canisters can be found in both countries. *Bencina blanca* (white gas) is available in Chile, but in Argentina multi-fuel stove users will normally be reliant on *nafta* (petrol) because searches for *solvente* (their term for white gas) often prove fruitless.

For carnivores who don't mind the limited menu range, food is a real highlight. Fresh veg is good quality too, even if most locals wouldn't dream of actually eating such an adornment. Thoughts of ice-cream will have you

---

THE KNOWING NOD

You're stopped at a corner shop in Catamarca, or a *dhaba* in Dehradun; friendly and inquisitive man ambles over.

"Where are you from? Where have you cycled from?" Reaches down to front tyre; gives it a squeeze. Look of approval spreads across face (*phew, got that psi just perfect*

again). "Get many punctures?"

"Nah, not often; they're Schwalbe, German tyres."

And then it comes, the knowing nod.

"Ah, German engineering" he says; "those couldn't fail to be good".

hallucinating during those desert sections between northern Argentinian towns, while in the south, raiding the bakery for *facturas* (pastries) is imperative immediately on arrival in any settlement.

CHILE

Over 4000km long but rarely more than 300km wide, Chile spans 38 degrees of latitude and has a huge range of climate and geography, from the driest of the dry in the northern Atacama Desert, to the Valdivian temperate rainforest and the Patagonian ice-sheets.

First impressions of the country aren't always favourable, as the Servicio de Agrícola y Ganadero guys at borders insist on searching panniers and confiscating any fruit, veg, meat and other produce you'd forgotten is prohibited. Processed food is allowed in no problem – more info can be found at ▭ www.sag.cl. Chilean officials are the most serious in Latin America, so don't even think about trying to deceive them.

Chiletur Copec are the best of the paper maps, while ATMs are more problematic than in most South American countries due to some only accepting MasterCard and not VISA. It's not an issue in cities but can be in smaller, one-ATM towns.

ARGENTINA

Iguazu Falls, Perito Moreno Glacier, Cerro Torre, Buenos Aires and Aconcagua are all to be found within Argentina's vast borders, but glancing at a map reveals that for most cyclists visiting every one simply isn't feasible – they lie on Argentina's periphery, separated by endless seas of flat pampa or desert. Fortunately, the majority of the big names are found in the Andes, and most bikers choose to concentrate their efforts here.

Argentina's notoriously fragile economy has taken a battering in the 21st century. Recovery from the crisis and devaluation of the peso in 2001 has been slow, and at the time of writing a black market 'blue dollar' rate is available for changing US$ on the street in large cities. This is higher than the official rate obtained if you use ATMs or pay by credit card, meaning **you make significant savings by bringing dollars into the country in cash**.

Argentines are a loving, gregarious bunch, and unless your Spanish is non-existent, you never got the hang of sign language or simply don't want to engage, expect to have a sociable time. The camping culture is the strongest on the continent, so turning up in a small town and asking for somewhere to plonk your tent won't elicit an uncomprehending stare as it might further north – you'll be pointed to the campsite or *asado* (barbecue) area where families head to gorge meat by the kilogram at weekends.

Paper maps of the country are good; the ACA (Automóvil Club Argentino) series, available in petrol stations and larger towns, is best.

An Argentinian asado (for two ?)

TIPS FOR TOURING IN REMOTE AREAS

• Have a large water-carrying capacity, and don't put all your water in one vessel – best to carry a number of smaller ones in case anything leaks.

On the Puna de Atacama, five days since last seeing a soul.

• Take low-volume food – spaghetti and rice are better than macaroni.
• Remove as much food packaging as possible before you set off, to avoid carting lots of rubbish around.
• Tell someone reliable what route you're planning on taking, with clear instructions what to do if you don't get in contact before a set time.
• Take plenty of extra reserves of food and water in case of unforeseen difficulties. When cycling unfamiliar routes on the Puna, we calculate food rations based on only being able to travel 30km per day.
• If you're really remote, and after a while you realise you've overestimated how far you'll get each day, don't be afraid to turn back before the point of no return...

Some route ideas

Entering from the North

As always, the fastest way to make progress south is by staying clear of the mountains and sticking to the PanAm. Crossing the Peru-Chile border between Tacna and Arica, it's possible to shoot down directly to Puerto Montt. The northern part of the PanAm is through the Atacama Desert, and if after a few days you cease to be beguiled by the barren scenery, it makes sense to detour from the main Ruta 5 wherever possible, and opt for quieter coastal alternatives for some sea views.

Many riders enter Chile on adventurous routes from Bolivia's altiplano. There are great dirt road possibilities in north-east Chile, while further south, many a sand and salar-hardened biker's first experience of the country is en route to San Pedro de Atacama.

The most westerly crossing from Bolivia to Argentina is at Villazón/La Quiaca, which gives access to the striking Quebrada de Humahuaca in the north-west province of Jujuy. If you've pedalled down from Prudhoe Bay and crossing into Argentina feels like you're nearly done, the 'Ushuaia 5121km' sign will bring you back down to earth! Continuing on this low route through the Argentine north-west, you pass through Salta, a city with a strong colonial feel and folclórica musical tradition, and the wine growing region of Cafayate.

The Puna

Part of the largest accessible high plateau in the adventure cycle-touring world (Tibet and Antarctica being tricky to get to on two wheels at the moment – though see Trip Report p228), the Puna de Atacama is one of the wildest, most remote and exciting regions you're likely to find yourself pedalling through in the Andes. North of the busy paving linking Santiago and Mendoza there are six border-bisecting options of varying degrees of difficulty. All are serious undertakings, requiring planning for long stretches between food and water sources, and a willingness to cycle many kilometres at altitudes of over 4000m. If you're unable to resist wild Paso Sico or pootling past the highest volcanoes in the world on Paso San Francisco, you're likely to be emphatically rewarded with superb views and a memorable ride.

South of the Puna, in the centre of Argentina, are wine-growing regions such as Mendoza, and the mountains include Aconcagua, the highest summit outside Asia.

PATAGONIA

Patagonia is a vast, wild space, with mesmerising itinerant clouds and intense cobalt skies; a hallowed region of legend and biking dreams. Cycle through, with the wind roaring in your hair, granite spires reaching to the sky on one side and the sea or swathes of barren plains on the other, and it's easy to see why the area has imprinted itself on so many a memory. Almost all bikers opt for the continent's most famous cycle-touring road: the Carretera Austral, but a few hardy souls brave Argentina's Ruta 40 through arid pampa which comes with fierce wind and corrugations guaranteed. Only the *loco* attempt to cycle featureless Ruta 3 on the Argentine coast – strong sidewinds and traffic mean it has nothing to recommend it unless you really dig tarmac.

Northern Patagonia – The Lake District

South of Chile's Temuco and Zapala in Argentina, lakes stud the alpine landscape and snowy volcanic cones pierce the sky. Pucón and Bariloche are the two main tourist centres but there is no shortage of paved or ripio roads leading to a peaceful lakeside camp in one of the numerous national parks. The region's scenery makes it a magnet for local tourists in holiday season, meaning popular roads like the Ruta de los Siete Lagos are overflowing with old Argie bangers at this time. It's the easiest part of Patagonia to get to know on two wheels, with the availability of supplies and accommodation making it viable as a non-camping tour.

Central Patagonia – The Carretera Austral and Ruta 40

For cyclists, Patagonia is synonymous with these two contrasting roads. Most join the Carretera Austral part way down near Futaleufú or Lago Verde, two of a number of crossings which make border-hopping possible – particularly handy if you need to leave Chile to dry out those damp clothes in an Argentine gale. The Argentine side has fewer settlements and longer stretches between food and water.

CHOOSE YOUR CAMPSITE CAREFULLY

For most Argentines, a campsite is not a place to pass out after a hard day in the saddle. It's somewhere for *mate* and a fire, a cheeky beer or cup of wine. All of which is fine, until the guitars come out around midnight – there's only so many times you can listen to a heavily accented *Hey Jude* before you get driven round the bend. So, if it's a Friday or Saturday night, or the local holiday season (Christmas – end February), and you need to get some kip, choose your campsite well. A wild camp might be best.

T R I P   R E P O R T
PATAGONIA

Name	Matt Pierle
Nationality	USA
Year of birth	1975
Occupation	Field Biologist and Educator
Other bike travels	Thailand & Laos, Turkey, Germany-Czech-Poland, Hawaii, San Francisco-Tijuana, Seattle-Vancouver.
This trip	Patagonia (Santiago de Chile to Ushuaia)
Trip duration	3 months, including 15 days of trekking
Number in group	Started and finished solo. In between I rode with Brits, Swiss, French, Canadians, a Kiwi & an Italian.
Total distance	Circa 3200km. I didn't use a cyclo-computer.
Cost of trip	About US$15 a day in South America, including net cost of bike (see below).

Longest day	153km – nice tailwind on Tierra del Fuego
Best day	So many! Riding through volcanic ash outside Chaiten, then soaking in geothermal hot pools to stay warm was surreal, and is probably the winner.
Worst day	Being exhausted near the southern end of the Carretera Austral, after a lot of rainy days.
Biggest headache	Evading a potential robbery by a group of young bike hoodlums who encircled me south of Santiago. Escaped unscathed, with all belongings.
Biggest mistake	Buying a return air ticket…
Pleasant surprise	Linking up with other cyclists along the way.

Bike model	Jamis Cross Country 3.0
New/used	Purchased new in Santiago to avoid extortionate baggage fees of US$300 (each way!) from the US. Benefits: supporting the local bicycle economy and making connections with knowledgeable local bikers. Bike cost US$600, sold it later for US$420.
Modifications	Brought 'everything but the bike' with me – racks, panniers, tyres, pedals and saddle to fit to the bike purchased in Santiago. Fitted wider handlebars.
Punctures	Just one…which I fixed while crouching in a ditch to avoid the strong Patagonian winds.
Glad you brought	2 small photo albums from home in order to connect with locals; a well stocked spice cabinet.
Bike problems	Front suspension became stiff after a while.

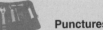

Any advice?	Eat well to fuel your body. Enjoy the local cuisine. Smile.
Road philosophy	A touring bike is like a flying carpet. It's a magical form of transportation that opens eyes and doors to both new horizons and new friendships.

Classic Route – The Carretera Austral

General Pinochet's ambitious project to force a 1240km-long road from Puerto Montt to Villa O'Higgins was begun in the 1970s. It slices through beautiful, verdant landscapes, passing beech and larch forests, lakes, glaciers and waterfalls, and there are a few boat journeys thrown in for good measure. The terrain is hilly, rather than mountainous, with short, sharp climbs, and a highest point of only

Passing one of the many lakes on the Carretera Austral.

1100m, just south of the region's largest town, Coyhaique.

It's a dramatic ride and, if you're not used to riding ripio, is a challenging one too. The route is slowly being paved, so if that's not to your liking get here soon. Riders who've made it through the Peruvian Cordillera and Bolivian altiplano will likely find the terrain less testing than the wet climate but in roadwork areas the surface can be frustratingly loose. It pays to find out in advance where these are and see if there's a way of avoiding them, though the chances of this are slim without a long detour to Argentina, as many of the roads branching off the Carretera are dead-ends.

Your main route choices are whether to head from Puerto Montt to the island of Chiloe then to Chaitén, take the direct ferry from Puerto Montt to Chaitén, or stick to the mainland route via Hornopirén and Pumalín, which still necessitates three boat rides. Between Coyhaique and Cochrane it's possible to remain on the main artery, or take a ferry over Lago General Carrera. Count on about three weeks from Puerto Montt to the end of the road at Villa O'Higgins, with Coyhaique's supermarkets and outdoor shops lying roughly half way along.

The Deep South...to Tierra del Fuego and Ushuaia

From El Chaltén, the terrain flattens, the sky expands, you return from the seemingly cyclist-dominated (though otherwise lonely) Carretera to tourist country, and if you've avoided those winds thus far, you won't for much longer. They're generally strongest in the January and February of mid-summer, so consider going a bit earlier or later, even though temperatures will be lower. On roads with traffic, it's wise not to cycle on really blustery days – see p114.

Make time for day walks from El Chaltén for close-ups of Monte Fitz Roy, and Cerro Torre – the most unlikely sheer slab of granite you'll

The downhill push to Lago del Desierto.
© Sarah Bedford

HIKE A BIKE TO FITZROY

The most aesthetically pleasing way of continuing south from the Carretera into Argentina is by taking the seasonal boat from Villa O'Higgins to Candelario Mancilla, pushing your bike over the border to Laguna del Desierto and taking the shorter boat ride across this smaller lake to link with the road to El Chaltén. This isn't the cheapest option, as the combined cost of the ferries is over US$100 – see 🖳 robinsoncrusoe.com for up-to-date schedules and fares for the Lago O'Higgins crossing. There's loads of hype on the road about this adventurous push through the woods, but it can be a lot of fun and stronger southbound pushers will find catching both ferries on the same day is not beyond them. It's a bit harder in the opposite direction but it may be possible to hire horses, so ask around if those arm muscles fail you.

---

ever see – before continuing on to the magnificent Perito Moreno glacier and Torres del Paine. There's a rich abundance of wildlife in these parts – flamingo, condor, rhea, foxes, guanaco; penguin breeding colonies and, out to sea, dolphins and whales can be spotted.

The Straits of Magellan are the last water barrier before Ushuaia – cross from Punta Arenas to Porvenir to avoid detouring far east to the main highway ferry at Punta Delgada. An overnight stay at the cyclist-bakery in Tolhuin is a must before hitting Ushuaia, the world's most southerly town. Those looking for full closure should continue on into Tierra del Fuego National Park and the end of the road at Lapataia. If you've made it this far from Alaska, pat yourself on the back, shed a quick tear, then head back to town for a cold *Quilmes* and to begin dreaming of the next big trip...

VENEZUELA
Laura Mottram

With high Andean peaks, Caribbean coastline, cowboy-filled plains and the table-top mountains of the Jurassic-age Gran Sabana, Venezuela's scenery offers much to cycle tourists. Most riders overlook the country, put off by its distance from the main migrating routes or deterred by high crime rates and the need to exchange cash on the black market; but with a little planning and care, those who make the effort to visit will be rewarded with a once-in-a-lifetime adventure.

Security
Security shouldn't be ignored or underestimated because the country has some of the highest crime rates in the world. Certain areas, notably the capital Caracas and its surroundings, are more dangerous than others but though elsewhere security is usually better, you'll still find most people stay indoors after dark. For this reason wild camping is not advisable, apart from in the Gran Sabana, which is generally considered safe. As is usually the case in places with a bad reputation, most people you'll meet will be warm and welcoming, and there are enthusiastic Couchsurfing and Warm Showers networks around the country which are great ways to meet locals.

Money

The official currency, the Bolivar, is fixed against the US$. Exchanging money or withdrawing cash at a bank will give you Bolivars at the official rate, but if you exchange money on the black market you'll get about double this. Travelling in Venezuela at the official rate is expensive so it pays to change money at the borders just before entering the country. Exchanging cash once inside Venezuela is possible, with shopkeepers tending to be the best to approach, but remember this is an illegal transaction so don't broadcast your attentions widely. European-run hostels are good places to exchange money at the parallel rate, especially if you have online banking.

Food and supplies

Venezuela is a culinary dream for cycle tourists, especially vegetarians, with big, hearty and not too expensive meals. Look out for *arepas* – stuffed corn cakes, *cachapas* – fresh corn cakes lathered in butter, cheese and often served with grilled meat, and *empanadas* – corn pasties oozing with cheese and other fillings.

The usual supplies are generally easy to find, but occasionally everyday items, like toilet roll or milk, disappear from shops. Venezuelans have the cheapest petrol in the world, so if you are using a multi-fuel stove you'll find your fuel bottles are filled up for free. In the bigger cities bike supplies are easy to come by.

The best ride

Start in Ciudad Bolivar with a trip to the world's highest waterfalls, Angel Falls. When the small plane returns you from the middle of the jungle, shadow the Orinoco towards Ciudad Guyana, then turn south along Route 10 towards Brazil. The landscape gradually becomes more tropical until you reach a winding road forged into the cliffs of the Gran Sabana.

This huge, wide, hilly plain sits above 1000m and is dominated by spectacular table-top tepui mountains and jagged waterfalls. Up here you can cycle for hours without seeing any other sign of life and will be spoilt for choice about where to pitch your tent. It is one of the few places in South America where you can feel truly alone whilst riding along perfectly smooth roads.

Follow the route towards Santa Elena on the Brazilian border to refuel on pizza and book your tour to climb nearby Roraima, a straight-side tepui that inspired Sir Arthur Conan Doyle to write *The Lost World*.

Continuing on through the Guianas to the Brazilian Amazon

There's no direct road between Venezuela and Guyana, so cross into Brazil and make your way, via Boa Vista, to the border with English-speaking Guyana. In the cowboy town of Lethem on the edge of the Rupununi Savannah, pick up 'The Trail', a dirt road that pierces through grasslands into thick, hilly jungle, and is best avoided in the wet season. Accommodation is found in the few roadside stops where you can pitch a hammock for the night.

From Linden you're back on tarmac and heading north to Georgetown, a city built from wood, where cricket rules and the food and atmosphere is Caribbean. Remember to arrange a visa for Suriname, if you need one, before

Encountering traffic on 'The Trail', Guyana's main interior highway. © Patrick Mottram

you leave 'Town', as they're not available at the ferry across the border.

You'll be dropped into Dutch-speaking Suriname where a flat ride through jungle will bring you to Niuew Nickerie. Head east towards pretty and peaceful Paramaribo, admiring canals built in colonial times and sampling spicy curries cooked by the descendants of Indian slaves who dug the waterways.

It's another river crossing to reach French Guiana, a French department where Europeans won't even need their passport stamped and where you'll be speaking French, spending euros and raiding Carrefour supermarkets for the best French wine and smelly cheese. As you cycle towards the capital, Cayenne, stop off at the old prisons where French criminals, including the famous Papillon, were once incarcerated. The European Space Centre pokes out of the jungle, and if you time your ride right you may get to see giant leatherback turtles lay their eggs on the sandy beaches, or the babies rushing towards the ocean after hatching.

You can get some good deals on flights from Paris to Cayenne, but not the other way around, and it's a good idea to find a Couchsurfer in the city to avoid expensive accommodation. Enjoy refuelling on traditional French food then head into the hilly jungle and into Brazil.

You'll be rewarded with your first view of the Amazon River at Macapá, at which point you're a very long way from anywhere. To continue, either hunt down a boat heading south towards Belém or, if you can't face cycling the interminable and roasting Brazilian interior, try jumping on one going in the other direction, up the Amazon to Manaus. In dry season there'll be a mixture of biking and boating from the Amazonas capital onwards to Peru, Bolivia or Ecuador.

7

TALES FROM THE SADDLE

The Wild Corner of Myanmar

Stephen Fabes *recounts biking the remote Chin State in Myanmar in the wet season where mud, leeches and landslides were the price worth paying for an adventure through an anachronistic, seldom-reached wilderness where hospitality abounds.*

Flat. F-L-A-T. That was how the pastor had chosen to describe this road that twisted through the remote reaches of Chin State when I'd pointed to it on my map of Myanmar. He'd even demonstrated, with a horizontal swish of his flat hand so there had been no misunderstanding: 'flat' is not Burmese for 'vertical'.

At every tree-shadowed bend in the road, my gaze lifted from the surface – a jigsaw of serrated rock and pot holes – to discover something more apt for base-jumping than cycle touring. Grades of insane percentages leered back at me, inviting me to regret, to turn face, to hurl curses into the icy squalls of mountain air. I wouldn't. I'd come too far, to quit now would be too spirit-sapping. I was still running on the fuel of optimism, the naive hope that things might improve, 'knowing' they couldn't get much worse, until, after each turn of the road, they did.

I remembered how I'd been offered an alternative to Chin State: a rod-straight temptress of a thoroughfare, flat probably, soothing my passage to India. I'd dithered at the junction, feeling beaten already – my t-shirt a leopard print of sweat and jungle grime.

STEPHEN FABES

Stephen is a medical doctor, award-winning freelance writer, hiphop DJ and adventure cyclist passionate about the world's back roads and wild places. Stories from his six-year, six-continent bike ride can be found at 🖳 www.cyclingthe6 .com. A book is in the pipeline.

Burmese women working in the rice paddies.
© Stephen Fabes

It had been five heady years since I'd waved goodbye to loved ones and seven since I sat in a London pub, site of many a life-changing decision, mini-atlas in one hand, a pint in the other and a plan playing in my mind. Seventy thousand kilometres later, I'd learned a lesson – the view shines more when you've earned it. Whether straining up 20% grades, through tropical heat or over rock-strewn roads, the old adage rang true – no pain, no gain. So with that in mind I'd paid a wistful glance at the easy option and set my sights on the hills.

I didn't have much to go on. Myanmar was a country in flux, not long open to tourism, and until recently it had been forbidden to enter Chin State without a guide. Few foreign cycle tourers had pedalled these back roads or crossed the country from Thailand to India. Google didn't surrender tour reports or altitude maps, and my gaze roamed the patch of green on my map – as blank and mysterious as a desert. A diminutive font signalled a few piteous settlements, joined by roads that, with their million sharp turns, looked like a tracing from a seismograph. I had 900km to cover in the eleven days before my visa expired, a job made grimmer by the unsealed dirt roads, the interminable climbs and the mud-making cloud-bursts of the monsoon: July was the worst month of the year to be here.

As Chin State loomed the country was still a lurid green but with primary forest that droned with insects, not the rustling rice paddies of before. Gone too were the scattering of oxen and women in rice hats, bent at the waist, toiling away for the prize of subsistence and crooked spines.

Traffic thinned. I was pressed into the road edge by the odd truck, thick with bodies. Curious eyes found me, brilliant white amid the shadows of their neighbours. Gaunt-chested men in *lungis* riding up to their navel nodded hello from the shade of teak leaf-roofed huts. I watched them consider me and walk off, revealing dragon tattoos from their shoulder blades to the small of their backs, returning to their women who wore shawls and had facial tattoos: a practice rumoured to prevent kidnapping by neighbouring tribes in years past.

The road skinnied down to a trail, and dirt replaced asphalt as a lone motorbike raged past. The driver had swiveled 180 degrees to assure himself of the best possible gawk at me whilst his un-chauffeured machine rallied off on a tangent. Satisfied, he turned back to find himself almost upon the forest. He jerked to the left, turned to me again, grin still sprawled, and disappeared.

The road began its steady twist into the clouds: on one side was a ragged cliff face, on the other a pale oblivion, sometimes bright and heavenly, other times leaden and dreadful, but always masking the spread of for-

Google didn't surrender tour reports or altitude maps, and my gaze roamed the patch of green on my map – as blank and mysterious as a desert.

est below. I climbed, expelling great, antenatal huffs, drizzle steeping my beard and making morning cobwebs of my arm hair. I felt the warm buzz that attends lonely adventures into the unknown.

Finally the wind gusted enough to vanquish the cloud, launching a vast scene of forested peaks dressed in cloud and menace, proving me minuscule. I was soon enclosed again, and a village gathered from the mist. The villagers came out of their stilted wooden

Enjoying the view, Chin State.
© Stephen Fabes

homes to watch me ride by: a colourfully-clad and muffled mountain people, an almost Andean evocation. Children and chickens dissolved and reformed from puffs of cloud that drifted through the streets as easily as swans. A few leery women in the road quickened their shuffles and men shrank into doorways.

I approached one man who'd stood his ground, offering him a smile so big it might have verged on the psychotic. He smiled back though and, with a 'come-in' flap of his fingers, I was invited for tea.

I crouched on my hams by a sputtering fire, the pastor's family gathered about me. The walls held a picture of a sad-eyed, lightly-bearded Jesus next to Avril Lavigne (her image in remote villages around the world is one of life's conundrums). Steam coiled off my clothes, blending with the wood smoke, as wind clattered the tin roof and we all wondered what I was doing here.

The village had no fresh produce, just stale biscuits, noodles and the suggestion of future scurvy. I opted for noodles, chomping them down as word spread and the curious were drawn in from the murk to shake my hand. People flashed me scarlet grins making me ponder the enamel-dissolving betel nut and another of life's ironies: the Burmese are a nation with the easiest smiles, and the worst teeth.

As I drank the tea a team of people busied themselves about me: a lady stoked the embers to keep me warm, a child filled my water bottles, whilst outside a man applied oil to my chain and another covered my bike in a waterproof tarp as the sky submitted cold and bloated drops of rain.

I noticed one elderly man was shouldering a rifle with a barrel that might have stretched from the ground to my shoulders, a thing from antiquity. It clashed with my evolving impression of Myanmar: that change was in the air. Even in this most desolate of settings I'd seen wooden boards declaring 'National League for Democracy' – Aung San Suu Kyi's party and one that, until recently, had been outlawed by the regime.

My few words of Burmese exhausted, with warmer knees ready to propel me up the mountainsides I said goodbye. A snake of voluble children followed me back into the clouds.

More villages marched by, draped over ridges instead of cut into mountainsides, perhaps because of a partic-

I felt the warm buzz that attends lonely adventures into the unknown.

The Burmese have used a cosmetic paste made from ground bark – *thanaka* – on their faces for over 2000 years.
© Stephen Fabes

ular peril of the season: landslides. I saw their aftermath every five or ten kilometres, blocking the road and allowing only motorbikes past so I no longer shared the mud with trucks or cars. I knew if there was a mechanical problem with my bike I'd be walking out, and that could take a week or more. This realisation collided with a new click from my right pedal: the bearings were shot. I couldn't make repairs here, and, deciding it was better not to listen, reached for my iPod. With Motown in my ears, a disaster felt unlikely.

I was still riding the precipice-edged mountain road an hour later when a flurry of fist-sized rocks cascaded down the mountain and into my path. I looked up, chose my moment, and pedaled madly past the raining earth and slate. I turned to watch the ongoing tumble. It was hypnotic: this mimicry of elements. For an instant land became water. The earth looked to flow and boil, a splash of rock here, a foam of shattering shale there. At once a huge section of soil slipped downwards, and then the entire slope subsided, bringing three trees crashing down the mountain and obliterating the road.

I spent the next hours pondering what-ifs and playing back that day's small events, giving myself reasons to have passed the road moments earlier, when the mountain would have claimed me within it. I came out of the clouds at last and cycled on a road furnished with mud and dozing buffalos, and I had to stop often to haul my bike through the gunk. This was no longer bicycle touring – it had degenerated into an undefined sport which combined the brutish power of sumo with the grace of care-home Pilates and the pointless cruelty of bear-baiting. By night I rough-camped, waking each morning to find bloody patches on the wall of my tent where leeches had attached themselves and feasted through the darkness.

I spent the next hours pondering what-ifs and playing back that day's small events...

The landscape calmed at last to low hills as I left Chin State, and soon I was back to the more commercial lowlands where adverts on huge plastic drapes announced the wonders of Grand Royal and High Class whiskey with their respective taglines: 'enjoy life!' and 'taste of life!' Given the state of the men loafing in shadows and glugging the stuff, these were ironic words indeed.

The torrential bursts of rains eased too and then ended, the fields beiged and were split by rocky gullies. The rivers dried to nothing, vast bridges ranged over sand and succulents. I camped one night in this dry shrubland where a nameless wild herb perfumed the air and for the first time in months I could leave the fly of my tent open: there were no mosquitoes in the gloom. In the dusk I watched hummingbirds zip in and slip their long beaks into funneled flowers backdropped by early stars and a bloodshot sky. Sleep was easy.

At last – a proper village, a place to feast on rice and curried meat. As I ate a girl shot to my side, armed with a dog-eared and faded pamphlet entitled 'English for Ladies and Gentlemen of Business'.

Buying chopped mango from a street vendor in Yangon. © Stephen Fabes

'Do you have any rubies or gems to trade?' she asked, reading from the book. I shook my head, took it and leafed through to find the appropriate response.

'I'm afraid, Madam, the matter is quite one-sided', I told her.

The girl, in her early twenties, struck me as unusually forthright for a Burmese lady. Her intentions soon became clear.

'Are you married?' she asked, again reading from the book before landing her eyes on mine.

'No.'

'Do you have fiancée or lover?' she fired back.

'Um, no.'

'I don't believe you! Give me your passport.'

I handed it over.

'Beautiful' she cooed as she appraised my photo, which was odd. I had always considered my passport photo to smack of a vagrant with several restraining orders.

'I want to travel so much', she continued. 'But I have no sponsor for my passport.' Then she looked me dead in the eye, her stare suffused more with determination than desire.

'My name is Maiah, you will remember me. This is where I work. You can come back here any time.'

I hadn't washed for uncountable days. My beard was of vagabond proportions. I smelt of feet and recently, when getting dressed, had inserted my entire leg through a rip in my shorts instead of through the leg hole. I could only look back at her, that poor girl. She must really, really have wanted out of Myanmar.

Cycling through Chin State I wondered if my being here would find its way into stories. My stories, of a country then unmarred by mass tourism, and those of the children of Chin State who may one day recount tales of the old Burma to the next generation. Their memories might include the flagship tourist they glimpsed as a child – a hairy, odorous man on a bicycle, tired enough to wear an air of disaster, but grinning manically too.

From my very first bike rides, as a woolly-minded youth with a rucksack tethered to a rusted bike frame, I've been hooked on the intimacy a bicycle invests in travel. It fells barriers and brings you closer to people. I enjoy how landscapes ease past my handlebars, each space slowly merging with the next. A bicycle reveals the world to be a place of joy-bright eyes, easy smiles and unwavering, and at times heart-rending, hospitality. In short, a bicycle is a great medium to explore a country in detail, and for a place like Myanmar – a country gripped by change and the wonder of it – that's the best way to do it.

I made it into India on the last day of my Myanmar visa with my legs aching, my lungs burning, and with the certitude it was only the pain I deserved. I was indebted. Myanmar had paid me back in spades.

Kidnapped by Comedians

Emily Chappell *left her job as a cycle courier in London to cycle solo across Europe and Asia. After 18 months she finds herself in northern Japan in the middle of winter. Not to be put off by a bit of snow and ice, she decides to head off into the hills.*

The plan had been to ride up to the shores of Tazawako – a mountain lake surrounded by hot springs and ski resorts – and find a secluded and hopefully picturesque spot to camp. Like so many of my plans, it didn't work out.

While I was still in Akita it started to snow and my host dolefully informed me that it probably wouldn't stop until next March. I looked out of his window. The whole city was white, buried under snowdrifts and hard packed ice, tucked in under a blanket of low white clouds that sent their endless snowflakes whirling through the air like feathers, and cast a dim, almost twilight fuzziness over the streets. Every pavement and every road was varnished with ice and people were shuffling carefully along them, wrapped up in scarves and coats and big, thick, insulated boots.

'You can stay longer if you want to', offered Sean. It was tempting. But this was what I'd come for. So I bade him a reluctant farewell, wheeled my bike out of his warm, cosy flat, and set off into the blizzard.

Akita Prefecture is one of the poorer parts of Japan, and doesn't bother with frivolities like clearing the roads when it snows. It's also an area that gets a lot of snow. As I struggled along the road out of the city, I felt almost smothered by it. There was snow in great heaps on both sides of the road – sometimes almost as high as my head. There was snow on the road, churned by the cars to a mess of slush, which then refroze in gravelly-looking ridges, frequently threatening to send my tyres sliding out from under me. There was snow piled precariously on every tree branch and rooftop I passed, every now and then losing its balance and tumbling off in a miniature avalanche. And there was snow in the air, pouring silently and relentlessly out of the clouds, battering me in the face as I rode along, and settling in drifts on every fold of my clothing.

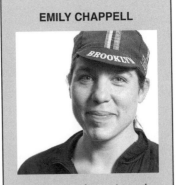

EMILY CHAPPELL

Emily is a cycle courier and a freelance writer based in London. When not on the bike, she can usually be found eating or sleeping. 🖥 thatemilychappell.com

Riding in conditions like this is rather challenging. There wasn't much space on the road so I was torn between wanting to hug the kerb and keep away from the traffic and wanting to find a bit of road that wasn't coated in ice. The best place to ride was in the ruts left by the car tyres but this left

Riding on ice demands a degree of concentration I had rarely needed to muster since I started cycle touring.

me further out than I'd have liked, and swerving in at a moment's notice was no longer an option – with all this ice, any sudden sideways movements were likely to end in disaster and loss of dignity. And a lot of the time there was no clear road at all.

My tyres kept their grip on the ice better than I'd expected. Riding uphill was just about possible, as long as I kept going. If I stopped though, it was impossible to get myself started again – as I tried to push off, the rear wheel would continually slip on the ice underneath it. A couple of times I faltered, or skidded, and then had to get off and push over the top of the hill.

Going downhill was worse. I'd replaced my brake pads but there was no way they were actually going to stop me. If I tried to brake, the wheels would lock, and the bike would carry on sliding along the ice. Each descent was accomplished slowly and painstakingly, my left foot dragging along the ground and my whole body tensed, ready to leap off the bike and into the snowy verge if something went wrong. I quickly realised that cycling up to a mountain lake, camping on its shores in the blizzard and then trying to ride downhill the following morning was a silly idea. I had quite enough on my plate as it was. So I wistfully rode past the turning for Tazawako, and carried on south.

The going was still tough but it was also curiously satisfying. Riding on ice demands a degree of concentration I had rarely needed to muster since I started cycle touring. Every twitch of bicycle and body has to be carefully controlled and monitored – if the bike swayed too far in one direction it would slip on the ice when I tried to right it. If I pushed too hard on the pedals the wheels would skid, so I had to be careful to maintain a regular rolling speed. Not too slow or the bike would slide sideways. Not too fast or I would lose control when I tried to brake. Every muscle was tensed, and my mind was hyper-aware of everything around me – the snow piled up on the verges and what might be under it; the cars and trucks thundering by, often sending a spray of slush over me as they passed; every little ridge of ice or pile of snow or pothole in the road – knowing that I had less time and space and friction than usual to respond to obstacles. I hadn't felt this sort of intense focus since I used to ride my bike in and out of the London traffic. For hour after glorious hour my mind was blank – concentration left no room for extraneous thoughts or worries. Rarely, I think, have I been so completely in the moment.

© Emily Chappell

PART 7 – TALES FROM THE SADDLE

And then I was kidnapped by Shun and Ken.

I don't know what Shun and Ken were doing, driving their car round Akita Prefecture in the snow. I found them lying in wait for me in a layby. As I rode past they flagged me down and before I knew it they were bundling me, bike and bags into their car, handing me a box of hot dumplings and a towel, and speeding off through the blizzard.

They were young, boisterous, hair-gelled and tracksuited, and driving far too fast, whooping with delight as the car bumped and swerved over the rutted ice, and turning round far too frequently to bombard me with questions. They didn't know what I was doing in Akita Prefecture in the snow either but I handed them my letter of introduction which they scanned earnestly and then commended effusively with broad grins, thumbs up and shouts of 'oh yeah!', 'very good!' and 'champion!' They didn't speak much English but they were using what they had to full effect.

The conversation drifted to our respective tastes in music – they bombarded me with a list of artists I hadn't heard of, and virtually applauded when I finally recognised the name Rihanna. To celebrate, they put on one of her videos, on miniature screens hidden behind their sunshades. They then introduced me to *Call me maybe* by Carly Rae Jepsen. I wished they hadn't. The song played, in a tedious and inexplicable loop, on their screens and through their speakers for the rest of the drive, and then in my head for the rest of the day.

...perhaps, with drivers like this on the road, I was safer inside their vehicle than underneath it. I decided not to worry.

I tried not to think about the effect all this distraction might have on Shun's already haphazard driving, along with the condition of the roads and the fact that he kept getting his smartphone out to try and translate things he wanted to say to me. Perhaps this was even more dangerous than cycling on ice. Or perhaps, with drivers like this on the road, I was safer inside their vehicle than underneath it. I decided not to worry. And anyway, they were extremely friendly. We exchanged all the details of our lives that we were able to with our limited common language and they filled in the rest with whoops and grins.

'We are Japanese comedians!' Shun informed me. 'Japanese comedians! Shun – and Ken! Shun – and Ken! Oh yeah!'

They bumped fists and bobbed their heads to and fro in time, then hooted with laughter.

We stopped for cigarettes at one of Japan's ubiquitous convenience stores and Shun insistently steered me towards the cake section. It was almost as if he knew how hungry one gets cycling through the snow for hours. I hesitantly picked up a packet of pancakes. He tutted and added another one, then a doughnut, then a chocolate bun and then cans of hot coffee (brilliant Japanese innovation) for all three of us.

I was in their car for an hour or two and their energy never flagged. For some reason they were carrying a selection of cheap plastic masks, the kind that might be given out a children's party, and whenever the car stopped for traffic lights or traffic jams, they'd put these on and try to attract the attention of the other drivers alongside them. They were usually ignored which seemed to strike them as absolutely hilarious.

They wanted to know where I was going. It was difficult to say really. Tokyo? Well, yes, but I didn't want to risk them offering me a lift all the way there. (Incidentally, I found I didn't mind in the slightest that I'd broken my line by accepting an unnecessary lift. This was a self-contained loop of Japan, rather than the world, and I'd amply proved to myself how comfortable I was riding in snowy conditions,

> **I found I didn't mind in the slightest that I'd broken my line by accepting an unnecessary lift... I'd amply proved to myself how comfortable I was riding in snowy conditions.**

which was my main goal for this leg. I think I'd have had a lot more trouble accepting a lift if I actually was struggling. And meeting Shun and Ken was an adventure in itself.) I settled for naming a town a few miles down the road, that I'd been sort-of aiming for anyway. But then they wanted to know where to drop me in that town and of course I couldn't tell them – if I was on my own I'd just have ridden around until I found a secluded (and hopefully sheltered) spot to pitch my tent.

We settled for a roadside service station which, this being Japan, was extremely comfortable, with spotlessly clean toilets and a 24-hour café. Shun and Ken prowled round the giftshop, playing with souvenir samurai swords ('We are Japanese comedians – and samurai!'), posing with statues and looking for presents they could buy me. I managed to talk them out of everything except a small lucky charm with a bell attached (which I thought might come in useful for scaring off bears in Alaska) and some chocolate (never turning down food is one of my most fundamental principles). They helped me set up camp in an indoor seating area before swapping email addresses and bounding off back to their car with big waves and grins.

I settled down for a pleasant and leisurely evening of reading books and eating whatever I could get my hands on. (You use so many more calories in winter, keeping warm and keeping the bike straight.) And then I fell asleep at about 7pm. I woke up shortly before 5am, to hear someone whispering my name or something very like it.

'Emiry. EMIRY!'

It was Shun. He handed me a can of hot coffee, gave me another of his cheeky grins and then disappeared, as if by magic.

I carried on through the snow. A couple of days later I crossed the final mountain pass before the east coast, and within just a few kilometres the clouds had lifted, the snow had disappeared and I found myself riding through green vegetation, under warm blue skies – as if by magic.

Shun and Ken. © Emily Chappell

Crossings and Encounters

In 2009, **Anna Kortschak** *set off from the Arctic Ocean in Alaska on an entirely open-ended exploration of the Americas; the following year, she was exploring the jungles of Central America. You can follow her adventures at* 🖳 athousandturns.net

The insect hum subtly shifts in pitch and tempo as black fades to grey in the jungle night. After days of indecision, followed by more days chasing hazy and conflicting information, I'm keen to be on the road, but a final bureaucratic barrier remains to be overcome.

My tent is pitched on the manicured lawns of the Tikal Archaeological Reserve, in Petén, Guatemala, but the compass of my desire is pointing north to the lawless borderlands, where few people venture. I want to re-enter Mexico, en route to Cuba, and the most direct route is due north. I am a little reluctant to tell Tikal's officials my plans in case, for my own good, they forbid me from carrying them out but the road I wish to ride is on the other side of a physical barrier. I need an official permit to go to Uaxactun, the neighbouring village and archaeological site immediately to the north of Tikal.

ANNA KORTSCHAK

An erstwhile Australian wanderer, if she ever writes a book Anna is one of those people who would have to include a long list of quirky dead-end jobs in her bio. In 2006, on a whim, she set off alone on her bike, from London to Prague and ended up travelling 3500km down the Danube, from its source in the Black Forest to where it enters the Black Sea. Absolutely hooked by the charms of travelling by bicycle, she has spent all her time since dreaming up different bike routes in various parts of the world and touring when she can.

It transpires that my fears are unfounded; the men in the office don't ask many questions, simply scrawling *extranjera* – foreigner – on the form and sending me on my way. Now, the only thing that momentarily impedes my progress is a thorn-induced puncture.

In Uaxactun I've been told to seek out Antonio, one of the few people who takes tours into the surrounding jungle and who knows the roads like the back of his hand. He is also a keen cyclist. I arrive in the middle of a pre-World Cup friendly between Guatemala and South Africa and Antonio's focus is painfully divided. With eyes flickering between me and the television, he agrees to talk later, in more detail, over some maps. And then, while he bears witness to Guatemala's doomed struggle on the pitch, I go out to explore Uaxactun under the merciless mid-afternoon sun. The living village is surrounded by ancient crumbling Mayan ruins but there is not a tourist to be seen. I wander in the afternoon heat, accompanied only by the birds and the beasts of the jungle.

I return to Antonio's place and, after putting up my tent, prepare for the road ahead by removing my mud guards. Antonio in the meantime has copied a map of the roads to the north. He shows me the location of a couple of work camps where I can replenish

The day passes slowly, with thick viscous mud sucking at my wheels... There is nowhere to stop and rest. The only place to sit is in the middle of the road itself, where it is not a foot deep in mud.

my drinking water and, probably, find a bed for the night. It rained heavily earlier in the week, but not for the last few days; the roads should be passable. He casually waves aside the suggestion that I will come across the bandits, rogues, murderers and rapists that the good people of El Remate – a tourist town by popular Lake Petén Itzá where I had started my research for this trip – believe haunt the jungle, waiting for an unwary cycle tourist to pass. The logistics of my journey sorted, Antonio donates a few tortillas to complement my avocado, completing my evening repast, and then cooks himself some eggs.

In the morning Antonio leads the way on footpaths through the village onto a road ankle deep in fine black mud. We push and drag our bikes through the muck until we emerge onto a larger road where the ground is firmer. Here, Antonio gingerly shakes my already muddy hand, wishes me luck and sends me on my way.

The day passes slowly, with thick viscous mud sucking at my wheels. Turkeys, guans and curassows stalk across the track, while monkeys chatter and rant above me, incensed at my presence. A toucan flaps from tree to tree overhead. It perches on a branch, head cocked quizzically to cast a curious intelligent eye at my bizarre doings – what kind of fool travels in the jungle by bike?

There is nowhere to stop and rest. The only place to sit is in the middle of the road itself, where it is not a foot deep in mud. But to stop is to be besieged by insects. Mosquitos are a constant high pitched tinnitus whine. Ants swarm over the ground, stinging and biting on contact with bare skin.

The track splits and branches around boggy sections and then reunites again. But at times the diversions wander far enough from the main road for me to start wondering if I am blithely heading, on some minor trail, into uncharted jungle. The constant bifurcations make a mockery of Antonio's instructions – they seemed so clear at his kitchen table!

When I spy a wooden sign with a bright yellow arrow seductively pointing left, I am torn. Hand painted and neatly lettered, it clearly states 'Dos Lagunas'. But wasn't there one more left hand turn to pass? Antonio specifically told me not to take the second turn because although it does go to Dos Lagunas the road is steep and round about...But why would anyone make such a beautiful sign directing people the wrong way?

The questions remain unanswered and unanswerable. I scout for clues

... what kind of fool travels in the jungle by bike?

After dinner, in the pitch black hammock shelter lit only by the red glow of cigarettes, they question me at length about my life and I, in turn, question them about crossing the border into Mexico.

and, eventually, since nothing is to be gained by indecision, I turn onto the path. The canopy closes overhead; there is no vista, no way to see the lie of the land or the scope of the forest. Nothing but a green tunnel of claustrophobic jungle undulating up and down over invisible topography. Just as I am considering turning back, another sign comes into view. I go on.

The track descends sharply as the shadows lengthen and the sun starts to lose its sting, and then, without further preamble, Dos Lagunas comes into view. The camp is deserted, so feigning a studied indifference I watch baby crocodiles by the lagoon until a couple of workers appear. I happily accept the invitation to cook my dinner over their kitchen fire and then collapse into the clammy confines of my tent in the hot humid night.

The following day the road presents no major challenges to progress and so it is early afternoon when I arrive at the Rio Azul work camp. Cabins and buildings surround a large cleared area peopled only by a young man, in Wildlife and Forestry uniform, deep in conversation with a girl, who flounces off huffily when I appear. I quiz the guy about the border crossing to Mexico and he assures me it is not far. It is still the hottest part of the day so when the young man points to some hammocks hanging in a thatched shelter, I am happy to find myself snoozing the rest of the afternoon away, swinging gently in the breeze.

As the sun sinks lower in the sky, the camp fills up with people. A man takes me to the kitchen where the camp cook rustles up a snack of re-fried beans and toasted tortillas. The Wildlife and Forestry guy returns and shows me a cabin where I can sleep. After this flurry of activity, the hammock shelter beckons again but my attention is constantly distracted from my book by a group of ocellated turkeys going about their noisy foot-stomping courtship rituals.

The dinner bell rings. We eat at long tables – the men a rowdy bunch of heavily-tattooed workers. A group of three Mexican archaeologists are currently on site and many of the labourers at the camp are engaged in various tasks to do with the restoration and preservation of the ancient ruins. After dinner, in the pitch black hammock shelter lit only by the red glow of cigarettes, they question me at length about my life and I, in turn, question them about crossing the border into Mexico. The men all agree that the border is close and that there is no problem with crossing it. And with that, I retire for the night.

In the morning I pass the Rio Azul site. Despite the massive work team at the camp, nobody is around and I wander about the overgrown ruins alone. Circling the pyramids, I notice

The Rio Azul work camp. © Anna Kortschak

that each one has an opening, brutally cut through the stepped stone walls, into the central chambers. I hope that it is possible to enter but I am thwarted in each case by a firmly locked steel door. On top of one of the larger structures, a rickety wooden lookout rises above the forest canopy. Standing aloft, I sail over an ocean of endless green.

Finally back on the bike, I head towards the border. Rounding a corner, the young Wildlife and Forestry guy from the work camp jogs along the road towards me. He stops in front of my bike.

'You're close now,' he says, enigmatically, before sprinting away.

Then, the road ends. Two of the tattooed labourers lurch out of the brush pushing a silent four-wheeler. They gesture urgently in the direction of the thicket and tell me that if I follow the path I will come to a road in Mexico soon.

'Quick, quick. Go now, the way is clear.'

They cast a hurried eye over my bike.

'You have water?'

Yes, yes, I have water. I'm a little mystified.

I push my bike into the thicket and a footpath – discreet but well-trodden – appears, winding away into the forest. With an almost audible click suddenly everything falls into place in my mind. Ah! So, **this** is the *Zona Roja* – the Red Zone – where drug traffickers and people smugglers do their business across the Guatemalan/Mexican border! This is what the good people of El Remate were warning me about!

Confused thoughts tumble around my brain. Have the guys from the camp come this way specially to check if it was clear of gangsters for the crazy *gringa* on her bike? Yes, it seems they have. But maybe these guys, my new friends at the camp, maybe they are the drug traffickers and people smugglers…. Who else is out here?

I stumble, blinking, into a bare deforested strip, twenty metres wide, carved out of the jungle. It stretches away in both directions, adorned at regular intervals by white painted obelisks. Each obelisk is graced by four gold plaques: Guatemala and Mexico are inscribed on opposing sides, while the others are bisected by the imaginary line that makes nations.

The setting is absurd. I laugh. I pose the bike against a plinth and take photos. I eat my packed lunch. I am a tourist – *what the hell am I doing here?* I locate the road on the Mexican side of the line by dint of wandering up and down for a while. But it is only as I am about to sail down the hill into Mexico that a real doubt assails me. What on earth am I going to tell the Mexican immigration people when I rock up to their office for my entry stamp? And what about the next time I want to enter Guatemala? How will I explain the fact I don't have an exit stamp? Standing transfixed, I wonder why all this hasn't occurred to me before.

The guys at the camp had told me that there were two options for cross-

The Guatemalan-Mexican border stretches into the distance. © Anna Kortschak

The road doesn't appear to get any traffic but my confidence in signs remains undented – a signed road must go somewhere, mustn't it?

ing the border and this one had the main benefit of being the closest. The other is at a place called Tres Banderas, the point where Mexico, Guatemala and Belize all converge, and the road, traversing the border, is clearly marked on the map. At the very least, the line will give me something to point at during a future confrontation with the authorities. I backtrack down the smugglers' path and set off to investigate.

At the junction, a sign informs me that it is 11km to Tres Banderas. The road doesn't appear to get any traffic but my confidence in signs remains undented – a signed road must go somewhere, mustn't it? I hopefully imagine a small shack 11km down the road. It will be manned by a bored official who will be surprised to see me, of course, but he will listen sympathetically to my tale and then indulgently rummage around in some desk drawer to find a rarely-used stamp that will grant me access to Mexico.

Leaves cover the road and the trees lean in overhead, another tunnel of tangled vegetation and filtered green light. As plant tendrils insinuate themselves into entrails of my bike, the wheels turn slower and slower. I get off the bike and push. It goes like this: push, tangle, stop, disentangle. Push. Tangle. Stop. Disentangle. The afternoon is dragging on. And then, ahead of me, I see a brown shape moving on the path. I grope for my binoculars.

The animal is walking down the track towards me. It pauses, rolls in the grass and then gets up and continues on its way, stopping again to rub its face on a vine hanging over the road. A cat. Lithe and graceful, taut, powerful, playful, curious, deadly.

The puma moves with a steady feline grace towards me. Most of me is willing to offer myself up to the beast and be devoured simply in order to get closer to it but at about fifty metres a wildly clamouring speck of self-preservation takes charge.

I wave my arms in the air and say, 'Hi, Puma!'

The animal stops immediately and regards me, motionless except for the barest twitch of its tail, for a full minute, before nonchalantly turning and disdainfully walking back the way it came. And then, like the traces of a fading dream, it melts away leaving nothing but the jungle.

I go on pushing my bike along the track peering at the living walls around me.

And then, regardless of the information provided by my map, the track, like everything else, is suddenly swallowed up by the forest and there is nothing left for me to do but attempt to get back to Rio Azul before dark.

The men at the camp are astonished to see me again. They crowd around.

'What happened? Couldn't you find the road?'

And I don't know how to explain to them that, really, an illegal border crossing simply isn't very convenient for me. I wonder why they imagine that I might need to cross the border here? What do they envisage I might be running from…? And then I wonder what other kinds of border crossings do they know? And, perhaps, the ways of conventional tourism are so opaque to them that they imagine 'tourists,' those unaccountable beings whose way is always paved with a magic ease, can go wherever they please?

Go with the Flow

John Burnham *and* **Gayle Dickson** *switched from backpacking to cycling in order to travel more slowly. Slothful by nature, they teamed up with Hungarian friend Gabor, who has fine-tuned the art of slow cycle touring, for a ride across Mongolia. They had only 30 days to reach Ulaanbaatar from the west of the country – a challenge none of them wanted. What they wished for was to ride through grassy steppe, swim in lakes and camp by rivers like true nomads. That's Mongolia, right? Just before setting out a better-informed friend e-mailed: 'Good luck with the sand and the winds'.*

We are sat behind a wall eating lunch, sheltering from the wind. (The wind!!) We've just crossed the border and it's freezing up here at 2400 metres. A young man, 'my name is Joy', rides up on his Chinese motorbike (Mustang model, of course) and starts chatting in broken English. Gayle is conscious that we know absolutely no words of Mongolian.

'Can you tell us the Mongolian for yes?'

'Yes.'

'No, in Mongolian.'

'No.'

'I mean yes.'

'Yes.'

Joy tells us he's Kazakh, so maybe asking about Mongolian is not the most diplomatic approach. He tells us there are 3 million people in Mongolia and 90 million livestock. We set off along the dirt road towards Olgii and immediately switch from the rocky surface to one of the dry mud tracks etched out in the grass parallel to the 'road'. When passing locals, I call out the one word of Mongolian I have learnt today: 'Sam-man-boo!!' No-one looks impressed that I've mastered the three-syllable greeting. In fact no-one even says hello back. After a while Gayle pulls alongside. 'It's *sain-bain-uu*, you idiot'.

JOHN BURNHAM & GAYLE DICKSON

John and Gayle have been travelling the world since 2001 when they set off for a 2-year adventure in South America. After that came 3½ years wandering along the Silk Road, ending with them buying bikes in Bangkok and returning to China on wheels. They free-wheeled down the Karakoram Highway and enjoyed it so much that the next time they set out on an adventure it was again by bike, this time from Tromso to Tokyo. 🖳 slothsonwheels .blogspot.com

The first night the wind howls and there are snow flurries. It was so cold when the sun dropped behind the mountains that we couldn't bear to cook a proper meal. Common sense dictates – instant noodles for dinner. Gabor has donned his down suit and is cooking with gloves on when we head for bed.

The dirt road heading north east from Olgii isn't too difficult. A bit of gravel, some rocky parts, washboard. There's pretty scenery as we follow a river overgrown with autumnal trees through a desert mountain landscape. The river is a long oasis. Towards the end of the day we have to climb away from its banks and load up with water just in case. I **hate** carrying extra water. A kilometre later we pass a herd of Bactrian camels; it suddenly feels comforting to be carrying that water. The track has become two deep sandy ruts. Gayle is trying to cycle the raised hard ground down the middle but tumbles painfully off. It brings tears to my eyes, never mind hers. Gabor is typically laconic: 'Mongolia!' I am convinced that the cycling cannot get any better than today.

✩✩✩

The next day we discover what variety can be found in the term 'dirt road'. Sand is the ultimate enemy. There's a certain skill required to cycle across sandy tracks and it's one I lack. My front wheel constantly catches and twists suddenly left or right, bringing me to an abrupt halt. A bit painful if your saddle is set so high you cannot just put a foot down to steady yourself. We discover the thrill of the fishtail – back wheel sliding this way and that and whoah! the front wheel goes at the same time! The sliding scale of difficulty with sandy tracks starts at 'Oh dear', rising through 'Oh 'eck', 'Oh blimey', 'Oh bugger', 'Oh shit' to 'Oh f**k' and finally 'Ohaaarggghhhh' as you crumple forlornly in a sand dune the size of Egypt at the side of the road. I am convinced that the cycling cannot get any worse than today.

> **The next day we discover what variety can be found in the term 'dirt road'. Sand is the ultimate enemy.**

✩✩✩

We calculate that with 1800km to cycle in 30 days we should be averaging around 60km a day to allow for a couple of rest days before we hit the asphalt closer to Ulaanbaatar. After two days' riding we realise this is not in our capacity. 'And why should it be?', we think resentfully. Why can't we just relax and enjoy the ride, go with the flow, float across the big landscapes? Surely this is the objective of all Slow Cycle Tourists?

When you're averaging 9km an hour on sandy washboard you get plenty of time to soak up the view. Bathe in it. The valleys are long and wide and there are magnificent snow-capped peaks off in the distance but as we mooch eastwards we enter a dusty landscape of low hills and sparse yellow grass, where even the hardy Mongolian herders are few and far between. A herd of animals breaks the monotony. Look, yaks! Or a passing motorbike. A nod, a wave. Ohhaaaarrrgghh! I'm off the bike again.

✩✩✩

Lunch outside a village after stocking up with supplies, sat beside a track unsure if it's the one we want. Gabor has lagged behind after a slow start to the day, and is possibly lost in the myriad streets of the village looking for the pump house. Or is he doing his usual stock-take and analysis of product ranges in the six little shops that line the main square of Khovd? Whatever – we are unable to check his GPS for clues so we sit down to eat and wait for that rare passer-by.

'What shall we have for dinner tonight?'

'How about veg and rice?'

'We had that last night.'

'Okay then, how about rice and veg?'

'I'd really like chicken curry, followed by apple crumble and custard.'

'What about goujons of beef in a red wine sauce followed by chocolate mousse?'

Getting directions. © Gayle Dickson

A motorbike interrupts our fantasy. A man and his wife are heading to the village wrapped up in their long Mongolian coats. Both are wearing colourful sash belts and boots. We point in the direction they have come and name the next village we want to reach and they nod in the affirmative. It beats the GPS hands down in my opinion, but it has taken over an hour for someone to pass by. We seem to have lost Gabor. He's probably still deliberating over biscuits in one of the shops.

☆☆☆

An old fella stops on his motorbike and rubs his fingers at me in the universal gesture that means 'money'. I'm struggling uphill at the time and wonder how to respond. I'm not sure exactly what he means. (Have you got any? Do you want some? I've got some!) When I see his rheumy red eyes I decide to ignore him and carry on. He's drunk, drunk as a lord. Slowly his bike tips over sideways and he struggles to squirm out from underneath, just in time to stand up for a very long piss. A simple hello would have done.

Later a Toyota Landcruiser passes and pulls up to wait. The driver and passengers want to have a gawk; they don't say hello, so we do. *Sainbainuu!* The driver asks in English, with a smirk 'One dollar?' I point at his car and then at my bike and respond in my finest colloquial English. But I'm laughing and he laughs too before zooming off in a cloud of dust.

In a village we are looking for the pump house to get water. Two young boys on bicycles happily lead us to the building, but it's closed. The pipe's empty. We look suitably disappointed.

Collecting water at the village pump. © Gayle Dickson

The boys indicate to wait and then speed off, returning ten minutes later with big grins and a woman holding a key. She opens up and switches on; water gushes out. The children in each village are curious, a little shy, invariably helpful. The adults mostly seem shy, incurious and reserved. It's hard to imagine their ancestors charging off to conquer the whole of Asia and half of Europe.

☆☆☆

There are several ways of pushing a loaded bike. You can grip the handlebars with straight arms, you can lean in to the handlebars with bent arms, or you can reach back to the seat post with your right arm while steering with your left. After two hours of this your shoulders will ache, your arms will ache, your right shin will be scarred by your pedal. You try cycling to relieve aching muscles and then remember why you were pushing in the first place. It's too sandy to ride.

The track is always firmer on the other side. You choose one and at some point realise it's the wrong one. But which is right?

The track is always firmer on the other side. You choose one and at some point realise it's the wrong one. But which is right? You cut across tracks, this way and that. None are any good – too much sand, washboard, gravel. 'It's like cycling through cat litter', Gayle complains. I am on a mission to find the right track, the way out of this ordeal. I jump sandbanks. I swoop through sand pits. I stall. I look around desperately. I feel like Steve McQueen in *The Great Escape* trying to find a way through to Switzerland.

'When will it end?' Gayle asks. Gabor corrects her.

'The question is not "**when** will it end?" The question is "**Will** it end?" '

☆☆☆

There's been an annoying sound coming from the back of my bike. It goes away when I put my earphones in and turn up the volume. Remarkably this is not a permanent fix. Eventually I discover my rack has snapped in an awkward spot. Resourceful Gabor suggests a splint using a tyre lever – it's the perfect shape so I cable-tie it on and set off cautiously. At lunch I check the rack. The splint isn't working. What I need is a short piece of thick wire to insert inside the tube of the rack. But where on earth am I going to find such a thing in the middle of Mongolia? Gayle reaches down to something in the dirt at her feet. 'You mean something like this?'

There's been an annoying sound coming from the back of my bike. It goes away when I put my earphones in and turn up the volume. Remarkably this is not a permanent fix.

The dirt roads begin to take their toll and we need to pause to make more repairs: Gabor loses a rear spoke and a screw on his sprung saddle snaps. A screw on Gayle's rear rack shears off, leaving the remainder inside the braze-on. Thank goodness for cable ties.

☆☆☆

Evening meals are incredibly satisfying after a long day in (or close to) the saddle, aided by the discovery of sweet chilli sauce, garlic sauce and soy sauce. We dine on pasta or rice with fried vegetables when we can find them. The staple vegetables are carrot and cabbage. Onions pop up now and again from underneath a shop counter. Eggs are a non-starter really, although one lunch-time in a village we take the time to boil up ten for later use. In Nomrog I walk into a

Camp cooking. © Gayle Dickson

shop and fall to my knees weeping at the sight of a sack of plump shiny red capsicum peppers. This shop turns out to be a veritable emporium of delights and we stock up with dried fruit and fresh veg. Oats are elusive in these parts so we experiment with a new breakfast of semolina porridge. Gabor road tests the cooking method and gives us a taste. Looking in the pan it looks like wallpaper paste. Eating it we discover it is wallpaper paste. Warm and filling wallpaper paste made palatable with raisins, honey, milk powder, jam and anything else we can think to throw in. Lunches are based around hard bread, a tin of unidentified but tasty fish and surprisingly good chocolate biscuits. Haute cuisine it ain't.

✩✩✩

Another tough day, with enough sand to make even a camel weep. The sky has been that eternal blue for which Mongolia is justly famed. Landscapes as big as they get. As the sun starts to dip the road brings us to a river with trees aflame in autumnal colour. The perfect spot. We push off the road, through the trees and out into a clearing beside the river. As usual we dither about which way to point the tent, which angle will capture the morning sun, which way is the ground sloping. It's not important. As the sky darkens the stars emerge and the Milky Way streaks across the sky. Who needs TV?

✩✩✩

In the night it snows again. We awake to a brilliant white scene. It's still snowing. Silence. No cars or trucks. No birdsong. We opt for a 'tent day'. Yesterday we reached asphalt: from here to Ulaanbaatar there's a proper road. We're tired and relieved but also sad to think that the real adventure probably ended where the asphalt began. It's been tough but rewarding. We snuggle down into our sleeping bags and talk about the journeys to come.

✩✩✩

In Tsetserleg we stop at the posh guesthouse. We know it's posh because there's clean carpet in the rooms. The plan is to rest a day and then move on, as in the end we know in our hearts that we will eventually take a ride to Ulaanbaatar. But none of us can resist another day off the bikes and the day after that it's snowing. Three days' rest. Just what we deserve, really.

PART 7 – TALES FROM THE SADDLE

Now or Never

Half way through his 4½ year ride across Europe, Asia and Africa, **Charlie Walker** *spent time in Bishkek, dealing with necessary Central Asian bureaucracy, before heading out for some adventure in the mountains of Kyrgyzstan.*

Time drifted by in Bishkek as I waited for four visas. I passed the days wandering the city and researching the road ahead. Evenings were spent speaking with other cyclists over big plates of rice and warm glasses of cheap vodka. Most of the tourists I met were awaiting visas to leave Central Asia before the winter temperatures set in.

Bishkek is a pleasant city with wide, clean streets and a surprising amount of greenery. The weather was clear, revealing the high snow caps that loom over the city's south. Each afternoon a shouted *adhan* (call to prayer) would blast from speakers on the minaret of a mosque neighbouring my guesthouse. The pre-dawn *adhan*, however, was from a different and audibly younger *muezzin* (caller); his voice timid and somehow hesitant while simultaneously beautiful and melodic.

☆☆☆

In the village of Tosor I stocked up on food and turned south, away from the water, on a barely credible dirt track which I cycled past twice without spotting. It was rough and steep; sandy in places, rock-strewn often and rutted always. It required all my concentration and my lowest gear to dodge the various obstacles and make painfully slow progress towards the mountain pass. I climbed into a narrow, crevice-like valley with a v-shaped wedge of snow cap floating in the opening at the end of it, luring me onwards like a carrot to a donkey. Next, I emerged into a gaping valley with grazing flocks and the track winding back and forth across it as it rose higher and higher. A hot sun beat down but when it dropped the temperature plunged with it. My water bottles were thickly iced when I crawled from my frigid tent in the morning.

As the switchbacks began at the head of the valley, a couple of 4x4s overtook me but soon returned,

CHARLIE WALKER

Charlie returned home to the UK in late 2014 after a 4½ year, 70,000km, bike journey across Europe, Asia and Africa. He's currently working on his first book.
⌨ charliewalkerexplore.co.uk

deeming the pass impassable. Each offered me a lift back down but stubbornness drove me on. The path became so steep, decayed and covered in ice that I often had to push my bicycle. Snowdrifts lounged across the way and the parallel stream had become a babbling trickle between well-established banks of ice. My speed slowed further, my breath began to wheeze and my head ached

> **...a couple of 4x4s overtook me but soon returned, deeming the pass impassable. Each offered me a lift back down but stubbornness drove me on.**

dully. I even felt my cracking lips throb. It wasn't extremely high but it had been over a year since I was at comparable altitudes, and I was unacclimatised; stopping every few yards to catch my breath. After seven hours of continuous labour (and only 18km of progress) I reached the pass, a little over 4000m, and pedalled between two glaciers. From the lake, the road had climbed 2500 vertical metres in the course of only 32km.

Layering up with clothes and freewheeling down the other side, I dropped to warmer climes in an empty valley following a westward river. A slightly sinister scarecrow figure on the roadside had an old cooking pot for a head; it was riddled with bullet marks. A lone horseman was nearly pitched down a rocky drop when he rounded a corner and his mount took fright at me and mine. I camped above the snowline and used my second sleeping bag for the first time.

At a boulder-bedded river crossing I lost balance and plunged my foot into the bracing water. Thankfully I soon saw a *yurt* where Maryn and her husband happily fired curious questions at me over homemade bread and *smetana* (Kyrgyz sour cream) while my socks and shoes dripped dry by the stove. My hosts were in the process of packing up to move to the lake for the winter months and were concerned for me, fretting about the inadequacy of my little tent.

The valley started showing signs of life: flocks of sheep shuffled around and gormless black yaks lazed on the dusty path. There were herds of horses; big, strong and fat from a long summer in the still-plentiful (but now brown) pasture.

A boy on a horse came and rode alongside me and soon asked to ride my bike. For the rest of the afternoon Max freewheeled for the downhill stretches while I rode his handsome horse, Tita, with a slender, whippet-like dog bounding alongside.

Max invited me to sleep at his home in the village of Uzun Bulak so we turned onto a side track to get there. The 3km he estimated to his home were closer to 15km and took us past an old Russian train carriage where a friendly old crone and her pretty, quick-eyed daughter served us

Scarecrow with a bullet-riddled head.
© Charlie Walker

PART 7 – TALES FROM THE SADDLE

Climbing to a 4000m pass. © Charlie Walker

tea. I have no idea how that carriage came to be stranded in the mountains, over 150km from the nearest railtrack.

Uzun Bulak turned out to consist solely of Max's home where we drank tea and looked through his family photo album. He also showed me a photo of his six-month old daughter that his parents are unaware of. He is due to marry next year but was reticent about the idea of married life. He lives alone and seems to like it that way. He is only 19.

We spent twenty minutes outside shooting at old vodka bottles about 30m away. I never hit but Max never missed; picking them off one by one, left to right. We ate a dinner of pasta and goat ribs by lamplight before sleeping.

I woke in the morning to Max's amused face and the question: *'Ty parydiosh sivodnya?'* (Will you go today?) The window behind him was white. I peered out at the formerly-brown landscape, now carpeted with two inches of snow. Heavy flakes were still falling. He suggested I stay for the day so, after packing cartridges with powder and shot, we both mounted Tita and went in search of wolves. I sat behind the saddle on a thin cushion with my legs dangling and a gun slung over my shoulder. As we trotted out into the whiteness, Tita's spine ground uncomfortably against my sit bone. It was going to be a long day.

The snow-muffled silence was profound and broken only by hoof fall and the sound of livestock tearing dry grass from the hard, snow-buried earth. Whenever we spotted another man, however distant, we would detour over to shake hands and discuss the health and whereabouts of livestock. Everyone was alert for the prowling black smudge of a wolf in the distance but we saw none and returned to the house after several hours with numb toes. It was still snowing when we sat down to *kartoshka* (a Russian potato dish) and a bottle of vodka. We made a different toast with each shot and called it a night when the last drops had graced our gullets.

The next morning the snow was even deeper but had at least stopped falling for the time being. I thanked Max and began pushing towards a small pass at the head of the valley. Some parts of the track were buried by up to a foot of snow and I floundered pathetically, often slipping and falling, for the 90 minutes it took to cover the one mile to the pass. Skidding down into the next valley, I had to brake with my heels as my brakes were locked in blocks of ice.

☆☆☆

From Naryn I was treated to a day of paved road before returning to corrugated gravel tracks once more. A herder insisted on struggling up a gentle incline on my bicycle for a couple of kilometres while I ambled happily alongside on his donkey. Soon I was rounding hairpin turns on a series of switchbacks that took me, at length, up and over a 2800m pass. I camped among trees with vibrant orange leaves before attacking another climb. As I neared the pass my stamina fizzled out and the sun set forcing me to camp above 3000m, using snow to insulate my tent. Another long descent brought me to a welcoming but extremely poor family who invited me for a potato lunch in their tatty yurt. The mother was only two years my senior but looked closer to 40 and had five young children.

Apple orchards and walnut groves lined the road for a stretch before wheatfields, mid-harvest, replaced them. Two donkeys reared and hoofed each other ferociously on the road in a village where tarmac began again. I cycled through the city of Jalalabad en route to Osh but, due to absurdly com-

Max and friends armed for wolf hunting.
© Charlie Walker

plicated Soviet border demarcations, I had to make a three-sides-of-a-square detour to avoid riding through Uzbekistan.

During this detour I saw a billowing dust cloud a little way from the road with a small crowd gathered beside it. Scrambling down a slope I discovered it was a game of *Ulak Tartysh* (known in surrounding countries as *Buzkashi*). This 'sport' simply defies belief: loosely akin to rugby on horseback with no teams, no boundaries and a headless goat carcass for a ball. The rules eluded me, but the gathering I saw had about fifty horsemen all thrashing their mounts (and often each other) with whips in the frenzy to get hold of the *buz* (the goat) and make a break from the mob. The prizes included carpets and Chinese televisions. Some men wore homemade, padded head gear and several had bloodied noses. There wasn't a woman in sight.

I was offered a horse and declined at first but soon climbed into the saddle after my brain was flooded with a heady mixture of adrenalin, testosterone and a 'now or never' reasoning. I drifted around the fringe of the violently seething throng, reigning in my foaming-mouthed mount, with no real intention of actually getting involved. However, someone must have spotted the hesitant white man at the melee because suddenly the fracas engulfed me and the *buz* was plonked across my lap. The carcass was unexpectedly hard with a mud-matted fleece and I looked up with terrified eyes as the frenzied horses and their indiscriminately whipping riders closed in on me. I believe another man must have whipped my horse's hind because he sprang into action, and charged through a gap in the mob. After only a few yards I had space to hang the surprisingly-heavy headless corpse down by my left side before swinging it up and flinging it over my right shoulder. I didn't look back but galloped on, regaining my lost balance, and looped back around to the crowd where I thankfully returned the horse to his owner.

People seemed amused by my unmanly conduct and I received a good-natured jocular cheer before having to shake many hands and pose for many camera phone photos. A little group of men sitting in the shade of a tree waved me over and I sat down to

I was offered a horse and declined at first but soon climbed into the saddle after my brain was flooded with a heady mixture of adrenalin, testosterone and a 'now or never' reasoning.

PART 7 – TALES FROM THE SADDLE

drink beer with them. Ibek, aged 22, was getting married the next day and we all toasted him several times. A friend of the group walked over leading a limping horse. A deep gash above its front right hoof needed attention so the men took turns to hose the muddy wound down with their sterilising urine. I was asked to do my part and, having just drank a couple of beers, I was able to oblige. Ibek then invited me to be the 'official photographer' at his wedding and we were soon loading my bike into a car to go and wash up for his bachelor party. While doing this, an intimidating man with semi-Slavic features arrived and asked in barked Russian who I was and what I was doing.

'I'm a tourist. I'm going to Ibek's wedding.'
'No. Where are you going with your bike?'
'London.'
'No! Where to on your bike?'
'Lon-don. I am cycling to London.'
'Osh next, yes?'
'Yes.'
'Go now! You are not welcome here.'
'What's the problem?'

He scrutinised me through his mirrored glasses but decided to say no more and simply stared impatiently at me. My new friends had fallen submissively silent and Ibek whispered in my ear that the man was secret police. I was left with little option but to say an apologetic farewell and good luck to Ibek before riding away. It was a sour ending to an interesting day but I was in formerly Soviet Kyrgyzstan; paranoia and distrust of foreigners from the authorities was to be expected.

Alaskan Epiphanies: Finding My Roads

In 2010, **Nathan Haley** *began a southbound Americas ride from Alaska to Ushuaia, a trip that would engender a love of dirt-road, wilderness riding. But first he decided a northwards detour from Anchorage to Fairbanks via Denali National Park would be a perfect warm-up for his first long tour. With what amounted to only a few weeks of bicycle touring in his locker, he hoped for a baptism of fire.*

May 19: My journey finally began today with a relaxed and easy spin out of the busy urbanity of Anchorage. Only 360 miles of isolated pavement now lie between me and Fairbanks. Things started in an easy haze of anticipation until just past Wasilla when reality dawned and I started to tense up. This is the point at which the comforting traffic of the Glenn Highway died, replaced by the more sedate George Parks Highway, which I'll follow through the heart of archetypal Alaskan wilderness all the way up to Fairbanks. Snaking through vast swathes of aspen and pine, it occasionally crests hills to reveal the true enormity of the surrounding terrain. I am finding the wilderness here to be intimidating, such lonely open expanses are flooding my brain with thoughts of only one thing: bears.

✩✩✩

To say that I was bear-aware is like saying that Bill Gates is comfortably well-off. I was obsessed. Growing up in the UK, where we don't have animals that can kill you, we sometimes dress up 'storybook' creatures such as bears in a cloak of exaggerated mystery. In my mind, they were bigger, fiercer and considerably more brutal than they really are. Even so, the reality is pretty serious, so one of the first things I did in preparation was research the bear threat.

The presence of both black and grizzly bears in Alaska confuses the situation immeasurably for newcomers. With perseverance, I slowly came to understand the different bears' weapons and hang-ups – the more I knew though, the more frightening they appeared. I tried to tame my fears with futile acts such as relentlessly practising drawing my bear spray, and attaching a bear bell to the stem of my handlebars.

In the US any form of danger usually means the presence of guns. Virtually everyone I talked with would ask me what I was packing. My casual nod to the small red can of bear spray hanging limply from my bar bag often caused people to recoil with embarrassed astonishment. If I thought I could coax some bear confidence out of the locals, I was very much mistaken. Every Alaskan I spoke to reveled in the chance to scare a tenderfoot, usually qualifying any survival advice with a horrifying bear attack story.

✩✩✩

May 23: I think I'm finally getting distracted away from my overwhelming bear anxiety. The last few days on the Parks Highway have been spent under vibrant clear blue skies, with incredible views of the Alaska Range. From the very first moment I lifted my head and witnessed these mountains' distant calling, I have been smitten. The waves of snowy peaks culminating in Denali itself are so intensely beautiful, how can riding towards such perfection be anything but carefree and easy? With the weather as perfect as it has been and the majestic Mount Denali burrowing into my heart, I am struggling to contain my excitement at the prospect of exploring Denali National Park.

✩✩✩

May 24: The calls of the Denali wilds have finally been met! I rolled into the park visitors' complex this afternoon and am prepared for the start of some true adventure. Six million acres of vibrant wilderness reserve surrounding the continent's highest peak await. Unsurprisingly, there are scores of tourists here, but I don't identify with any of them; I

NATHAN HALEY

Nathan dreams of big spaces, high mountains and remote trails. Intent on riding the journey of life to the max, he gave up a promising career in documentary films to cycle. After 5 years exploring dirt roads in the Americas, he still can't think of anything better to do. 🖳 velofreedom.bike

PART 7 – TALES FROM THE SADDLE

Denali National Park. © Nathan Haley

feel different and apart. My focus is on the 91-mile road that spreads west into the park, ending at the former mining camp of Kantishna. Unpaved and closed to regular traffic, this road provides me with a unique route into Alaskan wilderness, access that's otherwise the preserve of those with exceptional wilderness knowledge, planes, boats or money.

From a shed behind the Denali Visitor Center, backcountry rangers dished out the permits I needed, subjected me to a frightening video on bear essentials and then rented me the big, clumsy bear barrel in which I'll carry my food. Proud never to have suffered a bear-related death in all 93 years of the park's existence, the rangers aren't ready to take chances on me ruining that claim.

✩✩✩

May 25: This has been the most incredible day I can remember. It started this morning as I joined the throng of other tourists on a three-hour bus ride to Toklat at milepost 53 on the Park Road. The summer season is yet to start so this is as far as the buses are travelling, leaving the remainder of the road traffic-free. My plan is to ride out to the end of the road and then return back along its full length to the Parks Highway.

As I loaded and limbered up in Toklat, the other tourists milled around before heading back to the park entrance. I feel bad that heavy skies deprived them of their chance to view Mount Denali, but know their disappointment must have been blunted by the dall sheep, caribou, moose and bears we saw on the journey out. Watching them get back on the bus really highlighted my freedom as a cyclist: I have no bus to catch, just the infinite opportunities of the open road.

A 1000-foot, 5-mile climb to Highway Pass served as my uncompromising introduction to unpaved loaded cycling. It was a struggle as my wheels got swamped in the freshly spread aggregate and traction proved elusive. The bike I've become familiar with over hundreds of miles of asphalt suddenly felt like a stranger. With morale dropping, doubts crept in and I started to feel very alone. Around every corner lurked an imaginary mother bear ready to protect her cubs, and packs of hungry wolves.

The thought of others cycling the road ahead worked wonders in diverting my attention away from bears and helping me relax.

Then came the descent! The thrills of hurtling carefree down slick blacktop have been replaced by a timid dance of subtle leans and delicate nudges. I saw two bike tracks in front of me, and from their unsteady appearance on the ascents I could tell they were going my way. The thought of others cycling the road ahead worked wonders in diverting my attention away from bears and helping me relax.

After another slog uphill to Stony Overlook, I managed to unravel myself from my thoughts long enough to step off the bike and really take in the surroundings. By this point I'd left the mixed forest of the lower elevations far behind and found myself cycling through predominantly scrubby tundra. The lack of trees laid bare vast expanses of browny greys and yellow-tinted greens that spread up mountains and down into broad valleys. The road itself meandered over passes and snaked around valley bottoms on its relentless charge west into an enormous expanse of natural desolation. To the south skirted the Alaska Range, with Denali itself towering above Kantishna at the road's end. Thirty miles east from there, the colossal Muldrow Glacier charges down from the range, its reach ending abruptly at the McKinley River. Everything is huge, not least the sky. Slabs of thick cloud that have only unbridled the sun a few times all day, briefly let it loose to dance life into the drab colours of the dying winter. The air here is blissfully pure and every sound belongs to nature.

For a couple of miles I was accompanied by a fox, before it took off to clamp its jaws around an unsuspecting snowshoe hare. I enjoyed my own lunch in the company of a couple of maintenance workers at the closed Eielson Visitor Center. As I ate, ominous clouds gathered in the southern sky to my left, floating formations that were soon growling and spitting crackling bursts of electricity at the near mountains. I foolishly stopped to see if the storm would run past me, a strategy that was quickly modified into a frantic attempt to outrun the threat instead.

With renewed focus, I forged on until a maintenance vehicle emerged from the distant gloom, breaking my hard-found flow. As the truck pulled nearer I couldn't quite believe what I saw: two bikes, propped up in its trailer. When the truck came to a halt beside me, a couple of weathered riders emerged from within the shadowy cab. Florent and Aurélie set off from France a good while ago and are already 10,000 miles into an epic world cycle tour. With the thunderstorm bearing down, I had little time to do anything but exchange contact details before soldiering on.

The French bicycle tracks had been something of a comfort to me. Although they continued to fall beneath my wheels, I now knew they led only to ghosts. Alone again, I felt a hint of desperation start creeping into my bear cries, calls I've learnt to holler to alert bears. As the atmosphere darkened and the rain became heavier, my anxiety steadily swelled. By the time I zipped past the milepost 85 turnoff to Wonder Lake Campground, I was terrified, fearfully garbling all sorts of inane and insane cries.

A few miles down the road I reached a lodge, the first of a series of buildings that make up the old mining camp of Kantishna. As the storm

I managed to unravel myself from my thoughts long enough to step off the bike and really take in the surroundings.

Alone again, I felt a hint of desperation start creeping into my bear cries, calls I've learnt to holler to alert bears.

I now feel ridiculous for carting my full oversized load of shiny new gear down this challenging dead-end road.

steadily cranked itself up to full electric output, I looked wearily down towards the village and then up at the lodge where a light blazed invitingly. On inspection, there was no one about to squeeze for information, but I was happy to use their awning as a shelter from the worst of the storm. Twenty minutes later, things had calmed slightly so I took the opportunity to head back up into the hills away from town.

Those few miles retreat to Wonder Lake were hard. I was mentally exhausted, sweating profusely in my recently donned waterproofs, and the wet road surface was proving even more challenging than the dry road had been. To top it all off, fresh bear tracks had appeared since I rode down the road only half an hour earlier. These freaked me out, prompting a loud and frenetic babbling of expletives that I sustained all the way into camp.

Sat here writing I can feel my eyelids getting heavy as the day's adrenaline fades. Things smell mildly cheesy in the tent tonight and my mind is racing from exhilarated exhaustion.

✩✩✩

May 26: Unzipping my tent door, I opened the day to mind-blowing views: a huge, crisp, clear morning vista of lakes, creeks, glaciers and forest culminating in the southern side of Mount Denali, the largest base-to-peak rise of any mountain in the world. All yesterday's efforts quickly fall into sharp context. I may have suffered a little, but I'm doing it and the dream is most definitely alive. I'd never ridden dirt before yesterday but after that intense taste I am craving more. Also, having survived last night in the tent, I am feeling much more confident and even beginning to appreciate my proximity to wildlife instead of fear it.

I noticed fresh cycle tracks on the road this morning and was surprised to catch up with Florent and Aurélie. They were dropped off soon after seeing me yesterday and enjoyed a leisurely morning in camp. As we cycled together they filled me in on their incredible journey. After a year on the road, their pace is frighteningly fast, a fact helped by their canny use of lockers back at the park entrance to lighten their loads. I now feel ridiculous for carting my full over-sized load of shiny new gear down this challenging dead-end road. Humble and gracious, Florent and Aurélie approach everything with a relaxed and easy confidence. Everything they do seems in stark contrast to my unrehearsed scramblings. I wonder if I'll last long enough on tour to one day be like them?

✩✩✩

... it has introduced me to what I now know cycle touring should be... as if my soul has been jump-started back into existence.

May 30: I awoke in the Riley Creek Campground at the entrance to the park this morning, feeling worn but elated. The past four days of impromptu hiking with the French, then the solo ride back to 'civilisation' have continued to amaze. It is only a few days ago that I left the paved roads for the first time, but something has changed in me, it's like I've just gone through some sort of bicycle awakening. The Park Road has completely changed my cycling landscape. Tough, 'dangerous', remote and spectacular, it has introduced me to what I now know cycle touring should be. I completely forgot about statistics, targets and mile markers as the involved riding pulled me into 'the moment'. It is as if my soul has been jump-started back into existence. The months ahead are suddenly looking even more exciting.

Just Don't Stop!

A year into her ride from the UK to Cape Town, **Helen Lloyd** *arrives in Nigeria, a country renowned for its roadside checkpoints and corruption. In this extract from her book* Desert Snow, *she soon discovers a friendly, hospitable nation beyond the stereotype, but it doesn't take long until a first encounter with the authorities…*

Nigeria is dangerous, unsafe, corrupt. 'Expect trouble on the roads,' people said. When you are told something often enough, you begin to believe it. I had been conjuring up scenarios of kidnap and robbery.

Then I crossed the Nigerian border and my fears and suspicions diminished by the minute. Everyone waved as I passed or said hello or welcome or good afternoon. The sun shone, the sky was a clear blue, and it seemed as though everything was right with the world, so I smiled and waved back. Downhill the pace quickened – faster, faster. Then ahead, I saw what I had been dreading: a roadblock.

Overlanders often cast aspersions on the military and police and condemn them as corrupt. Whereas cyclists have a hard job mustering the energy to get from one place to another, so those in motorised vehicles have their own difficulties in the way of paperwork and vehicle registration, and because they travel much faster, they spend a disproportionate amount of time dealing with bureaucracy. There are, however, more overlanders than cyclists travelling through Africa, and it was their view that predominated my thoughts. When I was back in England, I did meet one man who had already cycled through Africa.

'So Dan, what about the roadblocks in Nigeria?' I asked.

HELEN LLOYD

Helen has cycled 45,000km through 45 countries – under the Saharan sun and across Siberia in winter. She has also made remote journeys by river and horse. *Desert Snow* is her debut book about her Africa ride. ⌨ helenstakeon.com

I flew past at 50kph with my head down, ignoring their shouts to stop. The bottom of the hill came sooner than I would have liked, and I was pedalling furiously to get up the other side...

'Oh, they're not that bad.'

'Well, it's alright for you to say that now. But like, how did you deal with the police?'

'Oh, it's fine. Just don't stop. Just cycle straight through and don't stop.' I had not considered that. I looked at him sceptically, wondering if he were having me on. *Maybe it's worth a try.*

There I was, rapidly approaching the roadblock of wooden planks, with long nails protruding upwards, laid across the road to stop vehicles in their tracks. There was a gap between the board and verge, enough space for a bike. *Shall I do it?* I scanned the canvas tent erected and saw several plain-clothed men sitting in the shade. I saw no uniforms, no guns, or motorbikes. *Go on, just do it. They can't shoot you without a gun or catch you on foot.*

I flew past at 50kph with my head down, ignoring their shouts to stop. The bottom of the hill came sooner than I would have liked, and I was pedalling furiously to get up the other side when two cars overtook and pulled me over, angry men shouting with arms waving frantically out of the windows. They were furious with me. *Little, innocent me? What have I done?* Already, I was conjuring up the lies that would diffuse the situation the quickest.

'Why didn't you stop? Why did you ignore us?' the red-faced driver roared at me. 'We are security and here for your safety ...' And so the tirade went on.

I saw his mouth moving and watched his face going redder and redder until I wondered if it were possible for a face to explode like an overripe tomato. I heard only noise, not words. *How the hell did I not see the cars? And how much money are they going to extort from me for this?* I tuned back in.

'... would you?' He was silent now, staring at me. He leant in close trying to intimidate me. His bloodshot eyes locked on me like a wolf that sees its dinner and knows it is just a leap and lethal bite away. My only thought was that his breath smelled bad.

'Sorry, what?'

'You wouldn't behave like that in your home country, would you?'

'We don't have roadblocks in England.'

'You have police though, don't you? And you wouldn't behave like that, ignoring to the police, in England.'

His bloodshot eyes locked on me like a wolf that sees its dinner and knows it is just a leap and lethal bite away. My only thought was that his breath smelled bad.

'Our police wear uniforms. How do I know you are police?'

He waved a filthy card, dirty from overuse or misuse with the laminated edges peeling apart. His tirade resumed. He still wanted to know why I didn't stop.

'I didn't know I was supposed to,' I lied. But he didn't hear me because he was shouting again. 'Look. It is done. What are we going to do now?' I raised my voice in retaliation. Not used to having someone answer back, he was silenced.

'Show me your passport.' Reluctantly, I showed it, and he grabbed it off me. 'You must go back to the roadblock,' he said. Now I was furious with this man I did not trust, and I refused to go anywhere until I had my passport back. Without it, I was powerless and at his mercy.

On the road in Nigeria. © Helen Lloyd

With a promise to go with them, he handed me my passport. But since my chances of escape were low, I pedalled back up the hill with one car ahead and one crawling behind.

The angry man gradually calmed down as he meticulously recorded my details onto a notepad of pink headed paper advertising a hotel. I calmed down too and suggested we start again. He ignored me.

The immigration official also needed to see my yellow fever vaccination card. His tight pink t-shirt, far from accentuating his muscular physique made him look like a big cuddly teddy. After scrutinising it, he informed me that I was fully vaccinated, that the vaccinations had not expired, that the signature was in the correct place, and the stamp there too. I tried to look enlightened, glad there was no excuse for a bribe.

Next the transport official wanted to speak with me.

'What is the registration of your vehicle?'

'I'm on a bicycle.'

'But what is the registration number?' he insisted seriously.

'It doesn't have one.' *Are you stupid?*

'I need a number.' I debated making one up, but decided against it.

'The make is Thorn,' I offered. 'Will that do?'

'No.' *Is this going to be the excuse for a bribe?*

'Can't you see it's a bicycle? Bicycles do not have registration numbers. Have you ever seen a bicycle with a registration number? No, of course not. It is black and has two wheels. So if you need a number, will the number two do?' I paused and held my breath. *Perhaps I should have just made up a number.* I used to be submissive in the face of authority – that was hard to believe now.

It was a relief when the other men started laughing. *And breathe.* The transport officer was silent with embarrassment.

'You are free to go, but next time you must stop. We are here for your safety,' the red-eyed officer reminded me.

'Have you ever seen a bicycle with a registration number? No, of course not. It is black and has two wheels. So if you need a number, will the number two do?'

✫✫✫

The huge green swell of Nigeria.
© Helen Lloyd

In the 160 km during my first full day in Nigeria, there were 21 checkpoints. Customs men wore grey uniform, the police were in black from beret to boots with an automatic rifle slung across the shoulder, and immigration had tank tops like your grandfather would wear with 'Immigration' knitted across the midriff. No one wanted to see my passport and some stopped me only to ask questions. *Where are you going? Where have you come from? When did you leave England? What is your mission? Will you marry me?* Some just wanted to shake my hand. *I love you! Be my wife! What's up? Can I have your number?*

The first city was the crazy, chaotic Abeokuta. The roads were a traffic-jammed maze weaving round the hills and crisscrossing at random. Police in bright orange bibs stood at junctions, supposedly directing traffic. Some drivers followed the hand signals while others decided for themselves. Mind alert, strong arms, steady balance, I held the bike upright and slowly negotiated the taxis and motorbikes jostling for position, putting a hand on the car bonnet to steady myself if I wobbled – determination to proceed was the key.

I didn't know which road to take and everybody I asked pointed me in different directions. Eventually, I despaired and employed the guidance of a taxi driver. Gradually, peace returned, and I rode through a sea of hills, over a peak and down to a trough, across the huge green swell of Nigeria.

Nigeria is seven times the size of England. With a population of 170 million, it means that one in every six Africans is Nigerian. According to projections, by 2050 its population will be the fourth largest in the world, ahead of the USA. Of the one hundred largest African cities, eighteen are in Nigeria and nine of these have a population exceeding one million. I passed through three of them. There are a lot of Nigerians.

And it does not go unnoticed when travelling through the country. I met Yoruba, Hausa, Igbo, and Fulani. I met policemen, customs officers and many other government officials, students, professional engineers, teachers, preachers, international businessmen, labourers working for the ministry of transport and many other ministries besides, truck drivers, families running restaurants, and countless people trading all things on the streets.

Despite its size, I spent only two weeks in the country, but covered 1400km. Had it been another time of year, I would happily have stayed longer. But it was the wet season, and I was racing to overtake the rain. Instead of ambling along lesser-trodden tracks and camping in the wild, I sped along tarmac roads and checked into cheap hotels at night. Without

Without food to cook in the evening or a tent to take down in the morning, I spent more time cycling and speaking with the people I met.

food to cook in the evening or a tent to take down in the morning, I spent more time cycling and speaking with the people I met.

At a guesthouse in Ibadan's run-down suburb, I met Tayo. He introduced himself when I sat down in the hotel restaurant. 'Would you mind if I speak with you?' he asked.

'No, of course not.' If I had wanted peace and quiet, I would not have sat alone at a table – it invited company. For time to myself, I had to stay in

A curious crowd. © Helen Lloyd

my hotel room and even then I was often disturbed. The desire to be alone comes from our western lifestyles and is not understood by most Africans.

The lady returned with a plate of rice and beef that I had ordered. The other option was rice and chicken.

'Oh, I see you are going to eat. Please, have your dinner. I will come back when you have finished.' When people sat down to eat here, they ate. They didn't talk. There was always enough time for talking afterwards.

'No, it's fine,' I said, but Tayo went anyway and came back later.

'Every two weeks I travel between Abuja, my home, and Ibadan for government work. I always stay at this guesthouse. It is cheap and clean,' he explained. That was why I chose to stay there too.

'My family lives in Abuja. I have a wife and two boys, eight and ten years' old. It is my eldest son's birthday next week.'

'Oh, that's great. They grow up quick, yes?'

'It's true, too quick.' He let out a sigh and went on talking, 'I don't know what to do. He keeps telling me that he wants a bike for his birthday. I think he's too young. I'm scared he will have an accident. Drivers are bad in Nigeria.'

Eleven did seem a young age to be driving a motorbike. *I wonder what the age limit is, not that anyone pays much attention to it, I suppose.*

'The drivers aren't so bad,' I countered, 'It's the vehicles that aren't road-worthy. I saw a lorry crashed today. The cabin had separated from the tanker and careered into the bush while the tanker just lay on its side in the road. The driver and his mate were sat on the top, mobile phones in hand, waiting to be picked up. I couldn't believe they weren't hurt.'

'How are you travelling?'

'I'm cycling.'

'But aren't the roads too dangerous?'

'You know, it's not that bad,' I lied. I had been run off the road by an overtaking lorry that morning. With

If I had wanted peace and quiet, I would not have sat alone at a table – it invited company. The desire to be alone comes from our western lifestyles and is not understood by most Africans.

With two lorries storming side-by-side towards you and a long deep air-horn blast of impending doom, it is surprising how quickly you can scramble up a steep bank with 50 kilos of loaded bike.

two lorries storming side-by-side towards you and a long deep air-horn blast of impending doom, it is surprising how quickly you can scramble up a steep bank with 50 kilos of loaded bike. 'If you take the smaller roads, there's not so much traffic. It's a great way to see the country.'

I went on to tell him about my journey, not because he had asked, but from habit.

'My son would love to hear these stories. All he talks about is getting a bicycle. His friends at school have them you see.'

'Oh, I thought you meant he wanted a motorbike.'

Tayo let out a laugh that burst from deep inside, as though he did not often find something to laugh about, and then he said seriously, 'No. I will never allow him one of those.'

We sat there quietly for a few minutes. I finished my Coke, sipping it from the glass bottle with a straw, and we watched the TV. There was always a TV in Nigeria's hotels. It was the sign of a modern establishment; wi-fi was another world away.

'I hope you don't mind, I think I need to go and sleep. It was a long day today,' I said.

'Of course. It is getting late. I should go to bed too. Thank you for speaking with me.'

'A pleasure.'

'You know, I think I will get my son a bicycle,' he said after a pause. 'There is a shop near our home. I could buy it when I return next week.'

'You changed your mind quickly,' I smiled.

'I think if you can cycle all the way from England, he will be OK on our street.'

'I think so too.'

'I will let him cycle, on the pavement, to the end of the road and back. No further,' he added adamantly.

'Oh I doubt you'll be able to stop him,' and I laughed a little.

Tayo looked serious and vacant and then sighed, 'My wife's going to kill me when she finds out.'

Bicycle maintenance

MAINTENANCE ON THE ROAD

At home, maintenance can be put off forever. On tour, you're covering much greater distances and need to keep your bike running efficiently. Rest days are a good time to keep up with maintenance on your bike, at the campsite or in a hotel courtyard. At the very least you want to be checking the '3Bs': bolts, brakes and bearings. Maintenance can be a chore but on the road it's much more satisfying when you have no distractions or time constraints and know that your work will ensure the smooth continuation of your trip.

Cleaning your derailleur drive train

Cleaning the chain and exposed gears is an important and rewarding task. Your bike will ride a little faster and more quietly and the drive train will certainly last longer and be less messy if you keep it clean. You may have one of those chain bath gadgets to wash the chain but on the road it's easier to give the chain and gears a dry clean using an old toothbrush (or the specialist brushes from manufacturers like Park), a tiny flat screwdriver and a rag. Working with everything dry makes far less mess.

With your bike standing upright, pick away at the grime on the chain and gears; if you have some WD40 or similar solvent spray, this will help loosen any crud. Hold the flat end of a small screwdriver against the side of the jockey and pulley wheels of the rear derailleur and rotate the pedal backwards to

---

CHAIN OIL

Convenient free supplies!

Instead of carrying your own chain oil, you might look around petrol/gas stations for discarded motor oil containers. You need only a few drops and there's usually enough in one plastic container for one or two bikes. In the developing world motor oil is sold in bulk so you won't find discarded bottles but you will find people who will part with a few drops from their oil cans, either at no charge or for the equivalent of pennies, in roadside repair shops.

Motor oil is not the most ideal lubricant but many long-distance tourers have managed for years with this low-cost method, which also spares you the risk of an oil spill inside a pannier, if you miss tightening a bottle top!

How much chain oil to use

Sprays like WD-40 are not good enough to properly lubricate a chain alone; they are not thick enough to protect the metal of the chain, cogs and chainwheels. Chain oil (especially the thicker formulations, such as 'Phil Wood Tenacious Oil') should be applied sparingly: a maximum of six drops, over the entire length of the chain (while backpedalling, by hand, two or three turns of the crank when the chain is in the large chainring). If a chain looks wet after you've oiled it, you've used waaaaay too much! Wipe off the excess or your chain will become a sticky magnet that attracts abrasive dirt and grit, and that defeats the whole purpose of lubrication: reducing wear.

Paul Woloshansky

scrape off dirt, as if you were working a lathe. If you can, do the same to the rear sprockets, cleaning each one in turn. It's harder to get in behind the largest chainring but be persistent and your efforts will pay off. Do the same with the chain itself; you need to poke and scrape every link, especially in between the plates.

Next, lay the bike down. Fold your rag in two and pull it tight to create a straight line along the folded edge. Use the rag like dental floss to 'floss' between the sprockets of the rear cassette. You don't have to remove the wheel and can use the rag to move the sprocket around when you have cleaned one side. Wipe off any excess muck and let everything dry, then add a few drops of whatever lubricant you're carrying (see box p345) to your chain.

Checking bolts

Some riders check nuts and bolts daily, especially for their racks, but unless you're riding off-road this is excessive except if you've noticed persistent loosening (either visible loosening or a wobbling rack). Checking all bolts (including the bolts on Ortlieb panniers) every rest day is certainly a good idea.

Rim brake maintenance

Brake pads have a much shorter life on tour – you're riding greater distances, and though there's hopefully less stop-and-start riding, your bike is heavier and you might be making some long descents. Wet weather is also very hard on brake pads and so they need frequent attention.

Fine tuning, which normally means tightening the brakes as the pad wears, is done by turning the small barrel adjuster on the brake cable anticlockwise to tighten the brakes. You might find the adjuster next to the brake lever if you have mountain bike bars, or they'll be by the brakes themselves. Over time, this fine tuning is not enough as the pad becomes so worn that it does not fully engage with the rim. Check after a big descent or a rainy day that the pads have not become dislodged. Brake pads can move out of position and in the worst case rub on the fragile tyre sidewall. If the pad is wearing unevenly you won't get good braking performance and should replace it.

Replacing rim brake pads

Rim brake pads come with a metal stud attached either to a brake pad or to a metal brake shoe into which you insert a rubber brake pad. The latter type is preferable for touring as you can easily carry the spare pads without taking up much pannier space. Most modern rim brakes are designed for brake shoes with a threaded stud (which are incompatible with smooth stud models – make sure you buy the correct spares).

Fitting new brake shoes is not especially easy as the pad can move around while you are tightening it, and you need near-perfect positioning. Attach the brake pads loosely to the brake. Hold the pad against the rim with a piece of thin card between the back of the pad and the rim (to toe-in the pad). When the pad is perfectly aligned with the rim, hold it in place with one hand and tighten the Allen bolt with the other. The pad will often turn as you turn the bolt so if possible get another person (whether it's your cycle partner or a random person who's hanging around watching) to hold it still (or to pull the brake levers tightly to hold it still) whilst you tighten.

Cleaning brake pads

Brake pads build up with grit and tiny scraps of metal – these act like sandpaper on the wheel rim, damaging it and reducing braking power. Using a toothbrush or a sharp tool, carefully scrape or dig out as much grit as you can from the brake pads. Cleaning the rim is also a good idea; it helps avoid damaging it, allows you to see when there is any damage, and makes wheel truing easier (see p351).

Brake squeal

Brake squeal is an annoyance but not usually a safety issue. It could be a toe-ing in problem – see p346 for how to set rim brake pads. Other causes of brake squeal are dirty or damaged rims, damaged or badly worn brake pads, loose brake arms (tighten the bolt attaching the brake arm to the boss on the fork or frame), or even the type of brake blocks.

Centring brakes

Brakes touching the rim unevenly is a common problem; usually one pad is dragging lightly on the rim. It may be that one pad is out of position and catching on the rim, or the wheel was not properly centred in the dropouts when you last put it in but, most of the time, a simple adjustment solves the problem. Look for a tiny Allen bolt (usually 2mm) on the side of one or both brakes – see illustration. Tightening that bolt on the brake that is rubbing will push it away from the rim. Alternatively you may have to loosen the

Adjust bolt to set brake pad

Tiny Allen bolt for fine adjustment of brake pad

© Stephen Lord

small bolt on the opposing brake. Experiment, but be careful not to over-loosen these bolts – it can release a spring inside the brake, and you'll need to remove the brake from the brake boss, dismantle it and reset the spring.

Replacing brake cables

Not a difficult job but make sure you have the right cables – brake cables are longer for rear brakes and different for mountain bike and dropped bar setups. Note how your brake cable fits into the brake lever when you push it out. You may have to squeeze the brake a little to see where the cable nipple fits into the brake lever.

Weak brakes

There are many possible causes. The longer cable on rear brakes reduces power – there's more stretch in the cable and also more chance of dirt in the cable housing, causing friction. The brakes themselves could be set in a position giving little mechanical advantage, or the straddle cable (older styles of brakes have a thick cable linking the two brake arms) may be too long. Grime in the brake could also reduce efficiency. It's usually possible to set the spring inside each brake arm in two different positions on the brake boss, so if you have a problem, remove the brake from the boss, see where the coil spring fits into a hole in the boss, and make sure it is in the hole that gives it greatest resistance.

Maintaining disc brakes

There is no routine maintenance to be done on disc brakes, they will work until they fail. The most common task with hydraulic brakes is bleeding or replacing brake fluid. While you will find instructions on the net for your brakes, you're much better off if you practise bleeding your brakes before your trip. You only need to bleed them on a long trip, but the thought of possibly carrying spares or tools such as syringes to do the job all argues for choosing mechanical disc brakes in preference.

Mechanical disc brakes will only need occasional cable replacement – the same as rim brakes – and pad replacement. Replace pads for all disc brakes when their thickness is between half a millimetre and 1mm. This can be a fiddly job but requires no great skill. It's possible that your rotors may become bent or warped, and there is a tool available to straighten them, but it is just a lever with an indent and you bend the rotor back by hand; the tool is unnecessary. Ideally you want minimal clearance between pad and rotor so anything more than a few mm in warp means replacing the rotor, which should not be too difficult to find or fit yourself.

Derailleur adjustment

As derailleurs have become indexed (click-shifting) and built to higher standards and narrower tolerances, they've become more fussy and in need of more regular adjustment. It's minor work but you might need to make small adjustments every couple of days. For a derailleur to work well, the chain, sprockets and derailleur mechanism (or 'mech') all need to be clean. A dirty cable will also stick and cause problems, and a kink in a cable can only be rectified by replacement. Manufacturers advise not to lubricate gear cables but if they are rusty or slightly damaged a squirt of spray or oil would be a quick road fix. Common problems include:

Limit screws

Barrel cable adjuster

Rear derailleur adjustment. © Stephen Lord

Noisy or poor shifting Assuming everything is clean, you need to look at the alignment of the mech and check it's tracking exactly in line with the sprocket carrying the chain. A mech feeding the chain a little to the left or right will be noisy and cause friction.

Turn the bike upside down and turn the pedal with one hand. By rotating the barrel cable adjuster one way or the other, the derailleur will move up or down the cassette – a few turns of the adjuster and it will jump into the next gear. Keep adjusting it till the derailleur is centred for each gear. It's easier if someone else shifts gears using the handlebar gear control while you pedal and experiment with the barrel cable adjuster – you'll soon get the hang of it as the gears run most quietly when all are correctly aligned with the mech.

Many gear shifters have a second barrel adjuster next to the gear shifter on the handlebar. On a long straight stretch of road where there's nothing but the sound of your gears chattering, try adjusting it on the fly – you'll soon be in the habit of listening out for gear noise and doing some fine tuning to eliminate it. To keep things simpler go for (non-indexed) friction shifters, for which you don't have to worry about the adjustments just described.

Chain comes off the cassette This is caused by loose limit screws (see illustration opposite) allowing the rear mech to move too far. These limit screws can work loose over time; tighten them so they only just allow the chain into the highest and lowest gear. The limit screws are at the back of the rear mech and are usually marked 'L' and 'H'. Screw in 'L' a touch to stop the chain jamming into the spokes and screw in 'H' to stop the chain going off the smallest sprocket (highest gear).

Chain skipping This might be caused by a tight link not articulating fully as it goes round the sprockets; it could have got damaged by the chain getting stuck in the spokes. Lubricate the tight link and prise it apart. If the plate on the side of the link looks damaged, you may have to replace that link. Sometimes your chain and/or sprockets are so worn that the chain comes off, especially during hard pedalling. There'll be no apparent damage, but examine your chain for stretch and check your sprockets too – see 'chain stretch' on p350.

Front derailleur

Front derailleurs don't have the fine-tuning adjustment of a rear mech, only the limit screws, but it's usually possible to move the cage (the curved plates which sit around the chain) while you're riding if they're rubbing on the chain. If you hear a clattering sound, it may well be the front derailleur and you can look down while riding and check if the cage is rubbing. Half-shifting the gear control on the left handlebar will usually shift the cage out of the way.

To move the chain over such large jumps between chainrings, the cage has to over-shift, that is, it needs to move a little further than the ideal position in order to push the chain onto the next chainring. That's when you need to give it a click or half-click to push it to a centred position for the ring you want to use. Very occasionally an extra push is needed when going up into larger rings or a click in the other direction to pull it back. Again, let noise be your guide and adjust it any time you can hear it.

Limit stop adjustment

As with rear derailleurs, tightening either screw moves the limit inwards, so if the chain is falling off the chainrings tighten the screw on that side. Note that the limit for the large chain-

Chainring remnants after a long tour.

Front derailleur limit adjustment. © Stephen Lord

ring tends to be right on the ring, whereas for the smallest chainring you have to set the limit a millimetre or two left of the ring itself.

Don't alter the height of the derailleur on the seat tube on the road, this needs doing only if you change the chainring or fit a different size. The cage should be about 1mm above the large chainring when set for the highest gear.

Chain stretch

Chains don't actually stretch like knicker elastic, but the rivets and collars around them wear out over time, allowing each link to lengthen and so effectively stretch the chain. Measure your chain using a 12" rule held at the centre of one rivet in the chain link. The 12" line on a new chain will be exactly in the centre of the twelfth link. More than 1/16" (nearly 2mm) over and it's time for a new chain and more than 1/8" (3mm) over, you'll more than likely need new sprockets as well. If you can see daylight between the chain and sprockets or chainring, your chain and the sprockets/rings are on the way out.

Headset maintenance

Paul Woloshansky

Headset maintenance is mostly ignored by touring cyclists, who are usually more concerned with how their wheels and drive-trains are holding up. Generally speaking, on shorter tours the bearings that allow a bicycle to be steered shouldn't require servicing or adjustment. On long journeys, however, ignoring an out-of-adjustment headset can ruin this component, damage a frame and fork, and negatively affect your bike's handling. A bicycle burdened with very heavy front panniers exacerbates the potential for harm so you need to recognise the problem early on in order to prevent or minimise damage.

The following advice is really 'an ounce of prevention' so you won't have to look for 'a pound of cure' out in the middle of nowhere:

Adjusting a threadless headset

Threadless systems are adjusted from the very top; tightening down the Allen-head bolt (in the centre of the top cap) drives the stem downwards on the smooth, threadless steerer tube. This action compresses the headset and eliminates bearing play. It's possible to over-tighten, so watch that there is no play but that the handlebar moves freely.

The golden rule is this: you must loosen the Allen-head bolts on the side of the stem (they attach the stem to the steerer) before you snug down the top bolt. This step allows the stem to move freely down the steerer. If you forget to do this, you risk damaging or dislodging the star-nut (the barbed nut that has been driven down inside a steerer tube, that the adjusting bolt screws into).

Also, before snugging down a threadless headset, check to see if any plastic or rubber seals are protruding. If they are, centre them so they aren't damaged or sheared-off during adjustment. If the seals are damaged the system will be less weather-proof.

Wheel truing

Because of the extra payload and rough roads it's normal for wheels to go out of true on tours. Squeezing pairs of spokes gives a very rough idea of spoke tension but should help identify any loose spokes. They'll also need some minor truing should a spoke require replacement. To do so without a truing stand or any tools other than a spoke key follow these instructions. Of all bicycle maintenance procedures, this essential skill is worth learning before leaving home as it does require a certain knack.

1. With the panniers off, stand the bike upside down.

2. Spin the wheel and push one brake pad towards the wheel. As you push it closer, it will probably make contact in one or several places on the rim.

3. Select the biggest point of contact to work on first. As the wheel rubs against the brake pad, it slows down and comes to rest on the biggest bump.

4. Slowly turn the wheel back and forth to find the centre of this bump. If it looks as if the bump is on the other side of the wheel, go round to that side and start there.

5. Bear in mind that though you're tightening the spokes, you're actually turning the nipples that the spokes screw into, so you tighten the opposite way. Turn the key **anticlockwise to tighten spokes**, and clockwise to loosen them.

6. Tighten or loosen in quarter-turn increments. Turn just past 90°, then back off in order to loosen the spoke in the nipple, as sometimes the spoke twists but does not turn in the thread. Lightly lubricate the nipple if necessary. Check the rim frequently by spinning the wheel to check on your progress, so you don't overtighten and risk a broken spoke or round off the nipple so the spoke key can't grip.

7. For small bumps, turning only the one spoke at the centre of the deviation may work, but you may have to slightly loosen the spokes either side of it. Be careful when loosening spokes: this is as dangerous as over-tight spokes in causing metal fatigue (and hence breakages) and allowing the wheel to go out of true.

8. Work around the wheel until all large deviations are eliminated. Once you can rotate the wheel and feel numerous tiny bumps, there is probably not much more you can do yourself. If you can get the deviations from true down to 1mm, that is excellent for a roadside repair.

Wheel truing takes a little practice. It's easiest with a proper spoke key (shown here). Turn anticlockwise to tighten; clockwise to loosen.
© Stephen Lord

Fixing a puncture

You'll need a pump to match your valves (these days nearly all pumps fit both Presta and Schrader valves), glue, chalk or talc, patches or old inner tube to cut a patch from, sandpaper and two (or three) tyre levers.

Most people on day rides simply fit a spare tube rather than repair a puncture on the spot and hold up their friends. It saves a few minutes. Even then remember to check the tyre for thorns or broken glass which might still be embedded.

To repair an inner tube

1. Loosen the brakes by pulling the brake cable out of its guide. Open the quick-release on the wheel and remove the wheel.

2. Remove the cap on the tube valve or locknut around the base of the valve, if there is one.

3. Loosen the tyre from the wheel by hand, squeezing the tyre as you go round it with your hands.

4. If the tyre is loose in relation to your wheel, you might be able to remove it by hand – the safest way to do so and rather satisfying too!

5. If not, use plastic tyre levers. These are soft and less likely to damage rims or tubes. The kind with a hook on the other end allows you to clip it to a spoke and free your hands to insert the second tyre lever – see below left.

6. Work your way slowly round the tyre with the tyre lever, bringing the tyre off the rim on one side only.

7. Remove the inner tube and pump it up. You can probably spot anything larger than a slow leak. Mark it or hold your thumb over it and keep searching in case there are more punctures. If you can't dip the tyre in water to look for escaping bubbles, you'll have to use your ears or try to feel the air rushing out if you hold the tyre up to your eyes or wet lips.

8. Rub round the hole with sandpaper, making sure you eliminate any raised edges running down the centre of the tube.

9. Apply a thin layer of glue to an area around the hole larger than the patch. Let it cure till it becomes tacky, then apply the patch, removing any backing

Left: Using plastic tyre levers to remove tyre. **Right**: Before resorting to tyre levers refit the tyre as much as you can by hand. © Stephen Lord

plastic or foil first on the side which goes on to the tyre. Hold it tight for a minute or two. If you have chalk or talc, spread a little on the excess glue. Or if there is some very fine soil around, crumble it to dust in your fingers and use that.

10. While you let the glue dry a little longer, check the tyre for foreign objects. Rips in the tyre can be reinforced with patches of old inner tube glued on the inside, though this may only work as a temporary repair.

A fabric tool roll is a convenient way to pack your tools and keep them from rattling.
© Stephen Lord

11. The glue will be dry within five minutes. Partially inflate the tube and stuff it back in the tyre and seat the valve in its hole.

12. Begin fitting the tyre bead back behind the rim. Go as far as you can around the wheel with both hands. Before resorting to the tyre levers to push the last bit of tyre bead over the rim, push the lever in between tyre and rim to make sure the inner tube is not trapped.

13. Partially inflate the tube then deflate it quickly to free the inner tube, should it be trapped. Inflate the tyre to full pressure, hope it stays that way and refit the wheel and the brakes.

Attaching and removing pedals

There are a number of situations where you may have to remove pedals during a trip: to box your bike for a flight or train journey, to avoid damaging other items of baggage when you put your bike on a bus, or to avoid damaging your

---

FURTHER LEARNING

Online

💻 sheldonbrown.com Excellent primary source of all reference information.

💻 madegood.org Videos and easy to follow instructions.

💻 thebiketube.com All the videos you could want for instruction on bicycles, repairs (including some innovative solutions), set up and anything bike related.

💻 parktool.com Good 'repair help' articles and some videos.

💻 youtube.com Type any bike-related problem into YouTube and you'll find heaps of videos from mechanics all over the world.

Books

● *The Bike Book*, (Haynes), Fred Milson. Good simple introductory text. Colour photos.

● *Zinn and the Art of Mountain Bike Maintenance*, Lennard Zinn. Very comprehensive, good for older bikes and components.

Bike maintenance courses

It's easier for most of us to learn practical things by doing. In Britain, CTC runs bike maintenance classes (💻 ctc.org.uk), as does the London Cycling Campaign (💻 lcc.org.uk). A week-long course will greatly increase your proficiency in many tasks and many classes encourage you to bring your own bike, so you will learn how to dismantle and service it before taking it on tour. 💻 cyclewales.net can provide customised classes for tourers at their Snowdonia workshop.

shins when pushing through sand. Pedals need a 15mm wrench to remove them, but pedal wrenches are normally about 30cm long as force is usually required. Most people balk at carrying such a long tool, and so don't. This means relying on finding a mechanic to lend you the necessary tool when needed, or (better) to take a wrench whose length you are able to extend (for instance by attaching tubing that you've brought with you to repair a broken tent pole) in the event you aren't getting the necessary torque. The wrench must be slim enough to fit in the gap between the pedal and the crank, but strong enough to apply sufficient force.

It's important to remember that right pedals have a normal thread, but left pedals have a reverse thread and so are loosened by turning clockwise. Grease your pedals' threaded spindles before fitting them to the crank.

Replacing a spoke

Replacing a front wheel spoke or non-drive side rear spoke is relatively simple. Remove your tyre, inner tube and rim tape to enable you to remove the broken spoke. Insert the new spoke and screw it into the nipple, then true up the wheel and refit the tape, tube and tyre.

If it's a drive side rear spoke that breaks, before doing the above, you'll need to remove the cassette. In a workshop, you would use one tool to immobilise the cassette and another to remove the lockring, but on the road you have no space for these tools, so you need a small cassette removal tool such as the NBT2 (or Stein Mini Cassette Lockring Tool). Follow the printed instructions that come with the tool for exact details of removing and then refitting your cassette.

GLOSSARY

Note: some of the terms used below are illustrated in the photograph on p33.

• **Bar-ends** Bolt-on extensions to handlebars to provide extra hand positions to straight/mountain bike handlebars. Available in many shapes and almost a necessity for touring on a bike with a straight (i.e. non-dropped) handlebar.

• **Bikepacking** Essentially mountain biking with overnighting equipment. Bikepackers tend to travel light, with minimal equipment carried in a frame bag, seat pack and handlebar roll.

• **Boss(es)** Brake bosses are the braze-ons attached to forks and frames for cantilever or V brakes.

• **Bottle cage** Metal or plastic drink-bottle holder that screws onto a bike's frame.

• **Bottom bracket** The large bearing inside the bottom bracket shell in between the cranks.

• **Braze-on** A small fitting on a frame which, on a traditional steel frame, was held on by brazing. Eg. bottle cage mounts, rack mounts, cable guides.

• **Cartridge bearings** A sealed ring-shaped unit containing ball bearings. Easy to replace, no need to service but no standard sizes and you will only find them in good bike shops while touring.

• **Cassette sprockets** The small gears at the back, also known as cogs. Used to be fitted individually into a cluster so that you could change the sizes of individual sprockets if you wanted, but these days the cluster of gears is produced in one unit which is known as a cassette.

• **Chainrings** The large rings between the pedals at the front of the drivetrain. Controlled by the gear shifter on the left of the handlebar.

• **Chainstays** The tubing connecting the bottom bracket to the rear dropout.

• **Chromoly** An alloy of steel, containing small amounts of chromium and molybdenum. Used to make strong, high quality bike frames and forks.

• **Cleat** A fitting on the sole of a cycling shoe that 'clips' into pedals (see SPD pedal, below).

• **Crankset** The chainrings, two cranks and stack bolts (which hold the chainrings onto the cranks).

• **Derailleur hanger** The place on the frame immediately behind the rear dropout where the derailleur is bolted onto the frame. This is a vulnerable point because it projects and if bent in an accident or in transit will badly affect gear shifting. Aluminium frames usually have a replaceable hanger owing to the difficulty of repair.

• **Drivetrain** The gear system considered as a whole.

• **Dropouts** The wrench-like ends to the forks and at the corner of the rear triangle on the frame, into which the wheel axles fit.

• **Groupset** An anglicised version of the Italian Gruppo, referring to the entire set of gears, usually in connection to the name brand and quality. Eg. Shimano Deore LX.

• **Hardtail** A hardtail mountain bike is one without rear suspension.

• **Headset** The bearings supporting the front wheel, one set being at the bottom of the head tube and one at the top. Almost all bikes nowadays come with threadless headsets, where the steering tube is not threaded but uses a bolt instead to pull the steerer up into the head tube, making it easier to adjust.

• **Hydrostatic head** The measure of how waterproof a fabric is. Eg. a fabric which can withstand the pressure of a column of water 2000mm high has a hydrostatic head rating of 2000.

• **Presta Valve** The narrow type of valve commonly found on road bikes.

• **Quills/stems** A quill-style stem is the old style in which a narrow handlebar stem fits into the head tube rather than around the top of the steerer.

• **Recumbent** Bicycle design where the rider lies back rather than sits in the traditional fashion.

• **S&S coupling** A coupling that enables a bike frame to be separated into smaller pieces.

• **Schrader valve** The standard car-style valve found on most bicycle inner tubes around the world.

• **Seat stays** The tubing running from the top of the seat tube to the rear dropout.

• **SPD pedals** Shimano's style of pedals that lock onto cleats in the bottom of cycling shoes designed especially for Shimano SPDs. They are the most common kind of pedal designed for cleated shoes. Undoubtedly efficient but some bike tourers like them, some don't.

• **Truing** The art of making a bicycle wheel true: perfectly round with no kinks or wobbles.

• **Wheel 'dishing'** When the side of the wheel has a saucer shape for greater strength. The left side of the rear wheel is more dished than the right side on a bike with derailleur gears, and the more derailleur gears a bike has, the less 'dish' to its shape and the weaker it will be.

ACKNOWLEDGEMENTS & CONTRIBUTORS

A special thanks to Stephen Lord for entrusting us with his much-loved handbook, and for always being there with sage advice and opinions. When we set off on our first tour, emboldened by having read the first edition of the *ACTH* from cover to cover, we never dreamt that seven years later we'd have the opportunity to update a new edition.

Producing this handbook is a collaborative, team effort and without the input of many, many kind tourers, it would never see the light of day. A big thank you to the 40+ contributors who gave up their valuable time to write about regions of the world and parts of bikes about which they are especially passionate. See below for a list of these generous folk from the touring community, with links to websites, blogs and books.

In addition, thanks to the following for photos: Janne Corax, Ben Dugauquier, Cass Gilbert, Andrew Grant, Roy Hoogenraad, Eszter Horanyi, Mike Howarth, Yoko Kai, Dominique Kerhuel, Archie Leeming, Peter Lighting, Daisuke Nakanishi, Jukka Salminen, Paul Schmidt, Peter van Glabbeek, Agnieszka Waligóra and Andrew Welch.

For helping out with advice and expert knowledge, thanks to Cass Gilbert, Janne Corax, RV Prakash, Grace Johnson, Tom Walwyn, Sylvie Bigant, Ben Dugauquier, Mark Elliott, Cherry Fitzsimmons, Guy and Susannah Halsey, the Pikes (senior) and Dr Natasha Jesudason.

Last but not least, thanks to Bryn Thomas, Nicky Slade, Anna Jacomb-Hood, Jane Thomas, Caroline Gray and Nick Hill – the crew at Trailblazer whose unflagging support and dedication to continuing to produce quality printed guides remains an inspiration.

CONTRIBUTORS

Tara Alan embarked on a mostly pedal-powered journey from Scotland to Thailand from 2009-2011 with her husband Tyler. She's the author of popular bicycle touring cookbook *Bike.Camp.Cook.* 💻 goingslowly.com

Tom Allen has undertaken bicycle journeys on five continents and is now a full-time travel writer and filmmaker. Reluctantly best known for the adventure film *Janapar*, and less reluctantly for his blog 💻 tomsbiketrip.com, he is currently attempting to move beyond being 'that guy who cycled round the world and got married to an Iranian girl', with several new projects in the pipeline.

Lars Bengtsson is a Swede who's ridden 85,000km on his bike, and canoed 600km on remote tropical rivers. He's also climbed a few mountains, three of them first ascents. 💻 lostcyclist.com

John Burnham & Gayle Dickson (see p325)

James Butcher & Sarah Bedford spent three years eating their way from Alaska to Patagonia, with occasional bouts of cycling in between. En route they refined their Colombian coffee addiction, developed a love of dirt roads and a hatred of Ecuadorian cobbles, collected almost every known intestinal parasite in Latin America, and learned their golden rules of cycle touring: pack half the kit, and allow twice the time. 💻 big-sur.co.uk

Emily Chappell (see p316).

Joe Cruz first started bike touring in the late 1980s and has pedalled the American West, Asia, the Middle East, and South America. He splits his home between rural New England where he is a professor of philosophy and his beloved native New York City. 💻 joecruz.wordpress.com

Stephen Fabes (see p311).

Peter Gostelow has cycled extensively in Asia, the middle East and Africa, covering over 90,000km in more than 60 countries. He currently lives and works in Tanzania, and continues to explore more of the African continent on two wheels. He occasionally blogs at 💻 thebigafricacycle.com about recent tours in Africa.

CONTRIBUTORS (cont'd)

Friedel Grant launched into bike touring with a tour around the world with her husband Andrew. They pedalled 48,000km through 30 countries before settling down to ride bikes and start a family in The Netherlands. Friedel writes about bike touring on her website ⌨ travellingtwo.com, has published the *Bike Touring Survival Guide* and occasionally writes guest posts for websites such as the Adventure Cycling Association.

Nathan Haley (see p334).

James & Jane Hall didn't start cycle touring till their late thirties. After circumnavigating the Iberian Peninsula they fancied a bigger trip – the 'Eureka' moment was a talk by Alastair Humphreys when they realised they couldn't risk waiting till retirement. In a nine month career break they cycled 95% the length of South America.

Steve Halton cycled from Cape Town to London over 18 months in 2013/14. He currently resides in London where he is planning his next adventure exploring the great mountain ranges of the world.

Loretta Henderson is an adventurer, author and speaker who founded the WOW (Women-On-Wheels) Wall at ⌨ www.skalatitude.com. She lives in the USA and is writing a book.

Lars Henning & Jenny Bell are an audio engineer/bike nerd and a singer/songwriter who left the London rat race to cycle the back roads from Mexico to Colombia in search of music and adventure. ⌨ tourintune.com

Alastair Humphreys spent 4 years cycling 46,000 miles around the world. He is an adventurer, blogger, author, motivational speaker, film maker and photographer. ⌨ alastairhumphreys.com

Jonathan Kennett has been exploring New Zealand by bike since the mid-1980s, and has written over 20 cycling books, including detailed guides on cycle touring, mountain biking and road cycling. For the last four years he has been working as a project manager for the New Zealand Cycle Trail network. He works with his brothers, Paul and Simon in Wellington, but spends approximately three months per year biking around the country. ⌨ kennett.co.nz

Anna Kortschak (see p320).

Maria Leijerstam became, in 2013, the first person to cycle to the South Pole from the edge of the Antarctic continent. She runs Multisport Ltd, an events & training company in South Wales. ⌨ whiteicecycle.com

Helen Lloyd (see p339).

Matt McDonald spent three years cycling the length of Europe, Asia, Australia and South America for The Cycle Diaries. ⌨ thecyclediaries.com

Anna McNuff is an adventurer, writer and speaker based in Richmond, UK. In 2013 she wheeled her way, solo and unassisted, 11,000 miles through each and every state of the USA. ⌨ annamcnuff.com

Scott Morris has been an obsessive mountain biker since the age of 14. He has a PhD in computer science and runs a number of websites related to mountain biking and touring: ⌨ bikepacking.net which covers lightweight singletrack touring; ⌨ trackleaders.com, a SPOT tracking based company; and ⌨ topofusion.com – a mapping application which is proficient in planning and visualising long and remote GPS routes.

Tim & Laura Moss spent 16 months cycling 13,000 miles around the world. Tim runs adventure website ⌨ thenextchallenge.org and Laura organises the Cycle Touring Festival ⌨ cycletouringfestival.co.uk.

Laura & Patrick Mottram spent 15 months cycling through every country in South America. Read about their trip in their book *Ipanema Turtles – A South American Adventure by Bike* and follow them at ⌨ pedallingabout.com.

Alia Parker is the editor of ⌨ cycletraveller.com.au and the developer of the 6000km Great Dividing Range Bicycle Touring Route (GDR Route) from Cape York to Adelaide. She has three bikes, loves classic steel frames and riding remote roads.

Andy Peat left the UK in 2005 to cycle and work his way around the world. Having crossed five continents, he's currently living and working in Singapore.

Matt Pierle is a field biologist who has travelled by bike on four continents and cycles largely in order to bird and botanize along the way. In addition to natural history he enjoys learning languages and connecting with people around food, farming and natural materials building.

CONTRIBUTORS (cont'd)

Scott Richardson cycled from the UK to India. He is now trying to fish as much of the world as possible. ⌨ worldbiker.blogspot .com

Lorenzo Rojo left home in 1997 wanting to cycle for a while in Latin America. He's still on the road, and currently touring in Asia. ⌨ munduanbarrena.blogspot.com

Mike Roy left South Korea on a bicycle and a whim, originally planning to cycle back home to the USA, but getting side-tracked just about everywhere along the way. He documents his attempts at eco-friendly living and travelling at ⌨ threeruleride.com.

Kurt Sandiforth has ridden the distance around the world a few times. His dirt-road wandering on a fat bike has seen him from Maine to Florida in the US, meander around Panama and ride the length of South America from Cartagena in Colombia to Ushuaia in Argentina. ⌨ bikegreaseandcoffee.com

Chris Scott is the author of Trailblazer's *Morocco Overland, Adventure Motorcycling Handbook* and *Overlanders' Handbook*. He's always had a sneaking admiration for the simplicity of adventure-touring with a 'pushbike' but his first bike trip was not until 2008, with former ACTH-author Steve Lord and a fresh copy of Trailblazer's *Himalaya by Bike* by Laura Stone.

Laura Stone is the author of Trailblazer's *Himalaya by Bike – A Route & Planning Guide*, which was the perfect excuse to cycle very slowly between Pakistan and Bhutan for two years. Laura now runs Greenrock, a cycle challenge events company. ⌨ himalayaby bike.com , ⌨ greenrock.co.uk

Shirine Taylor & Kevin Dugan are a young couple from Oregon who are currently cycling around the world in search of the most beautiful mountains and friendly people the world has to offer. ⌨ awander ingphoto.com

Rob Thomson is a human-powered world record holder who has travelled to over 30 countries. He currently lives and works in Hokkaido, Japan, with his partner. ⌨ 14deg rees.org

Elmar & Ellen van Drunen have travelled by bicycle all over the world, enjoying the total freedom and the great outdoors. ⌨ bicycle-junkies.com

Charlie Walker (see p330).

Logan Watts & Virginia Krabill changed direction in 2012 and set out on bikes through Latin America. The following year they cycled southern Africa, Morocco, and Spain. Recently they have been documenting and publishing off-road bikepacking routes on ⌨ pedalingnowhere.com

Bill Weir is a lifelong touring cyclist who has roamed extensively across North America, the Pacific, Asia, and Europe, yet dreams of still more rides. Travel writing helped finance his long journeys. He has links to recent bicycle rides in Asia and beyond at ⌨ arizonahandbook.com

Amaya Williams & Eric Schambion Amaya has pedalled more than 150,000km through 96 countries on six continents. Since 2006 she has been on a quest to be the first woman to cycle every country on the planet. With cycling partner and husband Eric, she's overcome altitude sickness in the Andes, survived malaria in Sierra Leone and dodged wild elephants in India. She's happiest setting off before sunrise to capture the magic of daybreak on a bike. Amaya is a native of Montana, a place she still calls home despite not having lived there since the late 80s. ⌨ worldbiking.info

Mirjam Wouters has been wandering the world on a bicycle since 2003; she gets sidetracked easily which is just as much (if not more) fun. ⌨ cyclingdutchgirl.com

INDEX

Abkhazia 155
Acute Mountain Sickness (AMS) 109
Adventure Cycling Association (ACA) 256, 264
Afghanistan 130, 140
Africa 229-54
myths debunked 232
airlines, bikes on 99-102, 204-5
air mattresses 93
Alaska 255, 258-9, 261, 334-9
Albania 125
alcohol stoves 95
Alan, Tara 97, 356
Allen, Tom 158, 356
Almaty (Kazakhstan) 170, 171
Altai Republic (Russia) 174-6
altitude sickness 109-10
Amur Highway (Russia) 176
Angola 254
Antarctica 228
Arabic numerals 237
Argentina 301-5
Arizona Trail (USA) 267
Armenia 155, 158-9
Asia 127-220
ATMs 27, 28, 29
Australia 221-6
Austria 125
Azerbaijan 155, 156-8

Baja California 274
Baku (Azerbaijan) 157
Bali 215
Balkans 125-6
Balochistan 143
banana flowers 189
Bangkok (Thailand) 207
bar-end shifters 49
batteries and chargers 98, 106
bears 259, 262, 263
Bedford, Sarah 279, 283-9, 356
Belize 275
Bell, Jean 122-3
bells, bicycle 73
Bengtsson, Lars 244, 246, 252, 356
Bhutan 148
bike bags 102
bike boxes and boxing 100-2
bike computers 73
bikepacking setup 71-2
ultralight 78-9

bike touring tents 89-91
bikes 32-47
accessories 65-75
components 47-64
documentation 26
maintenance 25, 345-55
security 115
tools & spares 73-5
transport of 99-103, 152, 191
see also name of component
Bishkek (Kyrgyzstan) 169, 170
blogs & blogging 24, 107-8
Bolivia 296-301
border officials 117
Borneo 217
Botswana 247
bottle cages 72-3
bottom brackets 58
brakes 39, 51-4, 67, 346-8
Brazil 309, 310
British Columbia 261
budgeting 18-20
Bukhara (Uzbekistan) 165, 166
Bulgaria 126
Burnham, John 160-71, 191, 325
Burundi 243
buses, bikes on 102-3
Butcher, James 265, 279, 283-9, 356

Cairo to Cape Town 229
Cambodia 208
cameras 98
Cameroon 253-4
camping 86, 103, 124, 263
see also tents
Canada 256-8, 261-3
Carretera Austral (Chile) 301, 305, 307
Casas de Ciclistas 291
cash 28-9
Caspian Sea 157, 171
Cassiar Highway (Canada) 261
Caucasus 155-9
Central Africa 248, 254
Central America 269-73, 275-9
Central Asia 160-71
chain oil 345
chains 74, 75, 349, 350
Chappell, Emily 21, 132-43, 316
children 23

Chile 301-8
chili con carne recipe 97
Chimborazo (Ecuador) 287, 288, 289
China 181-91
Chinese for bike tourers 186-7
Chongqing (China) 190
climate 16-17
clothing 81-6
coffee making 96
cold weather touring 175, 177
Colombia 283-7
Colorado Trail (USA) 267
comfortable cycling 15, 32, 58-64
CoMotion cycles 45
compasses 98
Continental Divide Trail (USA) 267
Continental Travel Contact tyres 57
contraceptives 111-12
Cordillera Blanca (Peru) 294
Cordillera Huayhuash (Peru) 294
corruption 117, 232
Costa Rica 277-8
costs 18-20
Cotopaxi (Ecuador) 288, 289
credit cards 27, 28, 136
'crotch rot' 110
Cruz, Joe 79, 296, 356
Cuba 278
Cusco (Peru) 295
custom-made bikes 44
customs & etiquette, Muslim 133, 136, 137, 235
cybercafés 106
cycling position, ideal 59
cycling shorts 81
Cyclists' Touring Club (CTC) 45, 99, 353
Cyrillic alphabet 173

Dalton Highway (Alaska) 257, 259, 261
Darien Gap, crossing 276-7
Dawes bikes 46
debit cards 27, 28, 136
Democratic Republic of Congo 254
Dempster Highway (Canada) 261

Denali Highway (Alaska) 261
dengue fever 108
derailleur drive train,
    cleaning 345-6
derailleur gears 39, 47-8,
    348-50
desert cycling 235, 252
Dickson, Gayle 172-80, 191,
    325
diet 112-13
direction of ride 17-18
dirt-road riding 71, 117-19,
    226
disc brakes 39, 52-4, 67, 348
dishing 52
documentation 25-7
dogs 115-17, 134, 248
dress code, Muslim countries
    133, 136, 235
drinking water 96
drop bars 40
Dushanbe (Tajikistan) 166,
    167

East Africa 241-3
East Asia 181-200
East Coast Australia 226
ebola 251
Ecuador 287-9
Egypt 237
electronic devices 98, 106-7
environment & cyclists 103
Ethiopia 240, 241
Europe 121-7
expedition touring bikes 34,
    40-5

Fabes, Stephen 311
Fairbanks (Alaska) 259, 261
fat bikes 36, 38, 78, 118
Flores 216
food 112-13
footwear 85-6
forums, internet 24
4 Rivers Bicycle Routes
    (S.Korea) 196
frame bags 69, 71, 72
frames 37-8, 46
France 124-5
French Guiana 310
Friendship Highway 192
fuel bottles 72

Gambia 251
gas stoves 95
GBAO permit 167
gear, weight & transport of
    75-80

gears 39, 47-51, 348-50
gear shifters 49, 349
gender relations 167
Genesis bikes 46
Genochio, Edward 179
Georgia 155-7
Germany 125
Geronimo Trail (USA) 269
gers, navigating by 179
Ghana 253
Gibb River Road (Australia)
    226
gloves 84
Gostelow, Peter 229-36,
    241-54, 356
GPS 105-6
Grand Trunk Road (Pakistan)
    143
Grant, Friedel 23, 278, 357
Great Divide Mountain Bike
    Route (USA) 256, 257, 264-9
Great Ocean Road (Australia)
    224
Greece 126
Guangxi (China) 191
Guatemala 275-6
guidebooks 24-5, 353
Guinea 251
Guinea Bissau 251
Guizhou (China) 190-1
Guyana 309

HACE & HAPE 110
Haley, Nathan 258, 287, 334
Hall, James & Jane 282, 357
Halton, Steve 229, 236-41,
    357
handlebar bags 70
handlebar rolls 71, 72
handlebars 40, 62-3
headsets 58, 350-1
head torches 98
health 30-1, 108-13, 235-6
heavyweight touring 79-80
helmets 85, 127, 222
Henderson, Loretta 238, 240,
    357
Henning, Lars 69, 357
hepatitis A & B 30
high altitude riding 292
Ho Chi Minh Highway
    (Vietnam) 210
Hokkaido (Japan) 199
Honduras 276
Honshu (Japan) 200
hospitality websites 19
Huascarán Circuit (Peru) 294
hub gears 39, 50-1

hubs 54
Humphreys, Alastair 184, 357
hydraulic disc brakes 53
hygiene 110-11, 113

Icefields Parkway (Canada)
    262
Iceland 126
India 144-53
Indonesia 213-17
inoculations 30-1
insurance 26-7
internet access 106-7, 224
Iran 130, 135-40
Istanbul (Turkey) 132
Italy 125
Ivory Coast 252-3

Japan 197-200, 316-19
Japanese B encephalitis 31
Java 215

kangaroos 225
Karakoram Highway 142-3
Kashgar (Kashi, China) 142,
    192-3
Kathmandu (Nepal) 154, 192
Kazakhstan 170-1
Kennett, Jonathan 227, 357
Kenya 242
Khardung La (India) 149, 150
Khiva (Uzbekistan) 165
Khorog (Tajikistan) 168
kickstands 73
Kinnaur (India) 148, 150-1
kitchen equipment 96-7, 98
Koga-Miyata bikes 42-3
Kortschak, Anna 269-79, 284,
    320
Kyrgyzstan 169-70, 330-4
Kyushu (Japan) 200

Ladakh (India) 148-9
Lagunas Route (Bolivia) 300-1
Lake Baikal Region (Russia)
    176
languages 131, 173, 186-7, 236,
    237, 256, 283
Laos 210-11
La Paz (Bolivia) 299
laptops 98
layering (clothes) 82-5
Leh (Ladakh) 149, 150
Leijerstam, Maria 228, 357
length of trip 15
Lenz, Frank 134
Lesotho 247
Lhasa (Tibet) 192, 193

Liberia 252
lightweight touring 76-7
Lloyd, Helen 175, 177, 339
Lombok 215
Lord, Stephen 1, 45, 70, 96, 268
luggage 64, 75

Machu Picchu (Peru) 295
McDonald, Matt 50, 298, 357
McNuff, Anna 260, 357
magic letters 131, 180
main routes
    Africa 229-31
    Americas 255-7, 270, 280, 281
    Asia 127-30, 201
    Australasia 221, 224-7
    Europe 121, 125-7
    see also route name
malaria 31, 108
Malawi 245
Malaysia 212-13
Mali 249, 251
Manali-Leh route 148, 149
maps 104, 204
    see also route maps
Marin County (USA) 268
Markham (Tibet) 193
Mauritania 249
mechanical disc brakes 53
medium weight touring 77-9
meningitis 31
Mereenie Loop (Australia) 224
Mexico 269-75
Mexico City 273
mobile phones 224
    see also smartphones
money 27-30
Mongolia 177-80, 325-9
moose 259
Morocco 249, 250
Morris, Scott 264-9, 357
mosquitoes 108, 259
Moss, Laura 139, 357
Moss, Tim 29, 77-9, 357
Mottram, Laura 279, 308, 357
mountain bikes 35
    adapted 44-5
    mid-range 46
Mozambique 245
mud 119
mudguards 73
multi-fuel stoves 93-5
Munda Biddi Trail (Australia) 226
Myanmar 130,148, 218-20, 311-16

Nagorno-Karabakh 155, 159
Namibia 246
National Highway 1 (Vietnam) 209
navigation 104-6
Nepal 146, 153-4
New Zealand 227
    Cycle Trail 227
Nicaragua 277
Nigeria 253
Nile Route 236-41
North Africa 235
North America 256-69
Northern Route (Asia) 172-80
North Sea cycle route 127
Nullarbor Plain (Australia) 225-6

off-road riding 119
Oman 139
online research 23-4
    hospitality 19
Osh (Kyrgyzstan) 167, 169, 170
Outback Survival (Cooper) 226

Pacific Coast Route (USA) 257, 262, 263-4, 265
Paiján (Peru) 293
pack animals 103
Pakistan 130,140-3
Pamir Highway (Tajikistan) 167-9
Panama 278-9
Pan American Highway 255, 256
    routes 258-69
panniers 64, 67, 68-70
Parker, Alia 221-6, 357
passports 25
Patagonia 301, 305-8
PayPal accounts 28
Peat, Andy 291, 357
pedals 85, 353-4
Peru 289-96
Philippines 217-18
Pierle, Matt 306, 357
Pike, Harriet 1, 32-98, 146
Pike, Neil 1, 11-31, 91, 99-131, 144-54, 255-8, 279-83, 289-308
Pinion gearboxes 51
planning schedule 18
polio 31
Power Grips 86
Prudhoe Bay (Alaska) 255, 259
pumps 73-4

Puna de Atacama (Argentina/Chile) 304-5
puncture repair kit 75
punctures 352-3

rabies 31, 117, 147, 236
racks 65-7
Rajasthan (India) 151-2
Ramadan 138, 235
recumbents 36, 43
remote areas, touring in 304
Repack Road (USA) 268
Revolution bikes 45
Richardson, Scott 116, 358
Ridgeback bikes 46
rim brakes 39, 52, 346-8
rims 55
River Danube route 125
road surfaces 14, 71, 118-19
road trains 224
robbery 115
Rohloff Speedhubs 39, 50-1
Rojo, Lorenzo 79-80, 202, 262, 358
Romania 126
Round the World trips 202, 238
route maps
    Africa 230
    Asia 128-9
    Australia 221
    Central America 270
    North America 257
    South America 280
    South East Asia 201
routes *see route name/place name*
Roy, Mike 148, 181, 182, 186-9, 358
Royal Highway (Laos) 211
rubbish disposal 103
Russia 172-6
Ruta 40 (Argentina) 301, 305
Rwanda 243

saddles 60-2
safari cycling 242
safety 30, 114-17, 124, 270-1, 283
Sahara 235
Salar de Coipasa (Bolivia) 300
Salar de Uyuni (Bolivia) 300
Samarkand (Uzbekistan) 165, 166
Samurai cyclist 116
sand 119
Sandiforth, Kurt 118, 358
Santos bikes 43

Schwalbe tyres 56-7
Scott, Chris 235, 358
seasons 16-17
    see also name of continent/
    country
Sea-to-Sky highway (Canada)
    262
seat packs 71
self-built bikes 46-7
Senegal 251
Shikoku (Japan) 200
Shimla (India) 149, 151
Siberia 174-6
Siberian routes 174-6
Sichuan (China) 185, 188
Sierra Leone 251-2
Sikkim (India) 147-8
SIM cards 107
singletrack tours (USA) 267
sleeping bags & pads 91-3
Slovenia 125
solar chargers 98
smartphones 98, 106, 107
solo travellers 20-1, 205
    women 21
South Africa 247
South America 279-310
South East Asia 201-220
Southern Africa 241, 242, 244-5
Southern Route (Asia) 130,
    132-53
South India 153
South Korea 195-6
South Pole 228
South West China 185, 188-91
Spain 126-7
Spanish language 256, 283
spare parts, bike 50, 74-5
Spiti (India) 148, 150-1
sponsorship 29
SPDs 85, 86
spokes 55-6, 74, 75, 354
Spry, Sonya 258
Srinagar (India) 150
Stone, Laura 148, 358
stoves 93-5
straight bars 40
straps 72
Stuart Highway (Australia) 224
Sudan 237, 239
Sulawesi 217
Sumatra 214-15
Sumbawa 216
sunburn & sunstroke 108-9
sunglasses 85, 298, 300
Suriname 309, 310
Surly bikes 40-1, 46, 66
suspension forks 63-4, 67
suspension seatposts 64

Swaziland 247
Switzerland 125

tablets 98
Taiwan 193-5
Tajikistan 166-9
tandems 36-7
Tanzania 243
Tashkent (Uzbekistan) 165, 166
Tasmania 226
Taylor, Shirine 156, 358
Tbilisi (Georgia) 155, 156
tents 87-91
tetanus 30
Thailand 206-7
theft 115
Thomson, Rob 197-200, 358
Thorn bikes 41-2, 46, 66
Tibet 130, 191-3
Tierra del Fuego 255, 308
Timor 216
toe clips 86
toiletries 97-8
tools 73-5
touring bikes 34-5, 40-6
touring gear, homemade 69
Tout Terrain bikes 44
tracking devices 107
traffic and safety 114-15
trailers 68, 266
trains, bikes on 103
    China 191
    India 152
Trans-Siberian Highway 176
travelling companions 20-3
trial tours 14
trigger shifters 49
Turkey 132-5
Turkmenistan 164-5
twist-grip shifters 49
typhoid 31
tyres 56-7, 74
    plus-size 38
tyre sizing 34

Uganda 242-3
Ulaanbaatar (Mongolia) 178,
    179
ultralight bikepacking 78-9, 267
unboxed bikes on planes 99
United Arab Emirates 139
USA 256, 257, 260, 263-9
Ushuaia (Argentina) 254, 308
Uzbekistan 165-6

vaccination 30-1
van Drunen, Elmar & Ellen 162
    358
Van Nicolas bikes 44

Venezuela 308-9
Vietnam 209-10
visas 19, 26
    see also place name
VSF Fahrrad Manufaktur bikes
    44

Walker, Charlie 330
water
    pollution 103
    purification 96, 113
water bags 98
water bottles 72
waterproof clothing 84
Watts, Logan 38, 71, 250, 358
weather forecasts 16
websites 24
weight of gear 76-9
Weir, Bill 151-3, 181-5, 188-91,
    358
West Africa 249-54
West Coast Australia 225
Western Europe 124-5
wheels 54-7
    size of 34, 38
wheel truing 351
wi-fi 107
wild camping 124, 263
wildlife 242
Williams, Amaya 193-6, 201-20,
    232, 358
Woloshansky, Paul 345, 350
women travellers 21
    health 111-12
'World's Most Dangerous Road'
    (Bolivia) 299
Wouters, Mirjam 126, 358

Yakutsk (Siberia) 176
yellow fever 31
Yerevan (Armenia) 158, 159
Yucatán Peninsula 275
Yukon Territory (Canada) 261
Yunnan (China) 188-90

Zambia 245-6
Zanskar (India) 150, 151
Zimbabwe 245, 246
zips, fixing 91

TRAILBLAZER

OTHER GUIDES FROM TRAILBLAZER – see overleaf for full list

Peru's Cordilleras Blanca & Huayhuash – the hiking & biking guide
Neil & Harriet Pike, 1st edition, 256pp, 60 maps, 40 colour photos
ISBN 978-1-905864-63-8, £15.99
The Cordilleras Blanca and Huayhuash boast some of the most spectacular
scenery in the Andes, and some of the most accessible high altitude trekking
and cycling in the world. Perfect pyramidal peaks, gargantuan ice falls and
turquoise alpine lakes are all easily reached from Huaraz, the region's capital
and centre of tourist comforts. This practical guide contains 50 detailed route
maps and descriptions covering 20 hiking trails and 30 days of paved and dirt
road cycle touring.
❏ **Trekking** – includes the classic treks: Huayhuash Circuit, Santa Cruz and
Alpamayo Basecamp, as well as lesser known, wild walks in valleys which see few visitors.
Ranging from easy day hikes to challenging routes of 10 days or more, all can be trekked independently or in guided groups.
❏ **Cycling** – includes the Huascarán Circuit, a loop of Peru's highest mountain, as well as four
other multi-day rides and five day-cycles from Huaraz. Covers all the information cyclists need to
pedal past glaciers on 6000m peaks or fly down 2500m descents from high passes.
❏ **Mountain biking** – includes two detailed downhill routes and information on organising guides
to lead you through the labyrinth of exciting singletrack in the area.

Himalaya by Bike – a route & planning guide
Laura Stone 368pp, 28 colour & 50 B&W photos, 73 maps
ISBN 978 1 905864 04 1, *1st edition,* £16.99

An all-in-one guide for Himalayan cycle-touring. Covers the Himalayan regions
of Pakistan, Tibet, India, Nepal and Sikkim with detailed km-by-km guides to
main routes including the Karakoram Highway and the Friendship Highway.
❏ **Route descriptions with detailed mapping** – Unique hand-drawn GPS maps
show distances between villages, altitudes, places to eat and accommodation,
water sources, fuel stations and points of interest along the way. Elevation profiles
for each 100km section and route overview profiles to get you training!
❏ **Town guides** – Islamabad, Kashgar, Manali, Leh, Srinagar, Shimla, Gangtok, Darjeeling,
Lhasa, Shigatse, Kathmandu and Guwahati.
'Inspirational guide' **Cycle Magazine** *'Rammed full of in-depth information'* **Adventure Travel
Magazine** *'Indispensable'* **LCC Magazine**

Morocco Overland – from the Atlas to the Sahara *Chris Scott*
2nd edition, 244pp, 50pp maps, 34 colour & 70 B&W photos
ISBN 978 1 905864 53 9, £15.99

Morocco Overland is a guide to 56 routes through southern Morocco's spectacular landscape – from the snow-clad High Atlas to the dunes of the Sahara and
right down to the Mauritanian border. With easy-to-follow routes ranging from
sub-alpine trails to arid canyons winding past hidden Berber villages and from the
Atlantic surf to former Dakar Rally pistes, this comprehensive route and planning
guide will appeal to both the seasoned adventurer and to the first timer.
❏ **Route guides with GPS waypoints** – Covering over 10,000km, this guide features 56 detailed
GPS off-road routes for 4WDs, motorcycles and mountain bikes with 100s of GPS waypoints. Each
route is reversible and is graded for suitability for mountain bikes. Includes fuel stations, restaurants
and places to stay. With over 50pp of mapping. *'The bible for off-roading to and
across this corner of North Africa'* **Wanderlust Magazine**

The Cyclist's Anthology *Nicky Slade (ed)*
1st edition, 160pp, hardback, £9.99, ISBN 978 1 905864 69 0

This anthology covering the subject of cycling and journeys by bicycle draws on
the writings of more than 50 literary figures from around the world – Sir Arthur
Conan Doyle, Ernest Hemingway, Jerome K Jerome, DH Lawrence, Dervla
Murphy, Eric Newby, Dorothy Sayers, Mark Twain, Quentin Blake and HG Wells
among many others. The perfect gift for any cyclist.

TRAILBLAZER

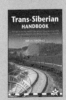

Adventure Cycle-Touring Handbook
Adventure Motorcycling Handbook
Australia by Rail
Azerbaijan
Coast to Coast (British Walking Guide)
Cornwall Coast Path (British Walking Guide)
Corsica Trekking – GR20
Cotswold Way (British Walking Guide)
The Cyclist's Anthology
Dales Way (British Walking Guide) – due mid 2016
Dolomites Trekking – AV1 & AV2
Dorset & Sth Devon Coast Path (British Walking Gde)
Exmoor & Nth Devon Coast Path (British Walking Gde)
Hadrian's Wall Path (British Walking Guide)
Himalaya by Bike – a route and planning guide
Inca Trail, Cusco & Machu Picchu
Japan by Rail
Kilimanjaro – the trekking guide (includes Mt Meru)
Moroccan Atlas – The Trekking Guide
Morocco Overland (4WD/motorcycle/mountainbike)
Nepal Trekking & The Great Himalaya Trail
New Zealand – The Great Walks
North Downs Way (British Walking Guide)
Offa's Dyke Path (British Walking Guide)
Overlanders' Handbook – worldwide driving guide
Peddars Way & Norfolk Coast Path (British Walking Gde)
Pembrokeshire Coast Path (British Walking Guide)
Pennine Way (British Walking Guide)
Peru's Cordilleras Blanca & Huayhuash – Hiking/Biking
The Railway Anthology
The Ridgeway (British Walking Guide)
Sahara Overland – a route and planning guide
Scottish Highlands – The Hillwalking Guide
Siberian BAM Guide – rail, rivers & road
The Silk Roads – a route and planning guide
Sinai – the trekking guide
South Downs Way (British Walking Guide)
Thames Path (British Walking Guide)
Tour du Mont Blanc
Trans-Canada Rail Guide
Trans-Siberian Handbook
Trekking in the Everest Region
The Walker's Anthology
The Walker's Haute Route – Mont Blanc to Matterhorn
West Highland Way (British Walking Guide)

www.trailblazer-guides.com
ROUTE GUIDES FOR THE ADVENTUROUS TRAVELLER